Third Edition

Sell Up and Sail

Taking the Ulysses Option

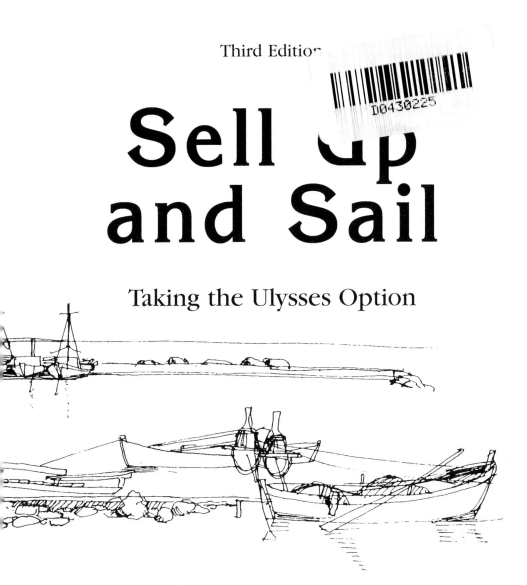

Bill & Laurel Cooper

SHERIDAN HOUSE

This edition published 1998 by
Sheridan House Inc.
145 Palisade Street
Dobbs Ferry, NY 10522

Reprinted 2000

First published by Stanford Maritime 1986
First U.S. edition published by Sheridan House 1991
Paperback edition with amendments published by
Adlard Coles Nautical 1994

ISBN 1-57409-046-1

Library of Congress Cataloging-in-Publication Data
Cooper, Bill.
    Sell up and sail: taking the Ulysses option/Bill and Laurel
Cooper.—3rd ed.
        p.   cm.
    Includes index.
    ISBN 1-57409-046-1
    1. Sailboat living. 2. Yachts. 3. Cooper, Bill. 4. Cooper,
Laurel. I. Cooper, Laurel. II. Title.
GV811.65.C66   1998
797.1'24—dc21   97-37677
                                                    CIP

Printed in Great Britain

ISBN 1-57409-046-1

Contents

Dedicated
To our parents and children,
who let us go.

Introduction

Not so many years ago the number of people living aboard cruising yachts was small enough for them to be considered very eccentric. The situation is no longer the same.

In 1980 a survey for an Italian marina company produced a figure of 4000 boats which were lived in all the year round in the Mediterranean alone. Of this number, 25% were British and some 10% were American. The number grows year by year, and to it must be added the substantial population doing the same thing in the West Indies, the Bahamas and the South Pacific, as well as the American community on the move up and down their East Coast waterways.

The significant words are 'on the move'. We are not concerned with houseboat residents, or even those who live in a yacht in one place. This is about mobility, and we try to go into it quite deeply.

It is about escapism as well. Too many moralists infer the escape is from obligations, but this view begs a lot of questions. Many of us escape from regimentation, from interfering bureaucracy, from cradle-to-grave suffocation: we want to look after ourselves. We are rebels from the Welfare State. We discuss that.

But an urge to go is not enough. To a lifelong sailor the act of setting sail comes naturally and easily. Most people are not so experienced, and we are often asked how we have managed to enjoy fourteen years of early retirement in this way, when many others have set out but have not managed to keep going. A good deal of the answer lies in understanding what you are trying to achieve, in defining your aim, in ordering your affairs to further that aim, and then finally having the capacity to cast off the last mooring and go.

This is not a book on technique — seamanship, how to sail, how to maintain engines — though we do indulge ourselves from time to time. It is about attitudes, about ways of ordering existence on the move.

We are not concerned with obsessive achievers speeding round the world on curried split peas, without touching land except to have their GREAT SAILOR ticket punched at the more spectacular blue-water stopping places. Nor do we have time for bathtub sailors, navigators of barrels or floating bedsteads, or voyagers in re-cycled cornflakes packets and other unsuitable craft. Our advice to nautical loonies is to stay at home, buy a plastic duck and give the rescue services a break.

There are some who for various reasons can be only partially or temporarily committed to wandering. Those with a sabbatical and no time to waste, and others with a semi-annual approach, wishing to live aboard for perhaps six months at a time. Though not suffering from a terminal case of wanderlust as we are, they have a minor infection: perhaps we can help them too.

We are writing for people who are out to enjoy themselves. So we concentrate on those parts of the world to which the live-aboards tend to gravitate, and where our voyaging experiences are more recent.

We write also for dreamers, for most of us were dreamers to start with, and we hope we may encourage them to realise their dreams. There may be those unsure of their ability, of their endurance, or uncertain that the lust is real. Those too who have to cope with the wanderlust in a partner, and how it might affect them. We try to help these people analyse their attitudes in Chapter Two, 'Test your U.Q.'. The two of us have very different personalities and we see things in different ways. To some extent, then, this is two books for the price of one, for we both express (as much between the lines as in them) what drives us on.

Preface to the Third Edition

Since we first wrote *Sell Up and Sail* almost 14 years ago, we have been delighted that, despite the lookalikes that followed, its popularity is undiminished. So why do we need a revised edition? As we predicted in a preface to the second edition, authority is now taking notice of the phenomenon, and wants to stick its oar in with regulation and certification. The psychology and the philosophy of sailing away remain the same, but the reasons change. If anything, the bureaucrats are getting worse, people of all lands are more and more fed up with the way they are governed, the speed and stress of cities, the noise and pollution. The incentive to get away from it all is stronger than ever.

The yachtie fraternity changes only slightly in emphasis. There are always the dedicated and starry eyed, always the adventurers, and the courageous pensioners who have waited so long for their reward. In the seventies there was a wave of Capital Gains sailors, afloat for one year to fulfil the letter of the law, and white escapees from African States, getting their capital out of the country in the only way they could, in one expensive package called a yacht. They were followed by Europeans laid off in the recession, using their redundancy pay to find a new life. Now, with the fall of Communism, a few brave hearts from Eastern Europe, with yachts stitched painfully together from leftovers, are joining the fleet. Prosperous Asians are appearing in boats, and we all continue to get on well together. The reasons for the Sell-up-and-Sail syndrome are so bound up with the economics of life that it is necessary to comment on the global economic situation as yachties are affected.

Traditionally the best cruising has been found in archipelagos. The Caribbean, the Greek islands, and the South Pacific are the three obvious ones. These places combined beautiful islands, less-developed economies where it was possible to live simply and cheaply, and generally hospitable inhabitants. It does seem that the last two of those advantages tend to go together. Many of the islands the yachties favoured were isolated, with small chance of profiting from conventional tourism. The visiting yachtsmen, while not themselves rich in terms of their countries of origin, enjoyed a comparative wealth so that their modest expenditure was welcome to their hosts. Communications in many of these regions were elementary, and very often there were extremely strong traditions of hospitality that were still apparent, helped because the yachties imposed few changes: they used generally unaltered facilities (they preferred it that way), and made local friends, and learnt some of the language.

Along comes commercialised tourism, and the investing vultures gather round the idylls the yachtie had 'discovered', and once had to himself. Islands which at one time had a ferry once a week or less, one simple 'ethnic' café-bar/general store to serve the locals plus half a dozen or so yachties, now have an airstrip capable of landing Boeing 747s. Strings of restaurants and jewellers' shops are owned by people who do not live in the islands, but who visit only in high season when thousands of tourists are broiling on the beaches. The local people, instead of a life of a bit of fishing, a bit of gardening and a lot of sitting happily under trees, now find they are rushed off their feet as waiters, chambermaids or washers-up working a 12-hour day throughout the season for the benefit of foreign investors.

And the berths previously occupied by the yachties? The anchorage has now been developed, and in the expensive marina (with non-resident owners and operators of course) the berths are filled with charter yachts and glass-bottomed boats. To which are added the world-wide mass-cruising fleets, such as the ARC (Atlantic Rally for Cruisers) and the Round-the-World equivalents, who put up the prices wherever they go, never to come down again, as appalled individual yachties following in their wakes discover.

So we long-cruising folk move on as another once delightful haven is off the list, except out of season.

It might have been thought that the European Union would have made things easier in Europe, and so it has from the point of view of bureaucratic procedures for citizens of its member states in other member states. But there have been two disadvantages.

The problems of entering and clearing countries and harbours may be simpler, but other kinds of bureacracy are galloping throughout the Union. Every country seems to have a pet area it wishes to regulate and by the time this has all filtered through Brussels we get not a distillation, not the lowest common denominator, but the Highest Common Factor, the sum of all the requirements.

New rules for skippers' certification, for inspection of boats, for hygiene, for insurance, for radio, life-saving equipment, fire-extinguishers: many of them not unreasonable in themselves, but boats and people are different one from another and we used to be able to use our own judgement in matters which were very personal and idiosyncratic to our own boats, which might vary from 66 year-old 60 tonne steel barges to new plastic dishes apparently weighing 60 kilograms.

The second disadvantage comes from the money that has poured from Northern Europe into the Mediterranean countries. Whether or not one approves of the massive corruption which accompanies these hand-outs, they have been on such a scale that the local people have been considerably enriched. We cannot cavil at the rising prosperity; they have come from a long way behind after all, but from the point of view of our own narrow interests the effects have been a dramatic rise in the cost of living in Greece (do voters in all the countries lining up to join the EU realise this inevitability?), and also the filling with locally-owned boats of all those lovely small harbours that were improved with EU money specifically to help visiting tourists. The world changes. Being fallible human beings, we grumble that others are bettered to our detriment. We should not. We move on.

We have noticed certain changes in the live-aboard fleet. In the traditional centres, the number of boats becoming quasi-immobile has risen, and these, too, take up berths that cruising boats might have used. A number have decided to call it a day and buy a cottage with roses. And the new recruits keep coming, and they keep being pleased, no matter that people shake their heads and say: 'It's not what it was'. It never is, was, or will be.

To those on the brink of departure we say: it is still a grand way of life, even if one has to go a little further afield to find it these days.

September 1997

Laurel.

LAMPARAS AT PETRITI

Chapter One

Why Do We Do It?

'What a greate matter it is to saile a shyppe or goe to sea.'

In 1976 we sold our house, waved goodbye to the family, and took to the sea in a boat we had built ourselves. We became long-distance, live-aboard cruisers, for whom no very accurate generic term has yet been established, 'Sell-up-and-Sailors' begins to be heard, though the nearest is perhaps 'Yotties'. Abandoning brick walls and gardens, property taxes, and interference from authorities who continually tried to order what we might or might not do, we took on the less comfortable but much more invigorating life of responsibility for our own actions, health, welfare and safety, and through this self-reliance achieved contentment.

Since then, the interest shown in our way of life has increased to a point where the number of people who wish to emulate us, and others like us, has become almost a social phenomenon. The idea of it seems to appeal to many. Although it is the antithesis to the collective responsibility of the Welfare State, that may be a perverse explanation for its attraction. It may also be why some people find they cannot handle the idea, since there is no doubt that great exchanges have to be made (we prefer not to call them sacrifices).

Sudden change is not good for the system. On a boat you can usually choose to change slowly, to stay a bit or go on as the mood takes you. An Atlantic crossing is a very slow change, giving you time to get used to the climate, and hurling no insults at your biological clock.

Have we not, some people ask, merely exchanged one set of problems for another? Yes, in a sense. We have exchanged the insoluble problems of politics, the pace of life, the battles with bureaucracy, and the appalling proliferation of paper which push one to the edge of madness; for problems of wind and wave and how and where to go next, which we *can* solve. That alone does wonders for your wellbeing.

When the wanderbug bites you, the symptoms vary from person to person. The acheing boredom and frustration of many of today's jobs — or worse, the lack of any job at all — produce understandable feelings of restlessness, and in some people a desire to travel. Many people in middle life feel that this is something they wish to do before they get too old. The young feel they would like to do it now, before family responsibilities and education become too great a burden. Many feel that it would be a great way to retire. All have differing requirements and expectations. With some, the idea of travel comes at the head of the list; with others, the escape vehicle comes first and travelling in it second. There is a third category to whom the building of the boat is a sufficient release. They dream of going but remain at home, quite content.

There was no doubt in Bill's mind that he wanted to build his own boat, and travel in it. There was a great deal he wanted to get away from: a 9-6 job, very stressful, complications of property and officialdom, winters of ill health, the speed of life, and the trauma of too much change too quickly and for no good reason. I could see his point.

Why a yacht? Because it is a romantic dream that has a chance of coming true: you can build it yourself. And when you've built it, you can travel in it, which is another romantic dream. Building a boat, or acquiring one and refitting it to your own requirements, seems to appeal to something very ancient and necessary in man. Your life, and that of your family, depend on how well you build it and how carefully you plan the voyage. In a world where someone else is always to blame for any misfortune (and where with luck, you can sue), to take responsibility for your lives firmly on your own shoulders and find out that the burden is bearable brings feelings of worth and confidence.

A yacht has a freedom of travel that no other vehicle enjoys. The sea is, by and large, still free to all to cross from one side to the other, starting and finishing where you please, or to stitch your way round its shores. There are extremely few restrictions and regulations specifically affecting yachts, and what few there are would be complied with by a prudent mariner in any event. Close to land and in harbour, you will find the only restrictions you are likely to meet. In or near big commercial ports you will find one-way systems, parking regulations and choked traffic just as on the busy roads of any city. Away from the big ports restrictions dwindle until they disappear altogether. A yacht marina is merely a specialized commercial port, and you can expect the same sort of restrictions; added to those of a caravan camp (no laundry lines, no barbecues). We avoid them if we can.

God help us if the day ever comes when we are all directed into marinas because commercial interests or overcrowding demand it, or indeed for any other reason. That will be the day when Bill and Laurel start building their kit-form space capsule. (Well, it's got to come, hasn't it?)

Until then, if your aim is carefree mobility, then a yacht is the ideal vehicle. Some people may find eventually that cruising is merely an interval between long stops in one place. Some find a place they love so much they never leave it. Would a caravan have been a better choice? It is certainly cheaper. To use a yacht to stay in one place means that you are not using to the full the expensive and specially designed equipment that was intended to give you mobility: like using the Rolls-Royce as a chicken shed.

If you find, after doing the UQ test which follows, that neither sailing nor travelling are really what you want, but that you would like to drop out of the Stress Layer for a while, or forever, and sink down to the quieter levels of the world, afloat or ashore, then it would make sense to search for your place in the sun by land cruising.

This involves driving at an average of fifty miles an hour instead of five knots. You need registration, insurance and a driving licence. In most places where you would feel like staying, caravans are strictly regulated into campsites. If you are not in a campsite, water and sanitation can be a problem. You cannot carry much fuel, and yet cannot move without it. You have to stick to roads, of more or less good quality. You are dependent on ferry services to get you across water, and filling stations for fuel, therefore you are at the mercy of strikes and industrial

Preparing Hosanna *for her maiden voyage. Note the Fiat 600 car — the smallest Bill could get inside.*

policy. But, yes, it is cheaper. Still, find your small village or town or island, and you will in some ways be less isolated than in a bed-sit in outer London.

We find that in a stay of one month in a tiny port we can, even if not accepted as part of the village, at least lose our tourist status. It takes care and tact, however. Try to change nothing. Watch before you join in. Does Baba Iannis always sit in the same chair in the Taverna? Then don't sit in it yourself. Do the old men like to cluster in one corner and gaze out over the bay? Then don't block their view with a table full of strangers. If the village turns in at half past nine, don't keep them up with noisy chat and laughter, ordering strange drinks that the Taverna has not got. Try to talk a little in the language, to assuage natural curiosity as to your age, marital status, and number and age of children. Don't go on too long, though; they have the whole world to run in their deliberations, don't forget, and if they missed an evening who knows what could happen? Catastrophe.

If Selene brings out her distaff to spin a little in the evening, I go and sit near her with my knitting, and we can exchange wordless admiration without making many waves.

Sense the mood, so that you do not behave inappropriately. One day, when the ferry came in, everybody stopped smiling. We, too, put on grave expressions. The men ran down to the ship and came forth bearing a coffin. The women came down to meet it and fell in behind. It was taken up the little alley beside the Taverna to a courtyard where three old ladies had been wont to sit on the warm stones in the evening. Now only two remained: Eleni had been whisked off to hospital on the mainland the day before, and had died there. She was very old, so faces were grave, but not tearful. 'Poor lady,' said the baker, 'I gave her half a loaf of bread many times. She was too poor to pay me, so I forget always to ask for the money.' Everyone came to her funeral, as she had no relatives left. The village cared for her in death, as they had done in life. Can one ask more?

Some people can. They want to go and spend another month at a different place, learn to understand another kind of village and another sort of people, drinking rum punch on a coral beach or rough red wine in a bodega, or 'island tea' in a Turkish tea house, or cook their stew in fumeroles in the Azores and eat lobster-in-the-rough off paper plates in New England. I cannot think of a better way of doing this than to go with your house on your back like a sea snail, at a speed where your surroundings change slowly and without shock to the system.

> *What is this life, if on our cruise*
> *We have no time to sit and booze?*
> *Conversely what, if full of booze*
> *We never get to sea and cruise?*
> *What is this life, I'd like to know*
> *If I am always down below?*
> *And if, upon the starboard tack,*
> *The loo is always out of whack?*
> *And what if I am ill at ease*
> *With not a ripple on the seas?*
> *What is this life? It suits us well.*
> *It's mostly heaven, rarely hell.*

To have built your boat, or at least lovingly altered and equipped her for such a voyage, is a process which brings in itself many rewards. For us, the real reward was the travelling. We held on to this aim through many black days during the building period.

This is a book for dreamers, but especially for those who would like to achieve the dream. We would like to take the stars out of your eyes, and use them to illuminate practicalities.

While anyone contemplating long-term cruising would be foolhardy to embark without some nautical ability, the effort of acquiring it can be eased by planning and dreaming. Indeed, dreaming may be one of the most enjoyable aspects of the whole enterprise. If you never get beyond the stage of catalogues and cruising books by the Sunday fire, enjoy the book. Just before we sailed, the Lifeboat Coxs'n said to us, 'A lot of people want to do what you're doing. Difference is: you've done it.'

We were dreamers once. Dreams can become a reality. It is hard work, rather than magic, that gets it done.

Chapter Two

Crucial Questions

'Make voyages! Attempt them! There's nothing else.'
Tennessee Williams — Camino Real

Part One: How Laurel was Persuaded to go to Sea

It was the insidiousness of it that got me.

From the day he retired from the Royal Navy, Bill began the 'one day we'll both go to sea' gambit. Over the years, punctuated by annual visits to the Boat Show (I always went with him — I almost always got migraine), the subliminal mention became less subliminal, and during his next two careers became friendly persuasion, then gentle insistence, and finally downright intransigence.

Not that I disliked either the sea or sailing; far from it, though my experience, while considerable, was largely on inland waters. I even liked the Boat Show. But I was entrenched in a comfortable little life and saw no reason to abandon it in order to get wet, cold and seasick away from my books, cats and children.

It became clear that if I was not to be shanghaied to sea willy-nilly, I should have to take certain steps. These were all backwards, and included countering every stated assumption that I would go by good-humoured negatives and careful references to '*your* boat' and '*your* voyage' and 'when *you* go, I'll have a cottage somewhere for you to come back to'.

After some years of this it dawned on my husband that I meant it, and that I did have good reasons for doubting my capacity at sea. With a sigh, he began to design singlehanded yachts. At this point I realised that he too meant what he said. My bluff called, negotiations began with frank and free discussions, and meaningful dialogues; and the next few designs were very different. If I was going, I wanted a say in the sort of boat I would live in.

The inevitable compromise

Bill says now that he built *Fare Well* round my books and my bath. For the next few years he worked on my sense of adventure and I worked on his sense of responsibility. We had two children whom we could not leave until it seemed they could do without us. We had cats (one horrid and one super) and a dog. How could Bill leave his tiresome, but very lucrative job? We had a large house that I adored. My life was busy and interesting, and I loved the work I was doing. It was going to be very hard to sell up and go.

Departure

In the end, as so often happens, some decisions were made for us by events. Bill became very ill for a year or two, able only to potter about the half-completed boat; and there was no longer any problem about breaking away from the job — the firm had already filled the vacancy. The children grew up suddenly and moved out, leaving us in a house far too big and expensive on our own. The horrid cat died, and we decided to take the other with us — one of our more brilliant decisions, as was the idea of giving the dog to Bill's widowed father, leading to one of those man-dog relationships worthy of letters of flame.

It began to look as if the sooner we went the sooner Bill would regain his health. There was the little matter of finishing a 55 foot ketch, and getting it to sea, but we had been working on that for some time anyway. (It took five years altogether and is quite another story.) Gradually the people who had been saying 'you'll never finish it' began to realise that we damn well would, and that we were damn well going.

Don't kid yourselves, it was hard. Morale was sometimes very low. It was as hard as I had thought it would be to sell the house, part with the dog, and say goodbyes to family and friends. On the plus side, our son Ben decided to accompany us for a while. A sense of excitement began to grow as we worked, planned and stored ship; and found some pleasant people to share our maiden voyage to Gibraltar. This being, apart from trials, our first trip, and nearly my first ocean trip, Bill had decided to be prudent and take some extra muscle.

When we finally set sail from Lowestoft, six people and the cat Nelson, a burden rolled off my shoulders that I had never been aware of. I smelt the sea, saw the first of many ocean sunsets, and felt a freedom I'd never known before.

I wouldn't have changed places with anyone.

Looking back

I had always loved the sea in rather a romantic and sentimental way. I was born and brought up by the sea, and dipped my toes in it nearly every day of my childhood summers, or sat in the shallows and let the little waves bounce in my lap. You could pee in it without anyone knowing. You could watch the storms from the cliffs and be amazed by the crashing noise of the breakers, the cold hiss and rattle and roar of grating pebbles; even at that distance you must shout to be heard. In bed you could hear the waves above the fitful pelt and spatter of the winter rain. How blissful to be warm in bed, and not out in the dark on the wild sea.

As I grew up I learned to sail, on the Broads of course, as did the young Nelson, but I was seventeen before I even crossed the Channel in a ferry, and the sea was still magic, and dangerous and attractive like an elder brother's motorbike.

That attitude was not very helpful when faced with a life at sea in one's mid forties. How would I cope with storms? How would I handle seasickness and exhaustion when we were short-handed? Could I stand my companions (let alone my husband) at close quarters and under stress? It seemed a good idea to find out about this sort of thing while the boat was still a-building. I do not advise anyone less dedicated to leave it as late as this. It is far better to do all this and more before you embark on a project which has a momentum as inevitable as the birth of a child, and to abort which is just as painful and a good deal more expensive.

Getting some sea-time in

My only real sea experience at that time (I discount dinghy racing where you are home and dry after a couple of hours) was a four week cruise in 1954 with Bill, our six-month old daughter and my brother.

The yacht was a 5-tonner without motor or loo. I felt that there was some basis for confidence here, as although it was July in the Mediterranean we had had one of those unseasonal summer storms, and a thick fog in the Sicilian Channel shipping lanes to boot. I had by no means disgraced myself; I had cooked, washed nappies, kept watch, steered and been useful. The baby enjoyed every minute. I enjoyed most of it. So far, so good.

I had the great advantage of faith in my captain. Bill is an experienced deep-sea yachtsman, and an ex-professional navigator. He is also a seaman of the old-fashioned kind, which he describes as managing without what you haven't got, and which leads to some amazingly ingenious ways of getting by. I felt I should have confidence in the boat, too; she was strongly built and looked seaworthy, and I was getting to know her by building her. I had had a lot to say about the design, and not just in the galley. The guardrails were to be very strong in case my hip failed me; and on the foredeck we had strong netting to prevent a body slipping through the guardrails. Below, the furniture was built strongly enough to fall against in a seaway without damaging it, the corollary being that such solidity can cause a lot of mayhem to bodies bouncing off it. Despite the numerous handholds that we put everywhere, strong enough to Tarzan around the boat on, I still sometimes ping-ponged off the furniture. Gazing at my doleful bruises, I insisted on more cushions, in the cockpit as well. Bill hates them, but they do cut down injuries, not only mine. We have mentioned the bath. For anyone with bone-aches a hot bath is a solace greater than any medicine. Salt water can be used. Since it is now believed that more yachtsmen die of hypothermia than drowning, and a recommended remedy for the former is a warm bath, maybe it's less of a luxury than we thought.

I wanted a corner for drawing, and I refused to share the chart table as I knew it would cause friction. I got it, a neat solution that was flexible enough to become a workbench when I started enamelling.

Double bunks were unusual at the time. You spend a lot of your life in bed, you might as well be happy there: we designed the first double bunk we'd seen that could be got at from three sides, instead of being shoved against the ship's side. I heard of someone who had an arm broken by a heavy bunkmate crawling over her in such a bunk, answering a night call. Twice.

Gaining experience

To get more confidence in myself, I went to the National Sailing Centre at Cowes (now alas no more) to learn some navigation (the coastal part of the Yachtmaster's qualification). Bill normally does all this, and to compete with him seemed foolish:

if someone can play the 'Moonlight Sonata' should you join in on a penny whistle? But I felt a lot better for knowing something, and it might have become vital.

I gained more experience. When we could we helped friends who were new to sailing by doing short trips round the coast or across the Channel. I began to realise I was not the first in the crew to succumb to seasickness, that pills and sensible precautions to prevent overtiredness and chilling were better than being frightfully brave, and that I was so hungry I *had* to cook something. I found that a little yacht flying down-Channel before a stiff breeze was great. I discovered that I did not much like going to windward. We remained on speaking terms with our friends. It looked as if things were going to be all right.

The house was sold. I still writhe with pain when I recall this period. Although planning and forethought went into everything we did, it turned out there was still a lot to learn. Much of it, twenty-odd years on, we are still learning by pleasurable stages, a little of it the hard way. Our happy years of cruising are witness to the fact that we did our homework, and that by the end of our maiden voyage a romantic dreamer had become something of a practical sea-person, and Nelson had enthusiastically embarked on the life of a one-eyed sea-cat.

Having described the process whereby I came to accept and enjoy living at sea, there are some relevant questions YOU should answer.

Part Two: Test Your UQ

Too little thought before you go,
And you'll be back before you know

We have devised a test to measure what we shall call your 'Ulysses Quotient' or UQ. While it should not be taken desperately seriously, it will nevertheless give you plenty to think about. You and your mate may even have your first disagreement over the first question. Ulysses, it will be remembered, roamed the seas for about ten years, looking for his homeland, the island of Ithaca. UQ can be described as a tendency to wander off for years in a small boat without actually getting anywhere much. (Though he was probably the worst navigator in history, he did, it is pointed out to us, suffer under the handicap of having an all-male crew!)

The desire, the will to go cruising is paramount. We realise that nothing we say will stop you if you are determined; whether you are an unskilled, penniless tyro, incapacitated by alcohol and agues, embarking in an unseaworthy boat with a sack of lentils and aiming to be the first member of Depressives Anonymous to round Cape Horn; or a thrifty couple with a small but well-found boat, making well-planned voyages that are triumphs of ingenuity, courage and dedication. However, we want you to enjoy your cruising; and time spent now on thinking and planning will save you money and misery later on. We cannot say this often enough.

You and your spouse, or mate, or lifelong companion, whatever (living at sea we have come across every combination of all four sexes) should do the test separately, in private, and without discussions or comparisons until all the scoring is finished. If you would like your children to do it, the same conditions apply: certainly they should join in the discussions which follow. Incidentally, I had better make it clear that I use the word 'Mate' throughout this book to cover:

wife, husband, son, daughter, companion, friend, crew, lover, consenting adult — whoever is going with you to be your team mate.

You each (or all) have a lot of decisions to make, and you might as well know what your sticking points are now. They may prove to be immovable, they may need hard work and compromise to find a way round them, they may in time vanish like smoke, but at least you will know what you are up against. Name your enemy and the battle begins.

Note that your scores are nothing to do with winning or losing, or with being right or wrong. The test is an attempt to assess: (1) your present situation, which may of course change, (2) practical considerations which may have a bearing on your future, (3) your abilities and capabilities, and (4) your attitude to mobility. The scoring comes under three different headings: Alpha (A); Kappa (K); and Sigma (Σ). Their significance will become apparent later.

If you cheat — have fun, and carry on dreaming. If you are really keen on the idea, take a good look at yourself, answer honestly, and this could be the first step in your voyage.

The Ulysses Quotient

Section One — Basic questions: Do you really want to go?

1   Do you really like sailing?
(a) Yes, very much.
(b) I don't know, I think I do.
(c) I don't know, I think I don't actually enjoy it.
(d) No, I don't.
If (a) score A4, if (b) score A1, if (c) score Σ5. If (d) score Σ15, and go to question (Q)3.

2   You are faced with a rough sea and a rising wind on a long beat into harbour. Do you:
(a) Grin and bear it?
(b) Say 'This is what it's all about' and call for eggs and bacon?
(c) Get sick and miserable, and let the others get on with it?
(d) Get sick and miserable, but try to produce the eggs and bacon?
If (a) score A2, if (b) score A1, if (c) score Σ1. If (d) score A1.

3   Have you ever been abroad? If Yes, continue. If No, score Σ4 and go to Q7.

4   Do you like travelling abroad? If Yes, continue. If No, score Σ4 and go to Q7.

5   When you are abroad, do you prefer to stay in:
(a) A pension?
(b) A campsite, or boat?
(c) A hotel?
If (a) score 0, if (b) score K1, if (c) score Σ2.

6   When you are abroad, do you:
(a) Like eating local dishes?
(b) Enjoy lots of olive oil and garlic?
(c) Prefer your normal diet?
If (a) score K1, if (b) score K2, if (c) score Σ2.

7 Do you speak any language other than your own (enough to be polite and do some shopping)? Score A1 for each one more than two.

8 Can you afford this venture?
  (a) Yes.
  (b) In time, or maybe.
  (c) No.
  (d) I've just won the Lottery.
If (a) score A2, if (b) score 0, if (c) score Σ3, if (d) score what you like!

Discussion on Section One

Q1-2 These are germane questions. If you are unsure, you had better find out the answers for certain, for your own sake and the rest of the crew. Do this by sailing with friends, in as many different boats and situations as possible. If you ultimately intend to go singlehanded, skip the next paragraphs and go to Q3. If you are going to sail with a mate, and your answers to Questions 1 and 2 differ widely from your partner's, the battle lines could be already drawn. If you like ear'oling (sailing with the lee rail under) and spray in your face, and your mate prefers to go over on the ferry, you have a compatibility problem which needs to be resolved. How much can (and will) Salty Sam or Sue throttle back to accommodate the natural fears of less adventurous members of the crew? We have known voyages founder on the fact that the skipper was too harsh, hard-driving and self-punishing. This is fine for racing weekends but unbearable for a long cruise, which ought to be a pleasant experience; and feeble, weedy crews do not contribute to this either.

Willingness is all, however, and much may be learned and achieved with determination. We have mentioned sailing with friends. Some might consider that a flotilla holiday would be the ideal way to do this. We do not. It makes a marvellous holiday and may tempt you into thinking you like cruising; but it is an artificial set-up. You will learn little that is of any use for your purpose, since flotilla sailing has less to do with long-distance cruising than the child licking the basin has to do with making the cake. While many people get bitten by the cruising bug on a flotilla holiday, you will need a lot of practice in situations where you must get out of trouble on your own. That said, bareboating (ie chartering a boat to sail without assistance and as you wish) is probably a happy medium. For Absolute Beginners there is a starter pack in Chapter 7 which will help you to be useful even on your first sail.

Q3-6 Do you really like 'abroad'?
We all love the thought of the palm trees, soft breezes, and swaying Hula hula girls. But do you enjoy new tastes and smells, or would you rather have your joint and two veg. and tea like mother made? (for Brits), or biscuits and red eye gravy (for Americans). You can get McDonalds, French fries and Foster's almost anywhere.

Do you find it all interesting and exciting, or do you worry about the drinking water and the loos? Are you happy in a pension, eating with the family and making a stab at the language, or do you prefer a coach tour or hotel where a courier takes care of all the hassle? Are you, in other words, a self-reliant traveller?

Q7 If you are not good at languages, you can always go West, where most of the continent of North America and a good many of the West Indian islands, plus the Bahamas and Bermuda, are populated by people who speak English of a sort. You can also go down to the Antipodes. If you go to the Mediterranean you will have to cope with foreigners on entry to a new country; and you will have to store ship, get water and fuel, and deal with spares and repairs. This will be stressful if you are impatient with people who speak little or no English. The other side of the coin is the fun of it. When I was much younger and prettier, I left our boat Phoenix in Syracuse harbour and went looking for a fishhook with my Italian Dictionary. 'Amo?' I said hopefully to the proprietor of the fishing tackle shop. His eyes lit up. 'I love you too!' he said. It was a while before I could get him back to the subject of fishhooks. When Nelson had a skin problem that I suspected to be a fungus, a young German came over to help. 'I hear your cat has the mushrooms,' he said.

Q8 Can you afford this venture? What is enough? Selling your house, if you own it, will provide enough money for a reasonable boat. But it has to be maintained, as you do; you will need to fit her out and store before you go, and you need reserves for contingencies — which may be drastic. Don't count on being able to find work on the way. The next chapter on Finance will give you some idea of probable costs, but a lot depends on whether you are in the Champagne or local beer and wine bracket. Perhaps you need more time to work and save, in order to sail with debts paid, mortgages discharged, some reserves and a light heart.

If you scored all (a)s in this Section, you have crossed the first barrier with ease. If you scored all (c)s someone probably gave you this book as a present. Tough. Enjoy reading it, however. If you came somewhere in the middle, you have some thinking to do. Now go to Section 2.

Section Two — Your job: Can you leave it?

1   Do you own your own business? If Yes, go to Q4. If No, continue.
2   Are you unemployed or retired? If unemployed score K2. If retired score K2. In either case proceed to Q7, otherwise continue.
3   How do you feel about the job you are doing now? Choose any of the following:
   (a) I have a strong vocation.
   (b) I really like my job.
   (c) It's just a job.
   (d) I'm in line for promotion.
   (e) I'll be glad to leave.
   (f) I'm ready for a change.
   (g) I've embezzled the tea fund and I'd better go.
If (a) score $\Sigma3$, if (b) score $\Sigma2$, if (c) score 0. If (d) score $\Sigma1$, if (e) score K1, if (f) score K2, if (g) score K10. Proceed to Q5.
4   Which of the following statements is nearest to how you feel? (Choose one.)
   (a) I can't let my work force down.
   (b) It's a family business: I have obligations.
   (c) I work all the hours God sends, and love every minute of it.
   (d) I used to enjoy it, but it's getting me down.

(e) It's a good living and I'm content.

(f) I'd sell if I could find a buyer.

(g) I'd be glad to be shot of it.

If (a) score $\Sigma2$, if (b) score $\Sigma3$, if (c) score $\Sigma1$, if (d) score 0, if (e) score $\Sigma1$, if (f) score K1, if (g) score K3.

5   Are you worried that you might lose skills and/or seniority while you are away?

(a) No problem.

(b) I'll catch up later.

(c) Yes.

If (a) score K2, if (b) score K1, if (c) score $\Sigma4$.

6   If you are a member of an occupational pension scheme, what happens if you give up your job now?

(a) I get a reduced secure pension on retirement.

(b) I get a return of contributions but no pension.

(c) I have no protected rights.

If (a) score K1, if (b) score 0, if (c) score $\Sigma1$.

7   Can you use your skills abroad? A skilled craftsman is welcome almost anywhere, but the Professions often erect barriers against foreign practitioners. See next chapter on Finance.

(a) Yes.

(b) To a certain extent.

(c) No.

If (a) score K2A2, if (b) score K1A1, if (c) score $\Sigma2$.

8   If in Section One (Basic Questions) you scored: As: more than 6, score a further K1. Ks: more than 5, score a further K1. Σs: more than 6, score a further $\Sigma2$.

9   Are you any of these, or do you hold similar posts: Justice of the Peace, President of the Women's Institute or Townswomen's Guild, Provincial Grand Officer in the Buffs or Freemasons, chairperson or officer of any Clubs or Societies, Mayor, Councillor or Alderman, etc? Score $\Sigma2$ for each post you hold. If you hold more than three, score a bonus of $\Sigma3$.

10   Do you spend more than two nights a week at meetings which are nothing to do with your job? (Here only, your job means what you are paid to do. In all other questions 'job' includes unpaid work such as housewifery, parenthood, voluntary work etc.) If Yes, score $\Sigma4$.

11   Do you spend more than two nights a week at meetings which are to do with your job? If Yes, score $\Sigma3$.

12   Can you give up the interests in Q9:

(a) Easily.

(b) With regret.

(c) No.

If (a) score K1, if (b) score $\Sigma1$, if (c) score $\Sigma3$.

Discussion on Section Two

Q1 Can you leave it? If you are unemployed, now could be your chance to go until the job situation changes, especially if your skills are such as to enable you to pick up work here and there on the trip. Although 'job mobility' is much in everyone's minds, 'serial professions' as envisaged by Alvin Toffler in his book *Future Shock* are not yet with us: that is, a series of occupations where you will change jobs at around five-year intervals. If and when such flexibility arrives, it will make leaves of absence or sabbaticals between jobs a much more feasible proposition, and probably improve the mental and physical health of all concerned. (In 1997 there are signs that insecurity of tenure of jobs is causing increased tension; frequent changes are with us, but they are not so beneficent as Toffler anticipated.)

Q3-5 If yours are technical skills in a fast-changing field, it will be hard to keep up while you are away. Technical journals are heavy: trusting them to foreign mails is expensive and chancy. We often ask friends to bring them when they visit us, and are smitten with guilt when their heaviest piece of luggage turns out to be full of yachting magazines, a pilot book, the Sundays, 'and a few paperbacks' plus several Royal Institute of Navigation Journals.

If you want to keep your options open, then leave of absence while you find out if you really enjoy the life, is the best answer. Otherwise you face a refresher course of some kind on your return, if there is one. This also applies if by leaving your job you lose status and seniority. It could be hard.

If leave of absence is not possible and you can not take your job with you, you should look on your voyage as early retirement, with the possibility that you might have to return to work later. If your skills are really rare and valuable you should have no trouble finding a job when you come back, and your employer will not care where you have been, so long as it wasn't in gaol. If your skills are less useful, you could face re-training for a new career. In either case, we don't need to tell you that your curriculum vitae (resumé to Americans) would need to be carefully worded. You will clearly be able to provide adequate, not to say impressive, reasons for your absence. The usual pack of lies, in fact. At least your health and vigour should have improved, and you might have acquired a whole new set of skills, but in the present climate you may face great difficulties getting back into the labour market, especially after a certain age.

Q6-8 If you are used to being a person of consequence, consider whether you will be satisfied with being 'just a yottie'. We tend to come a bit lower on the social scale than some of you are accustomed to. You will be 'of no fixed abode', can't get a credit rating, and end up classed with gypsies and chicken-stealers. There are many compensating and pleasurable feelings of achievement and satisfaction, but these do not scintillate outwardly in other than an air of contentment and relaxation.

And once having tasted real freedom, could you ever again settle to a 9-5 existence? We think we could if the devil drove — but he'd need a big whip.

AGHIOS EFSTRATIOS
EARTHQUAKE DAMAGE

Section Three — Your health: Are you fit to go?

1 Do you feel unwell a lot of the time? If No, continue. If Yes, score $\Sigma 4$.

2 Do you have a condition for which you regularly seek medical advice? If No, continue. If Yes, score $\Sigma 5$.

3 Do you have a condition which worries you and for which you have not sought medical advice? If Yes, score $\Sigma 4$. If the answers to the last three questions were all No, score K3 and go on to Section 4. Otherwise continue.

4 Do you remember your condition:
(a) Hardly ever?
(b) Some of the time?
(c) All the time?
If (a) score K1, if (b) score $\Sigma 1$, if (c) score $\Sigma 3$.

5 Would your doctor allow you long periods of self-medication?
(a) Yes.
(b) No.
(c) He doesn't give a toss.
If (a) score K1, if (b) score $\Sigma 4$, if (c) score 0 and change your doctor.

6 Could your condition:
(a) Prevent your standing a watch, night or day?
(b) Endanger the boat or fellow crew members?
(c) Necessitate expensive and/or time-consuming medical attention while on voyage?
(d) Cause over-tiredness or require a rigid regime or schedule?
If your answer to Q6 is No to all four, score K1. If your answer is Yes to (a), (b) or (c), score $\Sigma 2$ for each Yes. If (d) score $\Sigma 1$.

Discussion on Section Three

Q1–4 Are you fit to go? There is no doubt that we go to sea with the most amazing handicaps. We have met unbelievably courageous long-distance cruisers with diabetes, cancer, heart conditions and stroke, amputees, people with imperfect limbs and paralysis; not to mention those souls (perhaps more fool-hardy than courageous) who were obese or alcoholic or addicted; to which list we should add several who were clearly bonkers. Nothing short of coma seems to stop us, as long as we are willing and able to 'manage' our disability with long-range advice.

A positive mental attitude will assist one's fellows to make a few (oh, very few) allowances, as will a determination to excel in the things one can do, while not shirking those tasks which will cause discomfort but not damage. Realism is of the utmost importance here, and the quality of enjoyment one can expect must be considered as carefully as physical well-being. A long talk with a doctor who understands exactly what long-distance cruising is all about will be necessary. If you have not already consulted on anything that worries you, ask yourself why.

Q5–6 At sea you will have to care for yourself. This requires more sense than bravado. A golfing doctor who doesn't understand what is involved will merely tell you not to go: professional people must be cautious about giving advice in unusual circumstances, as they could be held liable for the consequences. Find yourself a yachting doctor to consult. Where do you find him? Offshore at the Yacht Club, of course, where his patients can't get at him! If you are in luck you should get a realistic answer; pointing out dangers to avoid, how to monitor your condition, what drugs or medication to take with you, how to inject yourself safely, and what to exercise and how.

Q6 Consider carefully whether you are a danger to the boat or crew. Red-green colour blindness, for instance, is a strong contra-indication since it is of vital significance on a night watch to be able to distinguish red and green lights on shore and on other vessels. A condition that causes you to tire easily, or requires a rigid regime or time schedule, should give you pause; since one of the great benefits of the life is being able to forget time and rigidity. Most of us long-term cruisers don't even know what day it is, and find that getting friends to airports is an unwelcome return to a scheduled world.

A word on drinking. Most of us do this with great gusto, the rum or wine being cheap and the company enjoyable. But note that air pilots are forbidden to drink before and during flying. Naval navigating officers are not so forbidden, but nevertheless have a long-standing tradition of not drinking at sea. (Of course, when let off the hook you'll find them drinking ashore and sinking a gin; but that's better than drinking at sea and sinking the ship.) Make up your own mind, but the sea is no place for alcoholics. We know of at least one yacht that was lost with all hands, where drink was a contributing cause, and a good many drownings from dinghies on the way back from the pub.

Don't forget that alcohol in the bloodstream increases seasickness. Not a few wild farewell parties have caused a postponement of the sailing day. Nor is it unknown for a yacht, after the gongs, bells and cannons have wished them Bon Voyage, to creep into a bay round the very first headland and drop anchor till their headaches improved.

Now the good news. On a well organized voyage your general health will improve, as the outdoor life and the lack of stress seep into your body and mind. You will probably be cured of your migraine (as I was), your asthma (as Bill was), or your hay fever, tummy cramps, eczema, PMT — anything with its true origins in tension and stress.

Section Four — Your family: How strong is the pull?

1   Have you parents, children, or near relatives living? If No, score K1 and go to Q4. If Yes, score Σ1 and continue.
2   Are you worried about any of them? If No, score 0. If Yes, score Σ3 for each one.
3   Are you the only child? If No, score 0. If Yes, score Σ2.
4   Has your mate (if any) parents, children or near relatives living? If No, score K1 and END THIS SECTION. If Yes, score Σ1 and continue.
5   Is he/she worried about any of them? If No, score 0 and END THIS SECTION. If Yes, score Σ3 for each one and continue.
6   Is he/she an only child? If No, score 0. If Yes, score Σ2.

7   What age will your child (children), both yours and your mate's, be when you sail? Will you take them with you? Score as follows:

	Taking them	Leaving them
0–5 years:	0	$\Sigma 5$
6–12 years:	$\Sigma 1$	$\Sigma 4$
12–18 years:	$\Sigma 2$	$\Sigma 4$
over 18 and/or independent:	K2	$\Sigma 1$
over 18 and dependent:	$\Sigma 2$	$\Sigma 4$

(The score is additive, thus if taking a baby and toddler with you score 0; and if you are taking one four-year old and leaving two of 13 and 15 years respectively, score $\Sigma 8$.)

8   Is there someone reliable to care for children remaining at home? If Yes, score K2. If No, score $\Sigma 4$.

9   Do you have children of school age? If No, END THIS SECTION. If Yes,
(a) Will you teach them yourself?
(b) Will you use a correspondence course?
(c) Will you send them to boarding school at home?
(d) Will you send them to local schools as you travel? And stay long enough to benefit?

If (a) score K2, if (b) score K2, if (c) score K1. If (d) score 0.

Note: Q8 There is a wide range of possibilities here. Boarding schools fill the bill in term time, but usually other arrangements must be made in the holidays if they cannot join you. Compliant relatives may take your child on for a while; this was a common thing in wartime, and most of us did not seem to suffer from being parked on aunts and grandparents and changing schools at frequent intervals. The criterion has to be that the arrangement is satisfactory to all parties, and you pay their way and extra costs.

Discussion on Section Four

Q1-6 You will not enjoy your cruise if family responsibilities lie heavily upon you. It makes sense, therefore, to solve as many problems as you can before you leave, so that on sailing you know that the situation is as stable as can be expected. Good communications after your departure are important; apron strings pull in both directions, and your family will sometimes be as anxious about you as you may be about them. Several cruisers we know have a clued-up person back home, who may or may not be a member of the family, to act as a clearing house for news; so that one phone call only, and that a short one, need be made. A fortnightly (for instance) 'How's things?' 'Everyone's fine, where are you?' is worth a lot, being positive and up-to-the-minute reassurance. Messages to ring home often go astray, and we find we do better by telepathy, and so do others we've met. I'm not kidding: we always obey any feeling that we ought to go and telephone, as we are so often met with a relieved 'Ah! you got my message.' It wouldn't be quite truthful to say 'What message?' but one always does.

Forwarding mail can be rather a chore. Some member of the family usually takes it on, sometimes quite gladly. Make sure they are reimbursed for any postage, and that they clearly understand what is junk mail to you and what is not, otherwise you might get the bulb catalogues and YOU MAY HAVE ALREADY WON (date of competition expired, of course) instead of a sought-after spare parts list and the OCC *Journal*. Written instructions with the address of the next mail drop are better than blurry orders over a telephone line that hisses and crackles like a radio star.

If you have elderly relatives that you have been in the habit of visiting, it is well worth going along to the DSS and pointing out that you will not be available after such-and-such a date. The Social Services can often help a great deal, and will do more if prodded: a talk with them may produce Home Help, meals on wheels, and a regular health visit, for instance.

If you think more help is needed, Age Concern can tell you what might be available. A good neighbour can be given the number of your communication link in case of need. The more people who know the situation the better: doctor, lawyer, fellow club members, fellow church members, and reliable neighbours: anyone who could help to hold the fort if need be. Don't forget great-nephews and nieces, and grandchildren, all of whom should be concerned, and encouraged to visit and give what assistance they can. However, they will all expect you (if you are female) to reappear and wave a magic wand if anything goes wrong, and this can be tricky if you are one donkey, two ferryboats and a bus away from an air terminal, as I was on one occasion. Let alone the expense. If you are male, then it is considered that you have a good reason for what you are doing, usually connected with the sacred word BUSINESS which excuses everything, and far less pressure is applied.

You may, however, be the only child and your relative may be isolated and friendless. The Social Services and Age Concern will be vital in this case, especially if the idea of moving to sheltered accommodation (for example with a warden) is met with resistance or is not possible for other reasons. What if, after all your efforts, your obstinate 90-year-old tells the meals on wheels lady where to put her gammon and mashed, and slams the door on the Health Visitor as if she were an itinerant brush salesman? What if your old person, in fact, insists on self-sufficiency and independence, in a mountain shack or the middle of Dartmoor? Presumably they do this from choice. You are a chip off the old block, aren't you? You'll be doing the same thing when you're their age. In the meantime you wish them good luck, and sail; also from choice. Only you can decide, but if things are unstable at home, it is particularly necessary for your peace of mind to have frequent communications, and a reserve of cash to travel home; and this will affect your choice of cruising ground.

Children: Take 'em or leave 'em? Many people have taken their children to sea, from birth to 13 or 14, and few have regretted it. Books written by survivors of wrecks can frighten you off, but note that the children DO survive. Read the many articles written for cruising magazines by parents who find, in the main, that cruising with their children has been an enriching experience. Their tales of sailing to new lands, meeting new people, and how the children develop self-reliance and confidence, and better yet, a stronger family bond, will be an inspiration for you. We also have a feeling that crews with children on board take more care.

Section Five — Boat skills: How able a seaman are you?

1 Do you own, or part-own, a boat? Or have you in the past? If Yes, score A2. If No, score Σ1.

2 Do you maintain, or help to maintain, a boat? (Hands-on, not just paying for it.) If Yes, score A2. If No, score Σ2.

3 Are you a qualified Master with a lifetime of experience and over 30,000 miles under sail in your log? If Yes, score A30, and go to Q17.

4 Do you potter about in boats? If Yes, score A1. If No, score 0.

5 Are you a weekend dinghy or small-boat sailor? If Yes, score A1. If No, score 0.

6 Have you cruised locally at home or abroad in a yacht for more than fourteen days? If Yes, score A2. If No, score 0.

7 Have you made a passage to a foreign country? If Yes, score A2. If No, score 0.

8 Have you kept a night watch by yourself at sea? If Yes, score A2. If No, score 0.

9 Can you take a compass bearing? If Yes, score A1. If No, score 0.

10 Can you make any of the following: bowline, clove hitch, rolling hitch, fisherman's bend, figure-of-eight knot, sheet bend? If you can do them all NOW score A2. If you can do three of them score A1.

11 If your car goes wrong do you:
(a) Call in the garage.
(b) Have a go at mending it.
(c) Read the manual and then have a go at mending it.
If (a) score Σ2, if (b) score A1, if (c) score A2.

12 Can you cook:
(a) Under difficult circumstances?
(b) With unfamiliar and limited ingredients?
(c) Without getting seasick?
If (a) score A1, if (b) score A1, if (c) score A1. If Yes to all three, score a bonus of A2.

13 Do you suffer from seasickness? If No, score A4 and go to Q17. If Yes, continue.

14 Is your seasickness controllable or reducible by drugs? If Yes, score A1 and go to Q16. If No, continue.

15 Do you recover after 24 hours or so at sea? If Yes, score A1. If No, continue.

16 Are you prepared to suffer the occasional day of misery? If Yes, score A1. If No, score Σ10.

17 Do you have a smattering of any of the following skills? carpentry, compass adjusting, diesel and petrol engineering, electrics (AC or DC), electronics, firefighting, fishing, food preservation, haircutting, how to move heavy loads, laundering (by hand), metalworking, meteorology, musical instrument (small), paramedical skills, painting, plumbing, radio, rigging, sail repair, scuba diving, sewing, soldering, swimming, upholstery. Score A1 for each three skills you claim.

Discussion on Section Five

> *'If there be more learners than saylors all the worke to save ship, goodes and lives must be on them especially in foule weather.'*

It seems to us that anyone who wishes to go in for the cruising life will have acquired some skills. Such is the availability of experience these days that failure to have done anything so far could indicate a lukewarmth: or maybe you are just dreaming.

Some definitions might be useful. In Questions 1–3 we clearly infer a sailing boat, though if for perfectly valid reasons you are thinking of going in a motor yacht, then adapt the question accordingly. Question 4, on the other hand, could mean any type of boat, which is clearly better than none at all. Questions 5–9 involve many conditions which might be borderline: you must use your common sense. If you haven't any, subtract A20!

Question 10 is a fundamental. At first we thought it should score very high; then we reasoned that we are not testing seamanship, but a kind of nautical wanderlust of which ability is only a part. Bill would not like anyone to go to sea without being able to do all these knots in the dark, or to drive even a motorboat away from its moorings without knowing the bowline at least.

If you are a novice and learn to tie these knots (or make these bends, or bend these hitches: what a rabbit warren old nautical jargon can get you into), then you will be already useful. We have come across many Yachtmasters who make their yachts fast with snowball hitches that melt in the sun.

In Q11 we are after your willingness to get stuck into a dirty problem with some chance of solving it effectively. Too many of us dash at a problem without thinking first. Always start with the simplest explanation, because that is often the case. And emulate John Guzzwell who was crewing for the Smeetons when their yacht capsized and was badly damaged rounding Cape Horn. His first re-constructive action was to sit down and sharpen his saw. There are rites of passage in all crafts: preparation before deciding what form the work will take is good thinking time.

Cooking Q12 is one of the basic skills of cruising. Skippers are not entitled to hide behind wifey's apron all the time. Poor food is as demoralising as bad weather and bad temper.

Seasickness Q13–16 must be taken seriously, since it can affect the morale and capability of everyone who suffers. A determined effort should be made to discover whether you start to recover after about 18 hours at sea and then are immune for the rest of the voyage, as the majority are; whether pills help you; or whether yours is the truly resistant kind, in which case you will probably hate the sea for ever.

The list of skills in Q17 are those that we have needed (or lacked) in a quarter of a century at sea in a yacht. (It is not definitive: if we have missed out your special expertise, sorry.) We intend the level of competence to be that of a conscientious amateur. Being a Pro does not score extra, but might improve your earning capacity. Moving heavy weights is an art worth studying if you don't want to get a hernia.

Laurel

GIGLIO, ITALY.

Section Six — Goods and gardens: Can you leave them?

1   Have you lived in your present house/flat for:
(a) Less than two years
(b) Two to five years
(c) Five to ten years
(d) More than ten years
If you love your house, score (a) $\Sigma 2$, (b) $\Sigma 3$, (c) $\Sigma 4$, (d) $\Sigma 6$. If you are ready for a change, score (a) 0, (b) 0, (c) $\Sigma 1$, (d) $\Sigma 1$.

2   Do you like gardening? If No, score K1. If Yes, score $\Sigma 4$.

3   Do you like horses and riding? If No, score 0. If Yes, score $\Sigma 2$.

4   Do you own antique furniture or fine pictures? If No, score K1. If Yes, are you prepared to sell it, or give it to parents/children? If Yes, score 0. If No, score $\Sigma 2$

5   Do you have a fine collection of anything too big or fragile to take with you: old cars, steam engines, carousels, mangles, Ming china, 13th century armour, books, bird's eggs or pornographic (excuse me, curious) literature? If No, score K1. If Yes, are you prepared to sell it, or give it to parents/children? If Yes, score 0. If No, score $\Sigma 2$.

6   Do you have a sport or hobby that you cannot take with you, eg billiards, model railways, pottery, hang-gliding, monumental sculpture or mink breeding? If Yes, score $\Sigma 2$. If No, score 0.

7   Can you manage without the local library?
(a) Yes.
(b) With difficulty.
(c) No.
If (a) score K1, if (b) score 0, if (c) score $\Sigma 2$.

8   Is there life without TV? Do you watch, per week,
(a) 1–2 nights.
(b) 3–4 nights.
(c) more than 4?
If (a) score $\Sigma 1$, if (b) score $\Sigma 3$, if (c) score $\Sigma 5$.

Discussion on Section Six

To some people, possessions are status. It is important to them to have a quality car, a house in the right part of town, and the latest gadget. They get a lot of fun out of their things, and are not likely to be reading this unless escape by yacht becomes frightfully fashionable one year, when they will buy a frightfully fashionable yacht to do it in, and have a lot of fun doing it for a short time before wanting to get back to their other gadgets. In our world, some people travel as light as a soul to heaven: Dan was one of these, he crewed for us from Antigua to Bermuda on his way to Europe and seemed to possess what he stood up in, a tracksuit and some running shoes.

Between these two extremes lie most of us, with a heap of rubbish that we could gladly say goodbye to, some useful odds and ends whose passing we might regret, and a further pile of junk that we cling to fiercely and beyond all persuasion. The more of it you can get rid of, the less hassle you will have on your voyage.

Q1 *Houses*. If you are going on a long voyage, your house back home will be a nuisance. Besides, you are probably buying your boat from the proceeds of selling it; since owning no property may give you tax advantages (see Chapter on Finance). Renting it in case you want to return can cause a lot of headaches: the Hiscocks tried this at first but eventually sold the house as the tenants caused so many problems. We have this spring met a French couple whose summer cruise to Greece had already ended in Fiumicino near Rome: they had to return and sort out some legal difficulty with their house. We sold ours. It was a wrench at the time, but the wound heals.

Q2–5 Those possessions that we could not bear to part with we left with various members of the family to mind for us. Funny, I can't remember what some of them are now. A few we took with us. So, we find, did other people; and it is surprising what a variety of objects mean enough to someone for them to find room and make a safe stowage for. We saw a cello on the 26 foot *New Life*, lovingly cradled on the forward berth (the second best cello, to keep in practice), an icemaking machine which worked by burning camel dung or any other solid fuel on *Northern Light*, an electronic piano for writing songs on *Clarity*. We carry my enamelling kiln. Eight year old Ben Lucas on *Tientos* had a most impressive Lego set. *Snow Goose* had a home computer before they got as small as they are now. Chess computers, TVs, guitars and bicycles are run-of-the-mill; golf clubs and tennis rackets rather less so. A dentist we know keeps a neat case of the tools of his trade on board, so do most doctors; indeed anyone with skills might want the wherewithal to use them, with the possible exception of lion tamers and nuclear physicists. The Sell up and Sail Collection Riddance Award goes at present to Mike and Carrie Hofman, who sold a collection of more than twenty British World War Two armoured vehicles and a field gun before setting off.

> *Beware of Grandsons, Goods and Gardens:*
> *Here your wife's resistance hardens.*

Section Seven — Attitudes: You've got to be crazy

1   Is your dreamboat taking shape? Are you (or your mate) currently:
   (a) Buying or building her?
   (b) Planning or designing or choosing her?
   (c) Still looking for the right one after ten years?
   (d) Designing for the tenth time in ten years?
   (e) Still building after fifteen years?
If (a) score K4, if (b) score K1, if (c) score 0, if (d) score Σ1, and if (e) score Σ3.
2   All of us have fears and uncertainties about such a voyage. Let's look them in the eye. Which one of the following statements is most true for you, concerning:
Keeping a night watch alone
   (a) I'll be OK.
   (b) I'm a bit nervous.
   (c) I'm rather nervous.
   (d) I'm not keen on the dark.
If (a) score 0, if (b) score Σ2, if (c) score Σ4, and if (d) score Σ7.

Becoming ill on the voyage (you or your mate)
    (a) We'll cope somehow.
    (b) I don't know what I'd do.
    (c) I'm going to first aid classes.
    (d) We'll have a check up before we go.
    (e) He/she would be helpless without me.
If (a) score K1, if (b) $\Sigma 1$, if (c) 0, if (d) 0, if (e) score $\Sigma 2$.

Bad weather
    (a) I'm used to it.
    (b) I think I'll be OK.
    (c) I'm a bit nervous.
    (d) I'm very nervous.
    (e) I'm scared stiff.
If (a) score K2, if (b) K1, if (c) 0, if (d) $\Sigma 1$, if (e) score $\Sigma 4$.

3   Pick whichever of the following best expresses your situation:
    (a) I'm determined to go.
    (b) I'm looking forward to it.
    (c) I can't wait, but I don't think he/she wants to come.
    (d) If he/she won't come, that's the end of it.
    (e) I love planning, but I'm nervous about going.
    (f) If he/she really wants to go, I suppose I shall have to.
    (g) If we go for a year, he/she might get it out of their system.
    (h) The idea is great, but I can't leave my grandchildren/dogs/cats/garden
        just now.
    (i) I don't think he/she has enough experience yet.
    (j) My friends seem dubious about my going.
For (a) score K4, if (b) K2, if (c) 0, if (d) $\Sigma 3$, if (e) $\Sigma 1$, if (f) 0, if (g) 0, if (h) $\Sigma 5$, if
(i) $\Sigma 4$, and if (j) $\Sigma 2$.

4   How long do you envisage doing this?
    (a) For the rest of your life?
    (b) For a year or two?
    (c) For several years?
    (d) Until you get too old?
    (e) For the foreseeable future?
If (a) score K4, if (b) K1, if (c) K2, if (d) or (e) score K3.

5   If you are not yet committed to going, how long before you do commit
yourself?
    (a) This year?
    (b) Next year?
    (c) Sometime?
    (d) Never?
If (a) score K3, if (b) K2, if (c) 0, and if (d) $\Sigma 5$.

6   Why haven't you already gone?
    (a) I'm really just dreaming.
    (b) For reasons I don't wish to reveal, or am not sure about.
    (c) I have.
If (a) score $\Sigma 5$, if (b) $\Sigma 4$, and if (c) you are fouling up the system!
If your score in this section is more than K15, you are somewhat imprudent:
subtract A4.

Discussion on Section Seven

In terms of partnership, one person is usually the instigator and prime mover of the Ulysses plan and the other (or others) the more or less willing follower. Usually the man is the instigator, and is going to be Captain. Usually the women and children are followers, and are going to be mate and crew. To the discussion which follows, it does not really matter which way round it is, but in order to avoid saying he/she too often we will go with the majority.

Trouble is clearly going to arise if the views of the partners are too divergent. Now, before you go to great expense and disruption, is the time to find out: if you disagree fundamentally about whether to go at all; or less radically about the kind of boat, the amount of time and money to be spent, what areas you will travel to, and the standard of comfort required.

Women have been home-makers ever since the first cave-wife hung a skin on the wall of her cave, instead of wearing it or lying on it. The habit, after 5000 years, dies hard, and it is too much to expect your wife to live in a production boat, stark as a railway station gents (and probably smelling rather similar), without letting her cosify it, within reason. The happiest boats we meet seem to be the ones with the homely touches. I have seen the sideways look in a woman's eyes when her man boasts that 'We haven't altered or added a thing since we got her at the Boat Show: keeps up the resale value, you know.' I am far more inclined to Hal Roth's view: 'the layout and detailing of the little ship on which a man lives and travels ought to be as personal as his fingerprints.'

I cannot see that curtains, covers, cushions and decor ruin the resale price. Nor has any production boat designer thought of all the extra gear you need to live aboard: indeed in many boats it is hard to find space for the oilskins and seaboots for every crew member. I shall say more about this later, when we talk about storage.

If you embark on this life with any hope at all, you have to trust and have faith in each other. It follows that there should be some basis for this trust, and that you should set out to acquire skills and experience that will justify it. It's no good sailing out into the sunset, Captain, with your manly hand on the tiller and your manly pipe clenched between your teeth, if your mate quickly concludes that you do not really know what you are doing or where you are. No good, Lady, posing like the yachting mag ads, in immaculate whites holding a rope that obviously goes nowhere, when your Captain needs knowledgeable help. You owe it to each other to learn as much as you can by sailing together and separately, with friends or by answering 'crew wanted' ads, for long or short journeys, in different kinds of boat with different kinds of skipper.

If you have both been living the nine-to-five life, you will be used to speaking to each other about five to six hours a day: less if you are silent breakfasters, TV addicts or in the darts team. How will you cope with being in each other's company twenty-four hours a day, barring night watches? When in such close quarters, a seventh sense needs to be developed. You should know when another person's space and privacy should be respected, and words that can wait half an hour be left unsaid. Long companionable silences should be easily achieved, and just as easily broken at the right moment. When we have friends on board we find that siestas are a great idea. Everyone separates to their own patch of space, and quiet activities, rest or sleep prevail for a blissful couple of hours. On meeting again later the chat is all the livelier, and the wit keener, for having had a break.

Fears and fancies we all have 2, and they need dragging out into the light where they can be more carefully examined. It is no good saying 'Cheer up, it won't happen!' because it probably will; no cruise is without incident. If you are aware of danger you have already taken the first step to prevent it; but be sure that you are guarding against realities, and not bogies under the bunk. You will reduce unnecessary worry to a minimum if you develop confidence in your boat, your Captain or crew, and yourself. Fear is allayed by encountering, and coping successfully, with trouble; this is what experience means. From the statistics, one ought to be far more terrified of crossing the High Street than keeping a night watch, but the first is a known and familiar danger and the second an unknown one. Eventually it becomes as ordinary as crossing the road, and rather less dangerous, though never to be taken lightly.

Illness on the voyage (either oneself or one's partner) is one of the thoughts that perturb us. Why do we not worry as much over becoming ill in our ordinary life at home? Because help would be available, in the form of doctors, hospitals, and friends. We have only to seek advice, and the burden is straight away on other shoulders: all we have to do then is follow instructions. If you wish to have the freedom that the cruising life brings, you have also to accept that you are going back to the pioneer days of being self-reliant.

Having said that; you will certainly be a lot healthier than if you'd stayed at home; and it's surprising how often there is a doctor in the next boat just when you need one. We have come to no serious harm in twenty odd years of cruising, some of it in very remote places. (See Chapter Fifteen for further comment on prevention of illness and accidents.)

I suppose most of us are afraid of bad weather, though some of us are reluctant to admit it. It's no fun at all to have your house bucketting about at all angles, and the corners of your galley attacking you when you cook; and when the cat burrowing on to your lap under your oilskin while you steer is the only bit of companionable warmth you'll get till the weather improves. But if your boat is strong and your Captain capable and prudent, and perhaps above all you have got your sea legs, then it's possibly a little better than two hours in a packed commuter train.

No blame attaches to people who are afraid to go to sea, any more than those who would fear mountain climbing or motor racing, or (in my case) pot-holing: I'm already not too happy on the Underground. Some people do these things precisely because they are afraid, and singlehanded too. To such brave hearts we give our admiration, but this book is not for them. Cruising is a game that two or more should play: no sane person goes mountain climbing or deep diving alone, and people who go off on journeys which they mentally label 'One Man against the Elements' or 'Alone in the Southern Ocean' are taking greater risks than we would care to. There is no need to be that crazy.

Nevertheless, if you want to undertake the life, you must develop a self-reliance that is unusual these days. We yotties are felt to be eccentric, a curious cross between hermits, voluntary exiles and adventurers. We feel very normal, of course; and only at gatherings of landpeople do we realise that we are perhaps a bit peculiar — when our answer to the inevitable question 'And where do you live?' is followed by an odd little silence, or a rush of enthusiastic clichés covering extreme social embarrassment. If you can't be classified, you are too alien to converse with. If they don't know where to put you in the social order you naturally go to the bottom. It's quite comfortable down there, there's no competition!

So, you do have to be crazy. But at least do it with planning, forethought and prudence.

Summary

Now, write down your scores:	A	K	Σ
Section One	..	..	..
Section Two	..	..	..
Section Three	..	..	..
Section Four	..	..	..
Section Five	..	..	..
Section Six	..	..	..
Section Seven	..	..	..
Totals for each type of score:	..	..	..

Now add up the totals for A and K, and multiply by 100. Divide this figure by your total Σ score: this gives your ULYSSES QUOTIENT, ie

$$UQ = \frac{100(A + K)}{\Sigma}$$

where A represents your APTITUDE and ABILITY for cruising, and K represents KINESIS which is the mobility force in your personality, while Σ (SIGMA) represents STASIS which is the inertia in your personality.

If your UQ is below 100, you are a static person from a cruising point of view.
If your UQ is between 100 and 200, you are moderately kinetic: go with someone who has a higher one.
If your UQ is between 200 and 300, you are kinetic: you'll get by.
If your UQ is over 300, you have marked kinesis.
If your UQ is over 1000, you are a bit weird; why haven't you already gone?

There is a possibility of obtaining a total Σ score of zero, which would lead to a UQ of infinity. This is only possible if you are already following the life of a Ulysses, and are thoroughly content. Go on and enjoy it in good health.

PS: If you can't do the arithmetic, you wouldn't be able to work out a sunsight: stay at home.

Chapter Three

Finance

*'The Purser doth keepe an Account of all that
is received and delivered.'*

When we were giving talks following the publication of the first edition, we were frequently asked about finance and it is clear that this is a pre-occupation with many prospective voyagers. Finance is a question not of income, nor of expenditure, but of balancing one with the other. It is likely that every reader's personal circumstances will be different one from another, so this chapter has to provide a broad coverage of the problems and factors as we have experienced them, or heard about them. Basically, running a boat to escape in is cheaper than running a house with car, garden, telephone, holidays and local taxes. It is when you wish to hang on to all of these things that serious money could be involved. We know we are writing now for an international readership, but different countries have a wide divergence of fiscal legislation. We are familiar only with British Taxes. Income Tax is one of the inventions that we have exported to the rest of the world. I hope everyone is duly grateful.

Laws have always been subject to change, but nowadays our parliaments seem to have contracted legislative cyclical vomiting, and ill-considered regulations spew forth too fast for even the experts to keep ahead of. What we write here must therefore be considered comment on what we perceive as the situation at the moment of writing, not as advice tailored to your particular circumstances. You have to make the judgements for yourselves. However, though Finance Acts and legal decisions come and go, certain principles of managing remain stable, so here goes.

Before leaving on a long cruise, make an estimate of how long you will be away. How reliable is your estimate? Things may go wrong and circumstances alter. Best to have several possible scenarios, each with its own mutually exclusive probability. You will want to adjust your finances, if you have any, to suit the most probable and most sought after scenario, but at the same time recognising that things may change, and you might need a fall-back policy.

Timescale is important. For those looking forward not to settling at sea for life but for having a limited break, perhaps a two-year sabbatical, financial consider-ations become different. When the break is for a comparatively short period like two years, one has to be careful to define the aim and what one can achieve. We think that to dismantle your personal finances for such a period would be unwise, because every major change involves fees and costs. You would not be able to become non-resident of the UK, so your strategy will remain that of a UK resident, so you would need to minimise any property (in its widest sense) that could cause problems while you are away. Many will want to keep their house, but it will need protection, and delegated authority to deal with problems is essential. For those going away for such a period a good and trusted friend or relation is very desirable.

Taxation

Apart from the actual provision of an income in the first place, the important thing on the income side is to stop most of it falling into the hands of governments or assorted middlemen. Since the first edition of this book, taxation in Britain has changed dramatically, the main change being the big reduction in personal taxation level. There comes a point when the costs of setting up schemes to minimise taxation make the process self-defeating. We do not think it is any longer necessary to devote one's energies to it when there are more enjoyable things to do.

When we first sailed away the marginal rate of income tax in Britain was 91%, and the basic rate was 37% under a Labour government which had been elected with all the enthusiasm attending that of the present one (1997). Since then, after 18 years of Tory misrule, the top rate has fallen to 40%, and the basic to 25%. In our wildest moments we would not have predicted such a change, nor will we predict what future changes may take place, but after so great a downward move, the next few years could well see a swing in the opposite direction. Once all the family silver has been sold, a government has to get income from somewhere else.

Talking of politics, we should point out that it is quite difficult to sell up and sail away and still retain your vote. We lost ours because of bad legal drafting under La Thatcher. You can keep a vote in Britain if you retain an address there, and you can vote as a resident abroad if you have an address there. We itinerant yotties are wandering waifs of no fixed abode, untrustworthy anarchists dedicated to the overthrow of democracy everywhere, and must not be allowed any civic rights whatsoever. Being deprived of any ability to influence events we tend to consider ourselves above politics, like most yotties with independent frames of mind, but that does not prevent us impotently fuming from time to time. So much for no taxation without representation. Oh yes! We are taxed, on pensions and royalties.

Non-residence

One way that British citizens can reduce personal income tax is by becoming non-resident. It takes three years of fairly persistent absence from the UK to achieve this status, though the Inspector of Foreign Dividends will grant provisional status if you bully him. An important factor in this persuasion is whether or not you have emigrated. The Inspector, who evidently is not strong on English, gets confused between emigration and immigration, believing that you cannot have one without the other. He will want to know the address of the castle in Spain to which you are emigrating. We succeeded in establishing, with some legal ballast behind us, that one does not need to emigrate *to* anywhere; mere emigrating, verb intransitive, is enough. But the Inspector never gives up. Every so often we receive a letter asking us if we have made up our minds where we wish finally to reside. We usually reply 'In Davy Jones' Locker', and that keeps everyone happy for another year or two. Once non-residence is granted, there are important restrictions on the visits to the UK that you can make in any year. In practice these are not onerous, but should be strictly adhered to. Keep your airplane/ferry ticket stubs.

Non-residence enables you to invest in those Gilt-edged stocks that are tax-free to residents abroad. This is advantageous if you are in the upper tax bracket, or have substantial joint holdings, but in those cases you will get professional advice. Usually the yield on these stocks is well above the rate of inflation except during periods of complete governmental madness. (Remember the late seventies?)

Incomes of husbands and wives are now taxed separately. It is likely there will be several changes in the rules because the Treasury never leaves any new procedure alone for long, but it seems at the moment perfectly possible for a husband to be a non-resident and to have all the non-taxable income while the wife remains resident and has all the inflation-resistant (but taxable) income in her name. If the husband has a good pension, then the position would be reversed. With present taxation rates (early 1997) we think double taxation arrangements are not worth the candle.

There remain other tax advantages to obtaining the status of non-residence. One is exemption from Capital Gains Tax. So if you have taxable property or business to sell, it is worthwhile starting the process of emigration and obtaining provisional non-resident status before the actual sale is legally completed. Here again you will need professional advice. Remember the important factor is to sell up and emigrate *from*: you need not immigrate *into* anywhere.

Other advantages concern inheritance taxes: get advice. Otherwise we do not feel that non-residence is worth the bother. One of the reasons is that when non-resident, susceptible income is taxed from the very first pound: one does not get any personal allowances. There is a complex formula which the Inspector should work out to decide whether you would be better off being taxed as non-resident or as resident (it is too difficult to go into here), and you pay the lower figure. Being non-resident also exempts you from jury service.

Do not forget that the British old-age pension is still very good value, though one cannot guess for how long. Keep up the voluntary payments if you can: the DSS has leaflets on this.

VAT

Value Added Tax is a major outgoing, and it is almost impossible to avoid. The exemption from VAT that can be claimed by non-residents when buying goods in Britain for personal export is no longer the great advantage it once was when it was available to EU countries. You now have to give a bona fide residence in a non-EU country to which the reimbursement cheque will be sent. Some yotties have an arrangement with an American or Swiss friend, but the penalties if one is caught cheating in this way are substantial.

The rules for VAT on boats in the EU changed in 1993. Consult the RYA's publication; and a special office of HM Customs provides documentation and advice in difficult cases. If the yacht has had VAT paid on it in any EU country, it may travel and change hands anywhere throughout the EU without incurring further liability. Any boats built or imported into the EU before 1985 are assumed to have paid VAT even if documentary evidence is unavailable. It is the problem of VAT while on the yacht itself that we worry about. Generally, except with a lot of effort it is difficult to avoid paying it on routine purchases.

Non EU yachts

The worst sufferers under European VAT legislation are the citizens of non-EU countries. The situation changes marginally in different countries, but the principle is the same. Whereas at one time an American (or Canadian, Australian etc) yacht could cruise the Med comfortably for years, her owners must now be a little more careful, and the rules are not nearly so convenient. In principle, a foreign yacht can stay in the waters of a country for six months, or in some cases a year. British yachts visiting the USA for example are given a six-month cruising permit, at the expiry of which they have to leave US waters or be formally imported into the USA by paying huge import taxes.

Non-EU yachts find the same in Europe. The Mediterranean is bordered by several different countries. Once one could stay one's six months in Italy, then do six in France, a few months in Spain, return to Italy, Greece, and so on. It was a lot less trouble than it sounds, and worked out quite well. Now all these countries are in the European Union, and they all have very similar laws governing VAT, though it is called different things in different countries (TVA in France for example). Nowadays, if you have done your six months in France, for example, you must leave for a country *outside* the EU, and you may not be allowed back into it until another six months has elapsed. We say may not, because in practice this is difficult to enforce. The Med is completely EU on the northern shore (except for former Yugoslavia which is still not wholly congenial), and is almost all inhabited by unfriendly Arabs on the southern shores (except for Tunisia, which is nice, but a little isolated), while the eastern end is engaged in the sort of intermittent hostilities in which the average American is a fair target for all sides: well, it ain't like it used to be.

The Med is still a good place to cruise, but the length of stay relative to tax etc, needs to be watched just as it does for European boats in the USA. The only difference is to treat the European Union as a United country for this purpose.

EU yachts

Nowadays the only awkward cases for European boats concern those which were exported from (say) the UK as an export without payment of VAT and have been passing their winters in Cyprus or Malta (both non-EU). Technically these vessels are liable for the tax on their first entry into any EU port, unless tax-exempt because of age. Whatever nationality you may be, if you are buying a boat, ensure that European VAT has been paid if you plan a lengthy stay in European waters or wish to sell your boat on to a European.

For a long time, the rules were not strictly enforced, especially in those countries which relied on income from tourism. Then Brussels got tough. We have established that British officials have supplied Greek officials (and we presume the same provision to exist between any pair of EU countries) with lists of yachts exported from UK free of VAT since VAT was introduced. We know of yachts arriving in Greek ports, being pounced on and being charged Greek VAT.

(The existence of the lists came to light as the result of an appeal.) This gives a strong disincentive to try to bluff your way through this particular minefield: you do not know where the mines are and the authorities do!

In one typical case, Greek customs waited some time before demanding the tax. They said it was to give the owner a chance to declare it. Then they charged double tax *and* a fine *and* costs on top for not declaring it. The sums involved are large; Get it right; it is not a tax to play about with.

One recent development (Spring 1997) concerns those of us who convert ex-commercial vessels for the purpose of living aboard. In an appeal to the VAT tribunal the Customs and Excise agreed that where a commercial vessel is so converted, and that the primary purpose is living aboard, while movement is secondary, then the cost of conversion and most of any subsequent maintenance work will be zero-rated for VAT. They even refunded VAT that had been paid on several converted barges, together with interest and legal costs.

This landmark decision is important for live-aboards in this category, but the process is not all that simple. Anyone who thinks they might benefit should contact an officer of the Barge Cruising Association (they ought to be members, anyway). What has not been made clear is how one will get on when navigating in other EU countries, which might want proof of payment.

Finance for USA Yotties

For citizens of the USA, the main problem in avoidance of US taxation is the possibility of losing citizenship. Having seen examples of correspondence shown me by American friends, I can affirm that the relentless po-faced tone of the USIRS makes the UK Inland Revenue seem like a friendly Agony Aunt. Our American friends still fill in their tax returns and send them off each March, whereas most English do not unless they have a pension.

On the investment side, given American freedom from exchange controls, it is surprising more of them do not look at the prospect of getting better net returns, while still retaining the financial strength of the dollar from some of the Scottish mutual funds invested entirely in the USA.

Earning your Keep

Earning one's living locally is theoretically possible but in many cases not wholly practicable. Unemployment is not a British monopoly: most places are far worse off, and elaborate precautions are taken to protect the local workforce from foreign competition. The problem needs looking at in three ways: first, how can one earn in a way that does not upset the locals, wherever one is? Second, what jobs, trades, or professions are generally welcome anywhere? And last, what about the Common Market?

Under the first heading come those various occupations that can be carried out aboard, the income therefrom not being obtained locally. Artists come under this heading, provided they are not seen to sell in direct competition with the locals, though even here there is often a degree of tolerance not evident in most fields. The keynote is discretion; it does not seem to matter how much you make, it is the degree of ostentation involved which is important.

We have personal knowledge of this field. Artists in general are very tolerant of one another, respecting talent in any form. The chief source of possible objection comes from the local art gallery or souvenir shop, but sales direct to other foreigners excite little attention. Only Bermuda has really restrictive laws. Places where the artist can make more than a little something are the West Indies and the Bahamas, where the locals do not do much towards providing a souvenir industry, and where the majority of tourists are comparatively wealthy Americans. Greece is interesting, for it can be chauvinistic or even xenophobic at times, but it is genuinely liberal towards artists and musicians. However, I suspect there exist several ways in which they could cope with unfair exploitation of this liberality.

Writing is not an easy way to earn, and we do not say this merely to impress our editor. She knows it already. Don't count on it for earning your keep. Best-seller novelists live like kings, but if you are merely well known you won't earn much for a great deal of labour. A couple of well known novelists living afloat in the West Indies do so very modestly. Writing for yachting magazines is hard work and badly paid. Unless you have a contract for a regular column you have to accept that not all your output will sell. This gives a poor return for the total time spent. One would need to produce a very large volume of words to make much of a living, and original, worthwhile subjects become harder and harder to find, leading to an inevitable fall in standards. Magazine writing has to be seen as a way of making an occasional bonus.

One yachtswoman we knew made couture bikinis for the boutique trade. She was talented, and is a good example of a well-planned, suitable home industry. Another couple taught themselves the craft of Scrimshaw, before Green laws demanded that dead whalebone should be given decent burial as carrion, and not immortalised into beautiful things. Laurel could probably make more from her enamelling than we do from writing, but the days are not long enough.

Carrying out services associated with boats for other foreign yachtsmen is worth looking at. Bill has made some pocket money adjusting compasses, and got the approval of the local Greek Coastguard officer, since no one else on the island was qualified to do it. Persons capable of doing electronic repairs are very hard to find, and thus welcome. A good working knowledge of technique, and ability to read a circuit diagram are required, while electronic parts are often easier to buy retail in less well developed countries. Anyone who can repair refrigerators will find much to do.

Those skills which are welcome anywhere are not numerous, but in yottie circles a jack-of-all-trades is welcome. Trained nurses are in demand world-wide, but doctors definitely are not; the latter seem to have devised some very restrictive practices. Mechanics can do well in some parts, though often it is a question of a direct job for another yottie, but really skilled men are almost always needed, especially in some West Indian islands. Shipwrighting jobs can be found, though these are usually in the busy season, which is when the dedicated cruiser wants to be doing his own boat. This applies also to casual labour, especially for start of season fitting-out; even if found it is likely to be when one would rather be sailing. Qualified teachers can sometimes get work, especially those with a certificate to teach English as a foreign language.

The European Union

Persons from one member country are supposedly allowed to work in the others. I am only aware of the situation round the Mediterranean coasts, where the French seem to be honouring the treaty. Not unreasonably, they demand that any foreigner working there should pay French taxes and social service dues; however, the bureaucracy is a wilderness for the foreigner to get lost in, and it is necessary to take care. In general I have found French authorities are sympathetic and fair about unintentional breaches of regulations, but they do not take kindly to attempts to pull a fast one.

If French bureaucracy is difficult, the Italians' is a complete enigma that even the natives do not try to solve. I get the impression that everyone lives illegally, and pays up when, or if, caught! It is a completely undisciplined society, and the illegal work going on is widespread. Italians, however, are the most tolerant and least chauvinistic people in Europe.

Greece is settling into the EU slowly and with difficulty, as the concept of fair play is totally alien to them. Their first reaction was one of enormous enthusiasm as money from Brussels descended on them abundantly. They called it Delors Drachmas. They didn't much like the fact that all those foreigners who had been moonlighting could now work legitimately, and even buy houses, but even this had its compensations. Quite soon more BMW's were being sold in Greece per head of population than in any country in Europe, as every Spiro, Nico and Dimitri traded in last year's donkey for a new car. If the EU money had come from Germany in the first place, it very soon got back there. Recently the reckoning came, the Greeks had to start paying taxes, and they are screaming the place down. Working in Greece is quite legal for Europeans, and it is not impossible to get work if you are prepared to work hard. It is easier if you have some skill, otherwise you are competing for the dirty work with illegal Albanians and people from less well off Balkan countries who will work for comparative peanuts.

The EU rules for working, starting businesses etc, now seem to be being honoured in law, even if in practice the process is not so easy. Levantine countries and West European methods and business ethics do not mix easily. But we do believe that they are trying to adapt. In the meantime be very wary of doing anything that could be wrongly construed: the Greeks are among the most hospitable people in the world provided they do not think their hospitality is being abused. Then they can become very nasty indeed. A Belgian couple we know started a modest restaurant and became far too successful. Their car was blown up.

Getting Money to Where it is Needed

> *It isn't funny*
> *To run out of money.*
> *Having some for contingencies*
> *Avoids stringencies.*

We now come to the problem of transferring funds and drawing money. In general it is necessary to have a bank account in any country where you have income originating. Transfer from bank to bank is hopeless. Transfer from an office of a bank in one capital city to an office of the same bank in another capital city is not much better. For example, a sum of US$7000 sent by the London office of the Bank of New York took 32 days to become available in New York, and that was fast going. Another sum took 53 days to get from the London office of Credito Italiano to one of their offices near Rome. Even Barclays took three weeks to get money from their head office in the City of London to their associate company in Antibes. All of these were telegraphic transfers: I have since abandoned all forms of bank transfer.

As if to confuse matters further, those old-fashioned bankers to royalty, Coutts & Co, once transferred a sum to Holland for me in two days, which is absolutely astonishing. It seems it can be done, perhaps only by bank clerks wearing frock coats. And we must remember that Anglo-Dutch banking has always been good, ever since the burghers of Amsterdam saved the Bank of England from default in 1697, in return for which we took William of Orange off their hands. In view of what he did to Ireland, it is doubtful if the deal was a good one from England's point of view, but the Dutch have always driven hard bargains.

Drawing funds for everyday living can be done in several ways.

1 *Eurocheques* can be drawn in Europe, also in Turkey and several unlikely other countries, which are not in Europe, but only on special cheque forms and with yet another card. The cheque is written in the local currency, and the limit is usually just over £100 (some banks will cash two per day). A service charge is made at every stage, which varies from place to place (22% is our record, in Romania). You need special forms from your bank. Eurocheques used to be cashable at Post Offices in several countries, notably France and Greece, but this no longer applies (Jan '97). In France the Eurocheque has become practically useless in 1997. France has turned retail banking over to machines in holes in the wall. Unfortunately the machines were badly designed and are apt to spit foreign cards out like a baby declining its breakfast.

2 *Travellers' cheques* are acceptable generally, but beware of cheques drawn on little-known banks, which means little known at the back of beyond. ('Who is this Barclay that he has a bank?' I was once asked.) These also have a ridiculous charge payable when you buy them, though in view of the fact that you are lending money to the bank, unsecured, the public ought to be paid a fee. A big snag with travellers' cheques is that they are difficult to get once one has left one's native banking scene. They can be bought abroad, but if you already have the money, why buy the cheques? Not unreasonably, banks will not send them through the post.

3 *Postcheques* are available to those with a National Girobank account. They come in chequebook form and enable withdrawal of up to £100 daily in local currency at post offices in Europe and the Middle East (with a few exceptions). There should be no commission on each cheque, but 50 pence is charged per transaction. This is possibly the cheapest way of getting funds at the modest level. Apart from Italy, I have found post office queues rather shorter than those in England. They are much the same length in Italy, but service is even slower.

4 *Credit cards* can be used for a variety of purposes. When we first wrote in 1985 they had limited use for ordinary shopping, since most shops in the scheme were the high mark-up luxury type of shop which we do not patronise. Cards still cannot be used for buying diesel oil at most marinas, though they can be

STONINGTON , CONNECTICUT

used to buy petrol at garages, which seems an anomaly, as this would be the most convenient use for such a card. In 1997 credit cards are accepted in Supermarkets, Hypermarkets and restaurants in France, Italy, and Greece, but not in Germany. (Near the channel ports they will ask for your passport as proof of identity, but not elsewhere: the Daily Gutter day-return Booze Runs seem to have engendered mistrust). On the whole, for retail use only VISA cards are worth the bother. I started out with a full set, and here are my views on four of them.

American Express This card has a very high annual service charge, and its administration is completely unsuited to the needs of the long distance sea-going traveller, being more geared to the casual tripper in capital cities and tourist centres. Like most cards, it can be used for airlines and luxury hotels: so what? I thought it would be useful in the USA, but shops refused it or asked for an extra payment if I wished to charge the purchase to the card. The same applied elsewhere. (An exception to this was car hire: it is virtually impossible to hire a car without a card, but it does not have to be American Express.) When I did charge something to Amex, there were so many billing errors and mistakes in exchange rates that the whole procedure became a nightmare. The only advantage of this card is that there exist AmEx travel offices in certain places where one can draw both travellers' cheques or cash in quite large amounts. Unfortunately these centres are mostly in capital cities or major tourist venues which, apart from Antibes, are unlikely to be of much use to yachtsmen.

Diner's Club Much of the above about American Express also applies, except that it is not nearly so widely accepted, and has no travel offices. I gave it up very early. The annual charge is too high.

Visa/Barclaycard This has been the most useful. I have used it for drawing cash in both the USA and Europe with good results, having once established that one needs a high credit limit, owing to delays in payments clearing and getting into the authorizing computer abroad. It is widely used in Europe without much difficulty, except in France where retailers are now using electronic machines which refuse some foreign cards, including British. We have corresponded with Barclaycard for some years now, and have been repeatedly assured that this is a hiccup which will not continue, but it does. However, a card is about the only way of drawing cash in France, though you may have to visit several dumb machines before you find one that works.

Access/Mastercard This is almost as good as Visa, but it is difficult to find co-operative outlets in France, while the Italian outlets limit the amount drawable to £200. Visa and Mastercard give good service in the USA. With both Visa and Access I have an arrangement with my bank in Britain to pay the accounts on presentation, which keeps one's credit limits up and avoids unnecessary interest charges on otherwise inevitable late payments. One problem with American Express was that they refused this eminently sensible arrangement, expecting travellers to pay within a few days from a position about a thousand miles west of the Canary Islands.

5 *Carry cash* There is a lot to be said for regarding the dollar bill as the perfect travellers' cheque. When we went down the Danube we did just that and managed splendidly. In poor countries it is necessary to have very small dollar bills, ones and fives at the most. As a peasant in the Ukraine could keep his family for a week on one dollar when we were there, you can see that to most people large bills would be meaningless. We were viewed with great suspicion in a British bank when we asked for dollars in one dollar bills, but when we explained the reason they found them for us.

There is no charge for getting them, unlike travellers' cheques, and they are acceptable everywhere, sometimes at a premium. A few years ago in Turkey, the up-market newspaper *Çum Huriyet* published the black market rates every day. There is, of course, no safeguard in the event of loss. Keep your hand on your halfpenny.

Getting a Large Amount in an Emergency

This is a big problem, but it is not very likely to occur. Possible causes might be a fine by local Customs (however undeserved, it sometimes has to be paid before being appealed) or the purchase of a major piece of equipment. Generally major repairs take long enough for money to be remitted by routine means, but it is possible for estimates to be exceeded giving rise to an urgent need.

As a precaution, negotiate the maximum possible credit limits on credit cards, which should be good for £5000 each at the very least, and this gives quite a good sum available at very short notice. Both Visa/Barclaycard and Access/Mastercard will make personal loans above the credit limit and are very prompt, so it might pay to carry appropriate application forms. However, because of fraud, foreign banks now limit the amount available over the counter or via a machine in cash against a foreign credit card. In Sicily not long ago we needed an expensive engine repair, and it took visits to ten different banks to collect enough money.

We have already mentioned that AmEx travel offices will cash quite large cheques for card holders. But I don't think this facility alone justifies the high annual charge.

In theory it ought to be possible to draw a certified cheque on the London (or New York) branch of a foreign bank and present it to the local branch of that bank for immediate payment. In practice it just doesn't work out.

Obtaining really large amounts (in this context) is an intractable problem; there is no certain solution that can be applied in all countries. I do recommend keeping a personal relationship with your home bank manager; if there is a crisis his understanding at a personal level can oil a lot of wheels. If you are going to be in one country for a fair time consider opening a local account and be known to the manager. Local advice at a friendly professional level is usually worth it.

All in all, the best way of getting a large amount in a hurry seems to be to get a lot of small amounts by various means and add them together. A nuisance, but effective. If you think it might be necessary, organise the methods in advance.

Banking Overseas

Considering the problem of getting cash country by country, I think it is fair to say the British will generally be astonished at the lack of customer convenience at retail banks in many parts of the world. On second thoughts I am astonished at the lack of customer convenience in any bank!

Banking in the USA

Here, banking is very fragmented and localised; almost village by village; there is no cheque card system, and cheques are uncashable outside the particular bank's immediate locality so Visa or Mastercard are essential for drawing cash. Foreign money is unwelcome anywhere in the USA; even the Canadians have trouble. Financially, the country is parochial; it is easier to make transactions between countries in Europe than between states in the USA.

Banking in the West Indies

One finds Barclays Bank generally very efficient and they will accept UK cheque cards. It is not generally realised that Canada does a lot to help the more backward islands and Canadian banks are common, well organised and helpful. In a world league of bank helpfulness I would put Canada above the UK. Apart from the French islands where French banks and currency are used, and there are no significant problems, most islands either use the US dollar as legal tender (the British Virgin Islands, for example) or tie their dollar to the US, and both currencies circulate side by side. Even on those islands with British sovereignty or strong connections, the pound sterling is not welcome, and this applies to the Bahamas and Bermuda too. Before leaving make sure to change local currency into US dollars as it can be difficult to do afterwards.

Banking in Europe

French banking used to be reasonable, but has now become rotten for foreigners. The most appallingly inefficient banks are in Italy, where modern banking is supposed to have been invented and the system does not appear to have changed since the prototype. Security is manic, commissions charged are higher, chaos and error abound, and it is one of the few environments in Italy where they are habitually rude to the customer. The best banking services for the tourist are to be found in the more backward countries that are heavily dependent, economically, on tourism. Greece is an example where the service is very good and getting better. In Turkey, everything is very polite and correct but takes a long time with much cross-checking and adding up of numbers. Spain and Yugoslavia are tolerable, but it is useless to try anything out of the routine in Yugoslavia. Tunisia, and most of North Africa, are based on the French system. Eastern Europe is keen on your money, but the transaction will take all morning.

Expenditure

Now let us have a look at expenditure. I would like to quote a cost of living figure, but tastes differ so much that it would be meaningless. We have met a couple who claimed to live (exist?) in a small yacht in the Med on about £50 per week for everything (approximate adjustment made in prices since we met them). I would treat this with a little caution because I cannot see how their craft could continue to be maintained properly, though at the time it appeared to be well enough. Such a life-support existence would be feasible if the cruise were short and no maintenance were done; no replacements, no emergencies to be met, no sickness or injury, and few, if any, excursions into the interior, which are certainly part of our life.

In the later chapter on victualling and marketing, Laurel will discuss the relative costs of food and stores from country to country. With a fair sized boat one can take advantage of differentials or bargains and buy some things in bulk. By moving from place to place many costs do average out, except between continents.

The Med is no longer the cheapest area to live in; the European Union has fixed that. In Greece particularly, we have seen the cost of living double in a few years, mainly because more sophisticated goods became available, pre-packaged items replacing the half-kilo in a twist of newspaper, and so on. Turkey is still cheap, but there is wild inflation, and the US dollar is much in use to try to cope with it. Yugoslavia is in chaos. Tunisia is cheap. France, Spain and Italy do not differ much from Britain.

One of the reasons why some countries are cheap to live in is that many imported and luxury goods are not available outside the big cities, which we avoid.

If we are having to budget for food, we allow £50 (1997) per person per week in the Western Med, £40 in Greece. This will cover modest food, and a moderate amount of wine, beer and refreshments, the main differences between countries being the cost of booze and meals out, see Chapter 9. The figure does not include fuel. It is, however, catering on a reasonably liberal scale: we could do it a lot cheaper and still enjoy life.

In the West Indies and the Bahamas, where the economy is dollar based and much is imported from the USA, the cost of living reflects this. One can live cheaply, but a bit primitively, on local fruit and vegetables (some of them rather exotic such as eddoes, dasheen and cherimoya), bananas, fish, rum, and pork if they kill a pig. And why not? In 1982 our budget for a longish stay in the Grenadines was US$30 per person per week, and in the USA in 1983 it was much the same. In 1997 all-in prices for food are a little higher than in the UK, but booze is cheaper. If you can manage with local produce and avoid expensive imports from the USA, Holland or France, the living is easy.

Insurance

The costs of insurance are substantial in the type of boat suitable for living in. In some countries, notably Italy and France, third party cover is obligatory, and there is talk of it becoming so in Greece, and I think anyone not so covered is an anti-social menace. However, many yachtsmen do not carry full cover.

We had good value for some years from the gentlemen of Lloyds, who behaved splendidly when we were struck by lightning. However, it became clear to them that they were not writing the right sort of policies, and instead of changing their policies they decided to write none at all. We switched to a policy with Groves, John, and Westrup, of Liverpool, who have given us good service at reasonable rates for some years now.

There is no doubt that it is becoming difficult to get cover for an ocean cruising boat, and virtually impossible if there are only two persons on board. I cannot convince underwriters that they are wrong here; they maintain that a small crew can get tired in poor conditions, but seem to forget that the Battle of the Atlantic was won by men, many of them yachtsmen by inclination, keeping watch and watch for weeks on end in appalling conditions. They overlook that insistence on a third member of the crew can be positively dangerous, leading to boats accepting an unknown as a pierhead jump. This happened to us once (we have a better arrangement now), and it led to the only time we have ever been robbed on board. We have known it happen to others too.

If you do get good cover, then keep in touch with your broker. Become known, get a track record. It seems to me unlikely that anyone will get good cover in the Med for less than 1.5%, and that rates will be a lot higher elsewhere. The ocean-going yachtsman badly needs a policy that will insure him against any third party claims, fire, lightning strike, and any structural damage, but excluding cosmetic finishing. It is often the latter that runs away with costs, and it is something many of us are prepared to do ourselves.

One odd feature is that US underwriters charge more for cover in European waters than for cover in the Western Hemisphere, while European underwriters rate the risks the other way round. Does this strongly suggest that rates are based entirely on personal hunch rather than on statistics? Of course they are!

Syndicates

The majority of craft we come across are manned by a married couple (the word 'married' being interpreted a little loosely), but there are a number of boats being sailed by syndicates, and as these are essentially financial arrangements this is perhaps the place for some comment. There are two broad kinds of syndicate.

In the Running Syndicate the expenses of running the boat and living aboard are shared, but the boat herself belongs to only a part of the syndicate, perhaps to one person only. In a Property Syndicate all the members have shares in the boat, though not necessarily equal shares. It is evident that it is possible to have a combination of the two sorts.

The Running Syndicate There is no question of ownership of assets, thus the syndicate is comparatively easy to start, break up or alter as it goes along. Many running syndicates have no formal agreement; they run happily on a shared interest and good fellowship. Given goodwill all round, a break can be just as easy: the person who wishes to leave just packs up and goes. Cautious people might like to have a more positive agreement; I would, but few actually do.

It has to be recognised that the boatowner(s) have the right to withdraw their vessel. But they cannot reasonably exercise this right suddenly in a completely isolated port and thus leave the rest of the syndicate stranded. Likewise, members must not leave the owners stranded, supposing the boat needs a crew to sail. A period of notice needs to be agreed, and it should be expressed in two ways, both in time and in geography; ie there should be a minimum notice of say, two weeks, but that the break shall only take place in a reasonably accessible port, to which the vessel should be taken as soon as possible. New members can be added at any time, but I know of problems, where, for example, one member wishes to bring in a marvellous girl he met last night, and the others just do not see eye to eye with him about her value to the syndicate as a whole.

The loose agreement might at least define what types of expenditure are covered, eg housekeeping, ship's stores, fuel, repairs, replacements and so on. It should certainly appoint a book-keeper. It should ideally set up a contingency fund to help meet accidents or disaster; the decision to use the fund has to be a majority one, and it should be used only for an item too large to be met out of two (say) months' total contributions. Most people would accept simple provisions like that otherwise there is no point in starting. If disagreement becomes serious, expulsion or dissolution has to follow, even if a somewhat different syndicate re-forms. In these circumstances the major problem is often the distribution of the contingency fund, especially if it is long standing and/or substantial. In theory it is possible to work out the refunds arithmetically, but many syndicates have fairly frequent changes, and few of them have a computer. One terminating syndicate I knew (a German one), threw a fantastic party, inviting all yachtsmen in the port to drink the fund which they eventually succeeded in doing. The real problem is that goodwill is often thinned on a dissolution.

A running syndicate problem occurred when an aggrieved party considered that a major repair that became necessary arose from neglect by the owner before the formation of the syndicate, and could enhance the value of the vessel after the syndicate broke up. He felt this was a capital matter, not maintenance; the owner thought otherwise. Such arguments cannot be pre-defined, or pre-determined. They are questions that have to be answered as and when they occur. All parties to a running syndicate must accept the vessel 'as is, where is', and they have to use their judgement as to future liabilities. Of course, an arbitration agreement would help.

The Property Syndicate is concerned not only with running a boat from day to day, but also with the ownership of, and responsibility for, a very valuable piece of property. In these circumstances an agreement *must* be made in proper legal form, for though there will be no problems if goodwill prevails, the scope for bitterness, anger and nastiness when tempers become frayed after some real, or imagined, injustice or slight is so immense that the exercise can turn into a lawyers' benefit. Better a small fee for legal advice at the start.

The syndicate agreement must, therefore, lay down clearly:

- Who is the skipper for purposes of running the ship (there can be only one).
- How decisions, other than navigational ones, are reached.
- Procedure for changes in the syndicate.
- How unforeseen liabilities will be paid, eg reconstruction due to previous neglect or hidden defects.
- Procedure for final dissolution.
- Arrangements for arbitration.

No syndication agreement should ever give any one person a right of general veto. When all goes well, such a right is exercised with tolerance. But if one person gets disaffected, or has a breakdown perhaps, then such a bloody-minded partner can ruin everyone's life. For similar reasons, agreements should contain a clause that in the event of a death the remaining syndicate members have the right to buy out the deceased partner's equity at a valuation arrived at by a stated method. Though all the partners might be the best of friends, this happy relationship may not extend to an executor, or to a legatee of one of these friends. If the capital values are substantial, and exercising the right is liable to cause embarrassment to a partner, then it is possible to obtain a temporary, contingency insurance on a number of lives payable to the survivors on the death of one of them.

I do not think the concept of time-sharing has any relevance to the type of cruising we are considering.

Marine Mortgages

Though vessels can be bought with marine mortgages, it would need much careful weighing up before sailing off with such a burden. The finance companies would not be overjoyed to see their security, mobile as it is, disappearing to parts of the world where they could well have great difficulty and expense exercising any rights in the event of a default. Even if they granted a loan, it would have to be considered less secure than a loan on a boat owned by a man in a steady job, and who never left the country in her, and this would probably lead to a higher rate of interest.

Think how you would pay the regular, very large, instalments. Out of a substantial pension, perhaps, if you are lucky enough to have one — but earning that sort of income while actually cruising is unlikely. It has been done by investing a large sum in property and using the net rental of the property to meet the mortgage payments on the yacht, but this presupposes that the former is greater than the latter. Remember that the finance company is in the investment business too, and in my experience it would be a very special investment opportunity that would make that sort of deal profitable after taking into account all the on-costs of the various arrangements.

To try to earn enough as one goes along to meet mortgage payments is crazy, other than for best-selling novelists, artists who can regularly sell a load of rubbish to the Tate Gallery or hard drug smugglers. The latter will assuredly have their yacht confiscated when they are caught, so the less equity they have in her the better. They should mortgage to the hilt.

What Does Cruising Really Cost?

I have been persuaded, against my better judgement, to be a little more specific about the costs of wandering abroad. This is, of course, to be on a hiding to nothing, for I will be trying to say how long your piece of string is. On the other hand I do have some data, thanks mainly to Laurel's elementary but effective accounting methods (women are far better than men at looking after money), and I do have a certain amount of both personal and borrowed experience of several boats, so here goes. The jargon may be mathematical, but I will give some examples at the end. We are forecasting, remember. Currency is immaterial for this exercise, provided you do not mix them; reckon using the same one throughout.

Let the price or current value of the craft be **P**.

Let the building material factor be **B** (see Table 1, below).

Let the rig factor be **R** (see Table 2).

Let the age (boat, not crew) factor be **A** (see Table 3).

Let the physical capability of each of the crew be **E** (see Table 4).

Let the displacement of the boat in tons be **T** (to the nearest whole number).

Let the cost of the sea-going inventory be **F**.

Table 1 *Building material factor **B***

Fibreglass (GRP)	1.0	Steel	1.35
Aluminium alloy	1.1	Teak	1.35
Ferrocement	1.2	Other timbers	1.4

Table 2 *Rig factor **R***

Sloop	1.0	Wishbone or staysail schooner	1.15
Cutter	1.05	Other Schooners	1.2
Yawl or Ketch	1.1		

If craft is gaff or sprit rigged multiply each of above by 1.1. For example a gaff schooner would be 1.2 × 1.1 = 1.32.

Table 3 *Age factor **A***

Less than one year	1.0	10 years but less than 20	1.4
1 year, but less than 5	1.05	20 years but less than 50	1.8
5 years but less than 10	1.2	50 years or over	2.6

Table 4 *How about the crew, Factor **E**?*

A really fit person well used to manual labour	3.0
Average person 16–40 years, according to fitness	2.0–2.6
Average person 12–15, or 41–60 according to fitness	1.8–2.3
Average person over 60, according to fitness	1.1–1.9
Someone willing, capable, but out of condition	0.9–1.1
A partially disabled person, willing and able to keep a lookout, pass tools, brew tea, and give first aid	0.5–0.8

Maintenance cost

The total annual maintenance cost is divided into two parts, of which one is dependent completely on the ship and her gear, while the other takes into account the capacity of the crew to do things themselves. Obviously they cannot do everything, or it is very rare that this is the case, and it would require unusual combinations and levels of skills. Our assumption is for an amateur and willing, but not specially skilled, crew. The formula works only for sailing craft because I have no data for motor yachts. The costs of engine maintenance in a sailing yacht are included with the broad assumption that the boat and her engine are proportional to each other in size and condition. Well, I do have to make some assumptions, don't I?

The first part, m_1 is

$$m_1 = 0.02 (P \times B \times R \times A + F)$$

which represents maintaining engine, structure, rigging, and replacing them from time to time. It is a long-term annual average.

The second part, m_2, is:

$$m_2 = \frac{B \times R \times A \times T \times 40}{\text{sum of E}}$$

The total expected annual allowance for the ship, **M**, is given by adding these two, thus: $M = m_1 + m_2$

If you are still with me, you must be keen, so let us look at some examples; we will take three to show a fair cross-section of types.

A A 50 year old gaff schooner, built of pine on oak, displacing 36 tons, costing in good sea-going order £30,000 and with an inventory of about £5000. So P = 30,000; B = 1.4; R = 1.32; A = 2.6; and F = 5000.

$$m_1 = 0.02 (30,000 \times 1.4 \times 1.32 \times 2.6 + 5000)$$
$$= 0.02 \times (144,144 + 5000)$$
$$= 0.02 \times 149,144 = £2983 \text{ per annum.}$$

She will have four young crew: a sporty accountant, and his wife who is something of an athlete, a bricklayer, and his wife who is not too fit. These might rate, in order: 2.6, 2.3, 3.0, and 1.4, giving a total crew worth, from this point of view, 9.3 as E.

Thus $m_2 = 1.4 \times 1.32 \times 2.6 \times 36 \times 40 \div 9.3 = £744$.

One might expect to budget for maintenance, then **M** = 2983 + 744 = £3727 per annum. (Always round up.)

B A bermudan steel ketch, 10 years old, displacing 20 tons, worth £50,000 with a £7000 inventory. She is crewed by a 54 year old fit man, his out-of-condition wife, and a 15 year old fit daughter. In this case P = 50,000; B = 1.35; R = 1.1 × 1.1 = 1.21; A = 1.4; F = 7000.

$$m_1 = 0.02 (50,000 \times 1.35 \times 1.21 \times 1.4 + 7000)$$
$$= 0.02 (114,345 + 7000) = £2427$$
$$m_2 = 1.35 \times 1.21 \times 1.4 \times 20 \times 40 \div (2.2 + 1.0 + 2.0)$$
$$= £352$$

So her total expected maintenance **M** would be 2427 + 352 = £2779 per annum.

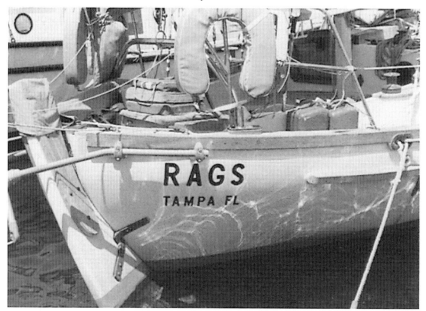

The owner presumably gave up a good job and went from riches to rags.

C A new fibreglass sloop, costing £32,000 with inventory costing £4000, displacement 9 tons. Her crew are an elderly couple; he is 64 and fairly fit, but his wife has arthritis and has difficulty with ladders.

$$m_1 = 0.02 (32{,}000 \times 1.0 \times 1.0 \times 1.0 + 4000) = £720$$
$$m_2 = 1.0 \times 1.0 \times 1.0 \times 9 \times 40 \div (1.2 + 0.7) = £189$$

So her maintenance might well cost £909 per annum.

Those examples are from the original edition, so the figures may look a little on the low side. However, all the relationships are relative so that the formulae stand whatever the level of inflation.

Since gathering the data for the foregoing the range of electronic gadgets has increased beyond all expectation, and the amount that has to be spent, not only on buying new, but on maintaining what has been installed is showing signs of getting out of hand. All consideration of electronic maintenance is excluded from the above estimates. The more you have, the more you spend, because modern electronics are based on the 'do not repair, fit the spare' outlook. It should read, 'Do not mend; go out and spend'.

Insurance again

If the boat is insured there will be another annual expense equal to the value of the boat with her inventory multiplied by the insurance rate, that is $i(P + F)$, where i is the insurance rate which, as discussed earlier, usually lies between 1.0 and 2.5% depending on cruising areas.

Even if the boat is uninsured, the crew should keep a contingency fund and start this off at the beginning with 1% at least of the boat's value; but they should add to this from time to time. I think it ought to be a budget item of about 0.25% of the boat's value. If the boat is insured, then a sum equal to the excess (the 'deductible' in the USA) should be kept on one side in a realizable investment, or in a deposit account on short call.

Personal costs

Other costs that have to be met consist of the housekeeping bills, that is feeding the brutes. In 1997, that appeared to be between £30 and £45 per person per week in the Mediterranean, depending on how much you drink and eat out (it could be a lot more if you lived in luxury), or $60 to $80 per person per week in the West Indies. (Currently £1 = $1.65). Again it is possible to go wildly outside the figures, but they are a guide, and they are heavily dependent on drink. The cost of a food basket on page 191 will give you some idea.

What your shoregoing pleasures are, and how expensive, I have no way of knowing, nor do I think I ought to tell you what ours are. You'll just have to sort this one out for yourself. There are other costs that have to be budgeted for, and these are particular to the person too. There will be the occasional trip back home to see the folks, which is coupled with buying spare parts, thus mixing sentiment with hard-headedness. You will have expenditure on any property or chattels you keep in the old country. You will perhaps have medical insurance, which is no cheap item. World-wide cover is wickedly expensive.

Fuel costs are coming higher on people's agenda these days. In most of Europe the low-tax diesel oil, previously available in many countries, has all but disappeared, and taxation on oil fuel has risen dramatically. And so has lub oil. Circumstances vary so much from country to country, from boat to boat, and from skipper to skipper; this is something one has to work out for oneself. Also, while on fuel, gas prices vary. Butane is subsidised in Greece, but heavily taxed in France, where it costs four times as much.

Obviously, I cannot comment on what allowances you make in 'your bits', but in 'our bits' above I would say that, if you do it all in a thinking way, you should not be more than 50% out. That is not a bad approximation in these circumstances.

Chapter Four

A Yacht to Live In

*'Were I to chuse a shippe for myselfe i would have her sail well
yet stronglye built, her decks flush and flat, and so roomy that
men might pass with ease.'*

The yacht is to be more than just a nautical vehicle: she is to be a home. This puts a very important requirement into the considerations, because many boats that are a joy to sail would make abominable homes, and of course vice versa. From reading accounts written by mile-hungry ocean voyagers, it is apparent that few, if any, spend more than 40 per cent of their time at sea. In our case, over twenty-two years of cruising our average number of days when we were at sea was 91 per year, which is about one day in four. In our busiest year with three ocean passages it was 118.

Many others spend less time at sea, especially those who stay in the Mediterranean where sea-going in winter is, to say the least, uncongenial and sometimes downright dangerous. It must also be borne in mind that even at sea one is living aboard the yacht, and that is a different thing from doing a fortnight's cruise. A degree of discomfort or inconvenience that is acceptable for a week or two rapidly becomes intolerable over a long period.

Size and Type

With the exception of the idle rich, most of us are subject to financial restraint. The reader has to balance the amount of boat to the amount of money and to the size of the available crew, and the answer has much to do with personal preference.

It is a mistake to try to live in too small a boat. Small size admittedly requires less energy to handle and to maintain, but the extra difficulty of moving about, the unavoidable close intimacy, and the obtrusiveness of all those stores for which there is no locker, make a breeding ground for irritation. We know a couple still living aboard a 25-footer after crossing the Atlantic in her, but they are young and very much in love, as well as being short of personal possessions. A German couple lived in a 24 foot boat with an Alsatian dog. Next year we met them in a 68 foot converted Baltic trader, having gone from one extreme to another.

A yacht that is too big can be a liability, of course. A couple limiting their cruising to sheltered waters under power could expect to cope easily with 75 feet, but one has also to think of mooring fees and maintenance. Surprisingly, gear does not always cost more in the bigger sizes; often chandlery for yachts is fancy, of materials chosen for their looks rather than their strength, and the ability to use fittings made for small tugs or barges can save money in some cases.

Fare Well is a 55 foot ketch of about 30 tons displacement. We sailed her a lot over ten years, and Laurel, my wife and mate, and usually sole crew, is a light-weight 5-footer with a congenitally dislocated hip. Since then we have motor-sailed our 60 tonne sailing barge, and though we have been less adventurous, we are beginning to find her a bit more tiring than we used to. Our boats are fine, but we age faster than they do.

Probably the ideal monohull for any age would have a waterline length of 33 to 37 feet, a beam of just over a third of that, and not too V-shaped in cross-section. That would provide a home that can be comfortable, have enough storage space, be easy enough to manage even when years advance, and be reasonably economical to moor and slip.

Multihulls

This is the time to mention multihulls. They certainly give more boat for the money, but they have compensating disadvantages. When heavily loaded, and in our life they always will be, they seem to lose proportionately more performance than a monohull. It is also necessary to go up in size to get enough headroom in the living accommodation. One can get by with a shorter overall length than a monohull, and whereas the latter might run to some 40 or 50 feet, a multihull might provide as good accommodation on 33 or 40 feet. But again there is a disadvantage in the multihull's beam: berthing becomes more difficult, and when it has to be paid for, much more expensive, the loading being 50 to 100 per cent. This is a big factor in the Mediterranean; it is less significant in the West Indies where one spends a lot more time swinging to a single anchor, and it is even less significant in the Bahamas where many of the best harbours are closed to the deeper-draughted monohulls. It's horses for courses.

Motor yachts

It is not easy to be a long term live-aboard cruiser in a pure motor yacht, partly because long passages are virtually impossible, and also because one must be much more cautious about the weather. We do know of several, split between the Mediterranean and the USA Intra-Coastal. In the former they have access to the attractive European canal system, and there is much scope for short sheltered passages. The Intra-Coastal waterway is rather a special case as, apart from a few Canadians, most yachts there are in their home waters.

As Laurel and I seem to be unwilling to give up this life, maybe motoring will be our eventual mode. Certainly in *Hosanna*, we have been motoring more as we get older. Of course a motor yacht provides considerably more comfort than a sailing yacht of the same length. I see no reason to adopt a superior attitude to the dedicated motor yachtsman. Typically he runs his boat well and safely, and conforms to cruising etiquette much better than the bare-boat charter people. Long-term cruising is an attitude of mind.

The motorsailer

There is much to be said for the motorsailer in the Mediterranean. The powerful engine capable of hull speed into a force 6 wind and short sea is most reassuring

" FAREWELL" S GALLEY

in the unsettled weather at the beginning and end of season, while the ability to set a fair spread of canvas on a long passage saves a lot of fuel and gives her a much easier motion. It is having the option of two adequate power systems that impresses me, but I think it important that both are efficient. I wish now that we had installed a bigger engine in *Fare Well* than 62hp. It's nice to be able to move about the engine room, but a bit more potential thrust would be a good use for the space. Modern engines, having much improved power/weight ratios, have more or less turned most present-day sailing yachts into motorsailers. Perhaps the term is beginning to mean less than it did.

I hope it is unnecessary to advise against the petrol engine. There was once a flotilla company in Greece operating boats fitted with these time-bombs. They seem to have packed up, thank God. I have swept up after too many nasty accidents involving petrol in boats, and I maintain that even in the hands of the experienced user the system is dangerous. In the USA where the low price of gasoline has favoured the petrol engine, there is at last a trend away from them. In the Mediterranean it is often difficult to get petrol except in cans.

New Boat or Old?

The process of selection introduces the alternatives: new or second-hand, one-off or a production boat?

This is the time for sweeping generalizations, and we will have plenty. It is a highly opinionated part of the book because it is impossible to be completely objective, for choosing a boat to live in is as subjective as choosing a wife. I suspect that these days it is becoming easier to correct an unfortunate choice of spouse than to change boats.

Production boats make less good homes than one-off vessels.

Professional yacht designers seem to have no idea how to design a yacht for long-term cruising.

Looking at these two generalizations, first go back a few years to the days when a designer would be commissioned by a gentleman to produce a yacht for a specific purpose. The designer would try hard to satisfy his client, and would go to some lengths to find out exactly what was needed. Now and then he must have succeeded, or we presume so, because in those days owners tended to keep the same boat for a longish time.

Nowadays people keep boats for a very short time, except among the live-aboard fleet where typically the boat lasts until the family come ashore again. We have had two boats in 22 years, and may well finish up with a third, but that is partly because we have erred on the side of having very large and unusual boats.

There is not so much profit for the designer in the modest one-off for a private owner. By designing a prototype for a production run the naval architect hopes for extending royalties and a wider dissemination of his name, for the designer is in the rat-race too. Because this is the market he is aiming at, his general arrangement plan will have more to do with production engineering and marketing than with real suitability for the sea. Though the word 'cruising' will appear in the advertising, fashion will dictate her shape and rig, she will have more than a nodding acquaintance with the IOR rating rules, and the marketing men will demand as many bunks as it is possible to get in.

Probably, when sold, she will spend most of her life at moorings, and that is about the right place for her.

Since we wrote the above we have been interested to read a paper by Hugo de Plessis, an experienced naval architect and ocean cruiser, pointing out the dangers of long-distance cruising in lightweight boats. To sum up his contentions, with which we heartily agree, he says that lightweight boats cannot carry the loads necessary to support a crew over long distances, and that when they are, inevitably, overloaded they become dangerous. His arguments are convincing. We know that the food and drink for four people on an Atlantic crossing weighs more than one tonne. We are surprised that his article has not been reprinted by a yachting magazine for wider circulation; it should be. The vast majority of so-called cruising yachts being marketed these days, particularly by continental builders, could reasonably be said to exemplify the description lightweight.

If one needs a ready-made boat I believe in going to the second-hand market, and even then picking a vessel that is capable of some alteration without losing her charm. There are good boats about, and they often have the advantage of a good inventory that saves a lot of money. In general boats from the boards of American designers tend to be more suitable for long cruising than those of other nationalities, though the Dutch are not far behind. The chief differentiating factors are that less attention is paid to rating rules, leading to more attention being paid to stowage, ease of handling under both sail and power, crew comfort and a nice appearance.

If you are building from new, or carrying out any major task and feel you have to have professional advice, then try to find a naval architect who has actually lived in a cruising yacht. They are understandably rare, because one would not make much of a living swanning about the Med, but it is quite an important point, like choosing a land architect who lives in a house of his own design. Have you noticed how most of them seem to live in Georgian houses?

There are now some designers who live in boats, though it would be invidious to give examples. But the fact that they exist is a healthy sign. What we need next is a live-aboard marketing executive.

If you are trying to buy second-hand, do not expect very much help from yacht brokers. Even if you itemise carefully exactly what you are looking for, you will be sent, for a time, details of craft that are manifestly unsuitable for your purpose, and then shortly you will be sent nothing further. This is because brokers generally do not understand what living aboard is all about, but then it is difficult to do so unless you have actually done it.

Britain is not the only place to look for a boat. There are many starters in this life, who for one reason or another do not get very far. Perhaps they have not done their homework. In any event there are often bargains to be picked up in Gibraltar, the Canary Islands, southern Spain or Portugal where they have been abandoned by a disillusioned crew.

Many yachts winter on the Côte d'Azur, and although most of these are likely to be holiday or luxury craft there is a substantial total turnover, so there are often suitable boats on offer. Brokers are used less in France because of the silly commission rate, and marinas often have many boats with *A vendre* (For sale) signs.

An area where live-aboard people are to be found in winter is round Elba, while the less well-heeled or more dedicated are to be found wintering in

Larnaca (Cyprus). Various Turkish marinas are popular too, but Turban, who run several marinas there, have increased their prices considerably. The Balearics and Alicante are further winter haunts.

In the Western Hemisphere, Fort Lauderdale and vicinity seems to moor as many craft as the whole of Europe put together, and the Chesapeake cannot be far behind. Given the high standard of US cruising yacht design, one should find something there.

English language magazines where suitable boats may be advertised are *Cruising World* (Newport, RI), and *Yachting Monthly* (England), *Yachting World* (England) for the larger boats, and *Practical Boat Owner* (England) is useful for the smaller sizes. *Boats and Planes for Sale* is a good source. *Fluvial* (France) has many advertisements for barges and rivercraft on the continental waterways.

Buying a Bare Hull

If the extent of alterations required is large, or one's requirements are very esoteric, one should consider buying a hull and then finishing it. This is basically what we have twice done, though I did have some say in the design of *Fare Well*'s hull too.

Completing a hull is not so difficult as may be imagined. Generally, the cost of the bare shell itself is a surprisingly small fraction of the total cost of a professionally built boat, often about one sixth. This means that there is a lot of work in finishing it, and it is a long time-consuming project. *Fare Well* took 4000 logged man-hours of amateur work, and *Hosanna* took even longer. A few jobs have to be done by professionals, but be careful: good free-lance professionals are hard to find, and you may end up as we sometimes did, having to re-do work. An intelligent and manually competent person with access to a good reference library can out-perform some of the ham-fisted cowboys who menace today's British yacht industry.

> *I will arise and go now, and go where the wind is free,*
> *And a fine keelboat build there,*
> *Of wood and metal made.*
> *Nine summers will I sail her,*
> *With a cat for the company;*
> *And live content in the awning's shade.*

Weatherliness

> '*A well bowed shippe so swiftly presseth the water as that it foameth,*
> *and in the dark night sparkleth like fire. If the Bow bee too narrow...*
> *she pitcheth her head into the sea; so that the meane is the best,*
> *if her after way be answerable.*'

I have already referred to the yacht that is a joy to sail but hell to live in. Understandably, most dreamers and planners contemplate a boat with good performance; yachting editors and cruising correspondents write endlessly about it, recalling with enthusiasm the drenching they got batting to windward for a few hours last weekend. A glorious sail! Yes, but they went home afterwards for a hot bath and change of clothes.

It's a bit different doing it for days on end, trying meanwhile to prepare and cook good meals, to do the maintenance and repairs, and to keep dry clothing. Many dedicated cruisers never beat to windward at all. Our own motto is 'if you have to beat, you're going to the wrong place.' Gentlemen do not tack. On a long passage it is occasionally necessary to compromise, but we have been known to heave-to in mid-ocean when confronted by an unseasonal heading force 6 and wait for it to change. Do not trust ocean sailors who bang on about windward ability: suspect them of being masochists.

It is a question of enjoying life and having all the time in the world to do it. Generally, in *Fare Well*, we did not approach closer to the wind than 55°; if we did it was usually for a short leg or to keep a better offing, and even then we tended to run the engine at half revs, which contributes some ever-welcome amps as well as thrust and gets the unfortunate episode over sooner. In *Hosanna*, we motor much more. There are eight sails in all, and in the Med it is often the case that we are too lazy to set them all for a comparatively short voyage, and setting only a few is not enough to maintain a fair speed. You will often see us with the upside down triangle in the rigging forward indicating that we are motor-sailing. Another reason is that she is a heavy boat to steer, and with an engine ticking over we get power-assisted steering.

High performance

One sometimes finds the opinion that high sailing performance is a potential safety factor. Let us examine this hypothesis. In 40,000 miles of cruising in *Fare Well* the following were our 'dangerous situations':

- A fire at sea
- A hurricane
- Damage from a heavy squall, or it could have been a waterspout, in the Gulf Stream
- A lightning strike
- A shaft coupling disintegrated, leaving a big leak
- I fell and hurt myself in a gale off Cap Corse
- The forehatch was left improperly secured and the forepeak filled with water
- The genoa furling gear failed, and at the same time I allowed the trailing sheet to foul the screw

In addition we have endured eleven other gales of force 8 or over, with no worries other than understandable apprehension.

At no other time in 40,000 miles over ten years were we in danger, and at no time at all would high performance on the wind have been of any benefit whatsoever. Nor any other high performance for that matter.

Let us contrast that with the racing fleet, which we suppose to be the exemplars of high performance. In the Fastnet Race of 1979 the fleet met a short summer gale of admittedly above average severity, but managed to score a world record for the number of distress signals per square mile of sea. The RYA enquiry served to encourage the already enormous complacency of the ocean racing industry. It

This is a modern glassfibre version of a traditional Greek boat, ideal for the Eastern Mediterranean

concluded that there was no firm evidence that any particular design feature was common to all the sinkings or damage, but failed to bring home that the lightness of construction was a common feature together with the flimsiness of spars and rigging, and even more so the unseamanlike nature of the sail plan encouraged by a rating rule that is dangerous. However, the enquiry failed to take evidence from cruising yachts that were in the area at the time. They, as far as we know because they didn't make a fuss, were all able to come through without assistance.

It is significant that a small American cruising yacht sailed through the worst of that storm with the owner, his wife, and two children under four on board, and wrote home merely that they had 'had a rough passage'. So far as I know the RYA did not seek their evidence, which was that of very experienced cruising sailors.

In the 1996/7 Vendée Globe Round the World Race, the yachts were heavily sponsored for the most part, designed by leaders of their profession, built and fitted out at enormous expense using so-called state-of-the-art materials... and their keels fell off, their rudders broke, their masts fell down, and several of them capsized and sank, with loss of life. The boats, sailed by first class experienced sailors, are built to win races, not to survive bad conditions. Does no racing yachtsman feel shame at the way the world's rescue services are being exploited to the tune of millions of pounds for someone's personal glory? Yes, it's rough down there in the Southern Ocean, but the designers know that, don't they?

For reliably safe cruising one should seek well tried and proven dispositions of sail, with everything much stronger than it needs to be in theory. Use of new materials should include a safety factor to take care of the unknown. So arrange matters that any sail can be furled or trimmed by one person without recourse to power assistance.

In Mediterranean conditions, where winds are often light and the seas can be unexpectedly and uncomfortably short and steep, we find we use the engine much more than we expected to. The number of engine hours per year remained fairly constant for a time, but has started to increase a little as we age. In any case with refrigerator, running lights and other domestic conveniences some battery charging is needed. In addition, in the Med many passages are of 30 to 50 miles, and if the wind changes or drops (it often does in the evening) there is a strong incentive to set the iron topsail for an hour or so to ensure timely arrival in a good berth before the whole port is full of noisy Italian motor yachts.

In the Bahamas and West Indies things are somewhat different. Winds are more reliable, it is easier to sail to an anchorage and/or weigh under sail, and the line of the Windward Islands runs as their name tells you conveniently across the wind, generally giving a comfortable reach in both directions.

Ease of Handling

A constant assumption throughout this book is a short-handed crew. The yacht must handle easily, whether sailing, motoring, berthing or unberthing. It is no good having a beautifully balanced sailing boat if your attempts to back her into an awkward slot in a strong cross-wind leave you tired, cross, and feeling foolish under the eyes of the whole town out for their evening stroll. These things are not incompatible; it is just that some designers, particularly those who have made their name in racing, have never learned how to relate them one to another.

To be able to handle sail quickly, and without too much effort, is vital to both comfort and safety. No matter how much you tell yourself that by keeping alert you will never have to do anything in a hurry, sooner or later you will slip up, as I have, several times.

We once rounded Cape Malea in southern Greece, leaving it close aboard, ghosting under every stitch of canvas we could set, including the poop awning. The cape is a steep cliff some 2000 feet high, and as we rounded we could see hissing white water ahead; as the Admiralty Pilot warned, on the other side there was a katabatic wind of great force. The log was reading 10 knots before I got the mizzen staysail down, and I never did furl the big genoa. It would not let me. As we sped south towards Africa at right angles to our intended course, the wind gradually eased and we re-established tenuous control.

On another occasion I fought that *maladetto* genoa for more than an hour at the end of the bowsprit which was dunking me every half minute. With each dunk the sea surged up my trouser legs leaving by the neckhole in my oilskins, and doing unmentionable mischief en route. Real cruising men are pledged to avoid such heroics, so shortly after these incidents we bought roller reefing/furling gear for the headsail.

Good roller gear, which can reef as well as furl a sail, solves a lot of problems, but in the large sizes it still requires a lot of physical effort, though reasonably reliable electrical winding gear is now available. Roller headsails are sometimes held to be less aerodynamically efficient than hoisted headsails. I do not think the difference when the whole sail is set is significant to the cruising yachtsman, while the ability to reef a headsail a little, a lot, or a little bit more or less, more than compensates for marginal losses. The whole system of roller reefing/furling is completely appropriate for short-handed sailing. Jams, snarl-ups and break-downs are not more frequent than conventional foredeck foul-ups, and the cost of the gear is offset by the fewer headsails required.

It would, I think, be advisable not to follow our example of fitting the headsail roller with a big, 175 per cent overlap genoa. *Fare Well*'s was 67 square metres and a lovely puller, but it was also a bit of a menace on occasions when the wind got up, being difficult for one person to tack it round the inner forestay.

For a cutter foretriangle I think the roller headsail should be a slightly oversize yankee. This means that arrangements must be made to set a light-weather genoa. If you have two forestays there will be occasions when the unused forestay gets wrapped into the furling sail, usually while rolling up before a strong wind, but one soon gets a technique for avoiding this.

It is impossible to recommend any particular gear because new ones come and go frequently. Unfortunately it is not advisable to seek sailmakers' advice, as most sailmakers either have their own gear or are agents for one or two, and objective advice is difficult to get. Very few people, and I am not among them, have experience of more than one or two different makes; real deep-sea experience I mean. You just have to use whatever advice you can get and apply your own judgement. Fortunately the technique of rolling has advanced considerably in recent years.

The long-distance cruiser's status symbol, especially in France. In my opinion such domes are little use. They soon become scratched and crazed, then more and more opaque. Better to have a proper wheelhouse.

Roller mainsails are not so good as headsails. The long luff of Bermudan main-sails means that those set externally to the mast tend to sag away from it, and to add very considerably to the compression strain on the spar without the vibration-deadening effect of the continuous contact via the slides or luff rope. Mainsails that roll inside the mast are available, and I have no intimate knowledge of them, but I would be much concerned about possible chafe of the sailcloth at the mast slot on the sort of voyages many long cruisers habitually make. Foul-up problems are probably not too significant and unlikely to be much worse than with a head-sail. Some gears have a serious problem in harbour, when with strong winds the mast slot turns itself into a gigantic organ pipe, and the whole place is disturbed with the hooting of a demented owl. Makers once notorious for this defect now claim to have solved the problem. Sometimes they have. Watch out when buying second-hand!

We have mixed reports of in-boom rolling. It involves having a rather over-size boom and a rigid kicking strap or martingale. Personally I would prefer it to in-mast gear because it is more accessible. I do not like climbing masts at sea.

Whatever rig you have, make sure there is no sail you cannot furl singlehanded, and quickly too. In these circumstances the divided rig makes a lot of sense, but remember that one cannot furl or reef all the sails simultaneously. Standing rigging should not be the flimsy affair of the racing fleet: it must be able to support full canvas in gale strength squalls, then as sail is reduced things will get better. There is one case to watch which I have found little appreciated nowadays: in gaff-rigged craft when the main is furled before reducing the headsails, there is still great compression in the mast and without the pull of the mainsail hoops to dampen vibration, it is quite possible to lose the mast. In spite of knowing all about this we still managed to lose *Hosanna*'s solid wooden foremast off the Kentish Knock, but it had been weakened by a soft spot round a small knot.

In general a well balanced ketch rig virtually eliminates the need for reefing. We almost never reefed in *Fare Well* because the possibilities are such that one can always find a comfortable way of setting whole sails, even if you use fewer and smaller of them. An exception was a very deep reef on the main which was meant to avoid the need for a trysail. We used it once in ten years. The mizzen had no reefing system.

If you have a mainsail that requires reefing, then the system depends on personal preference influenced by size of sail. For short-handed crews slab reefing is dubious above an area of 40 square metres, but sails that big are getting dubious in our context anyway. It is in sloops and cutters that reefing becomes very important, and the frequent necessity of getting up there on the high bit of boat in bad weather is a strong argument against the single-master. Reef points should be avoided: you have to be up there even longer.

All booms, but especially main booms, should have a stout gallows, not only for stowing in harbour but also with slots in the outboard ends so that the boom can be easily bowsed down to leeward to be worked on. It is far easier and safer to hold onto a rigidly fixed boom than to cling to one that is allowed even a little move-ment. If the gallows is fitted about two-thirds of the length of the boom from the mast it is possible to arrange a slot on the extreme end, so that the end of the boom when stowed is a foot or so outboard of the ship's side, thus providing a good lift-ing point for bringing heavy weights on board, or recovering people from the sea.

An extendable gallows allows the boom end to be held out over the water.

Extended gallows

RWC

What applies to furling, applies to sheeting too. When one is short-handed, all sheets and controlling cordage of all types should, so far as is possible, be led to a sheltered place, preferably a cockpit. It will not do to have one or more sails flog while you sheet the others. Even a few seconds' hard flogging in a severe squall can demolish a clew.

With roller furling, if heavy weather is expected then over-roll a furled sail by a few turns. I once left our 8oz genoa loosely rolled, with perhaps a square foot or so still off the roll. When a waterspout hit us in the middle of the night the force was enough to pull all taut and effectively unroll a little of the sail, which disintegrated into ribbons in seconds. An 11oz sail that was set, survived in usable state but a conventionally, though hastily furled mainsail was ripped out of its gaskets and was lost too. One cannot go about continually taking precautions against squalls of this extreme violence of course, but where their occurrence is possible or likely, then one should.

Roller reefing/furling does partially solve a problem of stowage, for sails so set remain above deck and also one needs fewer separate sails. Space below in a long-cruising boat is so valuable that many stow their sails on deck. It is possible to have a sailbag such that a headsail can be put in it while it is still hanked on its stay. It does not look very elegant, making the average yacht look as if she has a nosebag on. It is quite important that all sails should be covered when not in use. Simple light covers will do: all that is necessary is to stop ultraviolet light damaging the synthetic cloth.

Hull Shape

While for most passage-making a deep keel is desirable, except perhaps over the Bahama Banks, there are innumerable little ports and bays where the deeper boats cannot go but where a shallow draught can find most wonderful peace (provided the wet bikes stay away!). There are also opportunities for exploring canals and rivers, especially those of France, or the lovely Intra-Coastal Waterway of the US east coast. These factors point the need for a compromise, and I would opt for a monohull draught of 5 feet or so. *Fare Well* was designed for 6 feet and for her size that is quite modest, but she did not end up that way, and cruising yachts never do, because no one can ever believe the incredible weight of things that they need to carry on long voyages. *Golden rule: in every case, draught when cruising with full living load will be at least 6 inches more than expected.*

Centreboards are not an ideal answer. When the Bollay family took their Rhodes-designed c.b. sloop *Snowgoose* into the French canals they eventually exported a good part of the mineral wealth of the country, which had got itself jammed up the trunking, and it took a lot of getting out. Centreboards can be awkward to manage in larger boats because they have to be heavy to be strong enough to take the big lateral cantilever strains. In smaller boats the draught need not be so very deep anyway, so that centreboards are perhaps an unnecessary complication.

It is worth mentioning that *Fare Well* while drawing 6 feet 7 inches (say 2 metres) cruised the Bahamas and the full length of the Intra-Coastal Waterway without any serious problems. We found the bottom a few times; once we stuck on a coral head for a tide, but got off unaided by laying out two bower anchors.

Long overhangs have a sporty look, but are expensive in mooring and construction; they add to the maintenance and contribute little to usable boat. I do not think they are an advantage for our purpose.

The retroussé stern and spade rudder hung right aft pose problems for a cruising yacht. Not only does one lose a commodious locker and some very valuable deck space without any corresponding saving on mooring fees, but if one berths stern-to, as in most Mediterranean ports, this configuration can be a positive hazard. Lying bows-to is an alternative that has its own disadvantages, which I will refer to under anchoring. The problem with a deep rudder right aft is that quays in the Med (and elsewhere) seldom have vertical faces to their full apparent depth. Very often they are ballasted to just below water level, and odd rocks together with the assorted detritus of centuries extend some distance from the quay.

A deep rudder hung well aft near the transom is vulnerable when mooring stern-to.

The sloping transom makes landing to and from the quay more difficult, but on the other hand it is a very good site for a permanent bathing or boarding ladder, and a little platform there forms a safish place to stow a can of petrol (gasoline) for the outboard motor.

Twin screws are an unnecessary luxury for sailing yachts in the sizes we are contemplating, but for the pure motor yacht they would make a lot of sense. Although undoubtedly vulnerable in canals, there will be occasions in less frequented parts where the ability to limp home might be a blessing. Away from the British or US coasts help is not so readily available, or even not at all. In some parts we have visited, VHF channel 16 may be of more use for ordering a taxi.

Hull Construction

It is in craft over 10 metres waterline that steel becomes an economical material. Then it becomes possible to have a hull of plate thickness sufficient to stand a variety of abuses, including abrasion and impact. In fact the only short-term danger to a steel hull is the tin-opener effect typified by striking a sharp rocky pinnacle. It is the most effectively resistant material to ice, though that rarely concerns us. Once the plate thickness rises above 4 mm, this danger recedes for the speeds we are likely to reach. The bottom of *Fare Well*'s keel is 1½ inch plate, rounded up at the forefoot, and when we sledded up 60 cm out of the water after striking a coral head at 7 knots the scratches on the steel were less than a millimetre deep.

Maintenance is heavier with steel, but it is unskilled labour for the most part, and the dedicated cruiser is there all the time to do it. If the hull is initially shot-blasted to an even grey, then instantly coated with epoxy-based cover to a thickness of half a millimetre, you have a good basis, but it is important to touch up damage to this film as soon as possible. *Fare Well*'s initial paint job lasted eight years, and even then only needed redoing near the waterline. Some people like zinc or aluminium spraying, but I believe this actually weakens the bond of the epoxy to the steel, though there may be some merit in epoxy-zinc as a paint. I think one can get too clever over this problem; the vital thing is to get the strongest possible skin to adhere in the strongest possible way, and any minor damage to the coating below the waterline ought to be taken care of by fitting good sacrificial zinc anodes, the life and effectiveness of which can be periodically checked.

Steel hulls do not leak, except through contrived openings. Similarly, fibreglass hulls ought not to leak, but strength and reliability depends on the quality of the materials and also on the conscientiousness of the laminators; factors which are difficult to assess in a second-hand boat later on in its life. Hulls of this material have been known to crack, particularly where skegs or keels adjoin the hull, and this seems to happen irrespective of the reputation of the yard, and particularly with light-construction boats from weight-conscious designers. The material abrades easily, which is very important if one visits non-yachty harbours where there are fishing boats with sharp steel projections, like metallic porcupines. GRP burns, and is a poor conductor of electricity which can cause it to disintegrate in lightning strikes, which are much more common in tropical climes. Like steel, it is not habitually eaten by any known animal (except Greek goats), but it does have its equivalent to corrosion, osmosis, which can be difficult to deal with. It is expensive on a one-off basis but this can be ameliorated by using the sandwich method, which has the great advantage of insulating the skin and is therefore an appreciated method of building for the hotter climates.

Ferro-cement boats have a bad reputation, which is not fully deserved. The well built hull is very good indeed, but poor technique gives rise to nautical disasters. I would consider a hull made by the Wroxham firm of Windboats to be worth a second look, as I have seen some very good work of theirs, and some good boats have come from New Zealand builders. As for the material, abrasion resistance is poor compared to metal, though better than GRP. Impact resistance is quite good for boats with a heavy steel reinforcement, but chicken wire, often used by amateurs because it is cheaper, lighter and easier to shape, is very vulnerable. Maintenance is a lot less of a problem than with steel. Ferro is thought of as being the cheapest material for a one-off amateur built hull, but so much depends on standards. In any case the cost of the hull is likely to be between one sixth and one fifth of the total cost of building. Resale of these boats is supposed to be difficult, but those with experience tell me they are much like any one-off: it depends on the quality.

A wooden hull has a lovely feel about it, but it presents many problems. All sorts of things eat it, and it rots and grows fungi, problems which are all much worse in warm climates. Hulls built traditionally are subject to leaks. It can be easily repaired in backward communities, though often good hardwoods are hard to come by, and this is a worsening situation as the Greens gain ground. Abrasion resistance is moderate, and whereas impact is unlikely to penetrate because of wood's elasticity, it can lead to planks springing, or to distortion with multiple small leaks that can be hell to stem.

I have little knowledge of the more recent wood techniques, but I do use a lot of epoxy resin, and have had great success with priming wood with diluted epoxy resin, so I have a feeling that its use now as a sealer/adhesive bears examination. Boats built in the West System (a sort of epoxy-saturated wood method, which seems to combine the advantages of GRP with wood) have impressed me and their owners all seem satisfied.

An aluminium hull has some of the properties of steel, but is lighter and not nearly so resistant to damage, a fact that is apparent in many a large repair yard. One of its principal problems is that it is softer than steel and dents very easily. It is vulnerable to electrolytic problems if great care is not taken over the selection of alloys and fittings, and it is by no means unknown for the wrong alloy to creep in because the right one is temporarily unavailable at the yard. It is expensive to build and extremely difficult, not to say impossible, to get repaired neatly outside the major sophisticated yachting venues.

It is now possible to have hulls built of steel with superstructure of marine-grade aluminium, without all the bother of bolting, insulating (to prevent electrolysis), and worrying if it is all going to hold together. Aero-Spatiale of Toulouse have invented a way of welding aluminium to steel. It cannot be done on site, but they sell strips in the form of a sandwich of aluminium and steel with a filler of thin titanium, the three 'welded' together by the pressure of detonating explosives. This strip can be conventionally welded to steel on the one side and to aluminium on the other, and seems not to suffer from electrolytic action. It is easy to use, but expensive.

Decks should be made of sheet material and should never rely on caulking for their watertightness. If they do, they will leak, which is a catalyst for rot and marital discord.

Long-term Value

Whether a particular yacht will retain or lose pecuniary value depends on many factors. Investment analysts have a lot of trouble accurately forecasting future prices of quite simple things; it seems to me very dangerous to base decisions on projected future assumptions about prices of one second-hand yacht against another. Some points are worth bearing in mind.

A long-cruising yacht will get much more wear and tear than a similar yacht that is seldom out of its shed, or off moorings.

A strongly-built boat which is unfashionable today may well be a strong 'character' boat when today's fashionable trade-in models are in the scrapyard, provided hull, engine and gear are in good condition and she's not too massive.

Resale prices are heavily dependent on fashion.

Are you buying a boat for life? If not, how long do you envisage cruising? If over seven years, it seems to me that resale worries should not be allowed to cause sleepless nights. Almost everything I worried about seven years ago seems to have solved itself in the meantime.

The most important thing is to buy a boat that suits you well. You would not buy a car that was a bastard to drive just because someone suggested it had a good resale value. We once knew a couple who had started out to live aboard, and thinking that they might not like it they had chosen a Finnish production boat with a good reputation for being easy to sell. A moment's thought would have shown its complete unsuitability for long-term living aboard. Of course they did not enjoy the life; they had ruined their prospects by forgetting what was the principal purpose of the boat and instead choosing on other criteria. Still, they got a good price for it.

If you are not going long-cruising as a completely new way of life, but as a short break of perhaps two years in a working career, your attitude to resale prices will be somewhat different. You will still need to consider your aims carefully in order to live reasonably well, but you would be a hostage to financial fortune to ignore the likely proceeds from the sale of the yacht, which you are unlikely to want to keep forever. It is quite reasonable to forecast two years ahead, and a good broker's advice will be valuable in this respect. Do not, however, pay much attention to his advice on what sort of yacht to cruise in unless you are really sure he knows what living aboard is about; I have never met one who does. Your aim may be different from the aim of a long-term cruiser, but you will still have an aim that is not entirely centred on resale. You make the compromise.

A Yacht to Grow Old In

*'The saylers are the antient men... and nothing
but experience can poffibly teach it.'*

This is a difficult subject to find a name for, mostly because we have all got into the habit of using euphemisms for 'old-age'. My preference for calling spades spades has not changed much since becoming a pensioner, but I discarded the word geriatric because my elementary knowledge of Greek suggests to me that the word really means an old doctor.

When we originated cruising symposiums (organised by *Yachting Monthly*) on the 'Sell Up and Sail' concept, we were very impressed by the strong interest in the subject shown by people who had retired. We were in process of changing to a boat more suitable to our own increasing years, and were somewhat shamed by the ambitions of some of our fellow symposers. It became evident to us that there is a positive demand for boats suitable for retired people to do a lot of sailing in, even if not to live aboard full-time.

This is the time of life when living aboard becomes especially attractive. No more worries about careers, children growing up, and income, because you should have seen to all that by now. The only problems are to do with one's physical capability, and the fact that it can be expected to decline as the years go by. (You can also go bonkers, but many of us are quite a long way down that road already.)

If you are buying a boat to retire into, it is important to project ahead what you can cope with. Certainly your skills will improve to offset failing strength, but there will come a time when skills reach a plateau and strength goes on declining. It would be unwise to contemplate frequent changes of boat. God knows, it is hard enough to find one super-boat in a lifetime without giving yourself the task of finding several, and every change is expensive. Nevertheless it requires quite a lot of self-discipline to buy a boat that will not perform to the full extent of your present capabilities. If you are not ready to face this prospect yet, come back to the subject in a few years' time.

We say elsewhere that we find production boats not very suitable for the live-aboard. At the time we found ourselves at odds with the editor of *Yachting World*, who is no fool and not inexperienced. It just goes to show that opinions can differ; though not a long-term cruiser, he tells us he is now changing his mind.

We faced the problem of changing boats twelve years ago. We do not pretend that our personal solution has necessarily been the right one, but we feel it might help some folk if we described the arguments that led to our decision.

Firstly, prospective old salts should consider their personal qualities. For example Laurel is small, and somewhat lame. Her disability will not improve; rather the opposite. Bill is big and very strong in the short-term sense, but short-ness of breath prevents him exerting himself for long periods without resting. None of our problems will improve.

If we were each at 90% of our best-ever capacity when we first set sail as live-aboards in 1976, we were probably at about 65% at change-over time, which represents a decline of about 2% per annum. This had to be projected forward. We had owned *Fare Well* for about fifteen years, this meant that our new ship *Hosanna* might be our ultimate if she would last us another fifteen. What will be our physical capacity then? Probably not very good.

We have known and met a fair number of yachtsmen who have gone on cruising far and wide into very old age, and we have become aware of some of their difficulties. We have helped some with their problems, for example, diabetes, which is only one of the possible scourges of old age. Many of these problems can be coped with, at least until they become really debilitating. Some old salts we can think of clearly went on far too long. It is one thing to rely on other people's help in an occasional crisis, but when one can no longer cope without frequent and almost regular assistance, it becomes time to think about swallowing the anchor, however much it sticks in your throat.

With regard to the boat, the obvious solution to the problem is to settle for a smaller boat than would the younger person. I say obvious because it seems to be everyone's instinctive answer. I don't think it is necessarily the right one. A lot depends on what you think you will be able to handle. Surprisingly, size is not as important as, for example, whether the boat itself acts like a gentleman or a hooligan. Some boats are absolutely intractable yobs.

The process of adapting to decreasing faculties can be approached in two ways. One is to have a boat that will be easily coped with until death us do part, come hell or high water. The other is to have a boat that is comfortable and reasonably sea-worthy, but which will both require and allow one to modify one's cruising range when that becomes necessary. We chose the latter course, but let us consider the other option first.

Maintenance is not so much of a problem because it can be undertaken in slow time. Clearly it is unwise to take on an impossible burden, but apart from that, maintenance should not figure too largely in the argument.

Assuming one is going to come down in size, what is the right size? We have to have good living conditions, so the boat cannot get too small. Small sporty boats need quick physical reactions, something we tend to lose as we get older. Space is needed for the things one likes to have about one, souvenirs, photographs, small treasures and so on. On the other hand it is desirable that the boat should be of a size that can be pushed or pulled short distances in harbour by old-man power without gut-busting effort, and that her gear should be light enough to be handled without causing hernias.

These two opposing factors indicate a boat of up to fifteen gross registered tons, and sails that do not exceed 30 sq metres each. To get good living comfort in this range one is going to have to sacrifice some speed and sportiness. Good fat lockers lead to good fat boats. Inside, the accommodation should be arranged so that tired people do not have to step over things, so that a person falling does not fall far, so that edges and corners are padded, and there are innumerable hand-holds. It should not be necessary to demount the table in order to have a restorative nap.

Unless there is a deck-house configuration, which has its points, the whole accommodation should be on a level, thus avoiding those irritating little three-inch steps that all naval architects seem to think essential, and which even able crews are always falling over. Much better to have two or three standard sized steps, which keep you in practice, than a host of trip-you-ups.

There should be a good seat at the galley, and bunks that are not too difficult to make. A lot of the problems down below become the lady's problems; she may stay fit longer than her old man (she may well be younger into the bargain), but how many yacht designers have been deeply into the ergonomics of an old lady at sea? Going to the loo in a small yacht arguably produces more broken bones than any other nautical accident, strong handholds in the head and a sit-down shower are essential. Even such a simple thing as bed-making can be difficult with awkward enclosed bunks; fitted bottom sheets and a duvet can help here.

On deck we come to the real difficulties. Admiral Goldsmith, one of the earliest dedicated live-aboards, died hauling up his anchor. I had tried to talk him into having electrics in his boat, but he was adamant. 'Ampères are the curse of mankind,' he bellowed at me from a distance of about three feet. Admirals tend to do that. I am torn while writing this bit because if I had the chance to choose a way of dying, this would be it, except for the awful problems it would leave my devoted crew. But isn't it better for many reasons to have an electric windlass and a self-stowing anchor? Heart attacks apart, there are times when, caught perhaps by a squall in an anchorage, one is obliged to work cables and anchors under trying conditions. Getting exhausted doesn't help.

Nowadays there are some excellent little windlasses on the market. Of course they use a lot of amps, but not for long; most of them pull in at over 20 metres a minute, so weighing would not normally take more than two minutes. Forty amps for two minutes is less than two ampere/hours; not very much is it? Especially as one would almost certainly have the engine running at the time.

Sheet winches do come with electric motors, but the prices are prohibitive as one needs a fair number of them. It is better to have geared winches with plenty of power. When getting on it is easier to give six gentle turns than three hard ones; it takes longer, but so little extra in cruising terms. Winches should be just above waist height if worked standing up, which is the best position for the effort. If you have to work them sitting down, then even more power is required. Don't risk straining the back.

The steering position should be in a wheelhouse. There is positive evidence that old people can be distressingly unaware of the onset of hypothermia. I know that the evidence applies strictly to very old persons, but I do not suppose that the condition jumps suddenly to danger level overnight: its development is almost certainly spread over quite a period; its onset probably arrives with your bus pass. Do not suppose that hypothermia is unknown in the tropics. Of course on a star-lit night with a gentle force 3 blowing from the quarter there is no problem, but during Hurricane Alberto I was wearing a thick sweater down below. (I didn't go on deck; I was too scared.) And remember you don't always stay in the hot climates. In the Med in April or October it can get quite chilly. We lit our wood-burning stove on 15 May this year at Arles, close to the Mediterranean coast.

The wheelhouse should have opening windows for the good weather, and a good chair to rest in. In *Hosanna* we have seats from which both of us can see around at the same time, and why not? It is still essential to have somewhere to sit outside, and even to entertain on a small scale, but do not place too much emphasis on sun-bathing; one gets tanned quite well enough without ever going into the direct sun, though the process takes a little longer. Many people who have spent long periods in the tropics have dubious skin problems.

Sail plans must be arranged for ease of handling rather than sailing efficiency. All sheets should come to a cockpit. All halyards or roller furling lines too. It should be possible to douse a sail without having to put on an act like a chimpanzee in a circus. In my view this makes roller sails virtually essential, and means either leaving the spinnaker behind or saving it for when junior pays a visit.

Have really big cleats. Hands and fingers get less agile, and fumbling with irritatingly miniature fittings is bad for one's frame of mind.

Give a lot of attention to lifelines. The aged do not pick their feet up so easily as the young, and we have seen older people tripping over deck fittings; the average deck-level lifeline is a perfect tripwire. It needs some experimenting but a lifeline at waist height may be the best. One tends to crouch a bit in bad conditions, and it might be easier to duck under than clamber over.

Mooring is a pastime which can tax old bones. Though Old Tom will undoubtedly be more experienced than Young Fred, his reaction time will be slower. Ensure a boat that is responsive under power and steers well at slow speed. Even if the boat is less than 15 tons, a miniature bow-thruster is probably a better buy than a lot of electronic navigating equipment (though I do not discount the value of anything which takes some of the physical burden off a small crew).

A motor-sailer is probably the best type of craft, for one will need a good engine. Consider how you could manage if one of you had to cope on their own. I could just about have sailed *Fare Well* back to the harbour by myself, Laurel would not have had the strength. If the event had arisen then she would have had to motor, and it is essential that the boat has engine power to make headway in a rough sea. As one gets older one tends to use the motor a little more, whatever one's original intentions. I see nothing wrong in this: in my view the prudent mariner is the one who uses all or any of his resources to the best advantage.

We have written about this subject at greater length in *Sail Into the Sunset*, published by Adlard Coles Nautical.

So how have the authors solved their problem of the old man's boat?

First of all Bill designed a steel boat in accordance with all that we have said above. We never built it. We approached the basic problem by considering the cruising grounds we enjoyed the most, and those we had not yet cruised but wished to. Some would require more nautical effort than others; quite clearly some are getting too much to contemplate unless done soon. Having graded these by degree of ambitiousness we found we had more than a lifetime's cruising ahead of us, and we decided to cut down by removing those such as the China Sea, which are unlikely to become congenial to the casual yottie for some time.

Hosanna *under all plain sail.*

It was about this time that Laurel indicated that she wanted to bring all her library, so we threw away our lists and Bill proposed putting in a bid for the *Queen Elizabeth II*. When the argument settled down again we both went to look over the market in sea-going Dutch barges in their raw, unconverted state. Bill had seen several conversions in the West Indies and in the USA which had sailed there on their own bottoms, and it seemed to him that one of modest size might suit us well. When sea sailing got too difficult we would have all those European canals and rivers to potter about in. In the meantime we would be limited to the fine weather zones in their more reliable periods, but our list was mostly that anyway. We tend towards a quieter life.

When we found a beautiful little barge of 26 metres available for what was virtually the price of her engine, we dealt. It was our intention to cut out 4 metres of length and make a full motor-sailer of her. After the two of us had driven her in ballast across the North Sea in February in quite rough conditions we became very impressed with what we had bought. Bill looked again at Laurel's pile of books. He decided we could cope with the Little Dutch Barge under power under all but survival sea states, once one or two things were improved. The cost of cutting out 4 metres, if invested, would produce enough income to maintain 4 metres.

So *Hosanna* has ended up entire and whole and perfect, a token of our love, with three fixed keels and a sail plan divided into three low masts, and all sails rolling. She has three engines, three screws and a bow-thruster. And three tonnes of books.

Since writing the above we have circumnavigated Europe, cruised *Hosanna* all over the North Sea, the Med, the Aegean, and the Black Sea, as well as various canals and major European rivers, including the Rhine and Danube. Navigationally speaking, her size has caused us little anxiety. Occasionally in bad weather the two of us have found her a bit exhausting: the worst case was being dismasted at 0400 in a rough North Sea (where we are proud to say the two of us coped on our own), though the most tiring experiences generally have been in the great rivers.

Now ten years on we will have to contemplate another change because the maintenance shows signs of becoming too much for us. We do not want to allow *Hosanna* to deteriorate as we have sometimes observed in old people's boats. One has to be sensible. A couple ten years younger than us could cope well enough. We now need time to think, though we expect you will be able to see the likely direction of our thoughts. Pity about all those books.

Chapter Five

Above Decks

'For a man of warre a well ordered taunt-mast is best,
but for a long voyage a short mast will bear more
canvasse and is less subject to beare by the boord.'

Nautical Terms

Neither Laurel nor I are sticklers for using a lot of nautical jargon. We are both inclined to talk of our bedroom, windows or ceilings, to give three examples. But there are items or doings which are peculiar to the sea, which are well described by sea terms, and for which no other words are adequate. Sometimes these terms have been debased by yachtsmen using them wrongly; it is my intention, when discussing equipment, to be precise and to go back to the right ones. To avoid confusion, they are defined here.

Passarelle: a plank, gangway or brow leading from ship to shore, especially used over the bow or stern in the Mediterranean.
Guardrails are a 'safety fence' running round the vessel; they can be solid rails, or they can consist of wires supported by stanchions.
Lifelines are wires rigged between various rigid parts of the vessel so that crew can hold on or clip harness onto them when moving about.

The remaining words concern anchors. Apart from names indicating the design, such as Danforth or Bruce, anchors may be described either by their function or by the part of the vessel from which they are used. *Bower anchors* are normally stowed on either bow, and are the normally used anchors by which a ship comes to anchor. A *sheet anchor* is a spare anchor usually kept forward, for use only in very bad conditions. Though it gives rise to an expression much used by politicians, it is not necessarily noted for its size or unusual holding power; generally it was a last resort because it was a bit of a pest to manage (like politicians). A *stream anchor* is one stowed at the stern; let go from there, usually in conjunction with a bower, so that the two anchors and the ship lie parallel to the stream and do not swing with its changes. A *kedge anchor* is an anchor used to point the ship or to move her about. The rope used between ship and kedge anchor is called a *warp*, which is also used to describe ropes used between ship and shore or between ship and a buoy, also for moving the ship. The kedge, which in these days of tugs and bow-thrusters has largely died out, was usually lighter than other anchors because it was typically carried away from the ship to be laid by boat; the word does not mean a light anchor but defines the use to which it was put.

The big racing yachts did not want to anchor during a race unless the wind was light and they might have to stem the tide. As their lightest anchor was enough for this purpose they would save weight by landing their bower anchors, and thus the racing fraternity debased the word kedge because that was the way the professional crews referred to their light anchor. In the same way yachtsmen came to refer to the rope on the anchor as a warp, when the correct word is *cable* whether it is cordage or chain. In the US it is often called a *rode*, an older word, so also correct.

When two anchors (or more) are used we usually say the vessel is *moored*, which strictly means made fast to the bottom. The angle at which an anchor cable leaves the ship is referred to as its *stay*. If it is almost horizontal and enters the water a long way ahead of the ship, it is called at *long stay*. A *short stay* is when the cable hangs down almost vertically.

The amount of cable between the anchor and the ship is called the *scope*. It should not be dependent on the size of the ship but on the depth of water, though the relationship is not a linear one. With chain cable a scope of five or six times the depth of shallow water is prudent, but for deep water, over 20 metres say, this can fall to three times the depth. Double this for nylon unless a heavy angel is used. An *angel* is a heavy weight lowered down an anchor cable to provide an extra 'spring' to prevent the cable coming up bar-taut and snatching (see p. 83). I have been told some yachtsmen call this a 'chum', and discover this is because some enterprising manufacturer used this as a trademark. For Med mooring with an anchor, use as much scope as possible, but also try always to use an angel with nylon.

Lastly, watch the word *spring*. Though originally applicable to a rope that carried out the expected function of a spring, ie to stop the ship moving backwards or forwards at the quayside, it has gone through stages of becoming verb, adjective and probably a gerund too, and crops up in all sorts of places.

Rigs and Rigging

If one discounts the requirement of high windward ability, one brings into question the suitability of the Bermudan rig. Why do so many long-term cruising yachts sport this rig? *Fare Well* is so rigged, and as I designed it so, I suppose I should be able to answer this question. I cannot. It must have seemed the right thing at that time.

For tradewind cruising it certainly is not the best rig. For short-sea sailing when short-handed, the modern type of Bermudan rig with a small mainsail and a very large foretriangle may be very efficient when on the wind on a long tack, but it is far from convenient when putting about, and a period of short-tacking in a largish boat can exhaust a crew of two: the rig can become a monster. The perfect answer does not exist, because it is a very subjective matter, but I think it pays to look at the question from viewpoints other than maximizing tractive effort per square foot of canvas.

One of these is ease of maintenance and repair, and I will touch on this in Chapter Eight. Another, already mentioned, is ease of management, especially when short-handed or tired, in setting, furling and trimming the sails. On longer voyages there is the important matter of chafe. There is initial cost, as well as cost of maintenance of masts and rigging as well as the sails themselves.

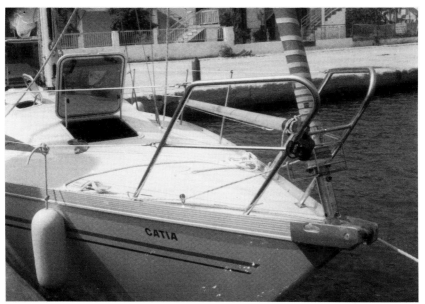

Can you believe that production boats are sold with navigation lamps tilting downwards like this? Well, they are. Just imagine what the bits you can't see are like.

With roller reefing/furling gear, some older rigs that did not prove altogether suitable for yachts, or which never caught on, bear some re-examination. Some years ago, Blue Bradfield circumnavigated the lovely little ketch *D'Vara*, just over 30 feet, which had an American designed wishbone rig, well sub-divided. He swore by this rig, saying that it gave him any combination or balance he required in any weather conditions. It seems to me that the wishbone mainsail with a downmast roller system would be effective and easy to manage with the wishbone set aloft permanently.

The spritsail also needs a revival. Being essentially quadrilateral, it could be set on a shorter mast with a vertical roller, and with vangs on the sprit. We tried it on *Hosanna*, and it set well, though we sometimes had trouble with the down-mast rolling gear. I needed to throw more money at it to get it exactly right, so I put up with its occasional misbehaviour. Shorter masts make a lot of sense when cruising, especially when off to distant parts, but one does need to keep a fair area of sail up aloft where the wind is stronger. I could like Mr Hoyt's cat-rigged Freedom boats but for the necessity of stepping heavy masts through the deck, which has never appealed to me. I favour the tabernacle; perhaps it is my East Anglian breeding.

A square-sail is a great asset on a tradewind passage, but it must be easily handled. The Dutch sailor Harm set a big one on his old Colin Archer using the 'drawing curtain' method of brailing the sail in from either side to the mast. I am told he did not keep it long, and others have said this way can be a nightmare in a squall. Has anyone yet set a square-sail from a horizontal roller gear inside a hollow aluminium boom? Such a sail, easy to reef and set, would appeal to me.

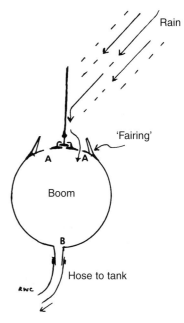

Rain

'Fairing'

A   A

Boom

B

Hose to tank

RWC

*Catching rain with the mainsail. The
fairing strips trap water next to the sail
track where it runs into the boom
through holes A, and drains away to the
tanks via an outlet B near the gooseneck.*

If one does have a shorter mast, then standing rigging is much simplified. It is possible to save a lot of money from this simplicity, and some of this will come with the sailmaker's bill. Sails made very simply for a rig that is not state-of-the-art (whatever that really means) generally last twice as long and cost half as much as those from fashionable sailmakers with gimmicks, big advertising accounts and another different gimmick next year.

With a boomed conventional mainsail it is possible to have a hollow aluminium boom made with a simple 'fairing' riveted on either side of the track to collect rainwater that falls down the sail and allow it to pass into the boom. A 1 inch BSP hole tapped underneath, close to the gooseneck, allows a hose to be connected and the water fed straight into a tank. One can collect many gallons during a squall.

Mast steps are seen on many long-distance cruisers; they have become, with windvanes and astro-domes, a status symbol of sorts. *Fare Well* has steps, but I would not waste money on them again. One does not want to go up a mast that often; a 60 foot climb at my age is no light undertaking; and at sea, when rolling, my moment of inertia at that radius is more than I can cope with and still do a job. Instead I use a cloth bag type of boatswain's chair. Nonetheless, a pair of steps conveniently placed about a metre or so below the cap or wherever work is likely to be needed would enable one to steady oneself, frap oneself down, and thus leave both hands free to work.

Running rigging is a great expense, and I prefer cordage. Wires are tolerable if turned on to a reel winch, but they have disadvantages. First, they have a tendency to spring into kinks which if inadvertently pulled taut, in the dark say, will seriously weaken the wire and also stop it passing easily through blocks or eyes. Second, when minor damage occurs, some of the small wires break and the ends project. The discovery of one of these can be painful and even disabling.

LEFT
This fairlead is not only a rope-eater, but one of the crew actually cut her foot on it.

RIGHT
Fare Well's *laterally pivoted side davits, an adaptation of the merchant ship type and much more practical than swinging davits. Note the strong guardrails. The fitting at top right takes the awning.*

Third, it is apparently impossible to find sheaves properly designed for wire rope. I once took part in some elaborate Admiralty tests to discover the best size and section of sheave for wire. It turned out to be a question not of finding the best, but of finding the least worse, but the trials did show a requirement for very large diameter sheaves, and a deep narrow groove of roughly semi-circular section.

Cordage, on the other hand, chafes. It also stretches, but in lengths up to 20 metres or so I have never found this much of a problem. It cannot be conveniently wound on self-stowing reel winches, and thus it can leave one with lengthy snakes about the deck. These can have their ends washed overboard where they will surely find the propeller; even if it is only trailing, it is doing enough revs to wind wool. (Someone defined a screw propeller as the perfect self-tailing winch.)

This leads on to winches. I believe in the self-tailing type, and have found those little blue rubber gadgets that can be added to existing winches to be less than perfect. This is a department where the money should be found for the proper job. It is not necessary to go for the metallurgically perfect, every part turned by a master-craftsman, models that cost more than the boat. For cruising, a sturdy well made job with simple bearings that can be kept clear of salt and well-lubricated without having to dismantle them into a kit of parts every few days, is what is needed. But do fit big enough ones. Under-sized winches cause accidents in squalls or emergencies.

Steering and Safety Arrangements

The chore of steering a boat for long periods is usually eased by self-steering vane gear or autopilots, which I will discuss later. One finds that they are in use for 99% of the time, but the occasion will arise when hand steering becomes unavoidable and a comfortable position is essential.

I am all for a wheelhouse. The open sportscar syndrome becomes less relevant as one matures. The Royal Navy were the last professionals to grow up, and it needed the atom bomb with its fallout problems to convert them. For my part, I do not like a wet shirt and a flowing sea. A first-class permanent awning is necessary over the conning position if there is no wheelhouse. Without an awning, the sun will boil your brains or else the rain will drown you. As the rain can also come at you horizontally, we are back to wheelhouses again. Of course the windows should open, and one of them have a substantial watershedding device. The Kent Clearview Screen is good, though in the smaller sizes the clear area is not big enough. There are also some very powerful windscreen wipers on the market which work well.

Even if a wheelhouse is impossible, make sure the cockpit is well fenced in. Some modern designers, obsessed with getting more berths and walk-through headroom everywhere, have put cockpits high up on top of the accommodation. It may surprise you to know that I do not object to this from the point of view of height (it raises one above a lot of the spray), but only because, to keep a racy profile, such yachts are usually given too little cockpit fence, either to keep a sea out or to keep stumbling, tired crew in. If you find a ready-made yacht with a high cockpit but which otherwise suits you, contemplate fitting a strong rail round it. The upper edge of the cockpit coaming should be at least a metre where one can stand up to it, but where a seat or bench is in front of it then a little extra is desirable.

Guardrails become even more important when short-handed or family cruising. In the early days of offshore racing we did not have them all round, and I went overboard one night, so I have intimate knowledge of this; not many of us survive to be able to discuss it.

There are some very expensive 70-footers on the market with guardrails eminently suitable for laundry lines, but not much else. From 10 metres LOA upwards, the minimum height of the top rail should be 75 cm and the maximum vertical gap 30 cm. Anything else is a perfect trip-wire. They need to be strong enough to arrest the progress of 100 kilos of body falling across the beam of the boat, assisted by flowing water, and that exerts a very large force indeed. This is not an area to take chances about: one has to consider the extreme case, and remember that disasters are rarely caused by something being too strong, only by being not strong enough.

Another aspect of guardrails is their vulnerability when mooring. Novices have an irresistible urge to push boats about by heaving on their stanchions, and given the apparent numbers of novices about it is desirable that the rails withstand this deplorable but widespread practice. Modern motor yachts are designed with high freeboard and considerable flare at the deck edge: for the comparatively low-freeboard sailing yacht, these features make mutual fendering very difficult. The ability to fender against one's guardrails is an asset. *Fare Well*'s guardrails are 80 cm high, that is 55 cm above the gunwale. The stanchions are 40 mm × 40 mm × 4 mm RHS steel welded on at 120 mm intervals, the intermediate rail is welded and the top rail is all teak. They are sufficiently strong to allow the unbraced top of a stanchion to take the sheet lead block of the 67 square metre genoa, and I feel happy about them. Up forward there is a different arrangement with netting, as the foredeck has less impedimenta to interrupt a fall, and netting is nicer to fall into than steel bars. Laurel has only one good leg and needs protection from falls. Don't we all.

Harness is very important on deck in rough weather. My opinion is that, given good strong guardrails as a back-up, one can move about better without clipping on to lifelines, but instead use two clips and move from one ringbolt to another. However in small yachts with light guardrails, narrow side decks, and the necessity to do a lot of work on the coachroof, some forms of stout wire lifeline are required. One should extend from cockpit to mast on each side, and another from mast to headsail tack. Wire of 8 mm diameter is about right, but must be made fast to strong fittings. I fear that a falling body could pull the mooring cleats out of some of the production boats I have seen, let alone the lifeline seating.

There is something to be said for a fair-sized yacht having a folding davit by her midship gangway rail-break. It would not only be of great help recovering heavy weights from the sea, but would be good in harbour for doing ditto from the dinghy.

One of the useful things to have on deck during the above type of emergency is a moderate length (50 metres, say) of light floating rope, about 8 mm diameter. This will not get in the screw, and given two circumstances, that manoeuvring is difficult and the victim is conscious, it is possible to come close enough and turn so that the rope is brought across the victim. If the yacht can be stopped, it is possible to haul him alongside. The rope should have a metre-long loop at the end, but the person should not normally be towed. Better to let the rope go from on board, and to pick it up again, if you have too much way on. There are some commercial 'kits' which perform the above function: they are not expensive and have the right sort of fittings.

I believe in use of engine in recovery. My experience is that even when running under spinnaker, the engine at full astern will not destroy steerage way and will save valuable yards while the sail is being furled: a point of importance for short-handed crews. But beware of trailing cordage when furling.

When we commissioned *Fare Well* there was no windvane steering gear strong enough, so we had a Sharp Mate autopilot which was the simplest I could find. In consequence I know little about pure windvanes, except that the Mediterranean's variable winds cause problems for them. The Sharp was a good companion; it only let us down once (on the first day out on an Atlantic crossing!) when a diode failed. (No dedicated cruiser should be without a stock of diodes, and a basic understanding of what they do: they are everywhere.) One little peculiarity of this autopilot (and others) is that it occasionally went barmy and took us round in a 360° circle before resuming the previous course on its own. We had trouble running before a big quartering sea, and I believe some vanes are not so good on this point; it certainly is a difficult point of sailing.

In *Hosanna*, because Sharp had gone out of business, we fitted a Cetrek, which is a much more complicated, all-singing-all-dancing affair with an 'intelligence' which measures weather helm and trim and automatically allows for them. After a measuring time, of course. For a sailing boat this is a big snag for the stupid thing cannot be made to anticipate a gybe, so that one has to steer by hand for a time, just when one should be tweaking sheets and things. Try to find an autopilot that permits you to adjust it with knobs, so that as you set the alteration of course on it you can also change the side of the trim. Proper knobs, not dainty little fairy buttons that gloved fingers cannot feel, and preferably dials in Light-Emitting-Diodes, which can actually be seen in tropical sunlight.

Knobs! Buttons were all right when you could feel the things with cold wet fingers, but now we have them hidden behind a sheet of smooth plastic looking like a Picasso painting, and often the best one can manage is to press about four at once.

Liferafts and Tenders

I suppose most people contemplating long cruises have read with interest, if not alarm, the accounts of yachts lost and the experiences of survivors. One feature that is worth stressing is that an inflatable liferaft is not designed for long-term survival, while there are several cases where persons have been recovered from rigid dinghies after long periods adrift. I have moved back to the view that the best liferaft for an ocean or well-offshore cruising yacht is a good rigid dinghy, even in the severest storm where survival needs an element of luck anyway. The dinghy must have first-class inherent buoyancy, and a stout cover or at least a partial one, and rope-loop handholds below the gunwales. The Panic Bag should be kept in it at sea (and it is the best place for the vegetable locker in any case). It requires no annual service, which is not only very expensive in some countries (it bears VAT in France and Italy for a start), but also difficult to arrange and check. It is also virtually impossible to verify that the work charged for has actually been done, and in too many cases it has not, or not properly at any rate. Also a dinghy has many other uses.

Which leads us to tenders. Once we had a rigid dinghy and an Avon, but we found that we used the rigid one for choice; and when we met a fellow traveller whose Avon had perished in the sun, we contemplated the inevitable deterioration of this asset and sold it to him. We have rarely missed it. Our dinghy is a small Norfolk lugsail dinghy, good for pottering up creeks and by-waters, but it is not a heavy load carrier. In *Fare Well* we hoisted it on side davits which I made myself. We had stern davits too, but a stern-hung dinghy is a nuisance in the Med, though a stern-hung inflatable makes a good emergency fender when lying stern-to a quay. The advantage of the side davits is that the dinghy can be turned in and stowed on deck in rough weather or when manoeuvring, where it is much safer and makes an extra locker.

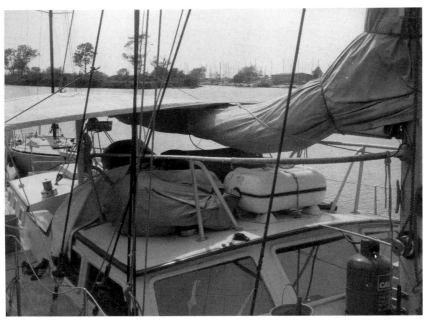

Note the good strong rail high up on the coachroof on Tientos. *Sensible sailors do not take risks.*

We still have the Norfolk dinghy (a super one built for us by Leslie Landamore), but *Hosanna* is a bigger boat and we hoist the dinghy out and in with a derrick, which is not nearly so easy as side davits.

We got rid of our 2 hp Evinrude outboard. We used it very seldom, it was noisy, always giving trouble, and in our view had more potential as an anchor than as a propulsion unit. Our dinghy sails and rows very well, and for when we were tired we had a very cheap Sears Roebuck electric outboard that ghosted us about at slow speed, needing no maintenance and not waking the neighbours. In the end we disposed of that too, because we find it fun to sail, and that the exercise of rowing ashore is good for us, helping to remove the results of too much Greek food and wine at the tavernas.

On the other hand, friends have a large Zodiac with a powerful outboard, and they tend to zip into some harbours for a little shopping without berthing the yacht. Unless the harbour is very encumbered I feel berthing is rather less trouble than fiddling about with dinghies. Once we returned to Gouvia very late at night, formally dressed, Laurel in long skirt and so on. The chap who was taking his dog for a walk and took our lines for us asked where we had been in formal dress. 'To the theatre', we said. 'What?' he said, 'In a 50 foot yacht?'

Another form of tender is a vehicle. Many dedicated cruisers are advertised by a bicycle on deck; larger boats sometimes have a mini-motorbike, which, if under 50cc does not require licensing in most desirable countries. In some it requires insurance (France is one) but no driving licences. The obligation of a crash helmet is spreading; France and Tunisia insist and there may be others. Motorbikes should have a painted sign 'Tender to...' instead of a number plate.

Sinclair makes a battery driven auxiliary unit to fit on the back wheel of a bicycle. This is, like the curate's egg, good in parts, but suffers from production engineering: they did not foresee that things fall over and break. *Hosanna*, being a barge, is able to carry a small car, a Mini or a Fiat 600, on deck (there we go, very one up on the Jones's that is!). In the canals it is worth it on occasions, but on the whole it was more trouble than asset, and the practice has been discontinued. It rusted before our eyes in the salt spray. For anyone living aboard a barge that is committed to the canals, it should be considered, but it must have its own loading crane. Second-hand hydraulic cranes can be obtained cheaply from truck-breakers.

Anchors

The long-term cruiser will have to take more thought to his anchors than the marina-based animal who probably never anchors at all. During 1982 we spent 134 nights riding to single anchor, and a further nine moored with two. In 1995/6 we spent 410 consecutive nights riding to anchors in one way or another. We dragged once or twice. *Fare Well* was fitted with two 75 lb (34 kg) CQR bower anchors which self-stow over rollers close either side of the stem. To port we had 45 fathoms (82 m) of 7/16 inch (11 mm) chain, and to starboard 40 fathoms (72 m) of ½ inch (12½ mm) chain, both handled by a Simpson-Lawrence 521 electric windlass. This layout owes a lot to big-ship experience, and it meant that Laurel, the vertically and orthopaedically challenged cable officer, could manage anchors and cables in all normal circumstances without any help. Foul anchors are another thing altogether.

The size of bower anchors is very important. Most published tables of recommended anchor sizes seem to have in mind the marina denizen or the ocean racer, and not the real sea-going yacht. For example, I followed the advice of Simpson-Lawrence, who are not noticeably incautious as a rule, but wish I had fitted larger anchors. Their table:

Length WL	Disp tonnes	CQR wt
40 ft (12 m)	25	60 lb (27 kg)
45 ft (13½ m)	30	75 lb (34 kg)

In my view, to enjoy peace of mind, one should have bower anchors larger than this. My table, in metric this time:

LWL(m)	Disp (tonnes)	CQR or Bruce (kg)	Cable link dia (mm)
10	17	25	10
12	25	30	11
13½	30	40	12
15	35	50	15

When moored bow or stern to a quay, and with an anchor out, the wind on the beam has a sort of sweating-up effect on the anchor cable, which in a strong wind can multiply the tension in it several times. Add to this the fact that a wind on the beam acts on a larger area of boat than a wind from ahead, and it is not surprising that anchors of apparently adequate size come home. If you expect to spend much

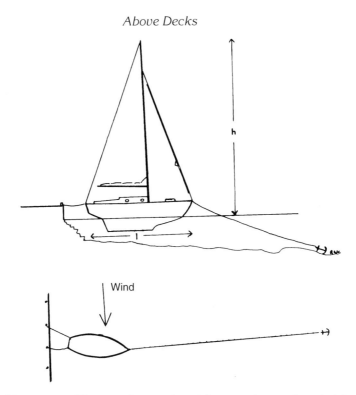

A yacht moored to a quay with an anchor out is not free to swing, and a wind from the side has more windage to act upon and causes far more strain on the cable and upwind mooring lines.

time in the Mediterranean an increase in size of both anchor and cable is desirable. The alternative, which we follow, is to have two bower anchors and use both if a strong wind is expected. The practice of waiting until the wind gets up and then laying out a second anchor by dinghy, upwind, may solve the layer's problem (if he succeeds, it's not always easy), but it inconveniences those across whose cables he lays his second anchor, who may justifiably call him names. Indeed we have seen this gambit not only fail to secure the yacht in question, but trip the anchors of several others, leading to drag acts quite as dramatic as anything on stage.

If I had thought further ahead I would have fitted *Fare Well* with a self-stowing stream (stern) anchor with its own capstan or windlass. It would have been useful on several occasions, especially in restricted tideways such as the Intra-Coastal Waterway. *Fare Well* had no kedge, and I saw no need for one as there is little point using a lighter, less secure anchor when the heavier, safer bowers could be managed more easily. She had a spare 75 lb Danforth which we never used. If the need arises to send away an anchor in a boat (after a grounding, say) I have always used a bower with enough chain cable; one does not need a lot if it is shallow enough to run aground.

On those rare occasions when the wind blows across the swell and rolling becomes a nuisance (it happened in Mustique in the West Indies, and also at Pargos in Greece), it is possible to spring the cable to point ship across a moderate wind (see diagram on next page).

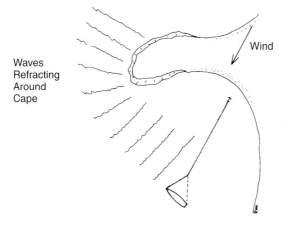

A stern spring onto the anchor cable is used here to point ship into the waves, which would otherwise be uncomfortable; however, the wind is now brought on the beam.

For *Hosanna* we have adopted a different approach to berthing end on. We use a stern anchor that is twice the weight of the bower. We go ahead into the berth with a stem fender over the bows, and nudge the quay with our stem. No matter what the wind we can leave the boat pressing end-on against the quay, leaning on Greece say, with the centreline engine going slow ahead and the rudder adjusted to allow for any cross wind. In this condition we have all the time in the world to put out head ropes, set taut the stern anchor cable and get out gangways. Of course this is only possible in straight-stemmed steel boats, but it enables us to berth a very big boat with just two people. However nothing comes free, and leaving the quay and weighing the big stern anchor while the bows quest in all directions can be a bit nerve-wracking in strong winds.

Choice of anchor type is a personal matter. They are mostly difficult to stow other than as described above. But the criterion of choice should not be a tabulated holding strength in one or two particular conditions, but a good all-round security in most conditions where sea sense indicates anchoring is worth considering. No anchor holds on smooth marble as one discovers at Xania in Crete. Taken overall I have found the CQR satisfactory, but respect that some friends prefer Danforth, Bruce or Fortress, though I would approve the latter very cautiously. It's their choice. All these anchors were very carefully designed. Avoid imitations. The CQR and Bruce anchors will stow over rollers. I have an idea that the Bruce is not so good in the smaller sizes as it is in the larger; perhaps this is another case where one should read the next line in the table. The Danforth will hang conveniently over the guardrails in a smallish yacht. Admiralty Pattern and Fisherman's anchors are really not worth it, except as rock picks, while ship anchors, such as the Hall's pattern, only come into their own over 100 kg.

Cable

I favour chain cable, though with frequent use the galvanizing does wear off and begin to look dreadful. When this happens, as re-galvanizing is not only very expensive outside the UK, and often very badly done too, turn the cable end for

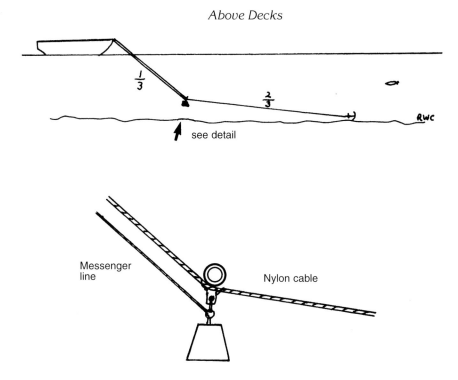

An 'angel' designed to hang on the anchor cable at about a third of the scope out from the bows, with its own light messenger line to lower and retrieve it. The weight should ideally be half that of the anchor.

end, wire-brush it and keep it soaked in boiled linseed oil, which is the only suitable oil without a nasty smell (it smells of cricket bats). Nylon has advantages, and for the lightweight yacht which is normally in a marina and does not often anchor, it is a good choice. There is on the market a coil of flat-braid polyester which I consider dangerous. Though the principle of rolling up a flat braid is excellent and practical, the material should be of nylon, which is highly elastic, and not of polyester, which is meant to be inelastic. The importance of elasticity in an anchor cable cannot be over-estimated. In doing anchor trials for the Admiralty, I found that anchors were started to drag very easily by a series of jerks; they would not move for a much greater steady tension in the cable. It is the weight of the chain cable in catenary that acts as a very good spring, and if you do want to use the polyester braid I would recommend lowering a weight (the angel, mentioned above), which should be about half the weight of the anchor, down the cable to about one-third of the scope from the bows. If you do need anything re-galvanising, it can be well done at Pireaus, near Athens, and also at Marseille.

One sees reference to nylon being subject to chafe or cut over coral, but I have no personal knowledge of this happening, probably because my friends are sensible enough not to lay out a nylon cable over sharp coral heads, which in any event are not good holding ground. More important is the fact that nylon will abrade over sand and fairleads, especially when strong winds have the ship

Heavy steel hook for holding chain. No moving parts.

A typical Dan Leno shackle, very useful for joining small chain to large rings, etc but hard to find. Chandlers that supply fishing and commercial craft may be a source.

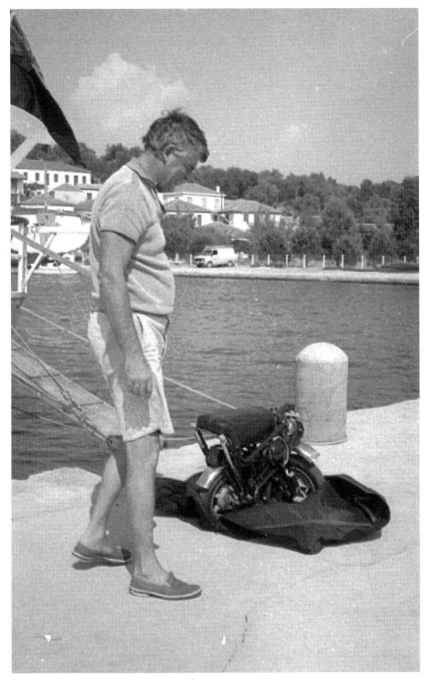

Fare Well's *folding motor bike in its folded state; it is a Di Blasi. Behind the typically scruffy author one can see the dinghy hung outboard on its side davits, freeing the poop for comfortable living.*

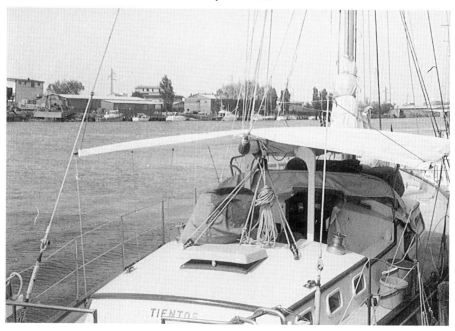

A simple, strong awning on Alan and Pat Lucas' world cruising cutter Tientos. *There is a lot of good sense in this ship.*

yawing. Nylon is more awkward to stow coming in than chain, especially as one needs double the scope, and another consideration in the Med especially is the question of security in crowded harbours when other boats are manoeuvring. Nylon cables lead at longer stay than chain, and thus enter the water much further away from the bows, and are easily cut by another vessel manoeuvring with difficulty. The question of legal liability is not the half of it: the case might well have to be argued in foreign tongues in foreign countries, and that still is not all. The reason why the cutter was in trouble in the first place was probably a strong wind, and the ensuing dance of yachts cut adrift and/or disabled with a rope round the screw soon develops the characteristics of a gang-rape among elephants, with comparable dangers to life, limb and property. Though legal opinion has it as the cutter's responsibility, that is based on big-ship cases heard before the days of nylon cables, and it could be argued that these, at long stay in crowded harbours, are unseamanlike and a contributory factor to trouble.

It is the ease of handling self-stowing bower anchors with a good windlass that makes berthing stern-to a quay the best proposition for craft needing an anchor of about 20 kg or more, even though skippers will find it simpler to manoeuvre ahead, rather than astern. If one had a self-stowing stream anchor the case might be altered, but a bowsprit does make boarding difficult and larger boats with normal sheer find the stemhead a little high. There will be more on anchoring in the chapter on navigation, because it is such an important feature of live-aboard cruising.

A simple board fender, for use against piling, rough concrete or damaging projections.

Other Matters

Backing into a berth (making a sternboard) is not as difficult as it appears and is soon mastered by most. Exceptions are yachts with an outward turning, off-centre screw. The secret is to get enough way on, for she will not steer until this is achieved. The speed required depends on the amount of cross-wind, and in very strong cross-winds it may not be possible at all. Most ship-handling text-books counsel a softly-softly approach until one has mastered the feel of her, but in this case it is not the best approach. The prudent mariner will go off somewhere secluded and do a bit of practice.

A recent development has been the introduction of moderately priced (comparatively!) bow-thrusters, and I have seen several fitted. For short-handed singlescrew yachts above, say, 12 metres such a device might be a better investment than electronics.

For serious cruising it is essential to have very strong bitts or cleats, because one is occasionally obliged to berth in harbours where the shelter is not perfect, and a swell or scend will have boats constantly dancing in their berths. Most deck fittings seen on production boats are criminally inadequate; this seems to be the area where the builder goes barmy to save a pound or two. The main centreline

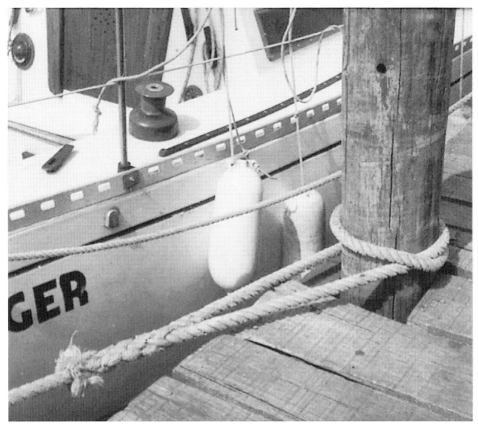

A complete turn round the bollard prevents chafe in the eye of the mooring rope. Not recommended if more than one vessel is on the same bollard.

bitts forward should be strong enough to take the weight of the boat, and one needs two shoulder cleats or bitts fit to spring on. Two midship cleats ditto and two substantial bitts aft, strong enough for towing. Spring bitts or cleats should be on the gunwale, thus avoiding the need for fairleads which are seldom as good as their name.

In many primitive harbours chafe of ropes on quay copings is a nuisance. A common Med practice is to have a loop of chain at the end of the rope, sometimes with a carbine hook. Unfortunately the size of chain equivalent to the strength of the nylon would be impossible to heave. In any event stand clear of people throwing chain about. A nylon rope of 16 mm diameter has a breakload of 4000 kg, which is a lot more than that of a 13 mm chain and more than twice that of the biggest carbine hook. One suggested solution to this problem is to use a soft wire eye at the end of the nylon, or if you wish to use chain, use a picking-up rope of lighter nylon and afterwards substitute the main berthing chain and/or rope which can be quite short.

Fenders seem to be cheaper in England than anywhere else; in the USA they are stupidly expensive, and no better quality. Most people use airfilled plastic fenders, and for lightness and convenience a few of these are more or less essential. But they are not ideal. Hot sun decomposes the plastic material of which they are made and they turn into sticky, grit-covered, abrasive puddings. Second, they are expensive; and third, they do not stand up to hard wear alongside rough concrete or chipped stone quays. A couple of small motor tyres are advisable for bad conditions, though it is not nice to use them against someone else's topsides. Of course we know that the marks are easy to remove, but some of the fancy yacht brigade get a little paranoid, and there is no point in causing offence. (We paint our tyres with white chlorinated rubber to avoid this.) Your neighbour may yet be happier about the grit-encrusted plastic ones.

'An awning... spread over their heads... especially in hot countreys to keep men from the extremity of heat or wet, which is very oft infectious.'

I have mentioned already the need for good permanent shade over cockpit or conning position. In harbour, where one spends most of one's time, temperatures are higher, breezes are attenuated, and some form of living in the open air is desirable in hot or sticky seasons. I designed *Fare Well*'s poop as a verandah: it is 4½ metres long and 4 metres at its widest point, planked in teak with very few impediments. It becomes a delightful living room under a big awning, with folding table and chairs. *Hosanna* is big enough to have a permanent covered verandah, which is where we live in the hot weather.

It is possible to have a simple awning which is, in effect, a sheet with a batten sewn into the hem at either end. When spread over the boom, and with the ends of the battens bowsed down, it is a very cost-effective solution. I prefer a long-term investment of a good heavy cotton awning, roped all round and strong enough to be set over the mizzen boom in all but very strong winds. *Fare Well*'s mizzen boom had a sliding gooseneck so that it could be raised up well above head height in harbour, and the awning had hose connections sewn in: in the West Indies, where fresh water is quite hard to come by, there are frequent showers and we could get 15 gallons from a half-hour rain.

The Americans have long had the Bimini awning, which is excellent, and it can be fitted to allow for it being spread under the boom and therefore valuable while sailing. British sailmakers are getting good at making these; for smaller boats they are the best. Remember that all boats are a compromise, and that you will never find the perfect boat. All you can do is to find one that is good enough to love, then you can ignore her faults.

Chapter Six

Below Decks

'On each side of the Stearage roome are divers Cabins... with many convenient seates or lockers to put any thing in, as in little Cupberts.'

Keeping Water Out

Though there is a natural emphasis on comfort in a long-term cruising boat, it is essential not to lose sight of the requirement that the comfort should extend to comfort at sea, otherwise we will end up with something like a Chelsea houseboat. So important is the ability to maintain efficiency and safety at sea, that the question of comfort, whether in harbour or offshore, has to be fitted round the requirement to survive such rare testing moments that the yacht might be expected to encounter. Important factors in keeping going at sea are minimizing both physical and mental strain; and minimizing the possibility of water entering the accommodation, which in effect will comprise most of the hull.

In our view, watertightness is a vital part of living in a boat. Inevitably one has more possessions on board than the holidaymaker, some of which are perhaps precious even if only for sentimental reasons. Sea water is the great destroyer, and it has allies with which it works. Dampness breeds mildew, mould and rot. And bad temper. Avoid it. It may not always be possible to stop every whit of water entering the bottom, but do get a watertight deck and windows. (It surprises us that in this day and age this still needs saying.) The aim is to be able to clean one's bilges with a hoover, and it is perfectly achievable.

But water *will* get in. Spray flies, waves do wash over the deck; a moment's inattention when tired and there goes the sea water, slopping down the hatch or skylight. Only a paragon can maintain eternal vigilance and what a bore he'd be to live with. We once had a terrible night beating down the Ionian Sea toward Kephalonia into a rising force 6 to 7, the spray flying the length of the ship as her head ploughed into each short sea, making us duck rhythmically behind the spray shield to avoid the worst of it. Then, worried because she seemed to be diving a little more deeply than usual, Bill misjudged a duck and was able to see the forehatch lift, only an inch or so but enough to swallow a gallon or two from the water swilling about the deck. We bore away instantly, forgoing the pleasure of mutual recriminations, and investigated the forepeak which is fortunately separated from the accommodation by a watertight bulkhead. Bill later calculated that there must have been four tons of water in it, and all because we each thought the other had screwed down the bad-weather fastenings. And that was not all: it was a night when Professor Murphy drove home several points. Detritus and mud from the anchor cables had blocked the pump intake, but then, they say there has never been a pump as fast as a frightened man with a bucket.

You could not enjoy living in a yacht with the watertight integrity of a submarine. There is a mean, and how far one goes in either direction depends on the chosen voyages, the chosen times, the chosen crew.

One way water can get below, even in harbour, is on the crew's clothing. A surprising dampness can build up this way over a period of prolonged rain or spray. Bill makes fun of Laurel's bath, but at sea it is an invaluable temporary drop for wet oilskins. Another source of damp is condensation, something that yacht designers have yet to appreciate fully. One modern Camper & Nicholson yacht in which a young couple were wintering in Corfu was dreadful: they were unable to use two of the bunks because of condensation dripping from the aluminium window frames. Now this is bad design and it is something to look out for when buying a boat. Older ships used to have 'save-alls' under scuttles and port-holes to gather the overnight condensation or the odd leaky drops. With plastics why are not save-alls moulded into the scuttles of the production boats that are often the worst offenders? A palliative is to cover the aluminium with some layers of masking tape, when the top layers will prevent the under ones from hardening out, but it doesn't look all that nice.

Insulation

The best hull insulation is to cover the interior above the waterline with about an inch of sprayed-on, closed-cell polyurethane foam, which is also an excellent protective coating for steel. Some years ago, this used to be flammable and gave off toxic smoke if it ignited. In *Fare Well* we sprayed it with fire-retardant paint, which coped with a small fire when an anti-mosquito candle was knocked over in the saloon. (A word on this: we had a blind girl staying with us, and of all the terrors, fire is one of the very worst for the blind. We were all so shocked by this experience that we never now use candle insect repellents.) The foam scorched but did not ignite.

While insulating *Hosanna*, we discovered that this foam is now available in a highly fire-resistant form. We used this and found it good, so much so that it was possible to make *small* welds on the opposite side of the steel plate without igniting the foam. We even cut a hole with oxy-propane, and the foam melted and blackened, but did not burst into flame. Of course we drenched the area with water immediately. In these circumstances, and with care, this foam is ideal for boats that are going to be lived in.

Other insulation methods are to line with glassfibre wool (Rockwool), which does nothing to protect the steel. I have seen an old steel ship with hardpacked natural straw and another with scrumpled-up newspapers packed behind the linings (and she was A1+ at Lloyds, which gives one pause for thought). In my opinion, the sprayed foam is best.

How to protect the steel behind the insulation? The foam will adhere well to an epoxy based holding primer which should be sprayed on immediately after sand-blasting. New steel which it is inconvenient to sand-blast is best treated with a 20% solution of ortho-phosphoric acid, the surplus acid neutralised with industrial alcohol (>75% is best), and then painted with a good quality primer, but the foam will then adhere only to the paint skin. Foam is really effective only on sand-blasted steel. *Hosanna* is an old ship and the after accommodation (the *roef* in Dutch) was in excellent condition after 55 years untouched (we could tell by the dates of the newspapers jammed into the corners). She had been coated there, behind the panelling, with a mixture of old engine oil and paraffin wax. We tried to sand-blast, but the mixture had penetrated into the steel itself, and as there was no sign of rust, we slapped on another coat of the same gungy mush. The Dutch know a few things about steel boats, and they do not like wasting money.

Ventilation alone will not cure condensation when dewpoint conditions are really ripe. In fact ventilation can import dampness when the air outside becomes saturated, so some means of closing off ventilators is desirable.

Designers might well reply to my criticisms of them, that they do not attempt to design boats for living aboard in winter. This is probably true, but why not? A yacht should be capable of use whenever its owner wants, unless its unsuitability for a particular use is openly stated.

Seagoing Citadel Versus Open-plan

Our own solution of the comfort/seaworthiness dilemma was eased by *Fare Well*'s size, but I believe the principle is adaptable further down the scale. It is to recognise those bits of boat that are vital to the navigation, those that are desirable for harbour comfort in winter or summer, and then those that are common to both, such as galley and heads. Then design a layout with a sea-going 'citadel' separated from the rest of the boat, not completely, but so that in bad weather especially there is no need to go beyond it. In our citadel, mostly in the deckhouse which is at half-deck level, we had the galley, chart table, radio, refrigerator, switchboards, a sea bunk, a small table, tool chests, oilskin locker (big — 21 × 24 inches × full height), and close by but down a ladder, the bathroom. (This actually contains a bath, essential in our case for therapeutic purposes and, as we said above, it also makes a first-class place to dump soaking-wet clothes.) The deckhouse is also the access to the engine room, which is beneath it.

In the ends of the yacht (excepting the forepeak and the lazaret) are the saloon forward, and a small guest cabin and our own double bedroom aft. This latter is not a cabin; we use the word 'bedroom' deliberately to emphasize the comfort and peace of the place, which is the biggest single space in the whole ship. I do not say that our conception of the best (there is no perfect) layout is the only one, or even the right one for another couple. It has worked very well for us, for a long time, for deep-sea and short-sea cruising and winter living. The only substantial improvement we would have made would be to have had a real wheelhouse instead of the then shelter, which we subsequently did when we converted *Hosanna*.

Others we know have an open-plan layout, one enormous airy space. It's nice for a party, and it suits the smaller yacht. It does suffer from 'one place wet — all places wet', and there is a lack of privacy when one has guests. Some have a small, separate after cabin as guest accommodation. These are very good for children, but having once been a guest in a Seadog ketch where I needed a shoehorn to get myself into bed, I suspect their long-term use for the grown man is a question of hope rather than reality.

A more conventional use for the half-deck deckhouse is to make it the saloon. This certainly looks better on demonstration models at the Boat Show. It does feel nice to have a light and airy saloon, but in Laurel's view it is also nice to have a light and airy galley. Certainly the catering tends to improve if the cook is not condemned to working in an ill-lit, ill-ventilated dungeon. In the climate we aspire to, most of the living is on deck, which is the ultimate in light and airy. In a Mediterranean winter our saloon does have its disadvantages because our side ports are often blocked by neighbouring craft, but it is mostly in the evenings that it is used and it gets dark early in winter.

We are not really able to talk about *Hosanna* in these terms. Even a small barge like ours is almost big enough to hold a village dance. We have in fact as much space as a small flat and are in danger of becoming spoilt. But we are getting on now, and will have to move to a smaller boat soon, so the subject is very much in our minds.

The Interior in More Detail

The galley

A particular advantage of having the galley high up is that it enables the sink to have natural drainage, something which can be very useful. The galley need not be large, but it does need planning *by the cook*. When living aboard one needs a rather more varied menu than a perennial tin-mix sea stew, so food stowage has to be extended and a more comprehensive range of cooking tools is needed.

Fuel

This has to be done in conjunction with the heating. There are many good arguments for having only one fuel aboard, one that is easily and universally available, and easy to load. The commonest fuel, and one that most of us are obliged to have in any event, for propulsion, is diesel oil, so let us consider that as a sole fuel.

First, it not only drives the main engine but it can also drive an auxiliary generator if you should want one. It will drive an outboard; unfortunately these are heavy though powerful, and not very convenient. In the low power range one can have a battery-run electric outboard, thus using diesel oil at one remove.

There are very good diesel heaters on the market. At the simple end I like the Danish made Refleks heater, which requires no fan and is therefore silent, but of course it heats only the compartment in which it is mounted. English-manufactured Taylor's are similar, and actually look a little neater. There are American and Dutch heaters too, all having gravity feed and dependent on a sort of carburettor made in the USA.

I am not so happy with blown-air oil heaters, having seen a serious fire in Antibes which happened when the crew were ashore for a very short time. It is possible in a bigger boat to have proper central heating with a normal oil-fired boiler. There is a very good Dutch boiler working on the same gravity feed system we mentioned above (the Somy.) The basic boiler is quite small, but it can be installed in multiples. Very clever. Try Paul Holland of Energy Solutions, Rochester (01634–290772).

Cooking can also be done by diesel. There is a Canadian stove, the Dickinson which is a bit like a primitive Aga. But I think the Rolls-Royce job is the one by Perkins Boilers of Derby. Although no longer in production, it not only cooks but provides hot running water and some central heating too. It is pressure jet operated so makes some noise. It is expensive and very heavy, but the company give the most excellent service. There is no other single fuel arrangement.

To have bottled gas for cooking will save considerable initial cost and a certain amount of weight, some of which will be lost because of the price, size and weight of the necessary number of cylinders required for reasonable independence from the shore. It will bring problems apart from its propensity to explode, which can be controlled: practically every major country has its own size and design of gas bottles, very often with differently threaded connections. To change bottles at a retail supplier it is necessary to hand in a local bottle. Odd bottles can sometimes be refilled at depots, but then there is the problem of transport, for the depots are seldom conveniently placed for yachts. I remember helping another boat take their bottles to a depot in Greece, and beating a hasty retreat as I observed the workman pouring liquid gas into an open cylinder through a funnel while he was smoking a cigarette. Possibly the mixture was too rich to explode, and the fumes did not rise.

I would think very carefully before opting for gas as the sole method of cooking, except in a small boat when I would agree that it is the only solution. If the boat is big enough to have a powerful separate 240 volt generator, then one can maintain the one-fuel principle by cooking with electricity. We do this in *Hosanna*. It can mean a lot of generating, even in the evening, when it can cause bad feeling among neighbours in a quiet harbour, but it is becoming more and more common especially among charter yachts. We have a four plate hob, two of which are electric and two gas, and using the gas below and the barbecue on deck is a good way of solving the noise problem if too close to neighbours, the amount of gas required for this occasional use being very small. *Hosanna* has on deck a little sheltered summer kitchen with a single miniature gas ring for brewing up late at night. We do tend to swing at anchor rather than moor cramped up in harbours, and it's more peaceful for us too.

Paraffin is not suitable for the live-aboard. We have small oil lamps in gimbals which we keep lit at night at sea, turned very, very low, when they provide a faint glimmer which allows us to move about without switching on electric lights and spoiling night vision. Coarse, cheap paraffin is getting very hard to find because rural or isolated communities are changing to liquid gas, while the refined, treated anti-pong variety is available in little tiny bottles at high prices.

Alcohol cooking is a menace. It surprises me that the Americans have tolerated it for so long, and I am happy to note a trend away from it at last. In some popular Caribbean anchorages one can sit enjoying a Planter's Punch after sunset while watching neighbouring Americans tossing overboard their flaming alcohol cookers. Some keep them on the end of a wire so they can easily haul them back inboard.

The lovely old sloop *Diotima* in which the late Admiral Goldsmith lived the life of a dedicated singlehander (and on the foredeck of which he died, weighing anchor at Monemvasia) had a solid fuel stove which was lovely in winter but noticeably warm in summer. Fuel was never a problem for him, he just gathered it from the beach. What a lovely little yacht! We last saw her in Hydra, now owned by a Greek sculptor who cares for her. *Hosanna* has two wood-burning stoves for winter evenings; we can sometimes find enough driftwood to feed them for free. We have a derrick and finding a full-sized eucalyptus tree floating off shore, we hoisted it aboard, at the same time removing a danger to navigation, and then landed it to cut it up with a chain saw. We were told off by the Port Captain for making too much mess, but we swept up the sawdust which made good fire-lighters when soaked in old engine oil.

Electricity

Even if one does not have 240 volt generators it is worth considering a circuit powered from the DC batteries by either a rotary converter or an electronic one. It is easy to get 500 watts (or even more if you wish, but the converter prices rise sharply with size), which can be used for a food mixer as well as electric drills, sanders, blow-driers, vacuum cleaners, soldering irons and many other things that ease the chores for permanent residents. Usually this type of appliance is on for a few minutes only, so the battery drain is small. In any event, a 240 volt AC circuit is desirable if one is going to spend a Mediterranean winter on shore power.

Do not rely on all countries having the same wiring practice. The UK system of Earth, Live and Neutral is a good system in principle, but abroad electricians often do not wire up three-pin sockets in a consistent way. It is a good idea to have twin fast circuit-breakers, one on each load-carrying wire of your shore power connection, and to have a certain means of completely isolating the ship's AC generator when connected to shore supply. Also, do not rely on the third pin in a shore connection being connected to earth; use a two-wire shore power cable and bond the earth connections of all your shipboard outlets to your own earth.

Some professional electricians recommend the use of an AC to AC transformer when on shore power abroad. This provides all the power you need, without any direct connection with shore terminals, and can be made to step up the continental voltage which is very slightly lower than the British 230 volts. Of course this is safer, but I wonder whether the increase is cost-effective. I think our method, with reasonable vigilance is 99%: to improve that to 99.5% is not of sufficient significance.

In Europe generally the supply is 220 volts 50Hz, but voltage at the dockside sometimes falls as low as 170, especially in Italy where I suspect a lot of people tap into the supply illegally. In the US the supply is generally 110 volts 60Hz, but it is possible with some shore sockets to get 220 volts by connecting up the pins

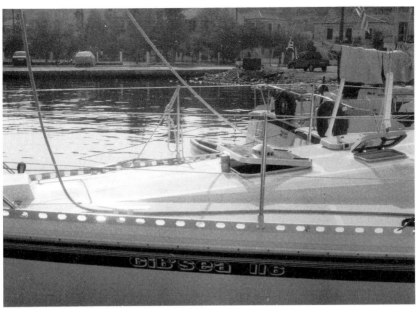

What builders do not provide has to be improvised, but one shouldn't have to use a beer can to adjust a hatch.

in a particular way. Local knowledge is necessary, as the pilot books say, but Americans are very obliging. We found that all our 50Hz equipment worked without any noticeable ill effect on 60Hz, and I suspect that there is considerable tolerance in the design. Motors and clocks go faster: this is possibly what is meant by dynamic America.

Refrigeration

This is the biggest energy user in the boat, apart from propulsion. Nowadays there are a few families living without refrigeration, usually in a small boat. When you get acclimatised it is not too bad, as I remember from days of yore. But now I do like a cold beer, and both white wine and rum punch are better chilled. Some say that the only way to take retsina is so cold you cannot taste it.

In *Fare Well* we had a top-opening refrigerator of about 3 cubic feet, and beneath and accessible through it a storage freezer of 2½ cubic feet. This was a good installation, driven by a Grunert compressor unit, with a large holdover tank. The control was manual with an externally reading thermometer. The compressor was driven by 24 volts DC from the battery. It was mainly switched on during the daily battery charge. It was a robust system, as strong as a brick privy.

For *Hosanna* we could not get an American installation and had to fit one made in Italy (Frigoboat) which was a big mistake. The system works from time to time, but needs a lot of expensive attention, and the service agents (apart, we must say, from the one in England) have not proved noticeably co-operative or effective.

For smaller boats the 12 volt units working on the Peltier system marketed by

Simpson-Lawrence are very simple though not highly efficient, technically. They are unlikely to make ice, but they will keep a small amount of food cool using two miniature fans; take spare fan units as these do not last for ever.

That system sums up the custom-built refrigerator, which has as many variations as you care to give it. The alternative is to buy a conventional household fridge at low initial cost and run it via the AC converter referred to above. The custom-built is probably more energy economical as its insulation is usually better, and cooling the refrigerant is usually by sea water. The domestic system cools by air, which can heat up the accommodation if not ducted out. In the event of major breakdown the domestic system is much easier to replace.

If considering the alternative of an ordinary domestic fridge with power from a converter of some sort, be careful. The starting loads of most domestic fridges are about ten times their running loads. This means that a fridge with an advertised power drain of 100 watts will need about 1000 watts for a second or two while starting up. This would be enough to blow an electronic power invertor, but the rotary type will take it in its stride. I favour buying American refrigerating machinery; the country is so obsessed by ice that they seem to have solved more of the problems than anyone else.

There are refrigerators working on the absorption method, getting energy from a gas or paraffin flame. I once tried the latter, and though I was quite pleased at the time there is no doubt that the present system is much better. The absorption system can be troublesome at sea because tilting and movement inhibits its operation. Laurel will discuss our use of the freezer under victualling.

Water systems

In small yachts water systems are usually manually pumped; the larger boats normally have a pressure system. The best I know of is made by Godwin; like most really good jobs it is bulky and heavy, but again their service has been excellent. Power consumption is negligible, and in *Fare Well* we had running hot and cold via the Perkins cooker. In *Hosanna* the generator heats the water.

I know of some boats which use a header tank. One has a tall, narrow 5 gallon cylinder inside the main mast with a visual sight glass. The skipper pumps water up each morning and has a very exact check on consumption. Knowing him, I bet he has a lock on the pump! Usually live-aboards use more water than holiday-makers; again it is a question of wanting a higher standard of living for long stays. I would certainly make sure that the yacht has very capacious tanks; most production boats, being dedicated to weekend use, are very poorly fitted. *Fare Well* had 400 Imperial gallons and without any drastic economy measures we used about 10 per day. With two guests extra this rose to about 13. For an ocean voyage we exercised a little economy and used 5 on average, laundry day always being an upset to the calculations. Probably tankage of 200 gallons, or 1000 litres, is the minimum for comfortable living and water security.

Water-makers We investigated these, and decided they were out of our price range, and this may well apply to most of our readers. From comments made by yacht owners possessing one (most of whom seem less than delighted) we gather that they use a gallon of diesel for each gallon of usable, but not very nice-tasting, water. Catch the rain! It tastes better.

Stowage

One of the major factors in the accommodation aboard a long-term cruiser is the relationship between bunks and stowage. Ocean racers can get by on half a cubic foot per man, but such an allowance would make for marital discord, and in time a pretty smelly crew.

In tropic conditions, when humidity can be high (and the same applies during a scirocco in the Med) the best way of stowing clothes is the hanging cupboard or wardrobe. Though women's clothes are smaller and lighter, the female needs (and demands, and uses) rather more space than a man. If we were to decide on a requirement of 1 m 20 cm of wardrobe bar for a couple (and this is a bit on the mean side) it would indicate 70 cm for her, and 50 cm for him. Generally guests need only about 15 cm each.

The problem is that while living afloat one has to carry on board full outfits of hot weather decent, hot weather indecent or casual, the same for temperate climes, and finally winter garments for both sea and shore which are very bulky. Whereas a man is moderately content to put on a shapeless old sweater to do the winter shopping, most ladies prefer to look a little less like an itinerant scarecrow.

Each person living on board ought to have about 12 cubic feet of good dry locker or drawers for clothing, quite apart from the wardrobe and any oilskin stowage. I like to provide a guest with 2 cubic feet, enough for a two to three week stay.

Food stowage is not such a problem in the Med where one is seldom far from a good market, but in the oceans, or the West Indies or Bahamas, one does need a fair bit of tin space. The bilges are traditionally used for this. Without leaks, one need not go through the old ritual of marking tins with a chinagraph pencil: we don't. Also, with dry bilges tins keep for very long periods, years even. We did once have a labelling problem by stowing tins in the bilge just above the prop. The vibration made the tins rotate slowly and wore off the labels, leaving the tins brightly polished. It took some time to trace the cause for we didn't go down there while motoring.

Tools are very important, and by keeping the boat dry I have had few bad rust problems without taking any elaborate precautions. One has to keep some tools very handy. *Fare Well* had five large drawers, each one sub-divided, in the deck-house close to the main hatch. There is seldom a hardware store round the corner.

By the same token, spare parts are a problem. Most of the spares we started with are still intact in their wrappers: it has always been something else that has gone wrong. So the quantity carried has grown and grown, and the ship has settled deeper and deeper into the water. It is necessary to make a list of all those gadgets the lack of which would cause severe problems, and these are the spares to carry. Call them class A spares. Class B spares are from those suppliers who are so bad, slow or unreliable that one is obliged to carry them on board. Class C is for those companies who can be relied on to help you out of a hole if their product goes wrong, by sending a spare by a fast and convenient carrier. One should make a policy of buying the products of companies in class C: they deserve every encouragement. Unfortunately there are occasions where one has to patronise a mediocre outfit, and the more you do the more spares you have to carry.

Designers seldom give sensible thought to chart stowage. I have seen a claim for a boat to be well endowed in this respect with space under the chart table for 25 charts, which is about 12 cm. A yacht's outfit (a full one would be much larger) of charts for UK to the Med, in the Med, Black and Red Seas, the Middle Atlantic, the West Indies, Bahamas and the US comes to a stack 24 cm high, and is probably the heaviest movable item on board. And quite possibly one of the most expensive, too.

Navigational publications for the same areas, ie pilot books, tables, almanacs etc, occupy 10 feet of bookshelf; and while it is true that I have one or two old chums among these which are not a great deal of practical use any more, the figure is not far out. There are sixteen Admiralty Pilots alone. Catalogues, a few books giving advice on problems, multi-language nautical dictionaries, and instruction books for equipment. To the suggestion that one does not need all these charts or books at once, the answer is that they have to be on board because the ship is one's home. There is no other place: no shed at the bottom of the garden, no convenient storage at Grandma's that one can easily get to.

Other books can be a problem too. People who have been brought up to read seem to need books to keep in practice, and books abhor damp. The worst are those printed on glossy paper, whose pages tend to stick together. (Yachting magazines are bad offenders.) Thank heaven Penguin and others publish a good list of paperback reference books.

Ventilation

The frequent mention of dampness leads naturally to ventilation and light. We have already referred to the possibility of moisture coming in the ventilator, but unfortunately other things can get in too. A good wire mesh (which should be of bronze because rats eat plastic) is desirable, to exclude mosquitoes, rats and mice. Laurel will take up this point later.

In really hot weather it is nice to have windows that open, though our steel boat is often cooler down below than on deck, largely because she is well insulated. The problem with opening windows is that they are seldom completely watertight, nor are windows and openings of whatever type. Our fixed windows have aluminium frames, as do the skylights. They all give a little trouble from time to time because after eight years the sun has perished the rubber-like compound in which the glass or acrylic is bedded, and one has to come to the conclusion that the aluminium framed opening or window is not really good enough for the long term. Replacing seals is a tedious job, and sadly I cannot recommend an alternative system, though we all badly need a better one.

It is not strictly necessary to have windows of the miniature mousehole size so often counselled by the old salts in the magazines. I have heard tell of Messrs Camper & Nicholson selling a large yacht to an American who, to demonstrate that their windows were not strong enough, hit them and broke them with a hammer, telling the builders that that was the type of force that they would need to withstand. While having every sympathy with an owner in quest of confidence in his vessel, I feel also for the builders, who had already fitted extra strong glass, which was almost certainly adequate. Don't forget that the windows have to be very well fastened into the surrounding hull.

A desirable aid to ventilation.

We have had a couple of very severe storms, and been knocked down until the deckhouse was submerged, but our hull and deckhouse windows (considered too large by some) have done well. (A few squirts got through, but they were not particularly noticeable in the ensuing disorder.) The 10 mm toughened glass in the deckhouse windows measures 37 × 19 inches, while that in the biggest hull window is 17 × 12. It is possible to build the boat like an armoured submarine: the best thing for the nervous is to have removable deadlights of ¼ inch aluminium plate, and enjoy the pleasure of good windows during 99% of the time.

Though it may be very nice to contemplate a cooling breeze coming down a skylight or ventilator just over your bunk, do not do it. Sooner or later the breeze will come with water. It takes just one second to get your bedding wet; it takes ages at sea to get it even tolerably dry. One can tell the boats with this design fault as they arrive in Barbados or the Azores: their drying mattresses are slung across the main boom, and the telltale banners of their shame are drying in the rigging. Surprising how often these boats have been well reviewed in the magazines.

One sees a lot of boats with miniature electric fans. We have an exhaust fan above the galley stove, but no other, and I am not inclined to add one, though I must confess that visitors fresh from the cool of an English summer sometimes talk about the heat. When in a big ship I have had to sleep with two fans directed onto my uncovered body, but this should be unnecessary in a well ventilated and insulated yacht.

101

Heads

'The Beak-head is... of great use as well for the grace and
countenance of the ship, as a place for men to ease themselves in'
[This is the derivation of the sailor's term head.]

Two heads are better than one, for sooner or later one will become a blocked head, usually while guests are on board. This is not always due to items being put down without being eaten first (watch out for people who swallow their cherry stones), though that is often the trigger. The underlying cause is usually scale owing to the salinity of the water. It is necessary to dismantle the flexible tubing every six months or so and beat it against the quay, preferably when there are few people about, and when wearing a hat. An alternative method is to flush the loo a few times with a 10% solution of hydrochloric acid, which can be bought over the counter in most Med countries for just this purpose. It is not a way endorsed by the manufacturers.

We changed the heads on board to Lavac because this loo has a separate pump above the basin. We carry a spare pump so if a loo pump becomes blocked it is a comparatively simple task to fit the spare, leaving the unpleasant servicing job to a more convenient time. We originally fitted a holding tank head because it looked as if everywhere was going ecology mad, but well-meaning attempts to control yacht heads generally ended in an administrative shambles, as in the USA where, except for waterways with locks, the legislation was discreetly ignored.

Since then, the ecology war has hotted up. Turkey has become most aggressive. It seems that both the informer and the magistrate get a proportion of the fine levied for infractions; there must be some inducement for the local people to be so eager to shop foreign offenders even for emptying the washing up basin, and the fines are disproportionate. We accept that in certain marinas, such as Marmaris, where the enclosed harbour is anyway in a bay with little water movement, that some control is necessary at the height of the busy tourist season, but we have found the regulation being rigidly enforced in a quasi-open port where the town's sewage system already drains untreated into the sea.

We anchored in a bay in Grenada where it was forbidden to use the ship's heads. There were five other boats there, in a water plane of about 5000 sq metres. With a tidal range of a metre, that bay was flushed twice daily by 5000 tonnes of water. Just how sensible or necessary are some of the restrictions that the more barmy ecologists so enthusiastically impose?

Now, in *Hosanna*, we have a 30 gallon galvanised soil tank which will cope with a fairly long stay in port, especially with only two of us on board. And *no*, we have never yet been accused of pollution: we are not by nature polluters, we just exercise common sense.

Washing

If the electrical situation will stand it, it is worth having some sort of washing machine. There is a simple, small plastic one on the market in France for about £80, and many live-aboards have one, making a point of an occasional day in a marina in order to do the washing. A hand-operated one is sometimes available

A practical navigatorium with good shelf space for both large and small books. Because the shelves are athwartships shockcord is adequate for retaining books, and enables them to be withdrawn and replaced one-handed.

from UK mail order catalogues for about £30. Laundromats are rare in the Med. Smaller boats do the washing on the quayside, but in the larger boats, where the machine is usually plumbed in, take care that the whole system has some sort of drip tray under it, for almost all machines spill a little water, and even if your hull will not rust, the gungy soapy mush will soon expand like the Quatermass experiment and fight you for possession of your ship.

Most authorities recommend that sullage tanks, to take drainage from sinks, showers and washbasins below the waterline, should be enclosed. Our experience is the opposite. *Fare Well* had an open sump in the keel in which was a submersible pump, and an automatic switch operated by air pressure as the water level in the sump rose. (Float switches are unreliable.) Received opinion is that this is supposed to be smelly and nasty. It was situated in the engine room, which was well ventilated, and it did not seem to smell at all, or at least not as much as the engine, and it had the big advantage that any gunge could be easily observed and readily dealt with.

If at all possible, have all machinery in one compartment that you can get into. It is no joke having a diesel engine in pieces all over the living room floor, and it ought not to be necessary except perhaps in the smallest yachts. Nor should the machinery be fitted in like a three-dimensional jigsaw puzzle for this is a poor inducement to do maintenance. Ideally one should not have to remove A to work on B or vice versa. The engine space should be very well ventilated for hot climates. We once had a fair amount of water down the engine room ventilator when laid well over in a storm, but it was an exception. Even so it is as well to have flaps on the ventilators, and unlike me, remember to close them in bad weather.

Guest cabins

Some yachts equip themselves with guest cabins in the hope that they can do the occasional charter to help pay their way. I am in two minds about this. It seems to me that chartering is getting ever more professional and customers are demanding more and more facilities. In these conditions agencies are not too keen on the casual charter, which in any event is never so lucrative as the professional. They can also be hard to find just when the owner wants them. The alternative is to devote that space to more comfortable living. Of course when friends come to visit they have no super cabin, but our friends are the sort who would holiday with us in a 5-tonner, and we can accommodate them better than that. However it does not solve any financial problems for the owner.

Double bunks are now accepted but it is as well to have a method of dividing them, even for non-marital reasons. Part of our padded headboard can be lifted out and slotted fore and aft to make two very comfortable sea berths.

All in all, do not over-concentrate on the boat as a boat. Think of her as living room for a good deal of the time. If you can do so before buying or finishing her, sit aboard and use your imagination. Surprising what you might come up with.

How to Compare Cruising Boats

'Considerations for a Sea Captain in the choise of his ship'

It is comparatively easy to contemplate a yacht which one is going to use for a purpose which is already thoroughly familiar. However, not many people will be familiar with the complete dedication to the way of life required of a confirmed live-aboard, long-distance cruiser. If they are, then they are unlikely to need any help choosing a boat, but for those who would like to consider another person's outlook, I have devised the following rough assessment system. I do not expect it to stand rigorously when applied to any and every boat, but if it is used to give an idea of whether a yacht is a genuine or suitable design for long-term cruising, one can then eliminate a lot of the rubbish and end up by choosing on one's personal tastes and that feeling of attraction to a craft that is the foundation of a true boat marriage.

For my part, I like to say something is lousy if there is good reason for saying so. You could probably say it about this evaluation scheme: I know it's not perfect, it is just something of a contribution to the debate.

Cooper's yacht evaluator

Take a piece of paper and a pen. Draw two columns, head one *Sea* and the other *Comfort*. The questions are arranged so that an affirmative answer will score as indicated in one column or the other (sometimes in both), while a negative answer will not score. Where a question is complicated there will probably be a few words of clarification immediately following. The first part of the questionnaire is divided into monohulls and multihulls and combined, all types and anchors; obviously each yacht can be considered under only one of these headings.

Questionnaire

Monohull section

		Sea	Comfort
1	Length overall of ship: is it under 30 ft	0	−2
	30–35 ft	1	1
	35–40 ft	2	3
	40–50 ft	2	4
	over 50 ft	1	4
2	Draught: is it under 6 ft	0	4
	6–6½ ft	2	2
	6½–7 ft	2	0
	over 7 ft	2	−4
3	Is the length of the keel bottom more than half the waterline length?	2	0
4	Is the after lower tip of the rudder less than ⅕ of the length overall from the stern?	−3	−1
5	Is there a retroussé transom?	−2	−1
6	Is the keel bottom horizontal, or nearly so?	1	0

Multihull section

		Sea	Comfort
7	Length overall under 26 ft	−1	0
	26–33 ft	0	1
	33–40 ft	1	3
	over 40 ft	1	4
8	Is there an automatic sheet-release gear?	2	0

Combined, all types

		Sea	Comfort
9	Is there clear standing headroom throughout at least 50% of the accommodation?	0	5
10	Is there a wheelhouse?	1	3
	Or if not, is the conning position well protected?	2	1
11	Deck integrity. Is the area of cockpit (including seats) below the level of the main watertight deck: nil	5	0
	less than 24 sq ft	3	0
	between 24 and 40 sq ft	0	0
	over 40 sq ft	−4	1
12	For each hatch or skylight score	−1	1
13	For each Dorade type ventilator over 4 inch diameter score	0	1
14	For each hatch or skylight over a bunk	0	−4
15	Is the mast(s) in tabernacle(s)?	0	1
16	Is there a triatic stay?	−1	0

		Sea	Comfort
17	Is there room for a bicycle on deck?	−1	1
18	Can a rigid tender be carried aboard?	1	2
19	Is it easy to get aboard from the water?	1	1
20	Easy access from shore by either bow or stern?	0	2
21	Are there more than four openings below waterline?	−2	0
22	Add together the breaking strain of all standing rigging that reaches the deck (see table at end). If the total is greater than:		
	7 × displacement in tons	10	0
	6 ×	7	0
	5 ×	4	0
	less than 5 ×	0	0
	less than 4 ×	−6	0
23	Mast compression:		
	if greater than: 2 × dispacement in tons	10	0
	if greater than 1.5 ×	5	0
	if less than 1.5 ×	−10	0

Calculation of compression strain is somewhat complex; there are yacht designers who have never heard of Euler's formula. If you can find out from a mast maker, well and good; or you could try the approximation given in Skene's *Elements of Yacht Design*; or omit this question.

		Sea	Comfort
24	We define the foretriangle as the distance from the foot of the forestay to the foreside of the mast at deck, times half the height of the mast as far as the highest foresail halyard sheave.		
	If this is greater than 40% of area of all plain sail	−4	−2
	If greater than 50%	−6	−3
25	Are there running backstays?	−2	0
26	Is there a permanent gallows for the main boom?	1	1
27	Are there internal halyards?	−2	0
28	Is there roller reefing/furling on headsail?	4	3
29	Is there roller gear on main	3	1
	and mizzen?	1	0
30	For each sail over 400 sq ft	−3	0
31	For a yacht over 10 tons displacement are there two or more geared sheet winches?	2	0

Anchors etc

		Sea	Comfort
32	Is the bower (main) anchor self-stowing?	2	1
33	If the bower is over 40 lbs, is there a power windlass?	1	3
34	Bower anchor cable. Is its chain, more than 150 ft	4	0
	less than 150 ft	1	0
	all nylon?	−2	−1
35	Bower anchor size. Calculate frontal area of craft: multiply mast height from waterline by beam of hull, both in feet. (I know the boat is not that wide at the		

		Sea	Comfort
	top of the mast, but the wind is a lot stronger up there and this is a good approximation.) Divide this area by 8. This gives desirable anchor weight in pounds, and applies to Danforth, CQR and Bruce anchors. Anchors of other types score nothing, and that includes imitations of above.		
	If no anchor of above size	−5	0
	If one anchor of above size	4	0
	If two	6	0
	If three	7	0
	(One might reasonably have one or two additional anchors at about three-quarters this size for use as a kedge or lunch-hook.) Q 35 applies only to conventional sailing yachts.		
36	Chain cable size. Take one quarter of anchor weight in kilos, add 2, and this gives cable diameter in mm. Minimum 6 mm.		
	If chain diameter over or equal to above size	4	0
	If chain smaller	−4	0
37	Is the engine petrol (gasoline)?	−4	−2
38	Does fuel tankage in litres exceed 12 × engine hp?	1	4
39	Is there a second means of generating electricity?	0	3
40	Are deck and hull skin well insulated?	0	4
41	Are there two separate batteries?	1	2
42	Water tanks. At least two, with total capacity in litres more than 40 × displacement in tonnes?	0	4
	Two tanks but more than 6 ×	0	0
	One tank only (ignore rubber tanks)	−1	−6
43	Can you sit down on all four sides of the engine?	0	2
44	Do you have access to the engine without dismantling half the accommodation?	0	1
45	Is the heating system independent of electricity?	0	2
46	Is cooking by either diesel, paraffin or bottled gas?	0	1
47	Is the cooker either gimballed or fully fiddled?	0	1
48	Is there a fiddled draining board or putting-down space?	0	1
49	Is there a refrigerator?	0	1
50	Does total dry locker space for clothes exceed 6 cu ft (160 litres) per permanent bunk?	0	2
51	Number of permanent berths. Divide displacement in tons by number of berths:		
	if over 5	0	6
	under 5 but over 4	0	3
	under 4 but over 3	0	1
	under 2	0	−5
52	Is there separate saloon and sleeping accommodation?	0	3

		Sea	Comfort
53	Is there a wc compartment with shower?	0	2
54	Non-clothing lockerage, above the cabin sole: is there more than 1.5 cu ft per ton displacement?	0	2
55	Is there a good clear area of deck for lounging?	0	1
56	Is there an autopilot?	2	4
57	If no autopilot, is there a windvane?	2	2
58	Is an echosounder fitted?	1	0
59	Are there at least two deck cleats, eyes or bitts, each capable of taking a lateral pull of half the weight of the boat without pulling out? (How to tell? Well, it's a bit difficult to provide a complete answer: such a fitting will probably look too big, but won't be. If in any doubt, it's not big enough.)	4	0

Table of Approximate Breakloads for 1 × 19 stainless steel wire, for use with the above Questionnaire:

Circumference	Approx dia	Breakload
⅝ inches	4 mm	4,700 lbs
¾	6	8,000
1	8	12,000
1¼	10	17,500
1½	12	30,000
1¾	14	46,000

To evaluate the boat add the scores of each column separately. The *Sea* column is meant to give some estimate of whether the yacht is fit to go to sea at all as a cruising boat. Do not expect the score to be conclusive; I am quite sure that there could well be exceptions, but most really worthwhile cruising boats should score well over 50 points.

The *Comfort* column has a broad coverage of those factors which affect one's standard of living; the idea is not to provide sybarism to a grand standard but to try to achieve a living above the 'grotty squalor' level, the sort of compromise between comfortable existence at sea and relaxed life in port. A good score in the Comfort column would be 60, but 50 might be treated as a minimum.

We have inevitably leaned heavily on our own preferences and opinions but have tried to allow for other points of view. If you have a strong opinion on some factor that differs from ours, then give it your own weighting; the important thing is to use common criteria for all vessels surveyed.

For interest, we reckon *Fare Well* scores 58 + 65. Bearing in mind that all boats are something of a compromise between sea-keeping and comfort, it might be as well, after first making sure that there is an adequate score under each heading, to compare totals.

A problem with this 'evaluator' is that it takes quite a time to assess each yacht; it is a very detailed examination giving a weighting of some sort to most things

The Refleks diesel oil heater, which being fanless is quiet. Later models are a bit more elegant.

worthwhile in a live-aboard yacht. To save time one should have a means of quickly discarding unsuitable craft by drawing up a shortlist. Keep the two broad criteria, seaworthiness and comfort. I suggest the following are seriously on the debit side in assessing seaworthiness in the context of this book:

- Deep, short, fin keel which tends to directional instability.
- Rudder hung right aft, which is vulnerable to damage, and also becomes inefficient when pitching in a following sea.
- Large foretriangle with Bermudan rig is tough on small crews.
- Main shroud chainplates well inside deck edge (leads to higher tension in shrouds and greater compression in mast.)
- Anchors not self-stowing, hard on weaklings like us.
- Running backstays are a pain in the transom.
- Bendy masts often bend too far, right over perhaps.
- Two or more sails over 400 sq ft. Tough on small crews.
- Steeply cambered decks are a poor foothold. In theory OK on one side when heeled. In practice, at sea one is never at a constant angle.
- Guardrails less than 30 inches high are tripwires.
- Cockpit that is not self-drained, and adequately so.

All things are a compromise, but I think I would not like to trust my life in a yacht with more than five of the above debit points.

Items that detract seriously from the joy of living in a yacht are more idiosyncratic. Make your own list, but consider:

- Lack of good shelter at the steering position.
- Lack of separate sleeping/daytime accommodation.
- Cockpit that is uncomfortable to lounge about in.
- Lack of a simple heating system.
- Insufficient fresh water (less than 1000 litres).
- Poor hanging lockers.
- Poor ventilation.
- Engine access in living space.
- Pokey little galley, ill-lit or ill-ventilated.
- Less than 6 metres of bookshelves.

I would not be very comfortable in a yacht with many of these points. Set your own limit: five perhaps.

In the end, whether you are looking at the short assessment or the more detailed, you have to face the fact that logic often plays second fiddle to love in the choice of both spouses and boats. Did you really go through all this sort of thing before choosing your wife? Minus three for a long nose, plus two for good puddings? Of course you didn't (I hope). And you probably won't choose your yacht this way either, but you might have fun looking at a few.

Naming your Boat

When we came to registering our new home (*Hosanna*) we had to face up to the problem of naming her. We would have liked to keep her existing Dutch name, *De Tijd zal 'tLeren IV*, which means 'Time will teach you', but we do not like names which have numbers after them, and we had found it impossible to cope with the Dutch name outside Holland. Almost unpronounceable to the English, it would be completely so to the French, Italians and Greeks; it promised us a lifetime devoted to spelling it out in full and having radio messages garbled out of recognition. *Hosanna* she became. It is a word that is reasonably common to all languages, it is cheerful, and it doesn't tread on anyone's toes. Things which have to be thought of, or should be, if one is off to foreign cruising grounds. Also it is one of the traditional Lowestoft fishing boat names; names with a ring to them like Kipling's trawler-minesweepers;

> *'Call up Unity, Clarabell, Assyrian,*
> *Stormcock and Golden Gain'*

If you intend long-distance cruising it is as well not to give your boat names like *Ploughboy of Loughborough*, or *Pwllhelly Phyllis*. Make up your own little list of impossibles. We once came across an Italian yacht called *Titty*. And off the coast of the USA we overheard a distress call from a boat called *Sexy Lady*. It was very difficult to take it seriously, and who wants ribaldry if in trouble.

In the West Indies, where all the local traders keep watch on VHF, we heard a very aristocratic English voice calling 'Scuba Shop, this is Darling Two'. Eventually a deep bass Paul Robeson answered 'Hallooo Darling!'

Even our beloved old *Fare Well*, which you might have thought was straightforward enough, was written down sometimes as 'Fairly Well,' or 'Fairy Well,' and on one never to be forgotten document in Turkey as 'Fart Well'. Take care.

Chapter Seven

People, Pets and Pests

'There are so many young Captaines and those that desire to be Captaines, who know very little, or nothing at all to any purpose'

A great many preconceived notions can be left on the quay on departure, along with the cardboard boxes, empty beer crates, broken gadgets bought at the Boat Show and other cruising detritus. Among these could be stereotypes long overdue for discard, such as: old ladies cannot be expected to climb on board boats, girls can't row, children are not useful, and pets are a nuisance at sea.

You now enter a world where many a nippy Grannie leaps lightly into a dinghy and trims it without being asked as others follow. She has probably steered a yacht in a gale on an Atlantic crossing. Yon lovely girl, so slim and ethereal, can probably get the starboard jibsheet to the winch and hove in while you are still thinking about it, let alone row you a mile ashore. The rope you have just thrown to a likely-looking native, who is standing there looking perplexed while the wind carries you rapidly away from the quay, is apt to be seized by a tow-headed eight-year-old, who makes a bowline in the wink of an eye, drops it over the upwind bollard and disappears down the companionway of that little Dutch sloop. As for pets, my crew would never be complete without a cat. Without too much prejudice, then, let us look at who can do what on board, and how to avoid unnecessary conflict.

It is no longer true that 'Captain' equals 'male'. Many girls and women are Skippers these days, so when I speak of Captains please believe that they are not exclusively masculine. I am more familiar with a male Skipper, and being told what to do as regards navigation and ship-handling. Other areas are my concern: the feeding, health and welfare of the crew are in my charge. In case of bodily accidents, I take over; not because I know more than Bill, but because *in that situation* I have a cool head and don't mind the blood. Much. Also, Bill still has to sail the boat. (Ah! you say: but what if the Skipper has the accident? We'll come to these things in Chapter 11.) I am also in charge of victualling and storing for long voyages, which is as it should be since I am usually also the shopper and cook.

How to be Captain

'The Captaine's charge is to command all.'

Our good Captain Smith once again says it all in a nutshell. The one person who need not worry about his status is the Captain: it is never in doubt. No company president, managing director, or even eminent surgeon on his rounds tailed by milling underlings, can know the power of being Master Under God (as the Lloyds policy puts it) of a ship, however small. The rest of us, according to another well known source, are a little lower than the angels, which presumably puts the captain slightly above them. This gives him a natural authority instantly recognized by landsmen, which is not surprising. What is perhaps surprising is that the quiet authority of a good Captain is recognized even when he is in bare feet and ragged shorts, and by his/her spouse.

No ship can ever run satisfactorily as a commune: the job of a Captain is to be Captain. I have never been Captain (except for a few hours entering the Turkish port of Datca, when Bill had a bad attack of Saladin's Revenge), so of course I have every right to comment on the subject, especially from the point of view of the crew. I use the word 'Capting' to signify Bossiness without leadership, so if I answer my spouse, 'Yes, Capting,' he knows I consider he is merely throwing his weight about and not giving sensible orders. He does not do it often.

- A good Captain explains a manoeuvre in advance, and thus does not need to shout complicated instructions at a bewildered crew at the last minute.
- His orders are clear and unambiguous, thus he does not need to repeat them with rising hysteria and ever-increasing decibels.
- If his crew make a mess of it, he wastes no time cursing. He says 'All right, folks: we go round and do it again.' (He is allowed to grit his teeth, however.) Always start from *now*!
- If he makes an error of judgement he accepts it without fuss and does not blame his crew for it.
- He does not get too excited if the anchor cable comes in slowly, when it always does come in slowly.
- He shouts when ambient noise at the crew's end makes it necessary.

Having said that:

- Captains are the ultimate authority on everything connected with the ship and crew. Wise mates and knowledgeable crew may help him to make the decisions, but he is the arbiter.
- He should make sure all on board know his policy on certain important mishaps and events, such as fire, shipwreck and man-overboard.
- He should be able to delegate many tasks, but it must be clear whose responsibility they are, and he should be prepared to back up his delegate with authority. It is important that he should be loyal to his crew, as they are to him.

A good Captain is recognizable not by his autocracy and didacticism, but by the respect in which he is held by his crew. It is not necessary for him to be the best qualified one on board, since it is possible for highly qualified people to be bad Captains. This is not to say that experience and knowledge are not to be acquired wherever possible; but courses of instruction should be carefully selected by recommendation rather than picked with a pin from alluring ads in the Yachting Press: thus you will avoid those courses run by old and bold military men who are nutty about semaphore, and condescend to your wife: 'This the little woman?' they roar, 'Soon make a good cabin boy out of you, eh? Can she cook?'

The Yachtmaster's Certificate, for example, is all useful knowledge and updated at intervals; but to have gained it is not the be-all and end-all, nor is the Coast Guard Captain's Licence in the USA. There is a danger, in fact, that such certificates entrain dubious feelings of an all-powerful super-knowledge of the sea. Bill has occasionally had to be very tactful (which doesn't come easily), when given shouted and peremptory advice by Yachtmasters off their home patch, advice which would have been inappropriate at best, and dangerous at worst. Both these admirable qualifications tend to be oriented towards local waters and conditions, and should be regarded as forming merely a basis for a great deal of further experience: there will be much to learn about sailing in more distant parts, and much nautical wisdom yet to be aquired. After fifty years at sea, one thing we have learned is to give advice only when asked for, or when a real and unnoticed danger threatens. We, too, are still learning.

A good Captain conducts an orchestra in which he may not play the bassoon too well, but he knows its function as part of the whole and all the players look to him for direction. Or to her, since both conductors and Captains may well be women these days. This causes no bother to most people, as she is usually in this position because her crew feel comfortable about her being there. It is again a question of respect. If certain bigoted and reactionary people find it intolerable to take orders from a woman, they must go and find a bigoted and reactionary Captain who will suit them better.

Every Captain will make mistakes, and sometimes they will be serious. Apportioning blame may be balm to the wounded spirit, but it is unproductive. After disasters, start from *now*. He may find himself in dire straits through no fault of his own, or indeed anyone's, and he will still blame himself. We left Bermuda with an excellent weather forecast, heading north with the expectation of leaving the West Indies well before the hurricane season: June, the rhyme goes, is too soon (for the hurricanes to come). On the eighteenth of June, two days out, we got warning of a tropical storm which had rapidly deepened into Hurricane Alberto. After the vortex had passed us, with no great damage, we were struck by a violent squall and a flash of lightning, early in the morning. Bill's only crime was being on watch when it happened, but the shock of it, and the despair at seeing our sails in ribbons, laid him very low for a while.

We were three on board. The watch below, Nora and I, were precipitated up on deck by the noise and the knockdown. Even if richly deserved, recriminations are unaffordable luxuries at such times, and this squall had been far too sudden for any action to have been effective. Nora and I made comforting and reassuring noises to our stricken Captain, and as soon as I could get the stove going we fed him on quantities of scrambled egg, since we were in no immediate danger and all had headaches from the lightning strike. Then we took a deep breath, and under his direction began to restore the ship to order. We were still 400 miles from land and it was going to be a slow and uncomfortable voyage, but it had to be faced. Neither Master nor crew can say in the middle of a difficult passage 'I don't want to play any more.'

What if the Captain and crew really don't get on at all? Suppose your Skipper, at the Yacht Club bar so smooth and full of salty tales of successful voyages and dangers overcome, turns out to be sufficiently bogus to be a menace to both his ship and crew? Suppose he retires to his bunk at times of

PORTE DE PECHÉ
BEAULIEU, FRANCE

stress, abdicating to his crew decisions which he should make, and for which he will later blame them? (This is a true story, and happened to a friend of ours who is a very experienced crew, on passage from the Azores to Gibraltar. She continued to the end of the voyage, and even though the ship reached Europe some 600 miles north of the position the cataleptic skipper thought he was in, no physical hurt or damage occurred, probably due to a good crew on the watch for trouble.)

Suppose the apparently athletic girl taken on for crossing the Atlantic screams when the boat heels, or is afraid of the dark and won't keep night watches? Or the strong lad turns out to be impossible to live with? Most incompatibilities of this kind can be avoided by a shakedown cruise, with no commitment on either side. Living aboard is about long-term tolerance, so a series of weekends or holidays afloat are not really the answer, though they may reveal intolerably irritating habits or personality aspects. You need to fight your way through a few situations to find out how you are going to get on under stress. To be able to duck out of trouble too easily, as you mostly can on weekend and holiday cruising, negates the point of the exercise. Most of all, you need time to work together and evolve an everyday smoothness of running, so that routine tasks become second nature, and there is more time and energy to cope with unexpected surprises. Thus, while no one is perfect, you will not set off on a long cruise with someone who rubs you up the wrong way. I have said elsewhere that marriages may not survive the strains imposed on them by the cruising life (this goes for friendships and Captain/crew relationships too), but marital breakdown, mutiny and mid-Atlantic mayhem are outside the scope of this book. Not far outside, though.

As you will have noticed, a great many observations that can be made about Captains are inextricably entangled with those about Crew, since they are two sides of the same coin.

The pierhead jump

Should a short-handed Captain take on a 'pierhead jump' (an unknown crew who joins at the last moment)? It is a desperate measure, fraught with risk and uncertainty. Only the Captain can weigh need against risk. In the West Indies such a crew must possess an air ticket outward before being allowed to sign off the crew list of any vessel. It is the Captain's responsibility to ensure that such a ticket exists, or he risks being landed with the person indefinitely. We have sometimes taken on someone at short notice: all but one were a great success, all but one came with recommendations from people we knew and trusted. Many couples we know have had a very different experience, however, even resulting in vowing never to take crew again however short-handed they were. The sins of the said crew varied from drug abuse, smuggling, theft and laziness, to actually taking command of the yacht in mid-Atlantic, from a rather elderly couple who were powerless to stop them.

The only time we took a crew who had not been personally recommended by someone who had actually sailed with them and knew them well, but only by a man they had done some boat painting for, we regretted it all the way from Gibraltar to the Azores. (Our insurers sprang on us, at the last minute, a requirement to have more than two persons on board for ocean sailing, a requirement they have since modified).

Be aware that if drugs are found on your boat, the boat is liable to confiscation, even if you were unaware of the existence of the drugs. It is not necessarily the hippier looking people who take or deal in drugs. Which takes us back to reliable references, living with prospective crew for a few days, and discovering their attitudes and habits, with, these days alas, a certain amount of healthy suspicion of anything that does not quite add up. At close quarters one has a better chance of finding out before it is too late. We come, inevitably, to:

How to be Crew

'The saylors are the elder men, for hoising the sailes,
haling the bowlings, and stearing the shippe.'

There is no task in a boat that is sexually exclusive. Some jobs require brawn, and there are women who can do them and have enough breath left to whistle at the same time. Others of us are rather less muscular, but perhaps good at fiddly jobs requiring great patience. Apart from being helpful, tolerant, humorous at the right moment and tactful, it helps to have a little knowledge.

For *absolute beginners* and a few others we could name, we include a 'Starter Pack' on one or two essentials, see further on. While unlikely to prove the definitive work on the subject (indeed, this book is not about seamanship), *no one who has taken in the full import of this section is useless*. Anyone who can make a bowline, and has learnt the intelligent use of fenders without bumping into the rest of the crew is already of considerable help; I particularly address myself to those windblown lovelies who are so disrespectfully called 'crew's comforts' by their companions.

Laurel and Bill's starter pack for would-be cruisers

'Here mayst thou learn the names of all ship's gear'

No one should embark on a long voyage or a life afloat without having acquired a minimum competence, which should be got not only by study but also partly by doing some boatwork. It is all very well to plan that the skipper will sail the boat to all intents and purposes as if singlehanded, and that his chosen crew will be entitled to consider themselves solely for catering and/or decorative purposes. It never turns out that way.

Circumstances will arise when it is a case of 'all hands to the something-or-other' and a certain basic knowledge of somethings-or-other would be no bad idea. Likely areas of difficulty are when berthing, or when others are berthing on you. There are occasions when sails will not do as they should, and no skipper, however brilliant, can see to both ends of a rope at once. People do fall over-board, they also fall in in harbour, especially from dinghies, and things do break or part.

Let us look at a checklist for the absolute novice so that he or she has, at the least, a basis on which experience can build.

What a crew should know

- Learn the names of important bits of boat or gear, so that you know what the skipper is talking about especially if he is excited or overwrought. Examples: bows, stern, jib, genoa, mainsail, mizzen, sheets, halyards, topping lift, forward, aft, port and starboard. Know what he means when he says take a turn (or whatever term your own skipper uses to indicate bringing a rope to a cleat or winch), turn up, make fast, fend off, check or ease sheets, luff or bear away, haul, veer, cast off. Concentrate on the phraseology of your own skipper: it is more important to have certain and accurate communication than the precisely correct nautical jargon.
- Learn to tie a few nautical knots. We suggest the bowline is very important. Then comes the rolling hitch, the round turn with two half-hitches, the clove hitch, the sheet bend and the figure of eight. The reef (square) knot may be better than a granny, but it is a bad knot except for tying reef points, and perhaps also for tying two Boy Scouts together.
- Learn well that in boats over 10 tons, on no account try to stop them moving with hands or feet unless you have an amputation impulse. A fender is built for the job and does it very well if you play your part. Learn that when boats move towards a quay or each other there will be little or no damage if someone (why not you?) interposes a fat soft object (no, *not* you) so that the impact is absorbed. Learn that these fenders can be pre-positioned as a precaution and to save time, but that does not remove the need to see that in the event they are in the right position (where the impact takes place) and not too high or low.
- Learn to heave a line. Most yachts in the sizes we are writing about can be controlled by rope light enough to be thrown quite a long distance. (Remember to hold on to one end of it.) If berthing, when you have thrown your rope to the quay and some kind soul has made it fast there, adjust your end so that the rope has no slack and take one full turn round the cleat and back it up. There is more to it than this, but that is a basically useful thing to do: if the skipper wants the rope hauled or veered (tightened or let out), or made fast, he will say so.
- Learn to steer a compass course. It is not difficult and it gets easier with practice. It is a lovely feeling when you master the art.

When you are able to cope with the above you will be very useful on board if you keep alert and use your loaf. Your typical Able Seaman is no great genius. He has a few basic skills, some basic knowledge, but most comes as he sails. A lot of the mystique is pure bullshit.

With even this small amount of knowledge you would not be unwelcome in most yachts. Such happy beginners are more use than the theoretical know-all we once had on board, who while on watch and unbeknownst to the Skipper, devised a spendid new lead for the jibsheet which carried away the starboard rail when he tested it. He'd been to Evening Classes.

Next step: To be of real use as a trusted watchkeeper a crew member should know:

What a watchkeeper should know

- Where everything is kept, and what it is called.
- How to switch on the engine and use it for simple manouevres.
- What the normal reading should be for all dials and meters.
- How to lower and row the dinghy.
- The Rule of the Road at Sea (part B first, then C and D).
- Enough coastal navigation to put a fix on the chart.
- Basic sail and shiphandling.
- How to steer a compass course.
- The first steps to take in several various emergencies.
- How to use the VHF or other radio.

(The RYA publish brochures which list recognized sailing schools, with details and prices of the courses run. Go on one, or go to Evening Classes, there's nothing wrong with them, as long as you regard them as the beginning, and not the end, of your nautical education. You will learn some basics which will help you to understand a very rich craft, and words of the vocabulary you will need to learn the language.)

We now have to recall that the crew and Captain are likely to be members of one family, or friends (long may they be so), and there is a lot to be said for *everyone* learning *everything*. In *Freya*, whom we met in the Chesapeake and the Bahamas, the family, with two young daughters, changed tasks daily so they all had their turn at engine bleeding, navigating, cooking and so on. This system might suit you very well. Diffident crew members also appreciate being given an area of personal concern, and time to research and study it. Such areas could be meteorology, cooking and victualling, radio, engines or first aid. The Captain does not have to be the navigator.

Bill and I use the 'specialist and backup' system. He is such a good navigator that it is hard for me to compete; but it would be obviously stupid for me not to know my coastal navigation. In the old days I could take a sun sight and work it out, however slowly and painfully, but Satellite Navigation has changed all that. Our GPS (Global Positioning System) has taught me so much about navigation that I am probably almost as dangerous as someone who has been to two Evening Classes.

I am a far better cook than the Skipper so I do most of it, but when he has to do it for a while we do not starve. When Bill is upside-down in the engine room on a rough day at sea I am guiltily aware that I would far rather be steering, cooking, sail trimming and piloting (all at once) plus handing him his tools, tissues and tea, and receiving in exchange bad language, bad temper and blame. The 'dirty bits' of the boat are not for me, unless I am required to wriggle into some small corner that Bill is too big to get into. This gets me the job of packing grease into the shaft tunnel greasebox, and painting inaccessible holes and corners. In fact I do most of the painting, after Bill has done the preparation. The miserable job of Antifouling, so called because it *is* foul and most people are Anti, must be shared.

We are well aware that most cruising crews consist of one man and one woman, most of the time. It behoves both of you to be capable. Running a yacht properly requires teamwork of operating theatre calibre. Whether your crew is large or small, we will suppose that they have been chosen after a shakedown cruise, and you have weeded out (or selected, according to preference) smokers, vegetarians, flat-earthers and bridge fiends. Even when the crew has been tailored, as it were, to fit, irritating habits should be curbed. In a small space the utmost tact and tolerance is essential. Snoring, nail clippings, washing (either too much or too little), black hole filing systems and food fads are all annoying; make your own nasty little list. If the crew is the basic man/woman one, there should be room for you to sulk (as we do) at opposite ends of the boat till tempers are recovered. At sea, this is hardly necessary, since the days are busy, and we hardly meet at night except to hand over the watch and are usually pleased to see each other by breakfast time.

We have a little rhyme that describes the sort of crew we do not want to take with us. It goes:

> *No no-hopers, no topers,*
> *No one round the bend,*
> *No no-soapers, no gropers,*
> *No windbags (either end).*

Children and Babies

The children we meet who live aboard yachts are almost invariably courteous, at home in any company, pleasant to talk to, willing and reliable. They are integrated with their family in a way that is fast being forgotten when children no longer work alongside their parents at any demanding task; especially against time and the elements. Children in general now do not help with the harvest, mend the nets, help launch the lifeboat, or dig for victory as used to be the case; and so do not share with their parents the satisfaction of a difficult job well done. A sea voyage, however, is something that is achieved by the whole family; and the pride in it shines out of the children's eyes.

A single child often misses the company of other children, and plenty of opportunity should be found for mixing, since it is too easy in an adult environment where responsibility is the watchword, for the child to forget how to be a child, and to find difficulty in relating to his own age group when the time comes. If the child or children accompanying you are of school age, you have to face their education. Whether you do this alone, or with help from their teachers, or by correspondence course, you are in for a tough time. In Australia, France and the USA correspondence courses are quite usual. Ten-year-old Ben Lucas on *Tientos* was working on an Australian course, which needed assistance from his mother Pat. The parents of Grant Dawson on *Iolanthe* had tried both the Calvert system (USA) and the British PNEU course. They preferred the latter as being more of a challenge, though the Calvert system needed no assistance from parents since everything was provided down to the last pencil and rubber and the child could be left to tackle it alone. Most parents prefer to be more actively involved, however, though it costs many hours of work.

One British couple we met had had remarkable co-operation from the state school that their child had attended: a stack of about twenty books was provided and a syllabus of work covering the next two years — which must have taken some dedicated teacher a lot of time and trouble to prepare.

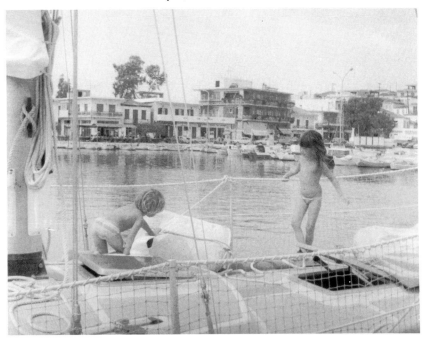

Good netting protects these French youngsters. It is quite effective for parents too.

However you go about it, it is no joke having to cope with lessons when you would rather be swimming; and this is as hard for the supervising parent as it is for the child; if you are temporarily in a yottie community it can help to run 'the school' on one boat, in rotation: the children benefit from interaction and competition even if they are doing different courses, and only one parent need supervise the gang. Mornings are best for the heavy work, while the minds are fresh (you will notice that a good school timetable puts the maths and Latin before the first break if they can), leaving the more pleasurable side of things till later.

Thank goodness, there *is* the other side of the coin. Great delight and interest can be found in visits ashore, studying people and places, the local museums, the customs and culture of many lands; and some of the language does not come amiss either. There is also a wealth of sea and shore life: fish, birds, plants, dwellers in rock pools and in sand holes, shells, trees and flowers. Recognition books for all these things should be part of the 'school library'. A scrapbook will find a place for exotic bus tickets, postcards, programmes, labels and so on.

A well kept log by each child combines many disciplines: writing, drawing, recording things seen, self-expression and observation are only a few of them. A rough book would help to lay out an attractive page. Since such a log will one day be a treasured reminder of the voyage, it would be worth presenting the child with a really important-looking hardcover book, such as are now available with unlined pages and attractive leather-type bindings, to encourage best efforts and the production of something to be immensely proud of.

121

Small babies pose few problems at sea. In a basic small yacht with a lack of gear that would raise eyebrows today my six-month old required only feeding, a change of nappies (no disposables then) and a safe place to sleep; nothing else. She did not seem to be at all worried by even quite violent motion, and was certainly not seasick: this seems to come with the toddler stage. At times of stress (ours, not hers) we put her in a carry-cot wedged between the two forward bunks where, to our amazement, she learnt to stand up — briefly, before sitting down suddenly when we hit a wave.

As for feeding: battling with baby bottles and a Primus on a stormy night is a very good way to get scalded, as I discovered. Bottled milk is not nearly so convenient as draught, especially at sea: I have yet to hear of any one coming to any grief through breastfeeding. You certainly don't get scalded. Nowadays I should probably use a cold-water method such as Milton for sterilization of the bottles, and think of a foolproof way of warming the milk. Baby food, in jars or tins, is widely available in the western Mediterranean, the USA and the bigger West Indian islands, but stock up if you are venturing farther, or to eastern Europe (especially the old Communist block).

When my mother took me sailing at six weeks old (a daring thing to do in those days) she put me in a box of bran with a muslin square under me, and tossed out the damp bran as necessary. I have heard of sawdust, sand and sea-weed being used in the same way. Kitty Litter is feasible, but a little lumpy, it is great in a bucket for adults when the head gets blocked, but is not available in the wilds. Nowadays we have disposable napkins (diapers to the Cousins) and you would think that washing nappies was a thing of the past. So it is, in many parts of Europe and the USA where disposables are readily available. If you are going to remote places, however, they will be expensive and hard to find. They are too bulky to store many on board. You may have to revert to the terrycloth or muslin squares of Grandma's day.

Mark and Felicity on *Scout* used a mixture of disposables and terry nappies for young Teresa. They were given a preliminary cleaning by towing astern, a watch being kept for dolphins who enjoy stealing them to play with! They needed a thorough final rinse in fresh water, or terrible chafing and soreness would result. At eighteen months, Teresa loves the shipboard life. She is used to being dunked in the water (many yottie babies can swim at six months) so she has no fear of going under water, but she cannot quite swim yet without her inflatable armbands.

Yachts with small children on board usually reinforce the guardrails with netting, to fill in the gap down to the toerail that a small child might slip through. We had netting on the foredeck of *Fare Well* as we felt it was just as well to stop adults and sails falling through. It has to be remembered that toddlers are all little Paganinis: great fiddlers. I watched recently, fascinated but unable to intervene, as three year old Suzanne on the neighbouring boat unpegged her mother's bikini from the guardrail and, chuckling, dropped it over the far side. We lent them our shrimping net, always handy for such events. Teresa loses tools and other objects by posting them into the rubbish bin. Sea mothers need even sharper eyes than their shore counterparts, since there are so many knobs, switches, buttons and hand pumps on a yacht; and they cannot all be put out of the reach of an active and curious toddler. I have seen a variety of ingenious devices to protect vital

Another good solution to the problem of how to keep little children safe.

switches: shockcord, wedges, Perspex lids over a whole bank of them: necessity is the mother of invention.

In times of activity or crisis, babies are plonked in a safe place. This is essential for parents to get any peace at all. It takes the form of a playpen, or a well-wedged carry-cot or 'padded cell'. The best idea, which I have seen many variations of, is the pilot berth transformed into a miniature nursery, well cushioned, with a strong net that snaps in place over the front. The baby comes to consider this as 'his', it is comfortable, full of his soft toys and comfort blankets or pillows, and he seldom objects to being put there for a spell. And even if he wimps a bit, you know he's safe and can be ignored till the rush is over or you have had your siesta. We have recently seen a toddler's car seat firmly fixed in the cockpit with the toddler happily strapped in, part of the family but safe in times of crisis or activity.

Children are people too, and while their skills are yet few they can be aided to feel valuable. They should join in all the activities they are capable of, and be taught the right way to do them. They should be given definite jobs to do, such as care of the fishing gear, teach them how to stick the hooks into a cork for safety. On long passages they can be asked to read the speedlog at intervals and record the result. It can be their job to identify and record birds, fish and sea creatures seen. The tasks must be seen to be genuinely useful or rewarding, and take them to the limit of their capabilities, so that they are not shrugged off when they are not in the mood: responsibility starts early at sea. It all helps to prevent boredom. (Yes, long passages can be very boring.)

How to be Navigator

'The Master is to see to the conning of the shippe.'

Traditionally a man's task, this is changing fast. There is no foundation for believing that women are less numerate than men: many of us were very badly taught. We can, however, learn. A female navigator is a threat only to very old-fashioned Captains who have forgotten that centuries ago no Captain, usually a moneyed aristocrat, would have been able to 'see to the conning of the shippe' since that was a well protected mystery known only to the Master, a mere professional. The wealth of published pilot books, tables and charts that we had when we were young did not exist. Only much later did the job of the Shippe man and the Captain merge, when it was realized that a practical seaman made a better Captain than the aristocrat who knew nothing.

Navigation is a practical skill. The theoretical side can be learned on courses (see the yachting press for ads) and there are also evening classes, usually associated with various Certificates. To acquire the practical knowledge, there is no substitute for doing it. Like driving, it is a skill that is probably *not* best imparted by one's spouse if peace is to reign. The practical courses at the National Sailing School at Cowes were excellent, what a pity they no longer exist. Similar courses are widely available and ensure that you do not remain an eternal student, without confidence in your convictions, but return with a self-assurance born of knowledge, coupled with a respectful wariness for those who have done it for longer and further.

A good navigator tries to be always aware of his ship's position in space, and he is always checking the instruments which tell him where he is. He checks his compass daily: in coastal waters against known transits, at sea against the rising or setting of the sun or moon. If something puzzles him or does not add up, he will not rest until he has solved the problem. He pays regard to a strong feeling that something is wrong. He is rigid about keeping his DR (deduced reckoning) going, and expects you to do the same when it is your watch. He will be very unhappy if you fib about the course and speed, whether because you nodded off and did not pay attention, or because you would prefer your helming performance to seem rather better than it was.

He checks his sextant for index error in case someone has fiddled with it. He is the one that notices what time the electronic log failed, and remembers to allow for the half hour you spent going round in circles when the jib furling gear jammed. The advent of GPS changes little of this: (you still have to spot when it's lying), only you now have to be really creative in explaining to the Captain why the boat is in the wrong place after you've been steering for an hour. ('Well there's a current, isn't there?') He never leaves anything to chance. You do not hear him say 'Yes, I think that's Cape Krio, we can alter course now.' He checks till he knows that it is Cape Krio. Otherwise you end up like the honeymoon couple we met in the West Indies, who mistook the radio mast on Union Island for that on Mayreau Island, and instead of (as they thought) entering harbour ran on the reef off Carriacou.

Harmony can be maintained at the chart table by not getting ink, cocoa rings, gravy, chewing gum, setting lotion etc on the charts. Pencils should not be allowed to drop, otherwise the lead breaks at half-inch intervals all the way through, causing terrible anguish as pencils are always sharpened when the Master doesn't know where he is, and the irritation effect is cumulative. Practise with a cheap plastic sextant, and you won't be worrying about damaging that gorgeous brass and varnish antique that your spouse is so dotty about. (And see Chapter on Navigation). Avoid using the Navigating notebook for shopping lists, and the dividers for opening tins, and perhaps the Cook's wooden spoon might not get used for stirring bilge paint.

How to be the Weather-man

'It overcasts. We shall have winde, foule weather.'

I don't think it is chauvinistic to say that women are (by my observation) much better at languages than men. It may be that we are more willing to try. Perhaps it is to do with having to make sense of what the very young and the very old are saying to us: we seem to have a greatly enhanced aural perception. That is to say, we can listen to a toothless old biddy in the marketplace speaking a thick dialect in a language we don't understand; then turn to our astonished menfolk and say, 'It's four and a half Filas for a Katlo, and please will we bring the container back.'

This leads to the women getting the job of listening to foreign language weather forecasts, which at times of bad reception sound far worse than the market lady and there are no nods, gestures and mime to assist comprehension. Thus, we get to be the meteorologist, too. If you have previously studied nothing more weighty, weatherwise, than your corns, it is time to find out why you can't break Buys Ballot's Law, why weather systems have fronts but no backs, and why:

> *When in port you choose to stay*
> *The Goddam gale will go away,*
> *But when to sea you choose to go,*
> *The Goddam wind comes on to blow.*

Courses in Meteorology for Yachtsmen in the UK are run mostly in conjunction with the Yachtmaster's Certificate. They are another subject that can be taken as evening classes (see your local Education Authority list, which usually comes out in August for classes beginning in September) or as practical weeks or weekends as part of a Cruising School. Courses can be of various lengths, with emphasis on met and practical forecasting according to students' needs, as well as the usual navigation, seamanship etc.

Since most weather forecasts are read at normal speed, you need a shorthand of some kind. While there are international symbols for weather phenomena, they are not adequate; and you will need to supplement them with your own. Do not believe the RYA booklet Weather Forecasts when it blithely tells you that the international symbols 'will enable you to appreciate at a glance the information which is contained on any weather map which you may see displayed in Clubs or Ports of call.' This applies (as do most RYA statements) only to Great Britain. Elsewhere in Europe, the Mediterranean, the West Indies and America (except for some huge and expensive marinas which rarely concern the cruising yottie) the weather reports are in words, on teleprinter or standard form, in the local language and often the local handwriting. Five years or so ago a very few Port Captains were beginning to have grey-on-grey Weatherfax reproductions, which were so appallingly smudgy and hard to read that they always put the plain words teleprint form up as well. Even in a foreign language it was easier to read. Now you get Navtex printouts (in English) almost everywhere except the western Med, which is the part that needs it most.

Both the RYA handbook and *MacMillan's Almanac* have a weather vocabulary in several languages which are very useful. Most weather handbooks explain weather symbols, and tell you how to take down broadcast information, link it to your own observations, and construct and understand weather maps. If you can record the radio broadcast report on tape, you can worry it out at leisure. You will get used to the orderly progression of it, and the sound of the words, and soon be able to take it down direct.

Italy used to get the Gold Sou'wester for the best TV weather report in the Med, on RAI Uno (Radiotelevisione Italiana Channel 1), but the old Air Force chap who did it with proper synoptic charts has been supplanted by the usual bimbo with pictograms. France (TF1) has a good one, after the eight-o'clock news, though the presenter's gimmick is to talk as fast as he can. Most of the European radio reports are good, and Greek Radio translates them into English after their early morning bulletin.

Nowadays almost every yacht has Navtex, whether the one that prints out and fills the boat with paper, or the one with a miniature screen. We find it invaluable, not only because I no longer have to get up at an unearthly hour to 'Get the Forecast' (except on the Italian Coast where Navtex doesn't yet work).

The only weather services which reach right across the Atlantic in either direction used to be in Morse, which is in process of being phased out. *The Admiralty List of Radio Signals*, Vol 3 is certainly the most comprehensive book of weather broadcasts in the world, both voice and CW (Morse), but it is usually out of date by the time it is published and is laid out like a Chinese puzzle.

If you do not know Morse, big ships have radio operators on board, most of whom are happy to pass the time of day with you and give you a weather forecast: they get bored on long passages too. Do not expect to see more than two or three ships, big or small, on your entire crossing, though, and do not try calling up US warships, as we did in mid-Atlantic. At first they would not even admit that they were there at all, reminding me of a large Newfoundland puppy trying to hide in a daisy patch. Then they seemed to think that the weather forecast was a classified piece of information. After much delay and seeking of permission they gave us a cautious description of the weather we were actually experiencing at the time. The Russian 'trawler' shadowing them was much more helpful.

The cruising yacht is very much on its own and must be self-sufficient. We act at all times as if there were no such thing as rescue services, which indeed is the case in mid-ocean. We are proud of our 20-plus years of deep-sea cruising with no calls for assistance: if we were in trouble we coped with our own resources. Judging what the weather was going to do next if you could get no forecast is an important and normal part of that resource.

Finally, if you ever need detailed weather forecasting in home waters, if you are looking for a weather 'window' to start a particular voyage for example, you can get expert forecasts tailor-made for your boat, your crew and your voyage, over the period of a month, from the British Meteorological Office at very modest cost. If you speak good enough French, Metéo Consult by telephone in France puts you in touch with the professional forecasters, who will advise you directly.

How to be Cook

'The cooke is to dresse and deliver out the victual.'

It is a poor cook who is not also a psychologist. This comes fairly easily to most women who, knowing how to cook on shore, have a head start at sea, and therefore get landed (not the most apt word here) with the job. Notwithstanding centuries of professional contempt thrown at the historical sea cook, and the extensive list of rude names for his dishes and his person, his contribution was vital and his lack of it often lethal. It is a job of immeasurable importance. Preserving morale in bad weather or other adverse conditions may rest heavily on the cook. 'Fate cannot harm me, I have dined today' said Sidney Smith. There is something unbelievably heartening about hot food and drink, and anyone who can rustle up an appetising one-pan dish in hell-and-high-water conditions is more to be prized than a Cordon Bleu. I've not noticed that men are any better at this than women: I have a strong feeling that it depends sometimes on who is hungriest. But the young male still tends to give cooking a low priority, and will stuff himself with anything that costs him no trouble rather than remembering the welfare of others, as a true cook should.

Practical help on cooking and victualling will be found in Chapter Nine, but before you embark be sure to take a few books to help you cope with the odder products of nature. You may not actually have to eviscerate a duck-billed platypus, or lightly kill an armour-plated turtle that is looking you straight in the eye; but you can see the way my mind is working. You may be leaving the fish fingers and pre-packed drumsticks far behind, and encountering unfamiliar fruits and vegetables as well.

Be sure you learn to make bread, in all its varieties. Fresh hot bread is as good for the spirits as the sight of land after a long voyage.

How to Steer and Keep a Night Watch

'Steer steady and keep your course so you go well'

Steering looks so easy. To some people, it is: they fall into the way of it immediately. Others find it hard. They wrestle and wrench the wheel; they oversteer and the ship hunts this way and that like a dog after truffles. The compass confuses them and the watch below groan as the ship's motion deteriorates. These hapless helmsmen chase the spinning compass card till they are dizzy, and seem to have no tenderness or coaxing in them, to sense the ship's needs. Naval Officers of the Watch of Bill's day had an order to deal with this phenomenon. They bellowed wrathfully down the speaking tube: *'Steer small, blast you!'* (use less rudder).

127

Fortunately, most of us learn to be at least adequate helmsmen. In bad weather half an hour may be quite enough at the wheel or tiller. It is hard work; you are likely to be steering because it has become more than the autopilot can cope with, however excellently (better than most of us, rot it) it can perform in calmer seas, and your concentration quickly tires. A certain mad exhilaration can set in with a force 7 behind you; you think you are doing very well indeed, like a drunken driver. It took quite a bit of persuasion to pry me loose from the wheel on one such occasion when it could be seen that I was tired, losing control of the ship, and likely to gybe all standing. I was soaking wet, singing loudly, drunk on the weather and indignant when firmly removed. They led me, babbling, below and quelled me with porridge.

Steering is more than just fooling about with the wheel. Unless told otherwise, the helmsman 'has the con'. This means that he is currently in charge. As well as steering the correct course, he should have an eye to the following:

- Are the sails flapping, or setting correctly? Has the wind or weather changed?
- If the engine is in use, are the revs, the fuel gauge, the oil pressure and temperature all reading normal?
- Other ships in the vicinity, the lights they carry, their probable course, speed and distance away.
- The sea: is it getting rougher, or a swell developing? Is the visibility getting worse? Can you see any shore lights or lighthouses?
- Odd noises or smells repay investigation: we have often prevented something dire by due attention to these.
- If the log fails, the time and reading should be logged at once, and thereafter you must estimate the speed as best you can. You will also have to be honest about the course you actually succeeded in steering, however reluctant you might be to admit less than perfection, since the DR (deduced reckoning) depends upon it. Check, similarly, if you have one, that your GPS is really working.
- Finally, the ideal watchkeeper will know when to call the Captain for something he really needs to deal with, and when he can be left to sleep.

All this probably seems a lot to pay attention to. It is just as well that it seldom happens all at once, and that a night watch can be a period of great peace or even paralysing boredom. The autopilot takes some of the strain, but conversely if nothing much is happening it can be a good idea to switch it off and steer by hand for half an hour, to keep you on your toes. If there is a moon and stars, and enough wind to carry you gently along: that is dreamstuff, and happens often enough. If you are in a nasty sea left by the last storm and slatting about with no wind, it can be exasperating. To pass the time some mentally write books, some listen to the Walkman (what a boon this is: no more do the loud-music freaks, whether adherents of Bach or Blur, Shostakovich or the Spice Girls, disturb the sleep of the watch below). Bill invents things, plans *coups d'état* and generally puts the world to rights. I have imaginary conversations with the Great, write poems and songs, which I sing (quietly).

It can be a long night.

How to be a Deckhand

'The younkers, or common saylors, for furling the sayles, bousing or trising, and taking their turn at the helm.'

If you are a team of two, it pays to do nothing in a hurry. Whether changing sails, or berthing, or any other bit of seamanship, take a little time to think. If you are entering a new harbour, the crew should check through the binoculars where any other yachts are, whether the mooring is likely to be stern-to or alongside, and whether the quay is provided with bollards or rings; or (as sometimes happens in remote Greek islands) a park bench and a lamp post.

It is also important to note where the ferry berths, and whether there is an irate little harbour official blowing a whistle and waving you off your chosen spot because that big freighter that you have only just noticed is coming in there and you are badly in the way. Having avoided these things, and the shallow end where all the little fishing boats are, you now get out what mooring ropes you need and place your fenders where they will do some good. If there are bollards, it is often a good idea to put a good sized bowline in your line before you even throw it, especially if there are no obvious sailors on the quay. Wait till everything is ready, and untangled. There is usually *time*.

This avoids the panicky hurling of tangled ropes at the last minute, which inevitably fall short; we see this happen countless times every summer. Since there is so often a rapt audience, it is nice to do these things well. It is sad to see a head-rope thrown towards the shore too soon, so that it stops short and falls in the water. Skippers should not expect a 40 foot line to reach across a 50 foot gap just because they say 'Now!', and deckhands would do well to practise (on a quiet quay out of sight of mockers) coiling and throwing a line that is at least 30 feet long. A good able seaman can throw an unweighted line 60 feet on the level.

A few good practice heaves will kill two birds with one stone (perhaps literally if you use that nasty ferryboat trick of having a weighted monkey's fist at the rope's end). One, you learn to heave the line with your whole arm; and two, you learn to judge the distance. Thus you avoid throwing too soon, and having the line snake out beautifully to its end, only to fall short into the sea; or that movement akin to closing a chest-high filing cabinet which gives the same result, the rope slithers into the (inevitably) oily water and heads like a homing pigeon for the screw. There should be no need, given the necessary forethought, to go through that rib-tickling performance that has all the other yachts in stitches: the last-minute disinterment of what seems to be a doormat knitted in 12mm nylon, heaved despairingly ashore for the dock committee to wipe its feet on, before the entire mat is dragged back into the water by the rapidly receding yacht attached to its other end. To bring the house down, the line has only to catch in the prop as the yacht circles.

Anchoring also stands a bit of secret practice before your public debut. You will still occasionally drop your anchor neatly into the dinghy (thoughtfully brought to the bow as you knew you were going stern-to, and subsequently forgotten) or get the chain caught in the hawse pipe, or fetch up a snarl which jams in the fairlead. But you will get it right nine times out of ten, and avoid the really calamitous things like failing to make fast the end or, as I did once, pulling an extra metre of chain cable up through the navel pipe, absentmindedly allowing it to slip off the gypsy that controls the links and onto the smooth warping drum. Since there was no longer anything to stop it, I watched aghast as with a thunderous roar the entire 45 fathoms of chain cable ran out into deep water. Right to the bitter end. Which was properly made fast and fetched *Fare Well* up with the sort of jerk you give the lead when your puppy is about to eat something disgusting. Bill achieved new heights, both in jumping up and down and in creative language, while we slowly got it all back in again.

Pets and Pests

'Hale the Cat!' — Captain John Smith

Of course he does not mean cat like our Nelson. Our egregious Captain, from whom we quote so much, lists the following on a man-o-war in 1627: the Cat, the Hounds, the Falcon (a kind of cannon), the Crab (a launching device), the Crow's nest, the Crow's feet, the Fish block, a Goosewing, Hogsheads, Marlin, Ratlines, Monkey, Sheeps' feet, Sheepshanks and Whelps.

Apart from these, many and various are the birds and animals we have met at sea. Their company is comforting, not only to singlehanders (who can otherwise end a three-week voyage talking non-stop for hours to the first person they meet) but to any crew who are not averse to animals. People will put up with a lot to have their pets with them; we have known a tiny yacht weighed nose-down with two enormous and beloved dogs, stowed forward like a couple of bower anchors. They had to be rowed ashore every few hours. Their owners got a bigger boat the next year. We met a Dane in Spain who swore he had rowed his dog ashore twice a day all the way from Denmark.

We have met parrots, large and small. Nelson is very fond of birds. So are we, but not to eat. The first parrot we met was a huge scarlet Macaw which came up our gangway on its owner's shoulder. On confronting Nelson: black, alert, chops a-slaver — it squawked and committed an indignity on its owner's shirt, and had to be shut in his car in hysterics. That was the start of a great friendship.

Moored next to us in Aegina, near Athens, a young circumnavigating family in *Active Light* had a tiny green parrot. Nelson was not hungry, but even a sleepy cat was enough to frighten poor Birdie across the street and onto the awning of the taverna opposite, where she had to be coaxed and climbed for. We met them again in Grenada in the West Indies, where we were all at anchor, and were able to exchange pleasant visits with bird and cat safely apart.

While birds are easy to look after, dogs are a horse of another colour, to mix metaphors. If you are doggy-minded you will take your dog with you and care for it like an extra child: which it will be, not being as self-sufficient as a cat or with the simple needs of a bird. A dog produces large turds which (unlike the cat) it does not know what to do with. It is theoretically possible to get your dog to use the scuppers, or to home in on a short length of tree attached to a stanchion, or a square of artificial grass. We have heard of all these being tried, with or without tempting bottles of 'Do it here, Doggy' perfume. In the cold real world, however, we observe that all dog owners have to use a shovel and hose the deck down pretty frequently; or row the culprit ashore at intervals which interfere with one's beer-time.

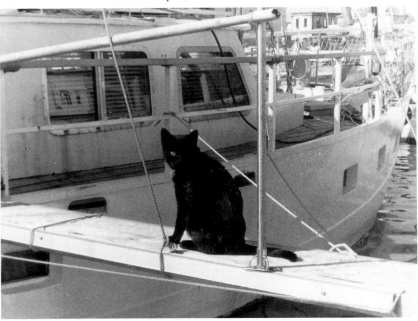

Nelson stands by to repel boarders with her one sharp eye. We have never had rats on board. (photo Tom Goedicke)

Dogs do not like being left. It takes only one of them, howling because its Dad and Mum have gone ashore, to turn a quiet anchorage into Banshee night in the Wolf forest. On the other hand they are a good deterrent for thieves (though our Nelson could be a bit frightening, with the eldritch shriek she used to fend off unwanted toms, and the moonlight glancing off her one eye, an emerald as large as a saucer). At least dogs are Faithful Pals. Cats are anybody's: if you upset them (by hoovering or varnishing, for instance) they go and live with someone else for a few hours, whereas a dog will grin miserably and put up with it. Cats are better in rough weather, it seems to me. They seem to be like humans as regards sea-sickness: some are and some are not. We know of one kitten that had to be found a shore home because it was very seasick, but we also know a very large number of contented ship's cats. At present we have one of each, one insouciant up to force 5, the other hibernates in the lifeboat the minute the motor goes on. As a matter of record, Nelson was with us at sea for ten years and upwards of 40,000 miles, and the present cats have clocked up seven years and 14,000 miles.

I have heard that Keeshonds (Dutch barge dogs) were trained to leap ashore with a headrope in their teeth and drop a bight over a bollard. We never managed to get ours to do this in the days when we took children, dog and all, out for the Sunday cruiser race. Ours was a good dog in a boat, so breeding helps a bit; he kept out of the way and did not moan, and when we were tacking up the narrow rivers of the Broads he would leap ashore on one tack, use a tree, wait until we tacked back again, usually having made only a few yards in two tacks, and jump back on board. He was so much a part of our racing crew that if we crossed the finishing line without him we were threatened with

Laurel

disqualification. For long-term cruising, however, cats take a lot of beating. They are neat in their habits, and when you run out of Kitty Litter they tolerate sand or pebbles. (This once led to a misunderstanding when a young pebble-trained cat, who was my guest while his people went home for a week or two, decided that my Christmas bowl of walnuts was The Right Place.) They are philosophical about bad weather; an example to humans, in fact. They find the warmest, driest spot on board (on your lap under your oilskin for example, or the airing cupboard, or the lifeboat) and hole up for as long as possible. When it's all over they emerge, all smiles and hungry. Nelson could suspend all bodily functions

FISHERMEN'S COTTAGES
CORFU

for about 36 hours when necessary: if only we humans could too. If she had to go and her tray was awash, she would come and tell you so, complaining indignantly until you put it right. Braced, intent and swaying with the ship's motion while producing her own, she then did her housework rather more rapidly than usual, skipping with relief back into her chosen hideout. Sometimes this was her box behind the compass (cats are not magnetic) but sometimes she liked to wriggle well down into some folded canvas; a bundled-up staysail became such a haven for her when on a transatlantic passage that we let it be until we reached the Azores.

Pet passports?

It is a difficult task to get your cat or dog vaccinated against rabies in England. At first I was told that it was impossible, but with a little persistence I got a bit higher up the chain of command and asked how, as we were going to sea, to get Nelson vaccinated. 'Oh, a Ship's cat' said the man. 'That's all right.' So Nelson became a ship's cat and was duly vaccinated. The vaccine is not normally used in Britain because at present the country is rabies-free and tests at once reveal an infected animal. These tests are much more equivocal on vaccinated ones and uncertainty would set in. When the inevitable happens and someone smuggles in a rabid cat or dog, or quite likely brings in a horse (yes, horse: they are allowed to enter and leave the country freely to go to race meetings, with no rabies quarantine restrictions) and rabies comes to Britain, the rules will change and vaccination will become normal. So said I in 1985, now in 1997 it seems we may be on the brink of change for other reasons. Vaccination against rabies has improved to the state of being trustworthy, as long as the animal is clearly identified by tattooing or microchip, and Britain cannot hold out much longer against usage in Europe. A green paper is soon to be issued (they say!), which envisages a passport for pets which will allow you to bring your animals back into Britain, comprising a 'same-day' rabies check and a microchip to prove it. The cost will be about £200, which is much better than the thousands spent on six months quarantine at present. In the meantime the veterinary headquarters of your county should be able to assist you with rabies vaccination if you are leaving Britain. Make sure you say it's a ship's cat as this cuts through a lot of red tape.

I have carried documents attesting to vaccination against rabies for any cat or cats on board for twenty years. No authority in any country has ever asked to look at them. In Gibraltar Nelson was vaccinated willy nilly; British rules then prevailed about bringing in animals, a bit odd considering that any squirrel or fox can trot over the border with Spain when it feels like it. Cats and dogs were confined to the yacht. Gibraltar has recently relaxed this rule: now if you are a resident of Europe visiting Gibraltar and your pet has a valid certificate of rabies vaccination dated not less than 28 days before your arrival, and providing you do not arrive from North Africa, it will be allowed ashore.

Malta still has the British regulations. Being an island, it makes some sense. However, they have no quarantine facilities and do not allow your animal even to be confined to the yacht. They employ the draconian solution of shooting them. This leads to a high rate of pet smuggling in Malta, which defeats the aim of the regulations. I recall a lady who gave both her small dogs sleeping pills to get them into Malta in her yacht. One woke up too soon and was duly destroyed, but she succeeded in smuggling in the other. She was not British, but Brits are not all blameless in this matter either.

Rats

Cats eat mice and kill rats. Until you have had one of these pests on board you have no idea what a good thing cats are. We met a yacht in Corfu in a state of siege after one month of Spanish Rat: they could buy only enough food for one day, which had to be kept in the oven, which was the only rat-proof place they had as it had eaten through clothes, flags, Tupperware, and even teak lockers. They were ready to sell their lovely little yacht for a song, rat and all, but they acquired a small cat and had no further trouble: they had already tried traps and poison.

In some parts of the world you are still required to sign a document concerning the health of any shipboard rats, in case you are carrying the plague. We found one of these in St Thomas's in the Virgin Islands, but rather piquantly rephrased: they wished to know 'if there was any unusual morality among the rates on board' (sic). Mice are almost as destructive, it just takes them a little longer to chew through your Tupperware. They are also fond of other varieties of plastics. We once had the saloon lights fused by a mouse that bit through the electric cable. This was one of Nelson's failures: she went through a phase of posting lizards and beetles down the forward ventilator into the roof space. Once, when she wasn't hungry, she posted a live mouse. It couldn't get out again and the roof space was only an inch or so high: too small to feed the cat into it.

Calling Nelson many dreadful and unpopular names, we removed a panel and tried some Italian Mouse Glue, a fearful substance that you spread on a piece of card which you then lay in the mouse's path. You then sit back and wait, hoping that the mouse is stupid enough to walk across it and stick, like Brer Fox to the Tar Baby. I must confess that I was not anxious to deal with the pathetic results that seemed bound to ensue. I need not have worried, the mouse was not that stupid. After some days the stuff slumped off the card and began to drip down the cabin wall. The regular scrotch, scrotch, of chewing mouse went on. We took the panel off again and threw the card, now dusty and ineffective, away. The drips down the wall remained sticky for weeks and appeared to have no solvent known to man.

I was relieved when the mouse, tiring of polyfoam, decided to try a change of diet, bit through the electric cable and fried itself. This one shameful incident apart, however, Nelson was all that one could hope for: she never allowed a wharf rat on board. In Mahon, in Minorca, she ratted diligently. After snoozing all the warm day, come Cat-time, that darker-than-twilight time when cats and shadows blend, she would yawn, stretch, test her claws on the rope doormat and slink down the gangway to vanish instantly. Other cats would appear from the waste land and derelict warehouses; a whisker here, a flash of white sock there; but Nelson, black as ebony, invisible, was marked only by an occasional sharp rustle, followed by twitters and squeaks as she pounced and bit swiftly through the neckbone. Rats were serious business, and she did not play with them as she did with lizards and mice.

Some people, especially in the States, have neat-looking metal rat-guards on all their mooring lines, usually an aluminium disc about 30cm across. Sorry, but to circumvent a determined rat, and there is no other kind, they should be at least a metre in diameter. It is hard to find stowage for four or five of those. I prefer a rat-guard that purrs. The purr of a cat is also a great tranquilliser, and has no side-effects.

Insects

Sooner or later you will have insect trouble; flies in the galley or midges round the barbecue.

Mosquitoes In a few places the mosquitoes are large enough to make life a misery. You will know where, because you will notice the screened verandahs, and the eerie blue light and sudden sputter of the electric bug frier. A very promising party of ours in Calabria broke up in disorder when, at dusk, swarms of mosquitoes drove us below decks. An hour later they were all gone, and we were able to reassemble.

On entering the Intra-Coastal Waterway in America we asked the advice of a weathered waterman about mosquito screens. 'Well,' he drawled, 'ya might put one on yo door there; but our mosquitoes are too big for yo windas.' As we did the trip in winter and spring, we had no trouble.

Where mosquitoes abound we have tried anti-mosquito candles, and nearly burnt the boat. We have tried Off and Autan and Oil of Lemongrass; Boots' Jungle Formula has been highly recommended. The bugs don't come near you but nor do your friends. A vicious little breed of mosquito is found in the Eastern Mediterranean. We went ashore to have a barbecue and noticed what appeared to be a shepherd's bed in the branches of a tree, about 2 metres off the ground. While our supper cooked we made many jokes about savage beasts that couldn't climb trees (we couldn't think of many), and became more and more uneasy as the sun set. Then, in the space of about one minute, we learnt the reason for the tree bed: we were set upon by millions of tiny but savage little beasts, kinky about ankles, none attacking above the knee. After the quickest clean-up and evacuation ever, we rowed back out to *Fare Well*, our tingling ankles peppered with bites as close together as the dots on a smocking transfer.

One gadget that seems to work in a small space is the mini hotplate on which venomous pastilles are warmed till they give off fumes. These are available in Italy. The warmer did not suit our electrical system, so Bill contrived one in a Kit-e-Kat tin which worked well. Then White Whisper told us of their simple and effective solution: put the pastille on some copper gauze above the oil lamp. Turned down to the absolute minimum, it makes the pastille fume nicely. There is a pocket battery device which is said to scare bugs away with ultra-sound. I know what I'd think about people who carry vibrating objects in their pockets.

If you are in an area where malaria is rife, then take no chances and sleep under a net. This at least does not smell, cause fires, or make your friends look at you oddly.

We are collecting more and more evidence that shows that taking tablets of Brewer's Yeast alters the taste of the blood to the point where mosquitoes say 'Yuk,' and cease to bite you.

Inevitably we come to *cockroaches*. When we built the boat we wrote to Shell asking them to recommend a long-term insecticide. We sprayed two coats of it on the foam that covered the interior of the steel hull, on top of the fire-retarding paint and inside the linings where no one was likely to touch it. It was obviously lethal, as it kept *Fare Well* insect-free for six years. Not until we were coming back from the West Indies did we finally 'catch' cockroaches: not (luckily) the 'Mahogany Mice' of the Caribbean but a smaller breed. However, like illegitimate babies, even little ones count. We took steps. Nelson ate some (they were crunchy). I took out the loose Formica linings from the galley drawers and sprayed them with Baygon (the Greek anti-katsarida kind which bears very little relation to the lily-livered stuff of the same name which is all they will allow you to have in the Western Med).

As a precaution, I had bought in the USA a trap called a Roach Motel, and I dug it out for use. It was well named: it seemed to invite them in for a hamburger and

a night's sleep, and then let them go with me picking up the bill for their entertainment, which was not cheap as I had bought two of them. I found only one
cockroach in it, and that was slightly bent as if Nelson had chewed it a bit first
and it had gone in there to have a martini and recover. When we came to the
conversion of *Hosanna* ten years later we found that the attitude to insecticides
had hardened, it was very difficult to get a long-term insecticide. Some of them
have been completely banned, and the use of the remainder is restricted to
industry, who are supposed to be more responsible about the use of such
dangerous substances than we poor mortals with only our cats and our children
to think about. It required great persistence to get it, and will now, we think, be
impossible. It will be necessary to use physical prevention (traps, cats, netting,
smoke candles and pastilles) and the rather watered down sprays with biokindly
propellant that are all you can get now.

We tried a secret anti-cockroach mixture imparted to us by the German
skipper of a charter yacht, alongside whom we had berthed in St Lucia. 'Haf you
cockroaches?' he asked us. 'No,' we said proudly. 'Now you vil haf,' he said, and
gave us his recipe, Jorge's revenge: sweetened condensed milk and powdered
boric acid. (Now wash your hands please.) The cockroaches yaffle the
mixture, and the boric acid concretes up their insides till it's like treading on
plum stones. (No, don't try it as a remedy for the runs. It is cumulative and
dangerous, so prevent the puss from eating doctored cockroaches.) I found
that Jorge's mixture dried solid and was ineffective after a few days, so I mixed
icing sugar with it instead. Hal Roth in *After 50,000 Miles* quotes entomologists
at the University of California as saying that any additives to the boric acid are
unnecessary and counter-effective. Well, my mixture, put in a flat tin and
wedged where children and cats couldn't get at it, must have got up the cockroaches' noses and choked them. Something worked, we have no cockroaches
at present.

It must be the size and obviousness of cockroaches which upset people and
cause a disproportionate amount of hysteria, since in fact they are not known to
be the carriers of any disease.

Flies are infinitely more dangerous, but do not cause the same reaction. A fly
alighting on the table to lick up a beer spill elicits a halfhearted wave of the hand,
instead of the panic and recourse to major artillery in the shape of slippers, pilot
books and even winch handles that characterizes the appearance of a cockroach.
And yet, friends:

> *The fly that on your bread has wiped its feet,*
> *Has also been and wiped them on the meat.*
> *But worse than that, this morning (for a treat)*
> *It trod in something nasty in the street.*

Whether buzzing round the galley, or groggily dive-bombing your nose in the
bunk, they have got to go. I keep the galley noticeably cleaner in warm weather
to discourage them, covering any exposed food or fruit and leaving no water in
the sink (flies too have to drink). We have a fly-swat, disgusting but non-pollutant.
We also have a flyshooter, which gives visitors endless harmless amusement and
even kills a few flies. If desperate, we use an aerosol spray. No need to gun down

individual flies: this is total war. Shut the windows, spray the area and go up on deck for a while. Then come back when it's all over, like the politicians. Of course you empty the rubbish as often as you can.

In Greece, every household keeps a pot of basil to keep the flies away. This is the little-leaved basil, not the one with large leaves grown in Italy to go with tomatoes. The Greeks tuck a sprig behind one ear or carry some in their hands; you will see the pots on their caiques and yachts as well. I have tried many times to grow my own pot of basil. It used to succumb to salt-blast, or else go overboard in a choppy sea (onboard gardening in *Fare Well* always ended like this, but in *Hosanna* we have a flourishing herb garden in a square metre 'frame' that flower pots cannot fall out of, protected from wind, and covered at sea to keep the salt out). Since Greece is one of the few places where you can still buy old-fashioned flypapers the pot of basil may be a triumph of hope over experience.

Wasps In September the wasps arrive, unless you are well out to sea and stay there. This leads to breaks in the conversation while you or your guests perform Kung Fu, ending with a wham on the table that makes the glasses rattle. Eating on the poop becomes a little less than perfect, and bare feet are inadvisable as wasps are dying all over the deck.

You can rig up a diversion in the shape of a tin containing enough soda pop, Sprite, or 7-Up for them to drown in: they seem very fond of it, but there will still be a few left to zzzz round the salad. After one especially efficient attack with the fly-swat we watched the stretcherbearers arrive in the shape of hornets, come to carry away the dead. One tried to carry two corpses at once and ditched slowly into the sea, like a crippled Lancaster with two bombs slung under it. It made nearly as much noise, too. The less ambitious hornets cleared our decks of dead and dying wasps in no time at all.

We knew a yacht that took on board a pathetic little Greek kitten, only to find that it was infested with pathetic little Greek *ticks*. Their bedding burst forth from below like spinnakers on the downwind run, and clothing bloomed in the rigging, scented with pyrethrum. I've seldom seen a gayer sight, even at Carnival. Frying ticks with a cigarette end is nauseating but effective. You can also use ether on cotton wool, but mind you don't anaesthetise the pet, or yourself.

Pests that come into the boat on fruit and vegetables, apart from those already dealt with above, can be reduced by discarding all cardboard boxes on the quay. Salt in the washing water deals with slugs and caterpillars (always make the fussiest person on board responsible for this chore, and see that they wear their glasses). Use clean sea water with a little permanganate of potash to pinken it.

Weevils are rarely come across in well packaged goods these days, but they will occur in the West Indies and the Eastern Mediterranean, when buying pulses, cereals or rice from the sack or in paper bags. If you can put the stuff in somebody's deep freeze for twenty-four hours, in a plastic bag, this will kill any eggs, and you can then transfer it to beetle-proof containers. Watch things like instant mashed potato and dry dog and cat food, which are very prone to attack. If you find a few beetles in something, you need not throw it out as they are not in themselves harmful; but never add coarsely ground black pepper to your risotto until you are sure there are no weevils in the rice: they look too similar. If there are more than a few it becomes psychologically unappetising and is better thrown away.

Other pests

Worms In the early days of 'abroad', when we were in our 'teens, both Bill and I caught roundworms, Bill from a Spanish paella and I in Morocco from heaven knows what. This caused a lot of excitement; passing a creature about 9 inches long and quite firm in texture is a startling event. My doctor reverted to alchemy and prescribed extract of male fernseed. It was not surprising, therefore, that I tried to find some remedies to take with me before we left on the Great Cruise.

When the chemist came out of his little white stillroom to find out what hophead was buying twelve packets each of Stugeron and Kwells, and decided that maybe this little sailing lady was not hooked on seasick pills, I began to ask him about worms. He backed off and disclaimed all knowledge. Fortunately, in ten years of cruising, not all of it in civilized places, we have not had occasion to use any remedy.

All the baby books mention threadworms, but not the round or tape variety, which in Britain seem to attack only dogs and cats. It is very easy to get multi-worm tablets for your pets, and you should take some as it is easy for them to pick up infestations on shore. Roundworm eggs are carried on fruit and vegetables, and tapeworms in undercooked meat. The eggs are not visible to the eye, but heat kills both types. Since we do not like to forgo our salads and raw fruit we wash them well, in a little potassium permanganate (a few crystals, enough to pinken the water) just before eating them. I'm even more thorough about washing raw food now, since one does not know what chemicals it has been sprayed with.

There is no great cause for panic if you do acquire one of the above internal guests, as those mentioned are more upsetting than harmful, unlike hookworm and other tropical murderers. If you are interested in herbal remedies, try 3-6 grains of fresh garlic bulb, or ½-1 fluid dram of juice. Or, to eliminate round and threadworms, and paralyse tapeworms: steep shredded pomegranate bark in a tightly closed container, reduce by half, and take 4 oz followed by a purgative. Better to use modern remedies such as Pripsen, which do not require purgatives afterwards.

A new pest has appeared since we first wrote. It is dangerous to swimmers and wildlife, aggressive, and extremely noisy, shattering the peace of anchorages wherever it appears. It goes under the generic name of a wet-bike, can be ridden uninsured and unrestricted by anyone of any age and at 60 mph. At present there is no remedy that will not land you in gaol, but the *Sunday Times* is running a campaign for safe waters which includes a ban on wet-bikes. Join it.

A word about monkeys. We were berthed close to a rather theatrical family in a small yacht in Sicily. They had two young children, and two monkeys. They were bad-tempered, noisy and ill-disciplined. (The children, however, were charming.) The parents ego-tripped up and down the quay with the monkeys on a lead, getting lots of attention. Nelson watched from her top-of-the-gangway sentry post, with distaste. Next day the parents were bored with their pets and sent the children to walk the monkeys. They got a little too far from their boat and were cut off by a large friendly dog, who barked at them playfully. The monkeys' reaction was instantaneous: with shrieks they shot up to the children's heads, where they loosed their bowels ready for further flight. For the next hour the dock committee watched with suppressed glee as the parents, tight-lipped and grim of mien, scrubbed their hapless children under the dockside hose with magnums of shampoo.

Other people's unwanted pets, whether roaming toms after your maiden moggie's virtue or those rangy pooches who seem to be able to pee for half an hour on your freshly washed mooring ropes, are discouraged by the handgun in the form of a water pistol, or (the heavier artillery) a Squeezy bottle of water, if possible iced, directed at the active member.

I'm told that goldfish get seasick.

Chapter Eight

Maintenance and Repairs

'... Decayed by weeds or Barnacles... which will eat thorow all the planks if she be not sheathed.'

There is a class of yachtsman who says 'Get it fixed', and Lo! it is fixed, and he signs a cheque. He is usually one of the racing fleet, or he keeps his boat in luxury style. He is unlikely to be a dedicated live-aboard for we are fairly firmly in the do-it-yourself class. Nevertheless, at either end of the economic scale there are those who occasionally employ a little casual help, or who actually provide that help. In any case we are all watching pennies, and tend to spend winters or refit periods where moorings and living are cheap.

Sadly, it is in just those areas that spare parts are hard to find, that local labour, while cheaper, is not up to the latest techniques, and that communications with the industrialised world are a bit tenuous. Which is why those places are so attractive. It is important, therefore, that all maintenance and minor repair work be able to be performed using on-board resources, or at worst using comparatively primitive facilities.

It is not a function of this book to instruct in elementary nautical maintenance, so we will refrain from travelling too far down that path, though we will wander a bit now and then. Rather, we want to consider how the live-aboard can minimise his inevitable problems by appropriate action before starting out.

Engines

There are some companies whose diesels may or may not be the best, but whose engines are found world-wide and whose service is first class. In my view, chief among these is Perkins, whose engines in one form or another are found every-where in tractors, combine harvesters, trucks, buses and fishing boats. I have come across sheds in Rural Calabria (there is an Italian saying: 'si trova niente in Calabria' [one finds nothing in Calabria] and it's evidently not true) and huts in Africa piled high with every conceivable Perkins part. At every depot I have visited it has been 'Yes, how many do you need?', and I have not found any other make of any other thing anywhere near this standard. If you add to this that *Fare Well*'s Perkins 4236 engine did over 5000 hours without any major attention, you will understand my feelings. Since those days, the company Perkins has been bought or sold, and will probably end up losing this unique attribute as it falls further and further into the hands of accountants who do not care.

In the bigger boats, General Motors and Caterpillar diesels do well, and service seems to be good. Gardner still hold the best reputation for sheer reliability, though the company is no longer the majestic affair it once was. Ford suffer because there are so many differing marine conversions not all of which are well done, and though spares for the engine itself are not too bad the problems attaching to service of the marinizing parts are great. Fiat and Renault fail by reason of poor service away from their home ground. BMC reports are patchy. Mercedes have a good reputation, which seems not always to be borne out in practice; parts availability seems to depend on nearness to centres of prosperity.

In the smaller ranges, Volvo have lost a lot of their one-time popularity because of poor spares availability which is getting steadily worse. We have had two generators with Volvo 2002 prime movers, and I would never touch a marine Volvo again. Twice bitten, more fool I. The 2002 was a Mickey Mouse affair requiring constant attention and more than its fair share of blasphemy, and thank heaven it has now been discontinued. But any company which can cynically launch such a product is not to be trusted again by me, at any rate. Yanmar and Bukh seem to be popular. Farymann and Petter, whose engines are in use on so many agricultural pumps and farm generators, ought to have a good spares service for their marine versions, like Perkins, but they do not. Spares are hard to find anywhere for both engines, and even their local agents complain; one of them showed me his almost empty racks. He had been waiting months for valve springs. Engines of this type have been converted for marine use and not done well. In Petter's case the combination of aluminium cylinder head with raw water cooling and a world-wide scarcity of the anodes essential for marine use, was a perfect plan for trouble.

There are of course other diesel engines suitable for yachts: Lister, Westerbeke, DAF, among others. I have no personal experience of these engines, and have been unable to consult anyone who has, so I must refrain from comment. I refuse to discuss petrol engines at all in the context of yachts.

Beware of Gardner engines that have been reconditioned by backyard firms using poor parts and relying on the reputation of the basic engine to find buyers. Also beware when a good company is taken over by a bad one and the whole standard starts to fall. If there is an engine already fitted in a yacht you are thinking of buying, then in addition to the broad views I have given, view with suspicion any product of a small company that is the wholly-owned subsidiary of a major conglomerate holding company. The small company's managers may be competent and conscientious (though not necessarily: many of them are run by accountants) but in any case they are completely at the mercy of the management of their parent company, whose decisions will pay little attention to the interests of customers at the far end of an attenuated chain, but will affect such matters as spares availability and their overseas distribution.

Might I please appeal for someone to produce a range of marine diesels with all adjustments, controls and service points on one side and the top? It's not impossible. A German company called Fisher have a small diesel generator with everything brought to the front, but it has raw water cooling, and for me, that is not acceptable.

One reads about diesel fuel in backward places often being contaminated. I have never found it so, and suspect that water in the fuel so often written about comes from on-board sources, as it did on the only occasion when we suffered from this problem. But supply pipes should have very good water-trap type filters, preferably mounted in parallel, and each separated by cocks so that one can change one filter while the engine is running on the other. Other filters are needed in line, of course, preferably two. Carry a fair stock of filter elements, but change them frequently and in rotation, because most have metal in them somewhere and this is liable to rust while in storage, thus rendering the filter element useless. We recommend Racor fuel filters; they are expensive but much better than any others we have come across, and fishermen swear by them.

Make sure the fuel tank has a draw-off point above and clear of a sump. It should have an access big enough for a clenched fist, to enable the sump to be easily cleaned out. There should be a drain cock at the lowest point to drain off condensation which might gather over a cold spell.

Obtain from your engine's makers a world-wide list of equivalent filter elements and lubricating oils. Manufacturers do not like supplying such a list, and parrot cry that only their products are good enough for their engines. This is rubbish; all they are after is the chance of charging up to three times the proper price for a spare part with their name on, but which does not differ in any other respect from the original part manufacturer's model. But engine dealers like to make sales, so if you are buying a new engine, get the list before you deal. They'll say they don't have the information: they lie. Get it before you deal. It is in any event impossible to obtain the well known brands in many places.

Be cautious about devices containing Jabsco pumps, and fit pumps with rigid impellers if possible. Jabsco agents are found in many places, but there are so many different impellers that few retailers have more than a small number, which never includes the one you want. In addition the company plays amusing games and changes the numbers every now and then, presumably to baffle their own representatives, which they do very well. Any company which does that sort of thing and does not supply retailers with a list of equivalents cannot be said to care much about its customers.

Outboard motor (and all two-stroke) service is of a very variable standard. I think all companies appoint agents who are little more than salesmen, and mechanical competence varies from 0 to 100. The best I ever came across worked round behind Barclays Bank in Bequia, in the Grenadines. He was the only man who ever got our Evinrude working satisfactorily, and, sadly, he was getting on in years.

Spars, Sail and Rigging

First, a story. We met a modern yacht that had been dismasted off the Canary Islands. They were still there ten months after their mishap, waiting for a replacement aluminium spar. By contrast, an old schooner discovered rot in the heel of the foremast while cruising Turkish waters. A new heel was scarphed in in ten days, the labour cost then being around one pound per hour.

Now, new masts are not needed that often and one may well cruise a lifetime without the necessity, but those stories illustrate a general rather than a particular point. Sooner or later repairs will be necessary to something, and if those repairs can be effected from local resources then one gets sailing again cheaper and sooner. The lesson applies, though with less force, even when cruising to sophisticated countries where certain basic standards differ. For example, electrical

Back in harbour after losing Hosanna's *foremast. Bill sorting out the mess.*

replacements following our lightning strike in the USA were more difficult and expensive to obtain because our equipment is 24 volt, which is not common over there.

A good solid spar can be got almost anywhere trees grow, except in the sophisticated countries. I have heard of an impecunious French owner who stole a telegraph pole for the purpose; though this displays initiative it is not likely to enhance the reputation of yachtsmen. Nevertheless it makes a point.

Going together with a wooden mast will probably be a lower sail plan, cheaper galvanized wire rigging, and cheaper sails. Some people chop and change their sailmaker, looking for an advantage here, or a bargain there. My family have used Jeckells for several generations, and though we might get a sail that is less than perfect on rare occasions, I do get excellent service, and I think anyone else would. This would probably apply to a regular customer of any other old firm such as Cranfields. As an example, following loss of an old but reasonable mainsail in June, we had a replacement arrive in the USA within nine days, at a cost of approximately half the lowest quotation there, and that was when there were

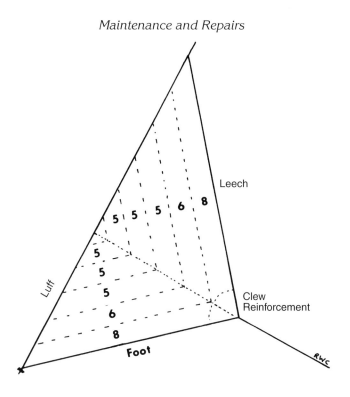

Roller reefing jib with heavier canvas in the outer cloths, for better·strength and longevity. Ample clew reinforcement is also necessary.

over $2 to the pound. The old sail, blown out in Hurricane Alberto, had lasted eight years; it is still serviceable as a spare. A good cruising sail, if protected from the sun when not in use, should last ten years.

That does not apply so surely to roller jibs, which somehow seem to get more unfair wear. Sacrificial strips along leech and foot are a nuisance. I designed our replacement genoa to be mitre cut with the cloths parallel to leech and foot, and with the outer cloths of stronger material. I have always found cloth to be stronger lengthwise, and old smacksmen knew this too, for it is the way they cut their 'tow foresails', which were the forerunners of the modern genoas. If the leech or foot deteriorates in the sun, it is comparatively easy to replace the affected parts.

Do not leave jibs rolled up when out of use for a long time or over winter. This is a common practice to be observed in marinas and a temptation with roller headsail gear.

Generally, sail and rigging maintenance is a continual process, mainly because it is one of the more pleasant chores. But once a year at least all sail seams should be checked, because they are the weak points. We have a modern Singer sewing machine capable of zigzag stitching, but it will not sew several layers of heavy cloth very well. Neither will our friend's Reads, which is sold as a sailmaking machine. I have a deep feeling that an old-fashioned hand-driven Singer would be best. Sew one's homeward-bounders in straight stitches.

Paint and Protection

If one is living aboard and cruising continuously it is sometimes easy to overlook passing time and the need for annual checks. In the Med these are done over the winter, but even then one has to allow for quite a bit of bad weather when work is impossible or inconvenient. In Corfu it rains a lot. At Bodrum, we had gales and even snow. One winter at Rome we had snow on several occasions and even ice on the deck. Painting in these conditions is not really a good idea.

Painting is important in a yacht. I have a feeling that a lot of fibreglass boats could have done with it from time to time, but for wood or steel it becomes essential. We try to keep a little paint in a small glass jar to touch up instantly any damage, and some is bound to happen. This way the annual chore, for that is what it is, is eased. GRP boats should keep on board two-part filler and gelcoat. The big paint job is so purgatorial that it has to be carefully planned. Part of it will be on the slip or hard, but upperworks can be done afloat, though we were dismayed in Porto Xeli in Greece to be arrested by the Port Police for painting our guardrails. As a Greek boat nearby was doing the same thing, it was clearly a bit of Greek xenophobia, and a bit of vigorous argument solved the problem.

The chief purgatory is the preparation: whether sanding, wire-brushing, descaling or whatever, bits fly and a door left open soon leads to marital disharmony. With sand-blasting it is even worse, and it is evident that one should respect one's neighbours.

I am going to interject a word on behalf of the mate here. It is necessary to work hard and long at this chore to get it over sooner, and if 'sir' expects 'madam' also to do a full ten-hour day with sander or brush, then it is unfair to expect her to cook the evening meal afterwards. We see as essential to the cost of the exercise having baths and a meal, however simple, at a local hostelry each evening.

Talking of sand-blasting, it is possible to buy portable equipment from a firm in Reading. In a large steel boat this might well be worthwhile, though a big compressor is needed too. The same requirement limits the use of a needle gun for cleaning steel.

Preparation, somehow or other, is the key. I have been concerned with painting steel ships for a lot of my life and have become disenchanted with paint companies. Apart from doing the job under laboratory conditions, the paint industry has made no real advance in protecting steel at sea since the First World War. The chipping hammer, red lead and oil paint routine I knew when I first went to sea lasted just as well as the latest advice and products of the industry. Here, for amusement, is a parody of a paint company's specification:

Steel should be sand-blasted to North Korean standard X24. This must be done with relative humidity below 10%, and in total darkness. All loose dust must be removed, and the steel should be coated with 5 microns of our No.7 priming solution within ten minutes of sandblasting. Because this primer is part-cured by moisture in the air, this coating must be applied with relative humidity above 70%. The primer should be covered by alternating coats of our 303 super-effective barrier, and our 404 semi-permeable undercoat until a thickness of 25 microns is built up. Overcoating time of the 303 and the 404 is between 12 and 13 hours, but the 404 should only be applied in bright sunlight and rising humidity. Failure to meet these conditions invalidates any warranty.

What I really want to emphasize is that paint companies make paint for use only in ideal conditions, and write their specifications sitting in an office. All too often conditions at the sharp end of life involve a worsening weather forecast and an obligation to be off the slip by tomorrow, inevitably leading to the decision to slap it on and hope for the best.

With *Hosanna*, a steel boat, chlorinated rubber paints have been successful. Their remarkably short overcoating time, 15 minutes in a Mediterranean summer, means the job can be done quickly, largely overcoming weather changing problems. You would not call it a 'super yacht finish', though it is effective enough.

Varnish is not compatible with our existence, at least not on the upper deck. Beautiful Italian yachts gleam from the attentions of vast crews of nautical char-women (this is how they solve their unemployment problem; they are all cleaning and varnishing the rich men's yachts). Sometimes one has pangs of envy and this leads to a token bit of varnish in the cockpit, but it is not really a practical affair in hot sun.

Antifouling becomes a problem as one moves from one area to another. Do not fall for International Paint's sales pitch that their paints are available world-wide. While I think their paints sold in Britain are among the best available, and paints with the International label are found elsewhere, they are not to the same specification in every country and one can come badly unstuck (and so can the paint). In the USA they print a full analysis of the paint on the tin, and this is very helpful. One wonders why there is no obligation to state the same valuable information in other countries.

Since there is now virtually a world-wide ban on Tri-butyl-tin (TBT) antifoulings for pleasure craft, owners of steel boats are in a fix. Paint companies are now advising us to use products they previously said were unsuitable! We do not have an answer, except that a boat over 25 metres is exempt from the ban. Considering how few small steel and aluminium boats there are, they could have sought exemption if the RYA had been better organised. In 1996 in various Greek ports there was a flourishing black market in merchant ship antifouling, to be delivered after dark. Presumably it had fallen off the back of a container ship.

Hauling Out or Slipping

The place where you haul out needs selecting with some care. In general, the more primitive the equipment the more it costs to haul out, an example where sophistication seems to have benefits for the yottie. The western Med, which is littered with more marinas than it seems there are boats to fill them, each with its own boatyard, is in need of business so competition keeps the price down; while the equipment, generally a Travelift or similar, is fairly new and reasonably well operated. It is in these places that a yacht of whatever type can be dealt with.

Further east in the Med the number of marinas decreases, and with it the number of Travelifts and their standard of maintenance. And the prices rise; it has never been properly explained why it should cost six times as much in Greece to haul a yacht as it does in Spain.

Yachts with a long straight keel can be hauled out on the old-fashioned ways, or on a proper marine railway. We have been out on the municipal slip at Barcelona, and at the de Gasperi yard at Porto Santo Stefano (surely one of the

With a long, moderate depth keel it is possible to haul out with primitive equipment, if used skilfully. A deep fin-keeler would be helpless in the more primitive parts of the world. This shows Fare Well *coming out over the beach at Erol Ayan's yard near Bodrum in Turkey.*

best yards in the world). At both of these the care and competence were of the very highest. We came out on an old cradle over a shingle beach at Erol Ayan's yard near Bodrum, one of the high experiences of our lives; a wonderful place, but the whole thing was hair-raising and not at all cheap.

In the Western Hemisphere, we hauled out at Hazzard's slipway in Georgetown, South Carolina, a lovely family boatyard and cheaper than Greece or Turkey. We had planned to haul again, but found that the high cost of antifouling paint in the USA made it pay to wait until we got to Spain.

I found the lift operators at the Club Nautico in Palma and also at Trehard's in Antibes to be good, and at both places the charges were reasonable. Facilities are not good in the West Indies. There is a slip at Grenada and another at English Harbour, Antigua; there must be others, but I did not see them. There is, however, a 3 foot tide in some parts and it is possible to do something of a job between tides. The big problem there is the long grass-like weed that grows close to the waterline, but it is no great chore to drop over the side and remove it every few weeks. I found a home-made scraper like a butter pat made out of ¼ inch ply very effective.

In the USA Travelifts are frequent, though as most Americans own boats of a similar size to those in northern Europe, most lifts have a maximum load of 20 tons (bigger ones do exist). Some American yards tolerate do-it-yourself, though most of them demand that you buy paint through them. In most of the Mediterranean DIY is considered the normal course of events. In Turkey, labour was so cheap that I employed jobbing painters who worked very hard but used about 30 per cent more paint than I did. Conditions are changing in Turkey; the

◀ *Greek hospitality at its best out of season. We are invited to an Easter lamb roast in Meganisi.*

The opposite extreme to 'Keep it Simple'. Hosanna's saloon in its winter clothes. ▶

One gains by the ability to haul out by traditional means. Hosanna in Levkas.
▼

One of the oldest cruising traditions: leaving your mark on the old breakwater at Horta. Not nearly as easy as the new one.

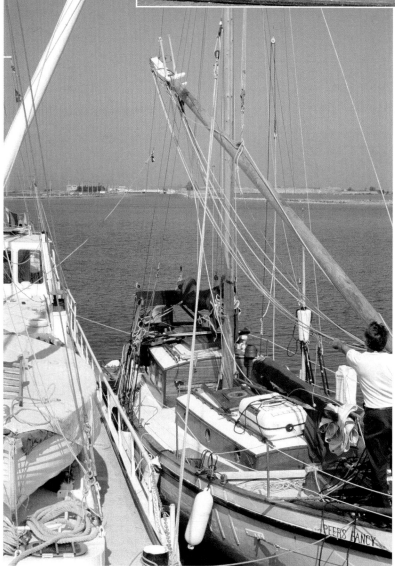

◀ *Help your neighbour: using Hosanna's derrick to re-step the mast in the little Canadian schooner* Peer's Fancy.

In island harbours there's always something going on next door.

Fair exchange: the loan of a sewing machine for an injection for tennis elbow!

This is an effective way of coping with the very young while continuing to do things.

◀ *The Intra-coastal Waterway in the USA.* Farewell *passing a big barge.*

Farewell *in Navpaktos.* ▶

◀ *If you go to popular ports in high season, things can get hectic. Here, at Hydra, much tolerance is necessary, but it's fun.*

marina at Kus Adasi has a Travelift, and one is planned for Bodrum now that harbour works have made the place safer.

Keep a few photographs of the yacht's underwater profile and section to help lift and slipway operators. They cannot always read line drawings, though in a good yard these are a help when slipping. Clearly mark the strength bulkheads on the hull. If you do not like a permanent mark, identify them with chalk when necessary, so that props and shores are wedged into the right places. It is a good thing to mark the gunwale permanently with the positions of the log impeller and any other sensitive device or projection. There is no reason why a steel boat cannot have lifting eyes welded to the gunwales, so dispensing with slings which often scrape off quite a lot of the paint that you have laboured so hard to put on.

Repairs and Failures

Quality of repairs varies enormously from place to place. The more primitive the place the more ready are the local craftsmen to undertake anything, usually with tolerable results. You do not buy spare parts, you have them made at half the price. It is only when one rediscovers the village blacksmith that one sees what Western sophistication has lost: the Mr Fixit, par excellence. In the West Indies, however, the development and education of the local people is such that there are very few local craftsmen. Exceptions occur: there are some good wooden boatbuilders at Bequia, and they get some good wood up from South America.

Let us stop to consider the skills that are likely to be found in all but the most primitive places. I suggest:

- Diesel mechanics of some sort. Most places now have diesel engines in trucks, tractors and fishing boats. It is rare to find somewhere without some diesel ability, though it might be a bit haphazard.
- Simple welding and brazing.
- Elementary woodwork, carpentry rather than joinery. Often there is shipwright ability, particularly in planking and caulking, the latter being competent owing to the roughness of the former.
- Metal turning, and casting of small parts, but seldom enough to turn up a new shaft for instance.
- A sewing machine, usually old enough to be strong enough to stitch anything bendable.
- Hydraulic knowledge. This may surprise you, but it is becoming a common feature in agriculture and trucking.

What is rarely to be found outside yachting centres?

- Aluminium welding.
- Stainless steel welding (sometimes at basic level but almost never with the right rods, which is important).
- Electronic capability and spares.
- Electric capability above household or car level.
- Swaging or Talurit wire fittings.

- Sand-blasting, except unintentionally in strong winds.
- Facilities for hauling out fin-keel boats.
- Fibreglass repairs.
- Spray painting.
- Spare parts for nautical equipment.

Unless one is going to confine one's cruising to the coasts of Britain, the Riviera, or the USA, it is worth pondering these two lists. To take to the out-islands a boat built of exotic materials, with state-of-the-art rig and electronics and the current racing-yacht hull form, is to run a big risk of having pleasure spoiled by non-functioning, non-repairable sophisticated gear, and a lesser but definite risk of disaster due to the inability of both local craftsmen and yourself to service or repair even quite minor damage. Insurance underwriters might well take more note of the repairability of the craft they insure, bearing in mind that the majority of claims are for damage rather than total loss.

If one tried, one could have a very pleasant boat that would reduce or cut out a lot of the payments the owner has to make to others. She would have shoal draught, a reinforced cutaway stem and a powerful stream anchor. She would avoid marinas; just drop anchor and put her bows to the beach. Rig the passarelle over the bows. Have four 5 ton screw jacks vertically in tubes through the hull next to the bulkheads and at refit time just jack her up clear of the water. I would not think they would cost more than a couple of haulouts, and from then on it's paying for itself.

Simple strong masts, simple strong rigging. Basic electronics, and electrics only. (Electric navigation lights are essential: no others are remotely adequate. Electric engine starting is also desirable. And see Chapter 12 on Navigation.)

Rigging and sail maintenance is not difficult, just absorbing. One will need, for sail repairs, a more substantial kit than those typically sold to the dilettante in Cowes. A yard or two of various weights of cloth to suit sails and awnings, and different weights of seaming thread on commercial size reels. Twine for whipping, roping, grommetting and serving. Each of the crew to have their own palm to fit, and practise how to use it. I have not found stay-put sail-repair tape effective for even temporary repairs, possibly because it had been in the locker a long time before being used, though round-the-world racers have access to much better products.

We find it convenient to fix sail repairs of seams with strong parcel tape and then to sew over the taped seams. This makes the job much easier, the stitching perforates the tape, making it simple to rip off afterwards. We have also had success with a temporary repair by glueing a patch on both sides with Evostik contact adhesive.

If travelling far afield, take spare cordage. Not only is it a consumable item that must be replaced, but it is also an attractive commodity in less prosperous communities; the theft of all of a yacht's running rigging is by no means unknown and one should be able to replace the more vital items at least. If your standing rigging is highly tuned, so that tension is critical, it is important to have some matching steel wire. Stainless steel wire is unobtainable in many places, and even when it is you cannot be sure exactly what you are getting: these steels differ quite a bit, and some are unsuitable for a salty environment.

Always use anhydrous lanolin for greasing shackles, rigging screws and other deck fittings. It is not only more waterproof than grease, it does not wash off easily, and it is cheaper and less messy. Never use graphite grease in a steel or aluminium ship's fittings because it can produce local galvanic corrosion problems.

Even in the tropics, use antifreeze in the cooling water because it has good corrosion inhibiting properties though it can be understandably hard to find.

As a logbook we use an A3 page-to-a-day diary. Those sold by WH Smith are glued together and do not last too well, but on the continent it is possible to get older-fashioned sewn and bound diaries. These will have the added advantage of giving Mediterranean holidays, and local phone numbers, but will omit the metric conversion tables.

These diaries or logs become also maintenance reminders. Put items that are time-critical on their expected days. Normally it will be highly inconvenient to do that job when that day comes round, and when the page is turned the job gets forgotten. This likelihood can be reduced (though not eliminated) by having a bookmark. When an item crops up which cannot be done at once it is added to the list on the bookmark, eventually to be crossed off when done. I have a very large bookmark.

If you have no engine hour meter, then whenever you use engine or generator note the time run in the log and keep a cumulative total. I record it only to the nearest half-hour, trying to be consistent about rounding up or down as appropriate.

Do not forget to keep your sextant lightly oiled, and attend to compass gimbals. Swing the compass yourself once a year to check for alterations in the deviation. If it is only a degree or so different just make a note on the card, but if there are some large differences, or if the differences are clustered in the same quadrant, then check to see if you have left anything magnetic about or have moved or fitted something significant. If there is no simple explanation get a professional adjustment done. Note that after passing through a violent thunderstorm or if the ship is on a cardinal heading for a long period, or after a large change in latitude, especially from northern to southern hemispheres, the magnetic characteristics of a steel vessel can be altered quite a bit. Take an early opportunity of checking, but you should do that daily in any event. Such changes are normally not permanent.

If one of the crew is contemplating having a replacement hip or knee joint, make sure to specify to the surgeon that the metal parts must be non-magnetic. No joke!

Homeward-bounders

Repair problems are best avoided by keeping things simple. What you cannot repair yourself with on-board materials and facilities is probably going to cause trouble sometime. Things do go wrong; even well designed, well made items break or fail for no apparent reason. Murphy's Law being certain in its effect, you can bet your life things will fail just when you need them. Here are a few examples of preplanned jury-rigs that can be used to manage temporarily. We call them 'homeward-bounders'.

Bulldog clips for rigging, or better still, double throat wire grips which do not cripple the wire. Keep quite a few of the right sizes stowed in lanolin to keep them usable, and a few lengths of wire rope or short chain to bridge a gap. If a wire parts and you have no spare wire, make eyes with the clips and close the gap with many turns of small cordage, which is better than one or two of larger.

Carry a little impeller pump of the sort that can be used on an electric drill. I have used one when the cooling water pump on the generator failed, and for other less important jobs.

Holes in rubber exhaust hose can be fixed with a short length (an inch or two is enough) of the right size steel pipe. Cut the hose, insert pipe and secure with hose clips. Holes in a rigid exhaust are best closed by a hose clip over a soft leather patch (if wet exhaust), or over a 'fearnought' pad (if dry). On wet exhausts, heavy cloth and rubber are usable. Hose clips have a variety of unofficial uses — they do not merely stay round, they can be bent and used to bind all sorts of things together.

Various advisory or regulatory bodies approve copper tube for diesel fuel lines. I think this is dangerous in a boat that gets a lot of use for copper not only work-hardens by vibration and frequent change of shape, but also time-hardens when liquid is flowing through it. In either case it becomes brittle and breaks when it will cause most trouble. Bronze pipe would be fine, but I prefer the flexible woven metal type, which is not overly expensive. Metal-clad plastic will only protect against accidental physical damage, but it does not proof the tube against fire. But when your copper (approved) tube breaks, and it certainly will before the plastic, that can lead to fire, too. For this eventuality (the break, that is) keep some strong plastic tube and hoseclips. If using the metal covered flexible piping, make sure that the metal cover is in contact at each end to eliminate static electricity build-up.

A frequent failure spot is a metal elbow in a wet exhaust system. Spares are very heavy, and the darn things go so often that one can get badly caught out. Look around lorry agencies for rubber cooling water elbows, which can be the right size. Indeed, they might be cheaper, lighter and better fitted from the kick-off.

Steering gear fails from time to time. This problem is mostly solvable by using the emergency tiller which you will, of course, have in the locker. It is not unknown for the rudder shaft itself to break, leaving the rudder intact but swinging freely. As a precaution against this horrible event, arrange a small V-shaped notch (open downwards) near the top after edge of the rudder. It is easy to lower over the stern a bight of rope with a few overhand knots in it, or with a length of light chain (6 mm section, say) in the middle. With one end either side of the boat, pull gently up and the knots or the chain can be jammed into the V, thus getting the rudder under some sort of control without having to go over the side to do it.

Spares and Tools

Finally, here is a list of the spare parts I have needed over the past ten years, which must indicate something. The tool list is somewhat longer than for normal cruising. If you become able to use all of these tools competently before you start you will be better off than I was at that point, for many of these have had to be added to my original outfit. Do not let the chores spoil the sailing.

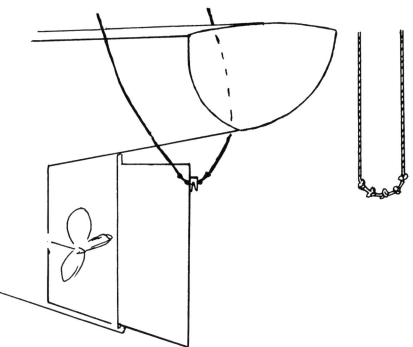

Jury rudder control, using a strong pre-fixed hook.

Spares used in Fare Well

These were used in more than ten years of continuous cruising. The number in parentheses is the number used where this is more than one.

On Deck
Oil seals renewed on SL521 windlass (2).
Shockcord, various sizes, over 50 yards.
Cordage for sheets and lashings.
Shackles. I mostly use galvanized, and replace them when they rust. But stainless
    ones do fail, and of course the pins I lose never match the bows I drop at other
    times.
SL hatch stays (3).
Canpa hatch handle.
Various hinges with brass pins (these are never strong enough).
Canpa hatch sealing round the acrylic.
Winch handle.
Deck caulking. Rotator for towing log (dropped overboard).

In the Engine Room
Submersible bilge pumps (3); switches (1) for same.
Water Puppy washdown pump (2).
Godwin fresh-water pump shaft seal and bearing.

Float switches (7).
Air-pressure pump switches.
Sight-glass plastic tubing on FW tanks.
Fuel-oil tubing, olives, cocks, bits and pieces.
Exhaust rubber tubing, exhaust elbows (steel) (3).
Dozens of hoseclips, all sizes.
Water pump on refrigerator (2).

On the Main Engine
Flexible lub oil pipe, set of cooling water hoses, numerous filters, shaft gland
   packing.

On the Generator Prime Mover
The Farymann needed: injector, water pumps (2), set of flexible mountings, fuel
   pipes, valves and valve gear.
The Petter needed: new cylinder heads (2), valve springs (7), new lub oil piping,
   water pumps (2), water pump impellers (3), set of flexible mountings, bleed
   screw on injection pump, injector, corrosion inhibiting anodes (22). A lot of
   blasphemy.

Electrical
Lucas AC5A alternator (3).
Lucas 440 regulator (6).
Lucas indicator bulb for above circuit (2).
Auto voltage control for G&M 3kVA 230 V alternator.
Transformer (1), rheostat, and bridge rectifiers (2) for G&M alternator.
Brushes for all motors.
Diodes in SL Shorepower rectifier (5).
Main batteries (2).
Battery isolating switches (3).
Japanese battery changeover switches (2).
A large-scale rewiring following lightning strike.
Diodes for Sharp Autopilot (2).
Solenoid spool valve in Cetrek hydraulic pump.
Ammeter.
Many switches, sockets and plugs of all types. Fuses.
Dry batteries by the dozen. New torches.
Fluorescent tubes 24 V (3); there are 10 fitted.
Bulbs — dozens, but especially the 24 V 6 W.

Navigating Instruments
Impeller assemblies for Walker Trident Mk 3 log (14!), and major repairs (3).
Wind instrument complete due to lightning strike.
Photo-transistor in anemometer. Vane blown off wind direction instrument —
   twice.
Rotator and flywheel for Walker Cherub log.
Echosounders: various small repairs, 1 new instrument and 1 transducer
   (Seafarer) and one co-ax plug.
Radio receivers (2).

Pencil sharpener.
Magnets for compass correction; they rust away in time.

Domestic
Weights for pressure-cooker valve, and seal.
Sewing machine driving belt.
Tap washers.
Photo-electric cell for Perkins Mate cooker.
Sealing strip for hob of cooker.
Fire-cement for cooker furnace.
Lavac WC: spare seat seals (2), flap valves (2), joker valves (5). Tubing for WC installation. Lavac WC bowl (the aluminium casting disintegrated, but they don't make that type any more, sensible people).
Fire extinguishers (3) — routine replacement.
Some Tupperware.
Thermos flask.

A spares list for consideration

For (each) Engine
Water hoses
Pump impellers
Any flexible pipe
Complete exhaust run
Filters
Pipe couplings and olives
Gaskets and seals
Mountings, if flexible
Valve springs
Plastic fuel pipe and clips
Hose clips, dozens
HP fuel pipes (from pump to injectors)
Spare belts
Duplicate flanges for hoses
Coupling bolts

Electrical
Terminal strip
Crimp terminals
Alternator regulator warning lamps
Circuit breakers, and fuses
Switches, sockets, plugs, light bulbs
Assorted resistors, capacitors, diodes, transistors: you may not be able to use them, but someone else might on your behalf.
Lucar connectors
Cable of all sizes
Windlass relay
Motor brushes

Other
Spares kit for all pumps
Rubber sheet (2 mm)
Paint, brushes etc
Soft aluminium sheet (3 mm), or copper in wooden boat
Threaded rod, nuts
Bits of plywood, timber
Sealing compound
Caulking
Stainless sheet (about 1.5 mm)

On Deck
Drive belt for windlass
Bolts, nuts for spreader roots
Shackles, thimbles etc
Canvas and thread
Cordage
Bulldog clips
Lanolin
Oar for dinghy (plus oarlocks, if of the loose type).
Flags and ensigns
Eyebolts
Clevis and cotter pins
Whipping twine
Shockcord and terminals
20ft of largest wire
20ft of smallest wire
Winch handle
Wooden plugs, assorted
Sail battens (if foolish enough to have them).

Tool list

I did not start out with all these. Many have had to be added on the way, which
tells one something.

Saws
A general-purpose, medium tooth
Large hack- and small hack-
Coping (if jigsaw not carried)
Spare blades

Hammers
Large ball-peen
Claw
Chipping

Screwdriver
For no. 4, 6, 8 slot-screws

Dumpy for no. 8 slot-screws
Small and large crosshead
Dumpy crosshead
Very large slot
Angled slot crosshead, preferably ratchet
Percussion

Chisels
¼ and ¾ in firmer
Hard chisels

Files
Small triangular, round and half-round
Large round and half-round
Half-round wood rasp (the wood-butcher's *vade mecum*)
Thread-restoring files

Clamps
Assorted, including adjustable opening
Vice, or a Black & Decker Jobber or Workmate

Bradawl
Bevel gauge
Square
Small smoothing plane, rebating plane
Pliers: large, small pointed, and circlip
Spanners: ring or open tube according to choice. Socket set. Large and small
    adjustable. Pipe wrench
Large and small Mole wrench or Visegrip
Nut splitter
Stud removers
Taps and dies
Hand drill
Steel rule, calipers
Allen keys
Punches, drifts
Sheet metal shears
Oilstone, rough and smooth each side
Dentist's probe
Long angled, surgeon's forceps (the best dropped-item recovery tool)
Funnels

Electric Tools, and Tools for Electrical Work
Two-speed drill up to 10 mm
Jigsaw
Orbital sander
Small angle grinder (steel boats)
Soldering iron

A corner on the quay can be very useful for painting a bowsprit, and for ranging anchors and cables so that all links can be checked.

Wire clippers and strippers
Insulated screwdrivers (lots)
Pointed-nose small pliers
Multi-test meter to read 0–25V DC, 0–250V AC, 0–10 ohms, 0–100 ohms, and
    0–1000 ohms
Crimping tool
Long jump leads (lorry type, say about 20 ft)
Short jump leads
Plenty of screws, bolts, nuts, washers, friction washers, self-taps, tacks, panel pins
    and nails to choice

Aboard *Hosanna*, which followed *Fare Well*, our needs have been rather different. We fitted out *Hosanna* while living on board, and even while cruising, so we carried vastly more tools than one would need for maintenance. This did not matter much for *Hosanna* is the size of a small factory; there is a wealth of difference in maintaining a small yacht and a large barge. Most of it is a matter of strength, not only of the barge, but also of the crew.

    Watch out you do not get a boat so large and heavy that she is beyond your resources, financial and physical. Laurel and I are twelve years older than when we bought *Hosanna*, and they are rather significant years. We are starting to find it hard going. Maintaining *Hosanna* (26½ metres LOA, and displacing 60-odd tonnes) has been hard work, but we feel repaid by having lived and cruised widely in a damned good boat. We could not wholeheartedly recommend such an undertaking to anyone who has not had some experience of big boats.

Financially, the difference is not in proportion to her size because one can buy second-hand, or from commercial suppliers who do not demand the same mark-ups as the yacht-chandlery trade, but that too suggests knowing where to look, experience that takes time to acquire. One will use different tools and the work will be on a different scale, often involving far more physical strength, lifting things for instance.

The most important criteria are to marry one's comfort to one's financial circumstances, also to one's knowledge, also to one's physical ability, and lastly a sense of joyous improvisation, problem solving, and being undaunted. If, however, you lack practical hands-on experience, gain it on something handier in size, and then work up.

Chapter Nine

Victualling and Domestic Considerations

'Many suppose anything is good enough to serve men at sea.'

The Galley

Apart from the heads, nothing will get more use on your boat than the galley. If you wish life aboard to be the peaceful and enjoyable experience we all hope for, it repays much thought and planning. You will not get it completely right to start with, but your first cruise will show up any design faults and mistakes in emphasis. These should be rectified. Even small inconveniences can become very irritating if encountered several times a day, and are intolerable in bad weather.

'The Cooke roome where they dresse the victual
may bee placed in diverse parts of the shippe'

Think of the following things:
Does the galley work at an angle of (say) 40° on both tacks? Will the lockers or cupboards open without depositing their contents on the floor? Is everything strong enough for the cook to hang on to, or fall against? Are the things that you need in bad weather easily and conveniently stowed? (If the pan you need is at the bottom of a pile of seven, Murphy's Law makes it certain that the 45° roll will come just as you have them all out on the floor to reach the one you want.)

Items in constant use should have prime space, closely followed by the mugs, bowls and stores needed in bad weather. Separate the pans (especially if they are non-stick) with cardboard picnic plates to prevent noise and scratches.

Drawers in the galley sometimes make more sense than cupboards or shelves, especially if they open fore and aft. All need strong catches of some sort: drawers can have a vertical retaining bar, a swing catch, or be the lift-and-pull-out kind. Magnetic catches are not usually strong enough against the G-force of a big wave.

If the crew is small, it is of great benefit to have plates and cutlery conveniently to hand. A washing-up plate rack (the low profile kind) can be held in place on the drainer with two strong hooks, I have found this to withstand even very violent motion, as does a deep cutlery drainer fixed to the wall, which holds the necessary knives, forks and much used kitchen tools.

The kind of stove you choose to cook with needs some thought. Bill mentioned the different fuel options in Chapter Six 'Below Decks' in some detail; I need not repeat them here. Top-of-the-stove cooking is fine for holidays, but for living aboard you will want to cook as you did on shore, and you will need to bake bread, which means an oven and grill is desirable. So are good saucepans, which should be tall and have well-fitting lids. They should not deform if dropped, and have well insulated handles. I have never regretted the expensive stainless steel pans I bought for *Fare Well* which after 20 years of constant misuse are as good as new, bar one whose handle rivets have failed.

Remember that your stove (and you) may have to cook at a sharp angle, or even crashing up and down (I had the dubious satisfaction of knowing that my diesel stove on *Fare Well* would function at a 60° angle: we were stranded in this position for a day or more, so it was quite important at the time.) You will therefore need well designed, high fiddles to keep your pans in position on the stove in a seaway. In addition, check that water cascading down a hatch will not put out the stove and prevent its use in a storm, as has happened on some racing yachts. At a time when hot food is most needed, you will be glad that your stove is in a safe, dry spot, and that you can brace yourself to use it without a waterfall descending on your head.

My diesel cooker had the added advantage that the stainless steel bolster that covered it would take a folded bedsheet. This meant that if I folded the washing carefully and placed it, still a little damp, on the warm bolster, I could walk away and let the ironing do itself. The stove was not gimballed, but was mounted athwartships. (Its fiddles always prevented a serious loss of soup.) It heated the water too, and had a strong crash bar.

That model had become too expensive when we fitted out *Hosanna*, and for the same money we got an electric cooker, a mixed gas and electric hob, and (having the space) a Microwave cooker, plus a generator to run them all. (Total weights were roughly the same.) I no longer regret the exchange, though the ironing no longer does itself quite so satisfactorily.

Gas stoves have the great advantage of instant heat and adjustability. Both the diesel cooker and the coal stoves still to be found in older boats are hot to use in the tropics; cold lunches become the order of the day. Many boats nowadays are thinking of installing Microwave ovens, as I have done. Their advantages are short cooking times, and therefore less power consumed, they do not heat up the galley in the tropics, and they fit into a small space. Though their output is measured as 600 watts, they will actually draw between 1000 and 1500 watts. They are now being made specially for yachts with a built-in inverter so that they may be used with battery power, otherwise an AC generator is needed. A drop-down door model, such as I began with, is best on a boat, but they are no longer on the market, so you must allow space for the sweep of a side-hung door. In case you break its accompanying glass tray or turntable (replacements are difficult to get and extremely expensive), take with you a suitable pyrex dish as a spare. Since the best way of cooking in bad weather is in two-minute bursts, you can see the handiness of a Microwave.

There exist small all-purpose oven-grills with a hotplate on top, some even combined with a Microwave oven. They are very convenient where space is limited, but their power consumption is as much or more than a full-sized electric oven, and at nearly 3000 watts is more than small inexpensive generators can cope with. In my experience the combined Microwave-grill works less efficiently than the two would as different items, but this must be balanced against the saving of space.

Whatever you choose to cook on, have another method of cooking, just in case. An all-electric galley is no good if the power fails, and it is possible to run out of gas. I have described the split hob I have in *Hosanna*, with two gas burners and two electric plates (these hobs are domestic and now easily obtainable, and we found screw down fiddles to marinise them). Our saloon is heated by a wood stove, on which we often cooked our lunch while converting *Hosanna* in the boatyard, using an upturned biscuit tin on a trivet as a Dutch oven, if it wasn't stew. In winter it now simmers a cheerful red beanpot, and a brass kettle. A small charcoal barbecue is not only wonderful for sunny anchorages, but can be a useful cooking back-up in good weather; or that old standby the single-burner Primus (the selfpricking one) or even a small Camping Gaz stove in case of dire need.

The sink, as Bill has said, is best with natural drainage. This has been a help to us on some occasions of emergency, such as bailing out the engine room. Since both were in the centre of the boat, it was a fairly easy matter, with two of us, to bail straight into the sink. When we were fighting an engine room fire it was possible to get water to it with a good deal of control, for the same reason. As regards one sink or two, while Don Street swears by a double sink even if they are too small to wash large pans in (it does make an extra catchall while working), I prefer one bigger one: if only because it drained one bucket of bilge water before the next one arrived. Don is right to point out that small sinks save water, but this is achieved at sea by placing a smaller plastic bowl in the larger sink, which has the added advantage of cushioning against breakages. I also get mad if the sink is too small to immerse a dinner plate.

Equipment

Avoid the temptation to clutter precious workspace with domestic appliances that will not work without shore power. Go back to the mechanical aids our grandmothers used, and if you want them handy create storage space for them. I would prefer to take such things as hand mincers and coffee grinders (rather than a bulky electric mixer or food processor which are too big for most galleys), a well-engineered hand beater and a wall tin opener that will not rust in a few days.

You will not, as on holiday, be either camping or eating out all the time, so be sure your equipment suits your style of cooking. If you are a dab hand at cakes, take your cake tins. I use the non-stick loaf tins, which I keep cushioned from scratches with paper towels or picnic plates and are still rust-free after several years' use at sea. If you are good at pâtés or potted tongue, take the containers you know to be the right size, and the piece of wood to press them with. Take an elegant dish for your speciality: sometimes one wants to splash out, joining the neighbouring boat for a combined dinner; and a little style is a welcome change. Not that a barbecue salad for twenty people does not taste just as good from a plastic washbowl: take several, they have many uses.

Spend time looking for your favourite tools in stainless steel. It took me years to find a pair of stainless tongs, without which I cannot even boil an egg, that fitted nicely to the hand. Chromium plate soon loses its shine when subjected to the chafe and roll of a boat, and then rusts disgustingly. Strong plastic can be a good alternative: sieves, ladles, and potato mashers come to mind, but strong is the operative word.

The Bamix 'Magic Wand'

As well as my tongs, the things I would not be without are: a pressure cooker; a wall-mounted can-opener, invaluable when fast sea stew is needed; a small spatula or butter spreader; a hamburger press (mine is plastic). Plus my only electrical kitchen gadget, which is the neatest handheld mincer and beater I have ever come across, called the Bamix Magic Wand. It consumes 100 watts on 240 V AC and used with a tall jar or jug will purée soup, beat cakes or chop vegetables. It was designed for the blind and is very easy to clean. I have not seen it marketed recently, Braun do a similar one if not quite so elegant.

You will need something to weigh and measure with. A set of stainless steel measuring cups are useful: I found the plastic ones too breakable, but a polythene jug marked in centilitres has lasted till it is all but illegible. Fortunately these are cheap and readily available. I once thought a miniature diet scale would be great for weighing at sea, but it was too small, too fragile, apt to capsize and extremely unreliable. I go for the compact battery operated electronic scale these days, it takes no more space than a paperback, can be used with any container, and weighs in kilos and pounds, which when cruising is essential. Mark One lasted eight years and is still working thanks to some rather dodgy amateur soldering (ours), so to be on the safe side we are on to mark two.

Apart from the pans already mentioned, you will need frying pans and lidded casseroles (good quality enamel seems to last well, but the cheap ones chip too quickly). Stainless or aluminium dishes of various shapes and sizes are handy, as they have many uses either for cold food or in the oven. Be sure to measure exactly the space available in your oven and get ovenware that fits well: it saves spills if the pans don't skid from side to side (most yacht ovens are too wide, imitating those on shore), and nothing is more irritating than finding that your two most used dishes don't quite fit side by side, or even one above the other. I use the brown rustic ovenware that you can buy almost anywhere now; used on calm days or in harbour we have broken only one in ten years. Mine are mostly oblong and the largest one fits the oven exactly and will do lasagne for ten or bake a huge fish.

On Don Street's *Iolaire* a very large aluminium pan is carried in case of lobsters. He says you can coil your dock ropes in it when not in use. We have one, but keep it in an inaccessible place with the large bowls that are required on such occasions inside it, since it is also useful for large quantities of rice and spaghetti. Lightweight moulded wooden bowls and trays from the Far East are worth the space, they are almost unbreakable and last for ever.

A board that fits over the sink for extra workspace is commonplace now, but was not when we built *Fare Well*. We invented our own, wood on one side and Formica on the other. When not in use, it slotted into a specially made groove alongside the stove. This board was for bread or pastry. A separate one, smaller but extremely thick, is carried as a butcher's block, and a cleaver goes with it, as meat and fish often come almost in their original state. It is difficult to have too many chopping boards: especially as we are now encouraged to use different ones for raw and cooked meats (for stop press on germ-killing boards see under Rubbish).

A minute timer, preferably the four-hour kind, can be invaluable not just for cooking but reminding you of watch changes, weather forecasts and even the noon sight. Fasten it firmly to a dry bulkhead, as landing in the washing-up bowl is not good for it.

Consider your gadgets from this point of view: Do I use it a lot? If it is electric, is there a mechanical substitute? Is it robustly made, of a rust-free material? If not, can I be bothered to cosset it by building a special stowage? Is it reasonably resistant to going wrong, breaking or getting trodden on? Is there a simpler way of achieving the same result? Having said that, I would be the last person to discourage you from taking any beloved device that you would be unhappy without. Be sure that it has a safe stowage, and try and protect it from the salt air.

Fare Well's Basic Galley Equipment

In use daily:
2 stainless steel saucepans
2 non-stick frying pans
Heat resistant mats with handles
2 wooden spoons, 1 wooden 'turner'
Stainless steel tongs
Kitchen knives and cutting boards
Plastic measuring cups
Small spice jar containing salt and pepper mix (5:1)

In use weekly:
Omelette pan
2 casseroles, enamel and lidded
Pressure cooker
Fireproof earthenware

Large and small stainless steel or plastic bowls and dishes
Assorted wicker baskets
Plastic bowls (for mixing, and rising bread in conjunction with a large plastic bag)
Potato masher, slotted spoon, ladle (with hook so it does not slip into the pan)
Wooden garlic masher (also pushes food into the mincer)
Wall or hand tin-opener
Hand egg-beater
Bamix Magic Wand
Non-stick loaf tins
Colander

In use less often, but worth their space:
Hamburger press
Huge paella pan, also good for frying enormous fish
Huge pot for lobsters or rice/pasta for 20

Before we leave the galley, let me remind you to find space for the indispensable roll of paper towels, and for the teatowel and handtowel which otherwise are always on the floor among the spilt sugar, rice and onion skins. There should of course be a better place than the floor for such things, which brings us to:

Rubbish, garbage, trash and hygiene

Some larger galleys have a free-standing rubbish bin just as you might find ashore, but this roams about in bad weather, and in smaller spaces it is probably better to have the kind that is fastened behind a cupboard door. The most convenient bin I have ever had either ashore or at sea is my present one, an exact copy of the one we had in *Fare Well*. It is fixed behind the bottom-hinged door under the draining board to my left, the door drops on a chain just long enough to allow the bin-lid to open, and it is in exactly the right place to scrape plates into as you place them in the sink. The galley floor is best kept clear and clean, since your dinner will occasionally land on it.

> *Always clean your galley floors:*
> *The portion dropped there may be yours.*

You don't want to slip on a greasy floor, either, so choose your flooring with care to be both non-slip and nice looking. It's hard to know if a soup-coloured floor is clean.

We may be able to cut down on chopping boards at last. In the wake of contaminated food scares we have been told to keep raw and cooked meats apart, and to use different knives for them, and I have furthered the aim by marking my boards accordingly, one side for raw and one for cooked, but on a boat washing up is not all it might be. Brand new in the supermarkets are state-of-the-art chopping boards with built-in bug-killer (Microban), incorporated into their molecules. Look out for binbags, towels, dishcloths etc similarly protected against salmonella, Listeriosis, E coli O157 and other unwanted bacteria.

We have a rule that engine room dirt is not to be washed off in the galley sink. Bill disobeys it constantly, so I have to provide a sludge-and-rust coloured towel which he carefully avoids using. So any diesel puddings are his fault.

When you are hundreds of miles from shore, rubbish has to be tossed overboard for valid reasons of space and hygiene. Paper and food waste will disappear very quickly, into the maws of fish. Tins if punctured will sink and rapidly disintegrate, two miles down. Bottles are filled with sea water and sunk. We do not throw plastic overboard anywhere. In harbour or near beaches and seashore, keep your rubbish and land it when you can, putting it in the appropriate containers if available. (It may, alas, yet end up in the sea. We have seen it dumped over a cliff by the local authority.)

Environmentally pernickety folk should realise that the law allows ships to dispose of rubbish which would otherwise become a health hazard, including dead bodies. This is eminently sensible; one must use one's judgement and discretion because nobody wants the seas polluted. When well off-shore one finds very little rubbish floating in the sea. It is different close to land, and we think this is evidence that most seamen are playing the game, unlike their landlubber counterparts.

If you have ever been woken at dawn by the relentless clonk of floating bottles along your hull; maddeningly loud and arrhythmic to screaming point (you are waiting not just for the proverbial second shoe to drop, but for the next ten green bottles), you will not, after a party, drop your bottles over the side to perform their *musique concrète* through the anchorage, waking more people than a change of wind among a ten-yacht raft-up. Perhaps the only legitimate use for firearms on board is for potting these offending bottles and sinking them.

While I am ordinarily rather a slob at washing up, tending to leave it till I feel like it, I get more diligent if there are flies or wasps about. If there is nothing to attract them in the way of sticky surfaces and leftover food, there is nothing for them to wipe their filthy feet on. Sometimes they even go away.

> *In fifty years there may be no more green*
> *The beach be hideous with oil and trash*
> *The air unbreathable, the sea unclean,*
> *And yet, I bet, appearing through the ash*
> *A yacht survives amid the polythene*
> *And in the rigging is a nappy wash.*

Keeping your cool: refrigerators, iceboxes and other coolers

Fewer and fewer long-distance yachts nowadays travel with no means at all of cooling food. A refrigerator is both a boon and a tyranny; it makes a lot of difference to one's life, but it eats power. (See Chapter Six for comments on fuels.) Top-opening fridges make sense on a boat, but most of them have poky openings which make both access and cleaning difficult. Our fridge on *Fare Well* could be defrosted in about ten minutes as it drained into the engine room sump. We had wire baskets made to fit it, four at the top and four at the bottom. If we cared to use the extra power, the bottom would keep food frozen. Defrosting and cleaning was done as a combined operation, both of us working fast: remove the eight baskets, hose down with fresh water, dry off and replace baskets. If the bottom was not full of frozen food, we put in a half-gallon container of 50% sea, and 50% fresh water, frozen if possible, to act as an extra cool bank. This also helps in case of a power failure. In this dire event, do not open the cabinet, and try to increase the insulation by covering it with sleeping bags or deck cushions while the failure lasts. After more than about 24 hours (given a tightly packed, well frozen and well insulated mass) you may have to decide if a big cook-up is going to be necessary to save the food.

Iceboxes of the type that take a large block from the fishhouse are found in many yachts, and the ice lasts a surprisingly long time: ten to twelve days in the tropics and three to four weeks in cooler waters. Keep the ice as dry as possible by draining off any standing water. You should have no trouble finding ice, either in the Mediterranean or the West Indies, but it is heavy. Anywhere there is a fish market, there will be ice. If you can get half-gallon containers of sea water frozen for you, as is sometimes possible in the specialist freezer shops in the Med and the USA, you can pack your box with these and obtain a drier cold. In the Pacific however, ice is harder to come by. I can do no better than refer you also to the excellent chapter on refrigeration in Don Street's book *The Ocean Sailing Yacht*: I have never read a more helpful or practical account.

To end with: *ice cubes* are worth a mention. The usual flat trays are of little use at sea; they spill when the boat heels. For years I searched for a top-opening untippable ice cube maker. When the answer appeared, it was, like all the best ideas, astonishingly simple, a compartmented disposable plastic bag, which you fill with water and then tie off, it then fits good humouredly into odd corners of the freezer without spilling. My present packet of these is French, and contains ten sachets of eighteen ice 'cushions'. This excellent idea is now available everywhere.

With no refrigerator or icebox we are back to Grandmother's meat safe, a wooden box with fly screen panels which was placed somewhere dry and airy, and if possible cool. An insulated polythene cool box in a dry bilge can be effective. Other cooling methods you will have are the sea water, which is often no cooler than the air, and the evaporation principle, used by the earthenware butter and milk coolers. A cloth or muslin dipped in fresh water causes rapid cooling as the wind passes over it, as does the Osokool type of porous box with a well for cooling water. (This water should be fresh, as salt will clog the pores, but little is needed.)

Marketing

This should be a pleasant experience, spiked occasionally with culture shock, and cushioned with coffee and cold drinks.

Those of our American friends who are used to the brown paper bags that go straight from the supermarket into the boot (trunk) of their car, will do well to acquire a capacious shopping bag, several in fact. The ubiquitous string or nylon net bag of Europe comes to mind, which is great for stowage on board but less good for bringing home the bacon, since sharp items protrude and bite the calves of the hapless marketer. The best sort of bag is something waterproof and rather shapeless, perhaps with a drawstring top, that will subside into the inevitable pool of water in the bottom of the dinghy without disintegrating or the contents taking harm. Such a bag can also be carried on the head, which is much better for your spine than hanging off-balance at the end of one arm. I often see yotties with rucksacks, another way to carry quite a heavy load safely. Europeans shopping in the USA, *per contra*, will soon realize that the paper bags, while ecologically sound, will not survive a soggy dinghy ride, and will take their own shopping bags with them to America where they can be difficult to find.

Entering a 'supermarket' on a Greek island, you will find a dim cave, smelling of wine, olives and sheep cheese. The shutters are closed to keep it cool. It is dark, the floor is uneven and the clutter is unbelievable. Only the owner knows where the lamp oil is, or what lies buried under the empty fruit crates, or how long he has had that dusty pile of rubber knickers for a previous generation of babies. (For today's babies he has a rather less dusty pile of Pampers.)

Be careful how you step back or you will be caught behind the knees by the weighing machine that stands on the floor and end up sitting in an open sack of rice. The bolts of cloth on the shelf are brown, brown and black; there are innumerable battered boxes of coloured thread and large hanks of natural wool for weaving the local rugs. Wine is from the barrel, olives from the vat and lamp oil from a drum: bring your own bottle. As it is several days since the last ferry, the vegetables are not what they were and the last of the fruit went this morning, but then you should have bought your produce on the day of the ferry, as everyone else does. However, there is wine, feta cheese and olives, and the bread that comes fresh every day, hot and redolent of the wood oven it was baked in. It makes shopping so easy when there is very little choice.

Compared with this, the supermarket in St Thomas really *was* a supermarket. The packets and tins were on self-service shelves and showed signs of having been wiped over fairly recently. There was a great deal of strip lighting though only a quarter of it was working. There were trolleys, some with a full complement of wheels, and there were a few baskets that did not snag your clothes with broken wires. Almost everything available in the States was available here: tins a little bent and packets a bit battered by the long journey, and rather expensive; but here were your hominy grits, your canned chicken-and-dumplings, your Hershey bars and Betty Crocker cake mixes. (Was that a beetle in the cornflakes?) Local produce was tucked away at the back in coarse grey paper bags: the dried beans, cornmeal, black-eyed peas and delicious transparent tubes of split pea soup mix, like a miniature barber's pole of orange, yellow and green. Here too were the bottles of Hot Pepper Sauce, and a cold box for the sows' ears, pig's tails and chicken gizzards. Were there beetles? Yes, some, but at least they would not be resistant to every known bug destroyer.

That was luxury itself compared with a supermarket in ex-Communist Romania (1995). The shelves were almost bare, with about six packets each of staples such as flour, sugar, powdered milk, and huge bricks of soap. After the previous night's rainstorm the pasta section was flooded, and tin baths were strategically placed to catch the drips still coming through the roof. A few tins of tuna, carp, and luncheon meat, plus locally made jam and honey, comprised the gourmet section. UHT milk was unknown, and there was no salt. I find it all intensely interesting from one extreme to the other. I love to know what people

Laurel

STREET MARKET, CIUDADELA, MENORCA

eat, and how they cook it, and where better to find out than the shady covered markets of Europe or the Western world, where a cool breeze wafts through with scents of fruit and spices, where the cries of the vendors are accompanied by the country tattle of chickens, goats and donkeys and good food is to be had at low prices.

I get my heavy shopping over early: it's cooler. (In Yugoslavia you may find everything sold by seven o'clock in the morning.) My 'donkey', who is only too anxious to leave, takes the load back to the boat, leaving me to the leisurely delights of tasting, chatting, balancing price with quality and discovering new things. No-one in a supermarket has time to chat as the market ladies have. They will tell you how to prepare and cook unfamiliar things, that if you wait a week the peaches will be cheaper, that the market will be closed tomorrow for a Fiesta, that the broad beans are new and tiny enough to be eaten raw with cheese. I discover treasures in obscure corners, I observe how things are bought and by what name, and what is in the cupboards at the back of the stall. With a bit of luck I come home with something cheap and delicious for lunch, which is well deserved since everything has to be logged in and stowed somewhere first, a time-consuming chore.

Having done it, though, you can then go off to quiet bays and not worry about shopping for a while; only about trying the new recipe one of the market ladies gave you. The language of cooks and those who are interested in cooking is surprisingly easy to follow: if you don't know the word a little mime helps. Before I learnt the Greek for eggs I had to act the hen admiring her product, which used to cause great merriment; perhaps life is less fun now that I know more words.

Stowage

'How the Ordnance should bee placed, and the goods stowed on a ship.'

Stowage is a fine art. There are three requirements. One: your goods should be safe from bending, breakage, beetles and bilge water. Two: they should be accessible. Three: you should be able to find what you want easily.

To take the last point first, I recall how Clement Freud, taken on to cook magnificent dishes for a long yacht race, prepared a splendid scheme of labelled lockers, a detailed inventory of every bit of food he had in them, and a delicious daily menu. Alas, the ship had to leave immediately the stuff was delivered on the quay. It was bundled in anywhere it would fit by the frantic crew and Freud lost all track of it, getting occasional nasty surprises during the trip.

Whether you keep an alphabetical 'where to find it' notebook, or a list of the contents of every locker and drawer taped just inside it, or have a phenomenal memory, it matters not as long as you can find what you want. A filing system by which everything beginning with, say, S goes in the same place sounds alluring, but has two practical drawbacks, one: you get incompatible substances oddly mixed together, like soup, sandals and seizing wire; and the other is that of nomenclature: B for butterscotch, or S for sweets? B for bandaid or P for plasters?

The Set Theory works well: stow like things together. It is logical, which helps other people to find things. Thus your paint locker is also the logical place for solvents, brushes and sandpaper; as the Bosun's locker is for all sorts of nautical bits and pieces which do not fit into the come-in-handy box, which all cruisers know and love if not by that name.

We start with the heavy things, which ought to go near the bottom of the boat. That means the dry part of the bilge.

Tins: You will read many an account, in books about world-girdling or Southern Ocean racing, of the tedious task of varnishing all the tins and painting on some sort of shorthand to indicate the contents. (This led to a friend of ours saving a tin of 'goose' for his birthday, only to find on opening it that it was gooseberries.) We do not do anything to our tins, other than group them by kind in different-coloured plastic bags. We then put them in the bilge, meat aft, fish forward and vegetables amidships. A dry bilge should be the norm for cruising; if you have reason to believe that your labels will soak off, change to a drier boat. The plastic bags are merely to help separate a batch of tinned soups from the sort of tinned meat that goes with salad. There is also a bag with party delicacies in it, for birthdays and such.

The portion of the bilge which contains the sump, bilge pump and/or strum box must be kept free of anything which could clog the pump if the worst should happen, so no plastic bags here. It is a good place to put hard objects with no extraneous bits to float off, such as drums of antifouling or gallon jars of detergent. Plastic containers should be well wedged in against chafe. If you have room, large flower pots and square plastic buckets make good separators, and the latter are always handy: we find we lose one plastic bucket per storm overboard, on average. Beer crates are also good, but too large for many boats.

Bottles: The bulk of these can stow in the bilge, too. If you get your duty frees there may be quite a lot of them. We used to pack ours carefully with corrugated paper, but when we ran out of it we found that jamming them in head to tail was just as effective: breakages are almost unknown, though a beer bottle popped its crown cap due to excessive fizz.

Those bottles that you want handy can be stored in cradles, on their sides as in a cellar, or behind a retaining bar, or in circles cut to fit or an arrangement of pegs. All these restraints need to be at least 3 inches tall if you want to prevent clinkage when rolling. Glasses go with bottles. They can go in similar circles, or be slotted into a holder if they are stemmed, or be packed fairly tightly into a drawer. The cheap French glasses will stack, but sometimes jam together unless separated by a leather tag. It is also possible to fit a bracket rather like a tooth-mug holder for glasses, and it's very good policy to have one to hold the helms-man's glass or mug in reach. We find these holders very good for jars of pencils and have them everywhere, with a circle of rubber or foam plastic inside the bottom to prevent rattles.

Plastic containers should be of flexible polythene rather than the hard trans-parent acrylic, which breaks too easily. The lids should fit well (Tupperware has been a boon to yachtsmen) to keep out beetles and dampness. A determined mouse can chew through them and a rat will be through in two bites. (Keep a cat.) Nevertheless they are indispensible for dry stores such as flour, cereals, pasta, rice and all the things that cannot be left in their original paper or plastic bags. The heavy polythene used for five-pound bags of rice seems to be beetle proof, provided you protect them from chafe. I have seen very impressive galley drawers built to fit their containers, all top-labelled and awesomely neat. My herb drawer is less orderly, as the jars and bottles are all different sizes and shapes; I've never known a serious cook who was able to stick with one brand of herbs and spices, ranged neatly in racks to fit as in the glossy magazines: we are not to be regimented like that. At least mine are all top-labelled and easy to find.

A combination of square and round shapes also means that you can get a jar out when you want it. This was not the case with a drawer I once saw packed tightly with square containers of the same height: it looked wonderful but you could not get a finger in to lift a container out. I find the plastic storage baskets now on sale useful for things that are not used every day. All the curry and Chinese ingredients go in one, to be got out when needed, all cake and pudding things go in another, and so on. If you are very short of space, put your herbs and spices into the small self-sealing plastic envelopes that are sold for jewellery, labelling them carefully. They should then be kept in the dark, so a biscuit tin might be better for your collection than tupperware in this instance.

A ready-use shelf near your stove should hold all the things that everyone needs constant access to, such as tea, coffee, cocoa, salt and sugar; it should also hold half a dozen tins of bad weather food (see Bad Weather Cooking).

In Spain, it is possible to buy strong polythene milk containers with a double-sealed screw-on lid. I found these ideal for large quantities of wholemeal flour and the like, the 3 and 5 litre sizes suited me best. Similar containers are obtain-able in Greece for storing olives. Being cylindrical, they stowed in the bilge and did not chafe as the squarish ones containing soft drinks or detergents did. We had supposed that the latter would stow beautifully in the bilge, and so they did, but after six months or so in close contact with their bedfellows they began to chafe and crack at the corners, and the resulting orange flavoured foam was astonishingly hard to mop up. We still use such containers, but are much more careful about protecting them from chafe.

Remember that foil packets of instant mashed potato and dried soups and vegetables are irresistible to weevils, which can eat through them with ease: put all your packets into a lidded box. Cardboard boxes and packets are also not beetle proof, put the contents into glass coffee jars, which though heavy seem very strong and we have not broken one yet. Take extra lids though: they do break. Cut out any instructions from the packet and tape them to the jar.

Oblong bins often sold for cleaning materials can be screwed in suitable places such as the engine room. A shelf or bracket for them to stand on prevents them breaking away from the screws if they are used for heavy items. (Use washers under the screw-heads). Ingenious use can also be made of flowerpot holders and deep sink tidies; for the brushes and scourers by the sink and in the heads or shower for organizing everyone's toilet gear.

Stainless steel and plastic tool clips have many uses, from preventing the washing-up liquid falling in the sink to actually holding tools. We wish the stainless ones were to be found in a wider range of sizes.

Nets are good for fruit and vegetables, since they are airy, and if strung horizontally help to minimize bruising. Net bags, hung from hooks so as to occupy those almost unusable spaces, can be used for a variety of awkward objects.

Cardboard boxes are not recommended. Some yachts will not even allow them on board long enough to unpack the groceries, but unload on the quay because they are believed to harbour cockroaches. While the cockroach, according to one of my authorities, is an innocent little creature and one of the few to whom no blame can be attached for carrying any disease, it breeds fast, is aesthetically unpleasing and crunchy underfoot. The Pests chapter will help you to deal with it.

Shelves: Other almost unusable spaces, such as behind linings, I have seen used to make little shelves for cassettes, hidey-holes for insecticides and rat bait where the cat and the children can't get at them, or once where there was a rather larger space holes were cut in the lining and various brushes stuck through them, with their heads on the inside and the handles in the space behind. Large shelves can be made more practical by the use of plastic baskets; you can even colour-code them. They are good for sewing materials, the bulkier items of first aid (bandages, rolls of adhesive tape) and personal gear.

Short-term Victualling

In previous editions we gave detailed lists, country by country, of what to buy where, what was hard to find and what to store up with. This seems no longer necessary, now that you can get almost anything almost anywhere in the West except ex-communist Eastern Europe. (You still won't get pork in Turkey, powdered ginger in Greece, soda water and cooking apples in France, and anything left alone and natural in the USA.) We give you instead later in the chapter a cost-of-living basket, which limited though it is, may be more useful.

Some people prefer to do all the shopping at once, and hire a taxi or donkey to get it back to the ship. On the Intra-Coastal Waterway in the States you can often borrow a 'courtesy car' to do this. In Europe, stores will sometimes deliver to the quay; it's worth asking. If the heavy shopping is done a day or so early there is plenty of time to stow things properly and choose your fruit and vegetables with care. They should last well if you handle and stow them with care.

Bread

Most Mediterranean bread is meant to be eaten the same day. If the baker takes the trouble to bake every day, he reasons that you should pay his bread the respect it deserves by buying it daily. Wrapped bread is looked upon with scorn and is only available in the larger centres. You can give your daily loaf a longer life, after you have enjoyed its first crusty day, by keeping it in a clean polythene bag, and thereafter placing a hunk of it for immediate eating in a lidded casserole in a moderate oven for a while. This needs a certain amount of judgement as you want the result to be close to fresh bread, not a dried-up rusk. A damp tissue in the casserole helps. When this has all gone, you will need crispbread or crackers, or bake your own. The long-keeping 'half-baked' loaves available in England and USA are beginning to appear in the yottier centres of Europe. The equivalent of *pain de campagne*, country bread, in almost any European country, keeps best.

Even for a week, put biscuits, crackers or cookies in an airtight container. There is something horribly demoralizing about soggy biscuits.

Meat

Meat for a week is easy if you have a fridge. With the possible exception of France, Mediterranean butchers do not hang their meat and it benefits enormously from a sojourn in your refrigerator of at least four days, especially lamb or beef.

If you have no fridge or icebox and the weather is hot, take raw meat for one day (perhaps two if you have a cool spot for it), cooked meat for one more day, and cook up a double batch of meat in the pressure cooker which you put somewhere cool and *do not open*. (The manufacturers frown on this idea because the cooker is not hermetically sealed, but we find the contents keep a day or so and are free of dust and flies.) Thereafter you will have to rely on tins, and dried and preserved forms such as hams and whole salami in its infinite variety; a boon to yachtsmen as they should hang in the air anyway. How long will salami keep? In 1944 we returned to the house we had left in 1939. In the deserted larder we found, hanging lonely under a shelf, a forgotten salami, given to us by a grateful Czech refugee at the outbreak of war. In that drear time of rationing we seized it with glee. It was used, slice by precious slice, in all kinds of ways; the smallest dice giving an exotic flavour, a bit chewy after all those years but still delicious.

Dairy products

Eggs and butter all keep well enough for a short cruise. Salt butter keeps better in normal conditions, but if you want to keep it in the freezer use unsalted butter. You will need a keeping kind of milk: condensed, powdered or UHT (Long Life); the same goes for cream if it is wanted. Enjoy good cheese, its life is short even under the best conditions: (5 to 10° C and 85% humidity is ideal). Soft cheeses last a few days, semi soft, such as Port Salut, St Nectaire and Provalone will last a week or more, the harder cheeses like Cheddar, Edam, the Tommes of France and the Gruyères will keep up to three weeks.

Long-distance Victualling

'Gammons of bacon, dried neat's tongues, Beefe packed up in vinegar...'

Long-distance means long enough to cross an ocean, though the same consider-ations apply to a long cruise among the more backward or isolated communities where supplies may be difficult to get; we were more benighted going down the Danube, especially in the ex-communist countries, than we ever were in remote Greek islands or the West Indies. A month to six weeks should encompass most ocean passages if one takes the more practical routes between ports.

Not enough attention is paid, I believe, to food for long passages. The lad who airily assured me in Barbados that he and his all-male crew had crossed the Atlantic on beer and cornflakes was pulling my leg (I hope), but there is more than a grain of truth in what he said. I've seen the least experienced youngster sent off at the last minute to victual the ship with a hastily compiled list in which liquor had clearly been discussed at length, but which was vague as to kinds and quantities of other items. I have sometimes been spotted as a yachtlady and asked for advice right there in the market a couple of hours before departure. If you are starting from England, explain to the manager of your local Cash and Carry Store that you need bulk stores for a long voyage, and you will usually be allowed to shop there on a one-time only basis. Lipton's in Gibraltar give a discount to long-distance cruisers if they spend more than a certain sum.

Where do you start? Where do you begin when planning food for a long voyage? Some swear by Frederick M. Gardner (see below); I went by multiplying a head count times meals times portions. On our Transatlantic crossing to the West Indies I was glad of the surplus remaining, as tinned and bottled stores were expensive and sometimes hard to find in the Windward Islands.

While we try to live on local produce where we can, to do so in the West Indies would have caused deprivation to the carnivorous males among the crew, despite the omnipresence of fried chicken; as steak dinners ashore were largely beyond our means.

I suggest that you start by reading the previous section on short-distance victualling, as much that I have written there is also relevant to long distances. I then have merely to underline and expand, without repeating myself.

How much do you need to take?

Carry food and water for *twice* the normal expected passage time, plus emergency provisions and water for a further *ten days*. You do not want to end up 'down to the last tin of corned beef and licking the dew off the deck', as one of our singlehanded friends described his landfall. Mr Gardner's famous list 'The care and feeding of a Yachtsman', lists items by weight and calls for 5½lb of food per man per day, of which 14½ oz was meat. To that he added a gallon of liquid per head per day for drinking. So he expects four people for 40 days to consume over a ton of food. It takes a bit of organizing. I studied this list with great interest before our first long ocean passage and came to the conclusion that our crew of three men and two very tiny women would consume rather less than that. No way can I eat nearly a pound of meat a day. So I decided to think in terms of

The bicycle that carries bulky gear ashore for repair can also save a long hike back from the market. This folding bike has a solid, simple frame and 3-speed gears that are useful on shore excursions; it has also survived immersion. (photo Mark Brackenbury)

the number of meals per day and the portions required, and allow a bit extra each time in case of extreme hunger. My deliberations are easily modified for larger or smaller appetites.

What should you take?

Tins If you have no freezer you will need plenty of tins of meat. These should be solidly packed protein, not the kind that is full of gravy where you find only two walnut-sized lumps of gristle with difficulty by using a magnifying glass. Good tinned meat and fish is expensive, but is worth the money especially if you have no fridge. Good buys are corned beef, chopped pork, sausages, stewed steak, luncheon meat, ham and tongue, and for special occasions steak-and-kidney pie, pheasant or grouse if you can run to it. Fray Bentos make an excellent range of pie fillings: steak and onion, steak and mushroom, and steak and kidney, which were extremely popular with the crew, much better than the tinned steak-and-kidney puddings, where the duff was of doubtful consistency and the filling rather meagre. Also popular was the stewing steak from Ireland brand-named Casserole, and Libby's Beef Stew. Newforge's Irish Stew tasted very good, but we had to add a lot more meat to it. Campbell's Meatballs which I thought would be great with spaghetti, turned out to be pasty and flavourless. I washed the gravy off them and replaced it with a good strong Italian ragu (spaghetti sauce) full of onion, tomato and basil, which made them a bit more interesting.

If you get tired of tinned hamburgers you can make much better meatballs from them. French tins of *cassoulet* (gourmet duck, pork and beans) are wonderfully ribsticking stuff, I wish I'd bought more. Add some pork boiling sausage (vacuum packed, keeps well) to pep up the protein. I no longer give space to tins of spaghetti. The real thing is so much better, and almost as quick and easy, especially if you cheat and use ready made sauces. The same goes for tinned soup, there is always something to make fresh soup from, even if it's potatoes, onions and milk, and a stock cube. There, too, is something worth its space: a variety of stock cubes of different flavours to add interest to soups, stews and risottos.

Tinned chicken is always a disappointment; it is too soft in texture and the flavour is changed. The best we found was the chicken and dumplings of the Southern USA. However I carry a few small tins of chicken in jelly, to add variety and extra protein to bad-weather soups and risottos. Tinned pâtés are always a good idea, as are hams and tongues if you can afford them.

Vegetables that survive canning best are *petit pois* (tiny peas) haricot beans (get some of them *au naturel* rather than in tomato sauce, for a wider variety of uses), *garbanzos* (chick peas), spinach, sweet corn, beetroot, celery (the texture is wrong but the flavour is good), tomatoes (very useful), lentils, green beans, broad beans and mushrooms (but dried mushrooms have better flavour).

In Spain, tinned cauliflower and brussel sprouts are available; we found them rather soft, but the cauliflower made quite good 'Crème du Barry' soup, and the sprouts, fried with onions, made an occasional change. Carrots are useful for a touch of colour, but fresh ones kept so well that I hardly ever needed the tinned variety. We carried assorted tinned Chinese vegetables, but missed the crunchiness of the real thing.

Tinned fish are very handy in all varieties. Octopus and squid survive canning well, mussels taste tinny. Tinned kippers and salmon make good pâté or kedgeree. Paella mixture (a small tin of mussels, squid and octopus, available in Spain) can make a good fishermen's risotto as well. Pilchard-and-potato pie is good. Sardines make a delicious 'spaghetti con le sarde', while anchovies make a good spaghetti sauce when mixed with garlic, chillis and olive oil. Tuna is useful.

Take a little tinned fruit; your fresh supplies ought to last well, but something like pineapple, raspberries or gooseberries can make a treat. Tinned fruit cake is worth taking, as it is time consuming to make.

Other tinned goods that I found valuable were the small tins or jars of spaghetti sauce available in Italy in four flavours, or the less good and rather sweeter ones now available everywhere in Europe and the USA, to which more meat, fish or mushrooms could be added to make a very satisfying meal, especially with wholemeal spaghetti. Many of these tins can, of course, be used for cold lunches, perhaps accompanied by a cup of hot soup if the weather is cool or a salad if it is hot.

Dried food, cereals, grains, pulses and flour

White flour keeps eight months to a year in damp-proof containers. Brown and wholemeal flour keeps less well owing to the fat content — keep it in the dark. The other grains and cereals will keep a year at least. Fresh water is necessary to reconstitute and cook them. They add texture and crunch to tinned food and have a fresher taste. Dried haricot beans, split peas, lentils and chick peas are all good in spite of the jokes. Rice keeps indefinitely and is essential in my cooking, both white and brown, but the brown takes longer to cook (soak it for 24 hours first). Dried pasta of all kinds keeps splendidly as long as beetles are kept away; they love it too. Wholemeal pasta is available and makes a more wholesome food, but it does not taste the same. Burghul (bulgar or cracked wheat) makes interesting pilaf as a change from rice.

Protein-rich cereals On long voyages among remote islands, such as the Antipodes—Red Sea run or across the Pacific, you can find your diet short of meat and fish. The same can apply if you cannot afford large quantities of tinned meat.

It is worth studying the following facts with care and in more detail than I have space to give here. (The Small Planet books listed in the appendix will tell you more.) Certain grains and legumes, eaten together, increase those proteins usable by the body to more than the sum of their parts, which explains why the poorer nations thrive on rice with lentils, cornmeal and kidney beans, bulgar and chick peas, and perhaps even baked beans on toast. So take with you dried haricot beans, lentils (all colours), split peas, soya beans and soya flour, chick peas, butter beans, peanut butter, and powdered milk; and combine them with brown rice, bulgar (called burgul or burgoo by sailors), wholemeal grains and pasta, for nourishing pilafs and spaghetti dishes; add small pieces of meat or fish if you have them, and plenty of spice and flavour. These can be excellent dishes and extremely varied and tasty. Recipes will be found in Middle East and Indian cookbooks, so do not be lulled into substituting tins of baked beans in tomato sauce, which make everything taste of ketchup and do you very little good. The pressure cooker will make short work of the dried vegetables, which can be cooked in stock or soup to add different flavours to suit whatever meaty morsels you have.

Muesli and similar mixtures keep better (6 months: the nuts in it deteriorate first) than crisp breakfast cereals (like cornflakes, which sog very quickly and take up much more room). Note that nuts go off much quicker than dried fruit, so do not mix them in advance. You will need bread flour, white and wholemeal, and ordinary flour, but take a tin of baking powder to make your own selfraising flour.

Wholemeal bread mix is worth its space. Cake mixes can be useful when time is short but keep less well than separate ingredients because the fat content spoils. Ready-mix packets, such as cake, pastry, scones and dumplings, have a shelf-life of about six months, but those with no fat, such as bread-mix and pancakes, keep about a year, and the bread-mix is usable for much longer if you add extra easy-blend yeast.

Sell-by dates

On long voyages you will outsail many sell-by dates, don't panic; they are the manufacturer's get-out, and need not be regarded as written in stone, unless they are dairy produce or certain meats. If it looks, smells and tastes all right, it probably is. The only thing past its date that has made me really ill is walnuts. In England.

Yeast Life is now easier with easy-blend dried yeast, such as Harvest Gold or McDougal's which keeps (they say) for nine months, longer in my experience. Sprinkle it in with the other dry ingredients.

Bread There are times when a loaf of really solid high-protein bread is worth a whole trayful of bridge rolls. Try this one:

High Protein Bread

1 packet (10oz, 280 grams) wholemeal breadmix.
 (Grannie Smith, McDougal's etc) or use 280 grams of wholemeal flour.
Add to the dry mix: ⅓ cup wheatgerm (a generous ½ oz)
 (this product does spoil rather quickly, unfortunately)
⅓ cup soya flour
⅓ cup instant powdered milk
½ teasp (or 1 sachet, 6 grams) instant dried easyblend yeast

Stir into the 6 fluid ounces of handhot water you will use to mix the dough, a tablespoon of molasses, black treacle or dark honey, add to the dry ingredients, mix well and knead for five minutes. You won't need a bread tin if you then shape it into a bunloaf or cob. Put it on a greased baking tray; place it, tray and all, inside a large polythene roasting bag (take with you several of the turkey roasting size), secure the bag with a wire tie and leave in a warm place to rise for an hour. Bake 35 to 40 minutes in a hot oven, and eat with enormous pleasure.

You will notice in the list of ingredients on the breadmix packet Ascorbic acid, vitamin C. This is not to do you good, but to cut out one of the usual two rises. If you make your bread from scratch, you can do the same, by adding a crushed 50mg Vitamin C tablet per 1.2 kg of flour, or a pinch of vitamin C powder for the recipe above. Vitamin C powder can be bought at Boot's.

Die-hard bread You have no oven? After kneading the above recipe, shape it into a round and put it in your pressure cooker, gently warmed and well oiled. Cover with a damp cloth. When the dough has doubled in size remove the cloth, put the cooker over high heat for three minutes, with the lid on but the pressure valve open. Turn down the heat to as low as possible, using an 'asbestos' mat or flame spreader if you have one, and cook, still with the pressure valve open, for 30 to 35 minutes. Turn the bread over and cook a further few minutes to brown the top. This really works, I've done it.

AFD (air freeze-dried) foods are made in quite a few varieties now. Apart from the well known dried soups you can get beef, chicken and shrimp curries, farm-house stew, savoury mince and beef Stroganoff, and all kinds of rice dishes. They need fresh water to prepare and take time to cook. Their texture tends to be rather monotonous, but they have their place especially for bulking out leftovers. It's worth reminding you that the average shipboard beetle gnashes its way through foil packets with disturbing ease, so keep them in a metal or plastic box, and be conscientious about putting the lid back.

In Italy you can get an excellent freeze-dried mixture of about ten diced vege-tables, intended for minestrone. There's an English equivalent, too. A handful of this in any soup or stew is good: you can also use the whole packet with a little salt pork, bacon, or boiling sausage and pasta, for a dish you can stand the spoon up in.

Dried fish is always heavily salted. Throughout the Mediterranean and in parts of the West Indies you will see boxes of rough-looking sheets of cardboard, vaguely fish-shaped, light on one side and dark on the other. It is, in fact, fish; called bacalao, baccala, stockfish or salt cod. It keeps forever and is very good when properly processed, but even if you get a preliminary amount of salt out by soaking it in sea water and then fresh, it still needs rivers of fresh water washing over it for 24 hours before it is edible, so it doesn't work at sea.

Dried mushrooms are a splendid idea: they have much more flavour than tinned ones. The French, Italians and the Chinese have very good ones, soak in a little warm water for 20 minutes.

Dried egg I have mixed feelings about. It's probably all right in cakes; otherwise use it to eke out the breakfast scramble or omelette. To make scrambled eggs entirely with dried eggs brings back too many wartime memories, but today's kids might like it, knowing that there are plenty of other things to eat, and bacon or Bacon Grill (tinned) to go with it. (Address in Appendix.)

Dried and salt meat is another matter. Whole salami has already been mentioned. If you have no refrigerator or icebox, a piece of smoked bacon will hang in an airy place, dusted with black pepper to keep the flies away. Hams are trickier, since the cut section dries a bit, but a leg of mountain ham we bought in Yugoslavia lasted all of a Mediterranean summer. It was heavily smoked and we hung it in a net inside greaseproof paper which was changed regularly. Similar hams are to be had in Spain, Italy and France. Vacuum packed smoked and salted meats keep from six weeks to two months and are worth their space for snacks: sliced ham, prosciutto (Parma ham), sliced salami, liver sausage, and that valuable standby, boiling sausage; the Dutch ones are excellent. Some vacuum packs of bacon will be useful for a few weeks, but a large piece of smoked streaky bacon (*poitrine fumée* in France) will keep much longer and taste better: keep it like the ham, in greaseproof paper.

Dairy produce for long voyages

Milk Long Life milk (UHT) and cream keeps for five months, and we think it is nearer to fresh milk than either powdered or condensed; it is a matter of opinion. (We were amused to find that it arrived in the USA while we were there in 1982: hailed, of course, as 'new', when we'd had it in Europe several years!) A little of the instant powdered milk can be useful in some recipes: ie bread, get the powder in plastic containers for best keeping. Long Life cream tastes better on tinned fruit than tinned cream, and is fine for cooking. Nothing beats fresh milk for cereals or just drinking, but I have yet to meet a cruising boat with a cow on board. Or even, come to that, a hen. Which brings us to:

Fresh eggs need no refrigeration: indeed EU regulations make the chilling of eggs illegal. Buy your eggs from a hen personally known to you, along with her assurance that they are new laid, ie this morning's or at a pinch yesterday's. Do *not* wash them. It is not an old wive's tale that eggs should not be washed: it is illegal in the EU for eggs to be washed before packing. The reasons are: a new-laid egg is protected from bacteria by a film thoughtfully provided by the hen for the purpose; this film is removed by washing. Also, a dry egg is impermeable to bacteria but this impermeability breaks down if the shell becomes moist, and while the egg is wet germs can pass through the shell and set up premature spoilage. (In the USA eggs are washed and dried at the packing stations under strictly monitored sanitary conditions.) In Europe, if you are fussy, you may gently brush off loose dirt and feathers, but leave any washing until just before you cook the egg.

BODRUM MARKET

It will now be clear to you why an egg that has been chilled should be avoided: on removal from the fridge condensation occurs, the shell becomes moist and bacteria can enter: shortening the life of the egg.

Keep your eggs carefully packed (we found fibre trays cut to fit square plastic buckets which we kept in the bilge were perfect) at a temperature of about 10°C/50°F; a cool dry bilge for example, and they will keep for a month with no further attention. On the average transatlantic crossing in either direction you should have no trouble.

How to deal with a bad egg As this is now a rare event in Europe and the USA, I revive some forgotten tips. After four weeks, start to test your eggs in a glass of fresh water. If they sink they are fine. If they float with a bit of the shell above the water, have ready a clean yoghurt pot or other disposable container: avert the nose and break the egg into the pot. If it is bad, you will know at once. Do not pour it down the sink: unless you have a salt water pump at the sink you will waste too much water flushing away the smell. Just deep-six it over the side.

If you are doubtful, you did use a clean pot, so the egg will be OK for well-flavoured omelettes or ginger cakes. If your egg is undecided whether to sink or float it is probably not young enough to be a breakfast soft-boiled egg, and the whites may refuse to whip, but it will still be usable for most purposes. A flattened-out runny yolk or white means the egg is old, but not necessarily bad. Broken yolks also indicate a stale, but not necessarily bad, egg.

No, you cannot test them in salt water because they would all float.

A new-laid egg (up to three days old) is very hard to peel when hard-boiled, and takes longest to cook, but you won't have that problem for long. If your journey is going to last longer than a month or five weeks, some of your eggs will need to be preserved. This is done by sealing the shell, either by putting the eggs in waterglass (a solution of sodium silicate obtainable these days only from very old-fashioned chemists) or smearing them with petroleum jelly (Vaseline.) Make sure you get the odourless kind: eggs absorb smells and tastes very easily. In waterglass, the new-laid eggs that my mother put down in wartime kept for a year. After six to nine months you could not count on unbroken yolks, but otherwise they were great.

Fats, and oils Outside the refrigerator, salt butter keeps better than fresh sweet butter but it is harder to get in the Med and more expensive as it is usually imported. Keep all fats as cool as you can. Margarine keeps longer and melts less easily. Both are available tinned, but require a bit of tracking down. Learn to cook with olive oil, which keeps a year or more, like other cooking oils. Lard keeps very well indeed, more than a year. Packets of suet do not melt, and keep about six months, or see sell-by date.

Cheese Sad to say, cheese is a problem. It is best kept in a cool humid place such as the vegetable drawer of the fridge (not the freezer, which is ruination to cheese). Any soft or semi-soft cheeses will not survive the first week, say goodbye to camembert and brie after three days. Semi-soft cheeses (St Paulin, Tommes, St Nectaire, Wensleydale) will delight you for a week if you wrap them tightly with clingfilm to exclude the air. Roquefort and other blues should be wrapped in a damp cloth and put in a plastic box, to keep a week, maybe longer. The harder cheeses need careful selection and dedicated care for their well-being in order to last; Edam, Cheddar, and Gruyère and similar are best in plastic bags with frequent attention to pare off mould and prevent sweating. Vacuum packs of grated cheese are very useful. Some of the industrial cheeses, vacuum packed or wrapped in foil, keep well until opened, such as Philadelphia and other cream cheeses: study the sell-by dates, and take small portions of wrapped processed cheese of various kinds for the Night Box.

If you can find a whole 'stoved' Edam cheese (Edam *étuvée*, available in France and the Low Countries), you are in luck, it keeps indefinitely. So do the granite-like Parmesan (in the piece) and Sbrinz, its Swiss equivalent, which will happily break your teeth after a round the world voyage. There are such things as tinned camembert and brie, made in Bavaria. If you keep them long enough you might have sufficiently forgotten what real cheese tastes like to find them amusing.

The only way to have yoghurt after a couple of weeks at sea is to make your own from a good Bulgarian culture.

Boil-in-the-bag and foil dinners Some are very good indeed, though they are expensive and the portions are small. They have an inestimable value for no-fridge voyagers, as they have a long shelf life. They then make good celebration food. Stowed so they do not chafe through they last almost indefinitely. Chicken and duck in these packs are infinitely better than tinned.

In Italy a boiling sausage known as Cotechino or Zampone is put up in the same way. It can be boiled in the bag, and is excellent hearty food sliced and eaten with lentils, mushy peas and mashed potatoes. All these sealed packs can be boiled in sea water. Other sausages such as garlic and liver sausage to be eaten cold are appearing in the UK in long-life foil packs too; no need to refrigerate these.

Do not rely on just one kind of food, and one kind of cooking even on a short trip. I heard recently of a crew almost succumbing to despair; they had been furnished only with boil-in-the-bag meals, but the alcohol cooker that should have heated them was ruined by salt water in a storm, and a single Sterno burner was all that remained to cook for ten people. Freeze-dried food is useless without the fresh water to mix it with, and even tins need an opener (carry two or three). As a last resort in storms you could take a few of the self-heating cans now available. They are very expensive, but in dire need you might feel a hot meal was worth the money. If you ring the changes with freeze-dried foods, tinned, vacuum packed, salted, and good old longkeeping standbys like rice and dried pasta, with fresh bread, onions and potatoes, you probably won't even need vitamin tablets.

Other ways of preserving

Vacuum-packed bacon and cold meats keep very well in a fridge or icebox, as does pâté. Even if you have no refrigerator there is a great deal of choice. Pâté will keep for a month, potted in jars under a layer of butter to seal it. You can keep a brine crock (I use Tupperware with a well fitting lid to prevent spills) and salt down pieces of pork, hocks, trotters, slabs of belly or tongues. If you leave them in the crock for three days they are mild enough to cook in the pressure cooker without previous soaking, and will then keep for up to two weeks in a cool dry spot, though my guess is that they will get eaten fairly rapidly. Not for nothing were the sailors of yore called 'salt horses': a little practice in the ancient art of salting and pickling may stand you in very good stead if you wish to cruise in the wilder parts of the globe; even in the Eastern Med and the north coast of Africa where the Muslim culture makes pork and *charcuterie* hard to find.

Bill and I became genuine Salt Horses on one Mediterranean cruise. I was looking for a tongue to salt before cruising eastwards, and in an Italian market allowed eagerness to overcome caution when I found one after a long search. I bore it back to the corner of the market where my 'donkey' was waiting with the heavy stuff. Beaming, I showed him my prize. He sighed, and pointed out the stall where I had bought it, where I could now plainly see the horse's head that adorned the sign. I had bought horse tongue. I pickled and cooked it just the same and it was excellent: we ate every bit with relish.

In the south-west of France they pot down goose and duck in the autumn; the meat is cooked gently in goose or duck fat, potted and covered completely with the fat in stoneware jars. It keeps for a year in a cool larder. My food bug authority worries about this, so if you want to experiment make sure you get an authentic recipe and follow the instructions carefully. The dish is known as *confit d'oie* (goose) or *confit de canard* (duck). I made some to take with us when we left England: we ate it and survived. In French supermarkets this duck and goose *confit* are now available in vacuum packs which keep well.

Bottling Bottling jars are quite robust. I take a few containing Bramley apples, and Apple and Blackberry, since they seem to be unavailable tinned. Supermarket apple sauce is woefully tasteless, and cooking apples are unknown even in Europe.

What to put in the freezer

If you are fortunate enough to have a freezer, and still more fortunate to have one that works, pack it with the solidest meat available. It is a waste of space and energy to fill it with bone, gristle and other bulky inedibles. Choose cuts with a minimum of bone or none, and reduce chickens to legs (or thighs and drumsticks) and boned breasts. Put them into packs of the number of portions needed for a meal. Do the same with chunks of stewing beef or lamb: you will be very glad at sea that you took the trouble to remove all the fat and gristle and pack it in convenient meal-sized portions. Chops, whether pork or lamb, should be parcelled according to crew numbers, or in two's, enabling you to add small amounts of protein to rice or pasta dishes. Shrimps are good packed in small amounts to add to fish soup, paella or risotto; even hundred grams is handy sometimes. Fillets of cod or haddock make a change if the fishing is not going well. Hamburgers can be made into meatballs, or cottage pie — get the best quality you can. The same goes for mince, get really good quality and put up in mealsized parcels which reflect the number in the crew. Keep a careful record of what is in the freezer, where it is approximately (baskets help, or different coloured bags), and cross it off the list as consumed.

I would grudge freezer space for prepared dishes, vegetables (except spinach and green beans) puddings and junk food such as pizza, but you might not agree. Morale is a funny thing — if you feel that frozen doughnuts or Black Forest Cake might at some point do the trick, don't let me dissuade you! In the freezer sweet butter will keep for six to eight weeks, salt butter rather less. (The reverse is true outside the fridge.) Margarine keeps longer than butter.

The Care and Treatment of Sick Vegetables

There is no reason why you cannot eat fresh vegetables from the Canaries to Barbados, or the West Indies back to Europe. Oddly enough, this will be more difficult coming east from the Americas or going across the Pacific, for it has little to do with the length of the journey.

It has everything to do with whether your fruit and vegetables have been wounded in the chill-room of the supermarket, or killed in the gas chambers of the commercial fruit merchants. If they have, then for keeping purposes they are not worth a damn, as you must have noticed. Regrettably since we first wrote 12 years ago things have deteriorated further, it is now very hard indeed in the Western world to buy genuinely fresh vegetables that have not been chilled.

You have only to compare the potato clamp at the frosty field's edge, the onions drying from hooks in the barn, the apples laid neatly on the attic floor to keep all winter (and what a memorable smell that was for the children!), the pumpkins stacked on the outhouse roof in bright orange rows, and the pomegranates and persimmons left on the tree to burn like lanterns in the autumn night, as used to be common (and still is where life is simple), and then think of the expected life of the produce you bought this morning at the Supermarket. If you don't put that cucumber in the fridge at once it will dissolve into a pint of greenish water by morning. The lettuce has suffered already in the car. The cabbage and oranges may last till the weekend. Not much else will.

Chilling kills fruit and vegetables. They die of hypothermia. Buy them straight off the tree, out of the ground or off the vine, from the farm or market (but *never* from the Supermarket of the western world). Choose them with the care you would give to selecting your next child from the orphanage, carry them gently without bruising them, and cradle them like babies in a cool and airy spot. If you wash them at all (to rid them of slugs or beetle eggs) dry them with great care and thoroughness to prevent mould. Unlike babies, you go through the whole lot daily and throw any doubtful ones overboard. We kept our main stock of fruit and vegetables in the dinghy under a canvas cover raised over the oars to give a through-draught; it was easy to check them over.

Fruit and vegetables

East-to-west Atlantic crossings, November to March: you will be buying your stores in a Mediterranean climate, in the markets of Spain or Portugal, the Canaries or Madeira. Quality and variety are excellent and prices are low.

Will last six months: pumpkin (if you do not pierce the skin). Potatoes, onions, lemons wrapped in foil; and carrots, Jerusalem artichokes and parsnips buried in earth or sand.

Will last a month or more: citrus fruits, tomatoes if you choose them hard and all shades of green and wrap them separately in paper towels or newspaper (but not foil because the acid in tomatoes eats through it), and put in a cool dark place. Check daily, eat the reddest and throw out any squashy ones.

Will last about three weeks: cucumber, marrow (do not pierce it), avocado pears, apples.

Two weeks: cabbage, carrots (kept loose), green peppers, melons.

Ten days: aubergine, globe artichokes, pineapple, courgettes. The latter benefit from wrapping as for tomatoes, and careful watching. If the flower has not dried off the end they are particularly subject to mould.

One week: lettuces (check for slugs etc): be sure they are dry and wrap firmly in Clingfilm. The big Romaine lettuces and the Iceberg keep especially well. Soft fruit, figs, grapes, cauliflower, green runner beans and celery.

Eat first and fast: spinach, cabbage greens or spring greens, watercress, Dutch lettuce. If you like chilled salad, and you have a fridge or icebox it is of course permissible to chill all these things just before serving. After all, you have to kill a chicken before eating it.

West-to-east crossing, in May to August: you will be buying your produce in the West Indies, North America or Bermuda. For the USA or Bermuda the notes on European shopping apply, with some alterations for the change in season. You will have to 'think seasonal' to avoid chilled produce. Remember: get it out of the ground or off the tree (or from under the hen).

Bermuda is a special case; you will find it harder to follow the rule that a chilled vegetable is a dead vegetable, because a large proportion of green stuff and fruit is chilled and imported from the USA for immediate consumption. At great expense, I might add. Never mind, it's only 18 days to the Azores. Actually, there are a few market gardens in Bermuda, but they require some hunting down.

The West Indies have some unfamiliar edibles worth describing. The large variety of roots (yams, eddoes, tannia, dasheen) keep well for months in a dry place. Yams and sweet potatoes are big enough to have doubtful pieces excised: use the mutilated ones first. Sweet cassava can be kept buried the same way as carrots and artichokes. (It is the Bitter Cassava from which the poisonous juice must be extracted; it is mostly used for laundry starch.) Pawpaw should be bought green, when it can be used as a vegetable until it turns golden, then it is eaten as a fruit after a week to ten days. Coconuts have a long life: while they come to no harm from a bump or two, it is worth stowing them securely or they crash around the boat like cannonballs.

Mangoes keep about a week. The huge bananas known as plantains are only for cooking; as they are very starchy you can treat them like potato. Breadfruit has the same function and keeps well. It grows on one of the most beautiful trees in the Caribbean. Christophene, in appearance like a pale green knobbly pear but a better keeper, cooks like a crisp marrow. Aubergine, often called melongene or eggplant, keeps up to two weeks.

The bunch of bananas that is the badge of all long-distance cruisers in the West Indies, hanging somewhere in the rigging, is something else. Even if you put a few 'hands' in the dark and cool to slow the ripening, you will still have to eat them fast when their time comes. You will need recipes for banana bread, banana curry, banana milkshake, banana cake, banana pudding, fried bananas and rum-buttered bananas, just for a start. They will cost you about a penny each, if you shop right. Be sure you hang them the wrong way up, which is actually the right way up (ends suggestively uppermost).

Other items

The best way to remember every item you will need is to imagine your way through a day, from the moment you rise till the time you go to bed, and write down every thing you eat or use. Thus you will not forget the toilet roll, can-openers, matches, washing-up brush, tartar sauce or salt. Then do it again going through events that crop up only weekly or monthly. (Yes, ladies, don't forget those; or your Pills either.) As Captain John Smith reminds us, at sea '...there is neither Ale house, Taverne, nor Inne to burne a faggot in, neither Grocer, Poulterie, Apothecary nor Butcher's shop.'

Transatlantic Food

My thinking went thus:
Meat for five people for supper for five weeks, using up the frozen meat first.
Supper
First two weeks: Day 1, Hamburgers. Day 2, Chicken. Day 3, Tinned. Day 4, Pork chops. Day 5, Steaks. Day 6, Party night. Day 7, Rice or spaghetti.
Following three weeks: Day 1, Tins. Day 2, AFD Curry. Day 3, Tins. Day 4, Steak-and-kidney. Day 5, Rice or spaghetti. Day 6, Party night. Day 7, Tins.

To my great astonishment we caught a fish, so one night we ate that. Party night food had been thought of, and was tinned pheasant or frozen duck (Bill's birthday), or national dishes mostly Chinese or Italian.
Lunch
These were bread (home-made when the bought bread gave up after the thirteenth day) and cold meats, galantines and pâtés, salami etc with salad as long as it lasted (till the nineteenth day), cheese and fruit. If it was a cold day we added hot soup.
Breakfast
Very important, after everyone had done at least one and maybe two night watches. We used combinations of eggs, bacon, porridge, sausage and beans, bacon grill, and kippers, plus toast and marmalade, and hot drinks. Bars made of cereal, fruit, and nuts, stuck together with honey and sold in the diet section of the supermarket make wonderful emergency breakfasts.
Nightwatch food (The night box)
Sweet biscuits, chocolate bars, cheese portions, wholemeal crackers, nuts and raisins, dried figs, fruit cake.

Transatlantic food: what we carried

For five people. We already had on board pickles, jams, sauces, salt and pepper, stock cubes and other staples bought in Italy, France, Spain and Gibraltar.

	SIZE	TINS		SIZE	TINS
TINNED MEAT					
Hot dogs/frankfurters	15 oz	6	Meatballs	15 oz	8
Stewing steak	15 oz	18	Irish stew	15 oz	12
Breast of chicken	3½ oz	6	Sausages	15 oz	6
Corned beef	7 oz	12	Roast beef	7 oz	7

	SIZE	TINS		SIZE	TINS
Bacon grill 6 x 12 oz, 4 x 7 oz			Roast pork	7 oz	7
Tongue	1 lb	6	Roast lamb	7 oz	4
Ham	1 lb	3	Pie fillings (15 oz)		
Steak-and-kidney pie	15 oz	2	Steak and Kidney		6
Steak and kidney pud	15 oz	6	Steak and mushroom		6
Steak and kidney pud	7 oz	12	Steak and onion		6

TINNED FISH

	SIZE	TINS		SIZE	TINS
Kippers		9	Crab	7 oz	6
Prawns/shrimps	7 oz	15	Mussels	3½ oz	3
Pilchards	15 oz	15	Oysters	7 oz	2
Salmon	7 oz	7	Sardines		12
Squid	7 oz	3	Paella Mix	3½ oz	2
Tuna	7 oz	6	Anchovies		2
Chopped clams	15 oz	2	Herring Roes		2

OTHER TINS

	SIZE	TINS		SIZE	TINS
Chopped pork	7 oz	6	Fabada (Spanish pork and beans)		1
Pork and beans	7 oz	6	Paella	15 oz	2
Sausage and beans	7 oz	6	Ravioli	30 oz	3
Pheasant	15 oz	1	Cassoulet	2 lb	1
Game pie filling	15 oz	1	Fruit cake	2 lb	1
Chinese goose	7 oz	2	Soups	15 oz	12
Liver pâté	3½ oz	2	Oatmeal	500 g	1
Pâté de campagne		3	Spaghetti sauce (Bolognese)		6
Sweet biscuits	3 lb	1	Spaghetti sauce (Matriciana)		6
Biscuits for cheese	3 lb	1	Spaghetti sauce (clams)		6
Spaghetti sauce (mushroom)		6			

TINNED VEGETABLES

	SIZE	TINS		SIZE	TINS
Pelati (tomatoes)	15 oz	12	Brussel sprouts	15 oz	12
Pease pudding	7 oz	7	Ratatouille	20 oz	2
Mushrooms	7 oz	9		15 oz	3
Leeks	5 oz	2	Red peppers	7 oz	5
Cauliflower	15 oz	7	Garden peas	15 oz	8
Spinach	15 oz	7	Petit pois	12 oz	4
Celery	15 oz	4	Water chestnuts	7 oz	2
Beans, green	15 oz	5	Bamboo shoots	7 oz	2
Haricot beans (natural)	15 oz	12	Bean sprouts	7 oz	6
Macedoine (mixed veg)	15 oz	6	Curried beans	7 oz	4
Butter beans	15 oz	3	Heinz beans	15 oz	3
Beetroot	7 oz	2	Carrots	15 oz	5
Broad beans	5 oz	2	Sweet corn	10 oz	12
Chick peas	15 oz	3	Red cabbage	15 oz	2
New potatoes	15 oz	12	Lentils	15 oz	4

	SIZE	TINS		SIZE	TINS
TINNED FRUIT					
Pineapple	15 oz	3	Peaches, large		3
	7 oz	4	Raspberries	15 oz	4
Pears, large		3	Fruit salad, large		3

	TINS		TINS
TINNED PUDDINGS			
Syrup sponge	8	Jam sponge	2
Chocolate sponge	2		

FROZEN

2 Large pizzas	5 Steaks
10 Loin of pork chops	1 lb Chicken pieces
2¼ lb Chicken breast	1 Duck
24 Beefburgers	

IN FOIL

Cotechino (sausage)	Chicken curry, 12 portions
Minestrone	

PERISHABLES

10 kg Potatoes	10 kg Onions
2 Cauliflowers	4 Cabbages
6 Aubergines	1 kg Green peppers
1½ kg Courgettes	10 Avocadoes
3 kg Sweet apples	3 kg Acid apples
4 kg Oranges	4 kg Green bananas
3 Melons	1 kg Red tomatoes
2 kg Green tomatoes	2 kg Cucumbers
1 kg Green beans	1 kg Carrots
1 kg Lemons	3 kg (10) Grapefruit
6 large White loaves	6 large Wrapped wholemeal loaves
12 Bread rolls	

FRESH GROCERIES

3 lb Streaky bacon	16 lb Butter 5 x 7oz
Vacuum packed bacon	3 lb Turkey galantine (whole)
3 lb 5oz Garlic sausage (whole)	2 lb Ham
1½ lb Liver sausage	1 Pork boiling ring
2½ lb Cheddar cheese	1½ lb Double Gloucester cheese
2 boxes Cheese portions	8 dozen Eggs
36 bars Bournville chocolate	36 bars Kit-Kat chocolate
2 pkts Crispbread	Nuts and raisins 24 small packets
Wholemeal crackers in packets of 4 x 24	

DRY GOODS

Plain flour	2 kg	Tea bags	250
Wholemeal flour	8 x 3.3 lb	Dumpling mix	½ lb
Rice	2 x 5 lb	Batter mix	6 pkts
Spaghetti	10 lb	Dried yeast	1 tin
Chinese noodles	4 pkts	(Add: Instant Easy blend)	3 pkts
Sugar	8 kg	Paper towels	6 x 2 rolls
Long-Life milk	36 litres	Toilet rolls	6 x 2 rolls
Long-Life cream	12 pkts	Nescafe	1½ lbs

DRINKS

Beer	144 cans	Orange squash	½ gal
Lemon and lime squash	½ gal	Wine	40 litres

What we actually used (23 days)

All the beer! All the fresh vegetables, and the following in tins:
(details in complete list)

Kippers	3	Mushrooms	3	Tongue	1
Ham	1	Corned beef	2	Jam sponge	1
Bacon grill	3	Bamboo shoots	1	Heinz beans	1
Pelati (tomatoes)	2	Chicken supreme	2	Roast beef	3
Sausage-and-beans	4	Soups	6	Brussels sprouts	2
Pease pudding	3	Crab	1	Roast lamb	3
Irish stew	5	Cream	1	Potatoes	1
Sausages	2	Bean sprouts	1	Salmon	2
Fabada (Bean stew)	1	Chicken breast	1	Pears	1
Game pie filling	1	Steak-and-kidney	2	Chopped pork	1
Steak-and-onion	2	Haricot beans	3	Steak-and-mushroom	2
Spaghetti sauce	6	Meatballs	1	Carrots	1
Stewing steak	1	Lentils	1	Pheasant	1
Water chestnuts	1	Prawns	1	Ravioli	2
Peas	4	Raspberries	2		

We had 2½ dozen eggs left, fresh fruit (oranges, lemons and grapefruit), and plenty of useful basic stores which stood us in good stead in the West Indies.

When we were within four days of Barbados the beer ration (jealously watched by the men) went up from one can a day to two, and then, to their great joy, to three.

Cost of Living

To give an idea of living expenses in some of the places we know, here is a basket of food that would feed two people for a week. As drink and meals out are far more of a variable than the food itself, and are anyway optional if you are travelling on a shoestring, I have kept them separate. The exchange rate is as on the day of shopping, and not necessarily current.

Cost of a food basket for two people for a week

	UK £1.00	France 9.20fr	Germany 375Dr	Italy 2750Li	Turkey 71.000Tl	Spain 230 ps	Romania 3250lei	USA $1.60
12 eggs	1.00	13.00	420	3400	64.000	226	1500	1.99
4 loaves	3.20	27.50	480	8500	60.000	920	1200	8.36
250g butter	.70	7.25	650	3280	60.000	272	2850	1.40
4l UHT milk	1.56	23.20	720	4464	56.000	480	unobtainable	5.00
1kg sugar	.78	6.70	275	1790	42.000	170	2500	0.90
1kg flour	.39	9.95	325	990	50.000	95	1250	0.72
200g Edam	.76	20.00	340	3240	80.000	324	unobtainable	3.20
100g Nescafé	2.17	24.90	1000	8950	213.000	450	unobtainable	2.28
3kgs potatoes	1.08	15.50	400	1500	60.000	60	1700	5.20
1kg onions	.80	9.90	200	1500	20.000	95	600	5.20
2 lettuces	1.60	7.80	200	1750	20.000	200	unobtainable	1.98
1kg tomatoes	.70	8.00	140	1500	38.000	115	600	5.48
2kg apples	2.00	8.00	390	5000	40.000	480	1200	3.48
4 pork chops	1.50	22.00	1200	7000	237.000	380	5230	3.89
2 steaks	2.10	12.00	2215	5230	315.000	550	3500	3.50
1kg mince	4.63	38.00	1600	13180	347.000	900	3000	6.00
1 chicken	3.50	25.00	2300	5930	230.000	520	5175	7.00
(A) sub-total	£28.55	£32.70	£34.28	£28.07	£27.21	£27.12	£9.30	£41.99
Drink								
12 botts beer	6.00	15.00	2220	12000	360.000	700	12000	7.00
6 botts wine	16.20	35.00	2340	11400	150.000	1200	21000	33.00
	22.20	50.00	4560	23400	510.000	1900	33000	40.00
(B) Drink	£22.20	£5.43	£12.16	£8.51	£7.18	£8.26	£10.15	£25.00
(C) Simple meal out for 2 with wine	£20.00	£25.50	£12.00	£18.50	£7.00	£14.00	£6.00	£18.75
TOTAL A+B+C	£71.75	£63.63	£58.44	£55.08	£41.39	£49.38	£25.45	£85.74
In dollars	$113.60	$102.00	$93.50	$88.00	$66.25	$79.04	$40.20	$135.47

Deep-Sea Cooking

SONG OF A SEA COOK

I think what pleasant thoughts I can
While bending o'er the frying pan
But truth to tell, I'm ill at ease:
It's hard to cook in seas like these.
But break the eggs and stir the pot
And try to be what you are not:
A cook with stomach not upset
Who hasn't lost her breakfast yet.

Why do they always ask for more
When half the stew is on the floor?
How can they eat so heartily
When I can't even drink my tea?
But peel the spuds and cook some duff
(Three pounds of flour should be enough)
They'll eat like the proverbial horse
Even if served with Diesel sauce

Cooking in bad weather

'... give every messe a quarter can of beere and a basket
of bread to stay their stomacks til the kettle be boyled...'

If you are the sort of cook that most of us are, fine on deck but subject to sickness down below unless horizontal, you have to develop a method if you are not to starve yourself while feeding the crew. One method is to bring all the ingredients up on deck, in one or more washing-up bowls, and do the preparation up in the fresh air. This is suitable for put-together meals like salad and sandwiches. Enlist help and it will be done fast, but half of it will be eaten prematurely.

A variation of this is the do-it-yourself buffet. Again washing-up bowls are used, to avoid everything landing on the floor of the cockpit. You cannot, of course, lay things out nicely on a plate, so recourse is made to smaller bowls and boxes with lids. Larger ones can contain potato or tomato salad, smaller ones sliced meat and salami, or tuna transferred from the tin. This is where I would use paper plates on the wicker plate-holders available in the USA, or wicker bread-baskets, which save washing up.

At some point in the day, however, you will have to serve something hot, since that is what is really popular in bad weather: a steaming pot of something rib-sticking such as soup, stew or risotto. For this I have a second method based on one-minute dashes to the galley, interspersed with fresh air up on deck until it is time for the next dash. (An extractor fan in the galley also helps.) There is no need for gourmet cooking under these conditions. Your crew will be more than grateful for that simple dish known to all sailors under various names such as lobscouse, slumgullion, potmess: in fact, Sea Stew.

Force 8 stew Choose a moment when you are feeling particularly strong, and make your first dash. Bad-weather stores should be handy in the galley, so if you also have a wall tin-opener it will take you no time at all to put in a large deep pan: one tin of meat, one tin of vegetables, one tin of soup and one tin of drained potatoes. (It does not seem to matter what kind any of these are, the result is invariably excellent, though some mixtures you may discover to be more favourite than others.) Light the stove and put the pan on, with lid. A pressure cooker is deep and works well — even without the lid. This mixture is very thick, and at intervals further dashes will be required to prevent it burning and to turn the whole mass over with a wooden spoon. When the entire contents are gently bubbling, serve in large mugs to three people.

This is the most delicious food you ever had if you are cold, wet and hungry. Starch seems to be needed for queasy stomachs to work on, so risottos and spaghettis are also good, but they are a little more time-consuming to cook.

Force 6 Stew, by the way, is made with fresh vegetables and potatoes instead of tinned ones, as the cook should be feeling stronger. Veg cleaning and preparation can be done on deck, using helpers, but watch your knives don't get chucked overboard with the peelings. Anyone who is too seasick to eat Sea Stew should be encouraged to eat at least some wholemeal crackers, and if you boil a kettle for a hot drink try them with bouillon or Bovril, which may go down better than tea or coffee. It is good to give the stomach something to work on: we find porridge and brown sugar very heartening too.

During Hurricane Alberto we had hot food the first day (eggs for breakfast with oatcakes and coffee, soup for lunch with fruit cake, and sea stew for supper); then water got into the Alkaline batteries and for the only time in ten years the stove would not light and we had cold food that day. The following day Bill got some of the battery cells going again, and as the huge seas were beginning to subside we celebrated with an enormous lunch of T-bone steaks and tinned raspberries and cream. Gosh, it was good. Once the alarms of the first day of the hurricane were over we drank a lot of coffee, some of it laced with brandy.

On the 'cold' day we had rum punch, which boosted morale without confusing the brain too much, and ate apples and chocolate and fruit cake, with the occasional ham sandwich.

It is noticeable that people who normally spurn puddings and cakes and sugary drinks, such as all three of us, turned in a time of worry and crisis to sweeter food and drinks. We were also immensely hungry, perhaps partly because it was hard to sleep through the noise and violent motion.

This brings us to: other useful ways to cope with bad weather when cooking:

- Use a damp sponge cloth or dish towel on the table or worktop to anchor plates and mugs.
- Pour drinks out fore and aft, not athwartships: who holds, also pours. Don't fill saucepans or mugs too full.
- Hand things up to the cockpit, either singly or in a wicker breadbasket for each person. This will take a mug of stew, bread, implements, and an apple or tomato. Mugs are better than bowls, which are better than plates.
- There should be somewhere the helmsman can put a drink safely, without it ending up on the deck.
- The high-friction Dycem plastic, which we call 'Sticky blue', can be cut to fit any surface. It has been so successful that we have been able to dispense with fiddles except on the cooking stove. (Address in Appendix.)
- Used and empty utensils should be put straight into the sink ready to wash up, so they do not roll underfoot and get broken.

Night watch food (the night box)

Night watches consume a lot of energy and except in pilotage waters they can also be very boring. You can count on the night watch losing all sense of morality and burrowing like alley cats in a dustbin through the cook's precious stores. If you do not want your menus totally disarranged, and large desserts intended for tomorrow to disappear without trace, you must provide a tempting and adequate night box. A large Tupperware bread bin might just be big enough.

It should contain both sweet and savoury items, such as dried fruit and nuts, cheese (wrapped portions are handiest), wholemeal crackers, chocolate bars and boiled sweets, cereal bars (a sort of solid muesli, available on the diet and health shelves of the supermarket. They keep a year and make excellent bad weather breakfasts); fruit cake and biscuits. If you are on a long passage where fresh fruit is limited, make it crystal clear whether fruit is allowed as an extra or counts as part of the daily ration, since it is impossible to satisfy a three-apple-a-watch man with the stores carried on a small boat. Some yachts fill Thermoses with soup and coffee for the night watch, others (if the autopilot is working well) find that the watchman gets a welcome break by making his own hot drink.

Food for morale

> *'And after a storme, when poor men are all wet, few of those but wil tell you a little Sacke or Aqua Vitae is much better to keepe them in health than a little small beere or cold water, although it be sweet.'*

When morale is low, break out some treat or delicacy: a tin of Dundee cake or shortbread, tins of Boeuf Bourguignon, Cassoulet or smoked salmon pâté. If the weather is fine and spirits need to be raised, pancakes, drop scones or new rolls with honey do wonders.

Find an excuse for a party: celebrate (or commiserate) something — the best day's run or the worst, 500 miles, 1000 miles, the day we saw the whale; and get everyone to help with the best dinner you can manage. Give a prize for the most inventive costume or headgear, or the best limerick. I always keep a bag of small presents on board. Whenever I see anything small and attractive ashore, I add it to the bag. Thus one can always cope with an unexpected birthday or find a suitable prize. You can also run a sweepstake on the noon-to-noon run.

Water

> *Skip will not let me wash my hair*
> *Nor yet my grubby underwear;*
> *'The water's getting low,' he shrieks,*
> *'We've just enough for ten more weeks.'*

Water, the lack of it, and where to get it, occupies the mind of cruising people a great deal. The habit of being mean with it must become second nature. If you run to the luxury of hot water, you cannot allow the tap to run hot without saving the cold water that comes out first. On our boat this is done by having a jug of the right capacity kept in the head: when the jug is full, the water will be hot and the jug of cold can (and must) be used elsewhere, in the kettle for instance.

The problem in *Hosanna*'s forward bathroom is much worse; this is miles from the tank. Bill has arranged a tap on a branch pipe which returns the running off water back to the tank.

> *'...a little pumpe made of a Cane, a little peece of hollow wood ... to pumpe the Beere or water out of the Caske, for at sea wee use no taps'*

194

Small toddlers love pumping water and turning on taps. So, unfortunately, do guests. Make sure that the water is not frittered away without your knowledge; a press-and-release tap would help, being harder for a toddler or guest to use than a Whale pump or a foot-button.

Have plenty of buckets. One cannot have too many, as one always seems to lose one (plus a doormat) in every storm. Then when it tips it down in the West Indies or the Pacific, you can fill your buckets and have a water frolic. Some people can plug their cockpit drains and turn it into a huge swimming bath.

If you are really short of water it is possible, indeed desirable, to use fresh water twice. First, where hygiene is essential, such as washing oneself or the dishes. Having done that, the resulting water, according to its state, may then be used for the galley floor, or engine room overalls. Hair needs a lot of rinsing, but the water used is usually still clean enough, if a bit soapy, to wash clothes in. Judgement has to be used here. To shore-people who have water to wash cars with, this must seem rather revolting. (We did say that the life is not all pâté and champagne.) I can assure you that Bill, coming up from the engine room with filthy hands, is quite glad of leftover washing-up water to get the worst off. All galleys should have a salt water tap, if only for fire-fighting!

A very refreshing gambit that takes a minimum amount of fresh water goes like this: heat a cupful of water to boiling and put it in the bottom of a warmed jug. Hold your face over the jug, under a towel as if you were inhaling balsam. Your face will be nicely steamed. Wipe off the grime and salt with a tissue and hand the jug to the next person in the queue, reheating the water as necessary. Water that has been used to boil potatoes or pasta can be used for soups or freeze-dried food, but go easy on the salt. Water drained from tinned vegetables can be used for the same purposes or to boil potatoes.

Can you cook in sea water?

To illustrate an important point: once in Yugoslavia we went on a Club Mediterranée sailing barbecue, the first of the season, which was going to be done in style, huge amounts of meat with rice and spaghetti cooked on a remote beach. Everyone helped. Well, nearly everyone. Some of the men went off to taste the wine at the local tavern three kilometres away, and returned disgusted. 'One has drunk a wine of the most execrable,' said a tired Frenchman, 'and one has spat all the way home.' He began to wash his mouth out with wine from the huge jars we had brought with us. 'Which one is the water to cook the rice?' I asked, looking towards the jars. 'That's all wine,' said the organizer, 'we will use sea water.' 'Have you done this before?' I enquired with some doubt. He brushed my worries aside with superb confidence: what do the English know about cooking? So we duly cooked rice and pasta for forty people in sea water. Both were so salty as to be totally inedible, and I have since found that the same thing happens with potatoes. You cannot cook vegetables in pure sea water. Not in the Mediterranean, anyway.

I have done some tests, and find that 5% of sea water makes it quite salty enough. That is 1 part in 20, or 1 fl oz of sea water to 1 Imperial pint of fresh. You would have to be pretty desperate for that to make any difference.

Washing at sea

Washing machines are not often carried by the long-distance cruiser. There is a small plastic washing machine that I have seen on live-aboard yachts, which seems to please its owners, being light but solidly made. As they don't heat the water they don't use much power; but they do use a lot of water, which is probably why I have seen them in use only in marinas or close to a dockside tap.

When water is pretty short, as it always is on long-distance cruises, the time comes when the Skipper's shorts are sufficiently redolent to be capable of independent movement and will come when you whistle, with the embarrassing affection of an elderly and appallingly smelly dog. Now is the time to consider washing in salt water. Any strong liquid detergent will wash satisfactorily. If it is choppy, put the clothes in a tub and let them slop around with the motion of the boat doing much of the work for you. You must get the salt out by a rinse in fresh water; otherwise your clothes will be stiff, the salt will attract moisture so that they never fully dry, and you could end up (particularly with tight jeans) with a painful skin rash caused by chafe, or worse, 'gunnel bum' (salt water sores).

In places where it rains, such as an east-to-west Atlantic crossing, it pays to see a shower coming and get out the clothes and buckets to benefit by it. To get one-self and the clothes one is wearing thoroughly soaked in fresh water can be very refreshing, and is usually an occasion for much hilarity and splashing about. The west-to-east crossing is considerably colder and normally contra-indicates such skylarks, but it would depend on the degree of desperation.

Acquire an old-fashioned washboard and that useful article known as a dolly or posher. Washboards are still found anywhere there are no washing machines, such as the Greek Islands and the West Indies. The dolly is rarer, but it is not hard to make one of the milking stool variety illustrated. If you were used, on shore, to a washing machine and a tumble-dryer, you will be surprised and pleased at how much longer your clothes last when you wash by hand, provided of course you don't lose them overboard when you've pegged them out to dry.

Before I learnt the art of secure clothes-pegging I lost overboard two good towels, a pillowcase and a woollen jersey. All sank to the bottom with extra-ordinary rapidity before we could seize the net. Spring-clip pegs, I learnt, are not

Washday ancient and modern. Greek wash board, a copper and a wooden 'milking stool' dolly, all-plastic clothes peg.

strong enough. Lead the washing line across the wind if possible, and use pegs that have no metal parts to rust, the old-fashioned Gypsy peg or all-plastic ones. Turn the clothes inside out (the strong sun will fade them quickly otherwise) and peg them firmly in such a way that they parachute across the wind. Lead the line through arms, legs or belt loops if you can. They will dry in no time. Bring them in while still a little damp, fold carefully and stack in a warm place. As they finish drying, they will 'iron' themselves with no further attention.

Some Practical Hints for Boatwives and Ships' Husbands

The WC and shower compartment Sea water used for flushing heads causes scale to form. Putting some vinegar in the bowl from time to time, especially if you are leaving the boat for a few days, helps to minimize this, as does a daily sprinkle with washing up liquid. An occasional cautious catharsis with the delightfully named Greek product 'Drastiko' (hydrochloric acid as far as I can make out), is abhorred by the manufacturers, but works absolute wonders.

The second most important habit to acquire (the first being not to waste water) is to put nothing down the loo that could lead to a blockage. It helps everyone to remember not to do this if there is a separate lidded bin for hairballs, cigarette ends, matchsticks, dental floss and even more unmentionable items. If your taste is for waggish notices on brass plates, now is your chance to let rip. Otherwise a simple green cross painted on the lid will indicate its use to most people. It will not stop children from poking about in there to see what it contains, but that all comes under the heading of a broad education. My children learnt a lot that way.

Thoughts about the accommodation Which is what the Yacht Brokers call your living space. We find we need safe places for spectacles these days. Pockets for them, and indeed for anything that needs to be readily to hand, such as seasick pills, sunscreen cream, finger plasters, bottle openers and so on, can be made from felt, leather, fabric or any suitable material, and screwed or stuck to the linings or cockpit in strategic places. Doublesided sticky pads can be used to fix not only these but digital clocks, perpetual calendars, navigating gimmicks, and even pictures and photographs if they are not too heavy. Fewer screwholes keep up the Resale Value!

You might doubt that magnetic racks would be of any use. We have one for kitchen knives and one for small tools. Only the big carving knife and the heavy ratchet screwdriver get jerked loose by a choppy sea: they are fine for smaller items. Don't site magnetic racks near a compass, it goes without saying.

Stow seaboots upside-down on dowels of suitable length. This not only helps them to dry but prevents them from filling up with rubbish and dead wasps. Keep a bag of plastic foam offcuts to stifle any clinks and bumps that can disturb your sleep in choppy seas: cassettes, bottles and glasses are the worst offenders.

A cylinder type vacuum cleaner has many uses apart from the obvious one. Ours helped us to build the boat. It was second-hand even then and has swallowed everything from wood shavings through nails and screws to lumps of rubbery caulking compound, drilling swarf, rust chippings and grinding dust. Put together backwards it can be used as a heavy duty blow-dryer for newly painted areas, or even damp bilges if you should be so unlucky. We are thinking of coarse painting, naturally. (We would not blow dust and flies on the sort of paint and varnish where dogs must not sneeze and cats must not tread.) There are now some battery-driven vacuum cleaners that are worth their space for light duties: crumbs, fluff, loose dust, even dead insects if they are small ones.

Few cottons and canvases can stand up to sea water and hot sun, but lining your curtains with heavy cotton prolongs their lives. Cockpit and deck cushions are usually vinyl covered, which lasts well but sticks to hot bare skin. Most people make loose cotton covers and accept that they will need replacing frequently. It's worth it not to find your thighs securely stuck to the cushions in hot weather.

A practical thought: you can buy sticky labels in the form of little coloured circles. Get several different colours, and use them to match plugs with sockets, so that a red spot plug fits a red spot socket. Or use them to highlight important electronic buttons that the designers try to hide from us by camouflage and incomprehensible icons: charcoal on charcoal seems to be flavour of the month.

Duty Frees

This has changed considerably during the past few years, and duty-free stores are now much more difficult to get. They are not supposed to be available for voyages between EU countries, though cross-channel ferries seem to get round that, at least for the time being. To qualify, one must be bound for a destination outside the EU.

The problem is that the number of bonded warehouses has decreased, and suppliers are hard to find. Those we did approach were scornful about supplying less than a truck-load. When we did find a willing supplier, we also found the procedures had become much simpler. No longer the embarkation under the eagle eyes of a squad of The Revenue Men; no more mystic passes with coded seals. The goods came on board just before sailing, and we pushed off.

To get the goods (and the savings are considerable), find a co-operative supplier, who will help make out the forms in a way acceptable to the Revenue. The further away your destination, the more you may take. Cheers!

And finally: the pleasure of it all

There are two occasions I shall miss dreadfully if I ever come ashore. One is the impromptu cruising barbecue, on a beach perhaps, with half a dozen dinghies hauled up on the shingle, and the yachts nodding at anchor a short swim away. The fire is already crackling under many and different grids and grills, bring your own meat or fish, something to drink, and 'a dish for the table' that everyone can share. The meal langours deliciously on into the warm afternoon or the cool night, with chat and laughter — memorable days.

The other is of wonderful meals for two after a good day at sea, not in them-selves so Epicurian, were it not for the beauty of the day, the good temper of the sea, the satisfaction in our progress, and the sharpness of our hunger. With such a sauce, anything tastes good.

Chapter Ten

Cruising Grounds

'One to the top to look out for lande.'

In discussing the type of yacht and her gear there has inevitably been some emphasis on voyaging and bad conditions. Your typical boat dweller is not out to score miles or win trophies, or even to get unnecessarily wet and tired; it is simply sensible to consider the worst, so that in the vast majority of cases the cruiser is well within tolerable limits of safety and comfort. In looking at cruising grounds the emphasis must be on the pleasant side of life afloat, although everywhere has its share of bad points which I will have to mention. Once again, there is a lot of subjectivity. How could it be otherwise?

Ocean crossing for the likes of us is not a case of long-lasting heroics. (They may happen, but are not part of the plan.) I am confining this to consideration of the more congenial places which can be reached without taking dubious risks, or by extreme physical effort. Thus our ocean crossings are confined to the nicer parts of the Atlantic, and I will discuss routeing later on in Chapter Fifteen.

The West Indies

Most people contemplating this life have a palm tree in the vision somewhere, so I will start with the West Indies. For our purpose, these start at Trinidad, close to the South American shore, and include the Windward Islands, the Leewards, Dominican Republic, Haiti, Puerto Rico, Cuba, Jamaica and a few smaller units. Most have a mixed colonial history, and the main population is of African descent from slaves, or in some cases of Spanish origin. There are many ethnic Indians in Trinidad. Some islands are very poor with unstable or uncertain economies, others have become more prosperous by exploiting tourism. It is a sad reflection that the islands in worst shape are very often those that were British possessions: the realization hits one with shaming force.

To nautical tourists such as ourselves, there is an inevitable pull towards the Windward Islands (the Grenadines, St Vincent, St Lucia, and Martinique) afterwards to the more diffuse Leewards; Dominica round to the Virgins. The parts farther west, Puerto Rico to Cuba, once less attractive for political reasons, are beginning to offer scope for visits, but most of the Central American isthmus is a part of the world best avoided except for the brave. It may be a long time before things improve there. There are also the islands off the coast of South America from Trinidad to Curacao, the smaller of which are becoming more popular; though being downwind of the main group they are not so readily convenient to cruise.

The major fly in the ointment for the private cruising yacht in this whole area is the large fleet of bare-boat charter yachts. Some are essentially private craft let out on the occasional charter and these are no problem: the difficulties arise from what I will call industrial chartering. The boats are almost always badly equipped, badly maintained and often badly sailed. The usual customers are Americans. Now, the USA probably has more private cruising yachts than the rest of the world put together, and probably more competent yachtsmen to sail them. In the same proportions she has also more boorish idiots, and it seems that many of these holiday in a bare-boat in the Caribbean. Search and rescue facilities in this area are scant (there are exceptions, notably Barbados), and these charterers, used at home to nannying by the very efficient US Coast Guard, put out a scandalous number of distress calls, many for trivial reasons and others for want of elementary prudence. British (and other nationalities) registered vessels are bound by law to answer distress calls. Sadly, the professional, crewed charter yachts, many of which are British flag even if only of a debased kind, have been driven to ignoring these calls.

In addition, the bare-boat fleets have established bases which reserve for their exclusive use facilities which were once available to all. Either that or they charge discriminatory rates for private boats that are not acceptable to live-aboards. People on a three-week holiday from a very prosperous country can out-bid longer term visitors for the scarce resources, and exert pressure for shallow sophistication and high prices, the main benefits of which go to external investors and do not reach the local people. Local politicians should remember that the local tourism that keeps their islands solvent was started by private yachtsmen, and it is ungrateful deliberately to squeeze them out.

The pleasures of the area outweigh the minor irritations. There are wonderful anchorages and beaches, and the sailing between is excellent. We found, almost without exception, the local people friendly, extrovert and cheerful, the officials good humoured and courteous. Generally the poorer the community the nicer the people and officials, and it was in the more prosperous Virgin Islands that we found the only examples of rudeness, and even those were not too bad.

Formalities are generally not irksome. Almost every island is a separate sovereign state, so that a lot of clearing and entering has to be done and a lot of expensive courtesy ensigns carried. Most islands make a moderate entry charge, and some yachtsmen resent this because harbours tend to be open anchorages with few port facilities; but considering that the islands are poor, such a charge is hard to find unreasonable.

The cost of living in the islands is based on the US dollar (apart from the French islands, which are heavily subsidized by France). Much of the foodstuff is imported from the USA, often by air, so that these items are expensive except the ubiquitous frozen chicken. Apart from the wealthier, more developed islands, up-market foods are hard to find. Yacht chandlery supplies have improved except in the more backward islands, but it is not cheap. Repairs can be undertaken at Antigua and Grenada, where there are boatyards with reasonable craftsmen, slip-ways, and berths with electricity for a self-refit.

Mail from Britain or the US to the islands is generally quite good, the telephone service is improving. Air communications are very good and air freight is recommended for parcels. European flights go regularly to Antigua, Barbados, Grenada,

Trinidad and the French islands; and the smaller inter-island services are very busy and really quite efficient, if sometimes a little hair-raising. Landing on Union Island or St Bart's is not for the faint-hearted. Montserrat Air Lines used to run a well-ordered air ambulance service that was welcome because medical services on many islands are not very sophisticated, but the erupting volcano on the island has put a stop to that and many other businesses. It is as well to have medical insurance in the West Indies because facilities in the islands are limited.

Diesel fuel is conveniently obtained in only a few places, but as the wind is so reliable, pleasant and free, diesel does not loom large in most people's minds. The most convenient points that I found were at Grenada (St George's), Martinique, English Harbour and St Thomas. If a really large amount of fuel is needed, go to Venezuela, where it is extremely cheap.

The weather is very pleasant during the European winter. The temperatures are moderated by the tradewind, which is usually about force 4 but does rise occasionally especially in certain channels. The most I recorded in one winter was force 6 off Kick 'em Jenny, near Grenada, where the seas were also unusually disturbed. It rains every few days, usually a sharp shower which should be used for topping-up tanks, for fresh water is not easy to get in quantity. During this season hurricanes hardly ever happen.

In summer the weather is not so pleasant, but to compensate there are fewer tourists. The weather is hotter, wetter, a bit more capricious, and hurricanes do happen though they are not by any means an everyday event. The old rhyme tells you when they start: 'June too soon, July by and by, August you must, September remember, October it's over.' Do not rely too much on this doggerel: we were damaged in Hurricane Alberto on June 18, 1982, farther north, off Bermuda. If you are in the Caribbean there is a wealth of local knowledge, of hurricane holes in which to get secure, and what precautions to take. These matters are out of the scope of this book; my hurricane experiences (two) have both been well offshore; the best place to be, we think. It is quite another thing close to land.

Charts and navigational publications are hard to get. For electronic or technical repairs, I found English Harbour the only worthwhile centre. Most services can be contacted on VHF. In fact, in the West Indies, almost everyone can be contacted on VHF: Sam Taxi, the Scuba Shops, the restaurants, and even hairdressers. Some restaurants make a general call on Channel 16 to inform all stations that their menu for tonight is on Channel 68, and bookings can also be taken thus. The radio is seldom silent, but on the whole the system functions very well: it is because everyone uses the radio that one finds it useful in a way not possible in over-regulated Europe or the USA. The radio discipline is better than on Long Island Sound on a weekend.

As one goes farther west the cruising gets less congenial. Big money dominates the Virgin Islands scene, and prices rise, marinas are found and sophistication starts to shriek. By the time you reach St Thomas you are in an American city and the supermarkets are well stocked, but the people lack the good manners of the poorer islands, and crime rates are higher. The welcome is often still good, but there is something missing.

The US Navy make a nuisance of themselves (quite unnecessarily) exercising north of Puerto Rico. Cuba used to be off-limits for British insurers, but I expect this is changing. I have not been to Jamaica recently, but have conflicting reports as to whether it is currently advisable. One reads a lot of alarmist articles in magazines about piracy, violence and robbery, and I will discuss our views on this later, in Chapter Eleven.

If one is required to leave a boat, say for an emergency visit home, the marina in St George's, Grenada has good security; alternatively there are facilities in English Harbour. Up-market marinas, at up-market prices, exist in Antigua, Tortola and St Thomas.

The Bahamas

Moving northwestwards from the Caribbean Islands, one comes to the Bahamas, another independent ex-British colony. It was peopled largely by loyalists from the revolting American colonies about 1778 and these white people with their black slaves were the forebears of many of the present inhabitants. In the north, the Abacos, much of the populace are so firmly Nonconformist that you might imagine you were in Scotland. You might, but it would be difficult, for the weather and scenery are very different. The Bahamas are flat, palm-clad, sandy islands set on a series of broad shallow banks penetrated by the odd deep-water tongue of ocean. The local industries are tourism and drug dealing, but the latter is a closed shop and the participation of amateurs from outside is much resented and dangerous. It can still be dangerous if you innocently see something you shouldn't. Be very tactful, and rather shortsighted.

The southern islands are more remote and less densely populated, with scope for some very quiet cruising, though provisions take some looking for. The northern islands are close to Florida and have large numbers of shorter term visitors. There is a bay called No Name Bay south of Miami which I selected as a good dawn jumping-off place for a day sail to the Bahamas: so did half a hundred others. The Florida Channel between that state and the Bahamas is one of the busiest waterways in the world, with some very long commercial multi-barge tows using it, and it merits some care when crossing, especially at night.

The Bahamas are islands where souvenirs are few and an artist/craftsman could earn a bit, but the cost of living, being so dependent on nearby Florida, is high. The Islands ought to be prosperous. The currency is at par with the US dollar, but there are local notes in circulation, as well as American ones. The officials are pleasant, courteous, but not noticeably industrious or efficient. Communications are good with Florida, and then from Miami are excellent. Mail and telephone services seemed to be good. The banking system, where it is of British or Canadian origin, is above average.

The other sort of banks, the coral ones, require care. Paradoxically, the old British charts are the best. One of these, no. 1496, was engraved in 1844 with the last new edition in 1907 and its detail is first class. I occupied myself for some time with checking several of the areas of the banks, and though there were some differences I would say that if used with a little prudence and common sense this chart is infinitely preferable to the US chart of recent publication. But any chart cannot cope unaided. The latest supplement to the British Admiralty Pilots should be carried, but even better are some of the recently published yachtsmen's guides. The Chart Kits published in Needham, Massachusetts by the

Better Boating Association are a good investment and based on US government charts. Care should be taken when using GPS in conjunction with older charts.

There are several places to leave a yacht in the Bahamas, but none of them are ideal and many are over-expensive. Unless one's departure is very urgent (in which case Marsh Harbour suggests itself), it would be better to head for Florida, a short trip away. There one finds every possible facility.

The East Coast of the USA

There are many people who spend their lives cruising the Intra-Coastal Waterway between Chesapeake Bay and the Florida Keys. The Chesapeake is a bay of great size, which can get very rough on occasions but has many delightful places to visit: Washington, which has been largely rebuilt by the industrious natives since my ancestors burnt it; Annapolis, the home of the US Naval Academy; Jamestown, St Michael's, Oxford and Cambridge. Some of these places are as delightful as their prototypical English towns. The Florida Keys are a string of islands connected by a causeway, extending round into the Gulf of Mexico.

The Intra-Coastal does extend north of the Chesapeake, as far as New York (where one can moor in the middle of Manhattan for less than the price of a hotel room), but the depths are not sufficient for most sea-going sailing craft.

It is superfluous to say much about the USA. The natives are friendly: however terrifying they may be as tourists, on their home ground they are charming, hospitable hosts, generous and efficient, with a vast and constant appetite for apparently tasteless food. But the country changes. The west shore of the Chesapeake, close to Washington, is rich, sophisticated and comparatively crowded. Progressing southward through the backwoods (literally) of South Carolina or Georgia, one finds people of less material wealth, and many of those at the supermarket checkouts are on welfare.

The waterway country is evocative of the Norfolk Broads on a vast scale, with trees, reeds, herons, bitterns, flat country, estuaries and a similar state of mind among the local people. It is sometimes a long way between settlements; there are remote anchorages, quiet and beautiful, oysters for the gathering, strong tides and many bridges which open very efficiently; the fixed ones have a minimum High Water clearance of 65 feet (except for one at Miami, which can be avoided by a short hop at sea). There is only one lock; at Great Bridge in Virginia. The water in the Waterway is spread very wide, but it is shallow. A draught of 2 metres (6¼ ft) is pushing the limit, and one must expect to touch bottom occasionally, especially near the southernmost inlets.

Provisioning is often difficult as in most US communities all the stores are now in out-of-town shopping malls. For this reason some isolated marinas have a (sometimes rather battered) 'courtesy car' which one may borrow free for local use.

The bigger yachting centres are crowded and made hideous by speeding water-hogs in fast power boats; which makes the southern part of Florida's waters less attractive. But there are plenty of good marinas where one can leave a boat to do some touring, and good facilities everywhere for hauling out and refitting.

American marinas are very different from those we have become accustomed to in Europe. The mega-marina does exist, of course, and is very much better run than its European counterpart, but the typical US marina is a comparatively small family affair, often with only 30 to 50 berths, sometimes a little scruffy but almost always with a real, friendly welcome.

The climate is surprising. In winter southern Florida is pleasant, but from St Augustine northward expect some very cold spells. It can be bitterly cold in North Carolina. In summer, the whole area is very hot and humid and has the world's biggest and hungriest mosquitoes. Spring and autumn are delightful.

US officials vary. We found Customs officers everywhere to be courteous, helpful and on the ball. The Immigration people were appallingly aggressive. Visas are no longer necessary for British citizens. US Customs will give the yacht a Cruising Permit on arrival, valid for six months, and though some states will renew this or extend it, others will not (South Carolina is one). Only yachts registered in countries with some mysterious reciprocal arrangement will be granted this permit, and it is difficult to get a definitive list. Britain is on it, so is France, but apparently Belgium is not. Yachts without a Cruising Permit have the chore of entering and clearing outwards in every state. Even with a permit, the obligation is to report by telephone every time one moors at an accessible place. In some states the Customs have a tollfree number for this purpose which is very considerate for the US public phones are bad. European mobile phones do not work, and it is difficult to get a US one without a permanent residence. We are familiar with this feeling world-wide: persons of *no fixed abode*, such as live-aboard yachtsmen whose boats may well be far more valuable than a house, are vagrants, gypsies, chicken-stealers, with no credit rating, and only a short way off being responsible for all the looting, pillage and rape reported to the local police. But let's not get carried away on that hobby-horse.

Do not fall into the trap of regarding US Customs or the US Coast Guard as merely benevolent nannies to the large number of incompetent skippers who crash from mishap to ineptitude on the coast. There is massive drug smuggling through the creeks and inlets of the Intra-Coastal, and the Waterway is well patrolled. The Coast Guard, though apparently staffed entirely by teenagers, is very much on the alert. They run the rescue service, maintain navigation marks, and keep watch on Channel 16 and also on 22A, which foreign vessels do not have. The US Coast Guard seemed to be permanently confused about our failure to reply on this channel. Note that several VHF channels have different user designations in the USA.

Buoyage is different, adhering to IALA System B.

The electricity supplied from shore in most marinas is another oddity. Voltage is 110V and is apparently world unique in using alternating current of 60 cycles instead of 50.

The regulations against pollution are strict, and in the case of yacht heads and holding tanks are so draconian as to be unenforceable. There being no pump-out stations, ordinary marine heads may be used at sea. I understand the whole situation is under review, when some of the ecological over-enthusiasm may be tempered with realism. On the Great Lakes, and in the canals and lakes north of New York where there is little outlet of water to the sea, the situation is different and the laws are enforced with vigour. There, marine heads may not be discharged overboard.

A brief word about the north, though these waters are not really our province as the sailing season is so short. Cruising the New England coast is delightful, though it does require alertness and good navigation because of the strong tidal streams, especially farther north, and the frequency of fog. Navigation marks are good and facilities are excellent. In fact the whole of the US coast is good cruising, and the people badly need to meet a few foreigners.

The Mediterranean Sea

The Med is a wholly different cruising ground to those we have discussed. History and scenic beauty rather than the quality of the sailing are the chief attractions. Generally navigation in small craft is not congenial in December to March, and should be indulged with caution in November and April. It is around the equinoxes that conditions become especially capricious, and quite like British weather. Depressions that come in from the Alantic are deflected at the last minute, and forecasts become unreliable. In high summer the weather is usually dry and stable. Winds over much of the Med are characteristically light and variable then though there are places where usable winds are good.

We have cruised the Med in winter, and we have not been alone. There are always a number of antipodean boats coming up through Suez, and some of these are on a limited time world cruise, so that they do not want to lay up for long. They form the nucleus of winter cruisers, and we have had some good social times out of season, sharing off-beat moorings with some very congenial fellow wanderers. This is what it is all about.

The Strait of Bonifacio, and the Sicilian Channel particularly close to Cape Bon, have predominantly west winds and east-going currents. In the Aegean, the summer (Etesian) wind, often called by its Turkish name Meltemi, can blow for three or four months from between northwest and northeast, sometimes reaching

A major disadvantage of the French system of mooring in marinas is that the visitor never knows the condition of the submerged chain. Here is a mooring chain in a marina that charged £16 per day for its use. Beware!

gale force, when ferry and even air services are interrupted. A particularly troublesome bit of sea, winter or summer, is the Gulf of Lions. It is not so much the wind strength that causes problems to the small-craft navigator in the Med; there is often a very short and steep sea going with it, and it is this which does the damage and causes acute discomfort.

We do not think we need to go into the Mediterranean countries in detail because, since writing the original edition, there are now many good guides (I hesitate, as a one-time professional, to call some of them 'pilots', but that is letting my prejudices hang out), so we will confine our comments to generalisations that are relevant to live-aboards.

The welcome for live-aboards has changed somewhat over the past few years. We have actually been blamed for this, being seen as having encouraged too many others to join in, but the increase in the numbers of live-aboards is not the reason for the cooler welcome. Where we live-aboards have pioneered yachting tourism in parts of the Med, others have followed us into the less well-known places. Easily accessible cruising grounds, such as the Riviera, have always been over-crowded and expensive.

For many years the difficulties of private yachting for short periods, such as are available to the ordinary family who have to work for a living, were such as to limit the number of yachts. This started to change with the flotillas which frankly saturated the more congenial places such as the Ionian Islands. These holiday-makers, who were not always well-behaved, changed the local culture during the summer. Tavernas changed their style, their menu, their service, and their prices. People on a short term holiday have, comparatively, money to burn. But it was the sheer numbers that tried to crowd into tiny little ports with no regard for local feelings that caused the problems. A few local people have profited, but many have seen their home villages spoiled for no personal gain. And so the yachtsman as a class has become unwelcome in some places, or at least not as welcome as was once the case.

An example to show what we mean: in the little harbour of Vathi in Meganisi one Easter weekend, the local people expected to enjoy their celebrations, which are as important to them as Christmas is to Nordic communities. In the middle of their solemn Good Friday procession two separate flotillas arrived unexpectedly. A population of about a hundred, marking the last days of a rigorous and austere Lent, was overwhelmed by a noisy invasion of about the same number in skimpy holiday clothes. The flotilla leaders were outrageously unsympathetic, encouraging their punters to push their way in to photograph the procession, and later the burning of Judas. They had not bothered to warn the taverna, which had to open specially to feed the unwelcome hordes.

There were two live-aboard yachts there, ourselves and a German boat, both of us long known to local families, both of us invited into the church and into their homes to share their Easter breakfasts, and help to roast the kokkoretsi and lamb for Easter day. We were informed that they might ask the harbour to be closed for Easter the next year.

The situation has been compounded by the growth of the bare-boat charter fleet. It is sad that the standard of seamanship of boat charterers is low enough to endanger other boats, and their nautical manners such as to render peaceable anchorages no longer congenial. While it is true that certain centres pose comparative over-crowding problems for those of us who were lucky enough to enjoy the Med in its uncrowded days, when it was much cheaper to live there than now, it is noticeable that the newcomer is still as enchanted by the life as we have been. So the harbours of the Balearics are overcrowded but, apart from the very high season, there is still pleasure to be had. Likewise in Greece.

We know of certain places in high season where the charterers do not get to. They are not necessarily as beautiful or convenient as the better-known spots, but they are often cheaper. No, we will not tell you our own secret places, but if you take to this life, and go to the Med for a long stay, you will find them. During the winters, when the yotties foregather, the word gets round. We are quite a strong, but friendly, union.

The cost of living has risen in the popular cruising grounds. Mainly this is due to the Common Market, the EEC or the EU.

> *It escapes no blame*
> *by changing its name.*

Things have not necessarily been all for the better as Brussels has come to the poorer parts of the Med. There has been, it is true, massive hand-outs to backward communities, but in the best Med tradition, these have often created a few millionaires, rather than benefiting the whole population. With Brussels has come more imports: marvellous! you can now buy packets of Krokkiweet on the tiniest island, but with it has come better packaging of everything, therefore much more rubbish, and higher prices.

Whereas prices in Greece and Turkey were once much the same, since Greece has been in the EU, her prices have risen to a much higher level. Nowadays the cheaper places are the less sophisticated non-EU countries, such as Turkey and North Africa. In the latter case it is as well not to visit Algeria owing to their tendency to kill foreigners to teach them a lesson, or Libya which is completely unreliable. Egypt is also not wholly secure, but Tunisia and Morocco will give you a good welcome, though the climate is desperately hot in summer.

The Dalmatian coast of Yugoslavia, as was, is getting back to normal. The boats returning are for the most part German. Alone of the northern yachting countries, Germany is close enough to ex-Yugoslavia for people to pour over the Brenner pass for a long weekend provided the boat is in Croatia. So, most of the berths in Croatia are occupied by boats belonging to Bavarians.

Military matters cannot be ignored further east. Insurers prefer yachts to keep west of longitude 33 degrees East unless an extra premium is paid. This puts a strain on visiting Israel and Syria.

All is not exactly rosy west of this meridian. Greece and Turkey are at it again. The Cyprus situation looks as far as ever from resolution. If there is one lesson the Greeks fail to learn it is that they cannot push Turkey too far, because if they do: Wham! The people of Cyprus are still suffering from this misapprehension. Further west the two countries still squabble. There is right on both sides, but in the main, the Turks cry 'so far but no further!' while the Greeks seem to be continually trying it on. It is the sort of thing that yachts can get caught up in as warships deliberately try to harrass each other, and helicopters dance like dragonflies in the hot air, with less innocence. But we were there recently and heard of no mishaps to yachts.

AGHIOS STEFANOS, CORFU

Wintering

The Med climate is cold on winter nights, even if sunny at lunchtime. Greatcoat weather in places, and at times. Most people like to find a good, cheap, safe berth to endure it. Many try to find work, and this is possible within the EU countries for EU citizens. Most have maintenance to do, perhaps a short trip back to the homeland to see how Mum is or the grandchildren are getting on. An extension of a previously mentioned problem is that many of the best winter berths are nowadays filled with laid-up bare-boats, most of which finish their season early enough to occupy the more congenial and safer parts of the harbour, doing nothing for the local economy for months on end. Further secure berths are pre-

Laurel

empted by those yotties who have given up all pretence to cruise anymore and who have taken a job ashore and use their boats only as fixed houseboats (this last is a noticeable product of the relaxation of restrictive labour laws within the EU).

More and more general harbours are using EU subsidies to turn themselves into up-market (comparatively speaking) marinas which, in Greece at any rate, charge local boats a preferential rate at the expense of the foreign tourist, for the attraction of whom the EU money was originally intended.

But one gets by. The chosen wintering ports change. And it has to be admitted that there is a type of live-aboard who does tend to foul the communal nest. Most of us tend to overlap onto the quay a bit, even if only temporarily while repairing

For wintering one can sometimes find a marina under construction where a reduced price can be negotiated. This is a view of Sibari in Calabria with only three yotties in residence.

something, for all live-aboard boats are encumbered. Some turn the quay into a junkyard. Others fall ill and cannot readily move on, or run out of funds and owe money, leading to their boat going rapidly downhill; as a class we have our share of personal disasters, and there is no welfare system to come and help.

In 1995/6 for example, many boats left Greek waters for Tunisia and Turkey, where they were made welcome. Greece had introduced an exorbitant scale of charges which led to open harassment by their Port Police (I have already referred to the incident of painting the guardrails), and though the worst effects were ameliorated, many found that a winter in Tunisia was a lot cheaper, the weather as well as the welcome was warmer.

Documentation

We have been taken to task by some readers of the first edition who had not yet set off deep cruising, for saying little about this subject, and several people at the early cruising symposiums, which we initiated, were clearly troubled by it.

There is a simple reason why we said nothing about it. Apart from the ex-communist bloc countries, documentation has never given us any real bother and we didn't think the subject merited space. There is no point in going minutely into it country by country because the detailed rules are constantly changing. Please let us reassure readers who are planning their voyages: Be sensible, but don't worry. The requirements are different in virtually every country, and often in different ports within the same country. Do not worry. I assume the

You never know what you'll meet and where. We come across a Viking long boat in Greece.

boat is properly registered in your own name, because boats registered in the name of companies in Panama, Guernsey, Gibraltar, etc. can get into difficulties, this being occasionally a signal of someone up to no good.

If the boat is in your name the formalities pertaining to the craft will give no trouble. They may take a long time, but time is not of the essence. You can save time if you make out copies (several) of your crew list. These lists should not only have the names in full of everyone on board but also passport numbers, dates and places of birth, maiden names (and once we were asked for names, dates and places of birth of our parents too). Do not worry. Stay calm.

We know of a Frenchman who cruised his yacht with an old British registration certificate of a yacht that had been scrapped. (The administration of the Small Ship Register encourages this, but the RYA dismiss this glitch as unimportant.) He had renamed his boat to match. He never had any trouble. You, being honest and essentially law-abiding, are not going to have any either.

No one has, so far, *ever* checked the number carved on our main beam, to see if it matches the ship's papers.

I assume you have proper passports that are in date. I assume you have taken the precaution of getting a visa for those countries who are scared to let you in without one, or who wish to extract the maximum cash from your visit. I assume you have found out if any vaccinations or inoculations are required, both for yourselves and any pets, and that you have the appropriate certificates. It's all tedious on occasions, but really quite simple. Do not worry.

If planning to go to both Israel and Arab countries, or if you wish to go to Northern (Turkish occupied) Cyprus and also want to go to Southern Cyprus or

Greece afterwards, then you can get a second passport in advance if you tell the passport office what you want to do. Greece cannot refuse entry under EU law to an EU citizen but they can be difficult. Don't mix the passports up, keep one for the sheep and the other for the goats.

Be careful about giving passage to persons of countries that are regarded as 'difficult' in the country you are heading for. Even this is not as bad as it sounds.

Stories

We arrived in Antigua with two South Africans on board in the days when the redoubtable Sergeant King was in charge of immigration there. Our friends wished to disembark and fly home. Within a short time, thanks to a friendly approach, our friends went ashore with the scourge of the Caribbean smiling happily and helping them with their baggage. People, even officials, are fundamentally approachable if you are tactful.

Some friends of ours embarked the young Greek boyfriend of their daughter for a short cruise and headed for Turkey without thinking. Their guest, when he discovered which harbour they were entering, was petrified. He expected to be decapitated or worse. The Turkish immigration officer told the quaking youngster he was very naughty to have come without a visa, then threw his arms round the boy's neck, kissed him and said 'Welcome to Turkey'.

Turkey now demands visas for Britons in retaliation for something they imagine Mrs Thatcher did to one of their diplomat's children. Visas can be obtained at the Port of Entry without any difficulty, and are more of an irritant than a penalty. Do not worry.

Some countries are beginning to demand evidence of third-party insurance cover. Not many. Italy is, I think, the only country to do it nationwide (get a certificate in Italian from your insurers), but some marinas are now demanding it as a condition of entry, not to the country, but to their *marina*. (Suppose you set the boat in the berth next to you on fire! France and Greece are the only places which we know to be affected.)

In all our cruising (except for ex-Iron Curtain countries) we have never been asked for documents issued by the port we have left, nor for de-ratting certificates, though once we were asked to produce evidence of good health. Any evidence. We wrote out our own certificate and stamped it with the ship's own 'official' stamp, which we put over the top of some left-over British postage stamps. It did the trick. Do not worry.

Check:

- Passports in date: visas.
- Boat registration.
- Boat insurance if applicable.
- Vaccinations and Inoculations.
- Yachtmaster or equivalent or evidence of personal competence (Europe only).

Remember that people do arrive in the most awkward countries improperly documented and still have a good time, provided they are not aggressive or tactless. So do not worry.

Celebrating the tenth anniversary of leaving England. Apart from the masthead dressing lines, the hoists from each upper spreader are the courtesy ensigns of all the countries we have visited, 23 in all. Note the precautionary use of two anchors, the prevailing wind in this harbour coming from the port beam.

We have made certain exempting clauses with respect to ex-Iron Curtain countries. It is likely these will be visited more and more in the future, and as they have not yet adapted their systems to the notion of freedom of passage, especially in yachts, you may find some difficulties. These are often soluble by the gift of a bottle of wine: costing (in Romania, for example) 80 pence, and well worth it.

One meets more and more yotties coming from these countries. One, Andreu, from Moldova, told us hair-raising stories of the problems he had getting permission to sail away from Odessa in the Ukraine in the boat he had built himself from government surplus items he had salvaged from the scrap-heap of an armament factory. (You do meet some interesting people in this mode of life.)

We have described in another book our experience of a recent impromptu visit to the port of Ismail in the Ukraine. They wouldn't let us enter the country, as we had no visas and could not go to Kiev to get them, but they were perfectly polite about it, and we could have obtained provisions and shelter if we had needed them. All we suffered was inconvenience.

In Romania, on the other hand, the bureaucracy was labyrinthine and byzantine: crooked in both senses of the word. The moral is that if visiting a country whose border forces are subject to political paranoia, you will need to have both patience and papers in apple-pie order, and probably have to drop dollar notes into various palms as well. This last is more difficult.

But *do not worry.*

Chapter Eleven

Misadventures

'... some accident that requires the help of all hands... which in most voyages doth happen.'

Crime

There are two sorts of relevant crime: those committed by yachtsmen and those against yachtsmen, with the occasional merger of the two. One of the features of long-cruising is its suitability as a way of life for the criminal who is either retired or resting. It is sad that in recent years the professional criminal has become aware of this: sad because inevitably the processes of identifying, tracking and arresting them will impinge on the freedoms of the cruising yottie.

When only a small number of retired criminals were involved the forces of international law and order did little, for attempts to track individuals would have been inordinately expensive. The occasional cigarette smuggler was arrested, but there was no great international co-operation for one country was not over-concerned about another's smuggling problems. But the alarming increase of narcotic abuse has brought yachtsmen into notice.

Drug smuggling is of two broad types: the highly professional operations of organised crime, and the more casual, small-scale activities of individuals. The 'casual' smuggler is of any nationality and can operate anywhere, though there is much activity close to the USA. The American authorities try hard, but they have a very difficult problem because of their closeness to some very anarchistic small states. Yachtsmen in the Caribbean become aware that Mr A, who was paid crew on the charter boat XYZ in 1990, appears in 1991 as the owner of a Swan 65. No-one checks on his sudden wealth; his boat is registered behind nominees in a British colony, and he is all set for a life of comfort. And a major contribution to his ability to enjoy the fruits of his dirty enterprise is made by the British government through its laws on colonial banking, company registration and ship registration.

These laws become a major factor in the activities of organised crime, and not only in its drug smuggling mode. Most of the hard-drug traffic in the Mediterranean and Caribbean occurs under the Red Ensign and there is no doubt that the British flag is falling into disrepute, to the inevitable disadvantage of British yachtsmen in general. Ownership of these yachts is vested in companies set up in Jersey, Guernsey or Gibraltar; the shares are held in the names of nominees, often living in Sark; the yachts are registered not only in these places but also in Southampton or London.

Laundering the proceeds takes place in many ways, but one is by buying and selling these yachts through certain brokers in the South of France, the transactions passing through banks in all the financially rotten parts of the world ie Switzerland, Lichtenstein, Luxembourg and the Channel Islands. A significant blow could be struck against organised crime by closing the secrecy loophole of company and ship registration in the Channel Islands and other British colonies. And our national ensign would enjoy a better respect.

That apart, most crime perpetrated by yachtsmen is petty, and typically against their fellows. French yachtsmen in the Caribbean have a poor reputation. This is hard on those pleasant, honest froggies who wish to enjoy civilized cruising, and in the Med, for example, these are more typical. What seems to have happened in the Caribbean was that, with the great expansion of yachting in France and the national hero-worship of such excellent seamen as Moitessier and Tabarly, many young Frenchmen set out to build cheap steel yachts for themselves. Hard-chine hulls could be seen a-building in the most unlikely rural sites all over France. Armed with a hundred kilos of pasta, a string of garlic, some salami and *vin de table*, they sailed for the palm trees with stars in their eyes and nearly empty pockets.

And then the money ran out. Jobs were not to be had. To return costs money, to go on to the South Seas costs money, and in a bind it becomes too easy to cut the painter on someone's Zodiac and sell it, and these are substantially untraceable. Though this activity is largely laid at the door of the French, others including the local people are not above a little of it. Given the fragmentation of the islands into dozens of little states, there is not much that can be done; the criminal can keep on the move.

So far as crime against the yottie is concerned, the wanderer is somewhat at the mercy of the petty pilferer. It is impossible to live in tropical heat and turn one's boat into a fortress: the open air is an essential ingredient. Fortunately there are few places where pilfering is a serious problem, for the more primitive the culture (assuming there is some culture), the more likely the inhabitant will have strong conceptions of hospitality and a lack of covetousness. Most of us try to steer clear of big cities. From the experiences of ourselves and friends, I think it unwise to leave a boat unwatched, even for short periods, in open harbours in big cities. By open harbours I mean those where there are no dock gates with police or Customs men controlling entry by the public. Typical among open harbours where care is needed are Barcelona, Baltimore (USA), Brindisi, Marseilles and Palermo, but there are many others. Most yacht marinas in or near a city are prime targets for thieves, and this particularly applies where the marinas are open to public access, such as Antibes and many others along the Riviera. This leads to boats in these marinas being fitted with intruder alarms, and given the intrinsic unreliability of marine electronics it means sleepless nights for all crews living aboard when these things go off semi-continuously. In fact, the intruder alarm when fitted to small craft goes off in error so often that no-one pays any attention.

In some countries, notably Italy where dishonesty is part of the culture, there is a very fierce desire to protect the property which a person has, even if he stole it from someone else in the first place. Marinas in Italy tend to have a more positive security system, sometimes leading to a sort of prison camp mentality. One, near Rome, was surrounded by a double chain-link fence, with vicious dogs running unleashed between them. There was only one gate, double locked, and a scrutiny before entry that stopped just short of body-searching. There was a

These Sunsail boats had been propped up on oil-drums. This is very bad practice and should not be done.

conscientious night patrol, but in spite of all this, thieves arrived by water one night and stripped several boats of their electronics. This marina, unlike some, welcomed live-aboards as reliable watchmen who actually paid the marina, not vice versa, for the privilege of keeping watch.

If you are frequently leaving your boat unwatched in any marina or large port, locking up becomes necessary. Doors and hatches in seagoing craft are generally stoutly made and good locks can be fitted. But these are not necessarily the whole answer because thieves are often adept at undoing them. It is worthwhile devising a complex door or hatch opening system that is apparently contrary to logic. We know of one case where such an entrance to a boat was attacked and battered without the raiders gaining entry, even though it had not been locked. For our own part, we have lost very little to the pilferer, which indicates that if sensible precautions are taken, too much worry probably attaches to the question. The total over the years was a teak-handled knife, a tape recorder that we left on deck while we were ashore, and two fenders which might have been badly made fast, and of all things, a steel derrick. Our total financial loss is probably less than the cost of a good lock. But note that we steer clear of cities.

Unfortunately one can no longer rely on scrupulous honesty anywhere in Europe. We have even had something stolen in a Greek island, something unthinkable twenty years ago. One point to watch in regard to petty theft: it does not pay to report it. Your chances of getting your property back are virtually nil, but to report it is to involve oneself with officialdom, sometimes to have one's freedom of movement restrained and, final indignity, in almost all countries the local Customs will assess you, the loser, as having imported the item and charge you duty on it, effectively multiplying your loss. This last unfair and unreasonable insult is the clincher.

The most common stolen artifact is an inflatable dinghy, with or without outboard motor. There seems to be a worldwide market for these items, and I am surprised the *Financial Times* does not list them under 'Commodities' with the day's range of buying and selling prices: 'The Zodiac market moved narrowly today with a fair supply from St Lucia which found ready buyers. Avons were in steady demand and gained 40. Metzeler deflated in early trading with a large batch of nearly new from Palermo, but recovered later to close the day 20 lower.' Normally inflatables are cut adrift from the parent yacht during the night. Old West Indies hands hoist their dinghies in at night, or else reeve wire painters, but these are difficult to make really secure to an inflatable. The ease with which they can be stolen and then hidden for later disposal is a very important factor in the choice of which type of tender to carry.

Liferafts are occasionally taken, for their cost is substantial, but as they are more easily traced they do not find such a ready market. Running rigging and on-deck gear is sometimes stripped from a yacht. In Brindisi this can be done by real experts while the crew are sleeping peacefully below. Brindisi is a bad port both from the point of view of real theft and pilfering, the latter being done both by local urchins and by the swarms of hitch-hikers waiting to embark on the ferries for Greece. The fact that Corfu suffers from thieves is due not so much to Greek dishonesty but almost entirely to young tourists. But it is in Italy that thieves have real chutzpah. At Palermo, thieves who had been locating the dinghy they wanted found to their dismay that the owners had chained it to the stern davits. They stole the davits too.

There is also an active market in whole yachts, mostly confined to those in quantity production, which are less easily distinguished one from another. The liability of having a particular type of yacht stolen is in direct proportion to its ready resale: so it does not necessarily pay to buy yachts with high resale values, which can anyway change.

In Antibes the yacht next to us, a German-owned Amel, was visited over several days, during the winter, by an overalled young man in a battered van, who did certain work aboard, and this aroused no suspicions. Nor was anyone alerted when the yacht sailed, ostensibly to the boatyard for slipping. It was by chance that a friend of the owner (who was at that time home in Germany) saw the yacht in Palma and went to greet his chum. He was an alert man, suspected something was wrong, phoned his friend and brought in the police. The thief was arrested, and it subsequently transpired that he had selected the yacht some time before and had negotiated a series of West Indian charters for her before actually committing the theft.

Many people contemplating long-cruising are concerned about piracy, which is the taking of a vessel or the robbery of crew, cargo or equipment on the high seas, ie away from harbour. This crime has been much played up by the press, particularly in the USA, to the level of mild paranoia. In the chandlery at Bahia Mar, Fort Lauderdale, I waited to be served while an American bought a rifle, a sub-machine gun, and two pistols for about $1200. While they were being gift-wrapped I enquired where he was bound with such an arsenal and was told the Virgin Islands. I could not help observing that he would be better off without them, which led to a frosty attitude on the part of the shopkeeper, who furnished, in season, many such armouries.

From which, you may gather, we are not armed. In my experience firearms are a positive liability; or to put it another way, gun-toting yotties have more problems from carrying weapons than the unarmed get by not doing so. For consider the question of how to use these weapons. 'To be a good gunner, you must learn it by practice.' Guns are killing weapons. It is no use having one unless you are prepared, instantly and without stopping to think, to point it at someone and fire to kill. The typical handgun is a very inaccurate weapon, and cannot be used to wound without seriously hurting. It is only possible to pump bullets in the general direction of the target and hope one of them will do sufficient damage to stop an assailant, if it is in fact an assailant. A rifle is not a close-quarters weapon (unless it has a bayonet: God help us) and is designed for comparatively accurate longer-range work. Anyone with any experience of naval gunnery will know of the great problems attaching to sighting from a platform moving randomly on three axes. Skilled naval gunners with complex control gear hardly ever hit anything: what chance has an excited amateur?

All these weapons must be kept clean, lightly oiled, and ready for instant use if they are to be effective. In many ports they must be declared, probably landed under police control and collected again before sailing. There are heavy penalties for transgressions of firearm laws, which differ from place to place so that one is never sure what they will be. In real life one is also faced with the problem of identifying an assailant as such. An American yachtsman (it is almost always Americans who get into trouble with guns) panicked and shot dead one of the crew of a Spanish trawler near Alboran. The trawler was approaching to swop fish for foreign cigarettes, a common practice at that time. That trigger-happy yachtsman became a sadder jailbird.

So how do you tell if the boat approaching is friendly or vicious? Do you shoot anyway? Hardly. And do you think that if they are real pirates they will be unprepared for your rather limited self-defence? They'll be ready, and they'll blast the hell out of you at the first shot, or ram you. The only people you will discourage by arms will be friendly ones.

We once went into Agios Andreas Bay at the southern end of Ithaca to find an American ketch the sole occupant. No doubt he was irritated at having his solitude spoiled, but the situation hardly called for his appearance on deck with a shotgun, telling us to get out of the bay as it was only big enough for one. It is the impulsive exploitation of the enhancement of power given by a weapon that is so dangerous in the hands of a person who is temporarily, or even partially, unstable. What did we do in Ithaca? We told him to grow up, and we anchored. He became quite friendly later. This story, which we have related from time to time, recently came back to us as having happened to someone else, but without convincing detail. I hope there are not really two gun-toting nuts around the Ionian Sea. I believe that the very ownership of a weapon fosters paranoia. If someone already has that tendency, it becomes more accentuated and even dangerous.

What about attacks in harbour? These do happen. Whereas we have no personal knowledge of any authentic example of piracy, we do know of people who have suffered personal injury in harbour. It is necessary to consider whether

BOUZOUKI SHOP,
CHIOS

these incidents would have been prevented with firearms. They all concerned intruders boarding a yacht. At least one of the yachts carried arms but had no chance of using them. Two of the three cases were murders, in St Vincent and in Port of Spain, Trinidad. That in Friendship Bay, Bequia was almost murder. Two of the yachts were American, one was British. It is impossible to be sure, but I believe that the mere possession of firearms would not have altered the outcome of any of these cases, where the murderers had been able to get to close quarters before being observed.

Do not make too much of these terrible events. They are regrettable and deplorable, but are not really as common as all that. Sadly, the St Vincent government do not appear to investigate or prosecute crime against foreigners with any energy whatsoever. Trinidad did at least produce and sentence a culprit. The whole thing is a question of prudence once again. Nothing will eliminate robbery and/or violence. But in places where it is known to occur, then some vigilance will reduce both its probability and its impact. Port of Spain is a big commercial port and not a noticeably congenial place for a yacht. But in Bequia one would be visited by a lot of native people, very friendly for the most part, some begging, some selling, but fundamentally law-abiding.

Do not display ostentatious wealth. Even modest possessions by North American or European standards are wealth beyond dreams for many of these people. If you have any doubts about a place, you have the means of leaving or you can take precautions. There is no call for paranoia, just observe a little, ask a little, get to know the local feeling.

What precautions? Do not leave dinghies in the water, or leave boarding ladders down, or ropes and fenders overside while at anchor. If you are very seriously worried about a place do not sleep on deck, and fasten hatches and large openings in a half-closed position that will allow ventilation but not admit a person. Take reasonable care, but do not reduce yourself to a fortress mentality all the time.

Places where theft is virtually unknown are the rural areas of Greece and Turkey. The more isolated and rural areas of southern Italy away from tourist centres, the Canary Islands away from tourist centres, the Azores except for Punta Delgada, the out-islands in the Bahamas and the rural parts of Yugoslavia. In all other areas it pays to take at least elementary precautions against petty theft.

Theft of all types is endemic in the French and Italian Rivieras, and in or near any Italian town of more than 20,000 inhabitants or a Spanish one of more than 50,000. In Athens, in Egypt, and to a lesser extent Tunisia. In Morocco. In the touristy parts of Portugal.

Accidents

'Master, let us breathe and refresh a little, and
sling a man overboard to stop the leakes.'

Not all damage to boat or person is caused by a criminal. Mishaps happen. In our experience most accidents between craft are trivial, most are clearly defined as to fault, and in most cases the defaulter makes amends instantly and without quibble. Three times we have suffered minor damage while made fast. Once in

Boulogne from a member of the Royal Motor Yacht Club, who departed shouting 'Sorry, old man' and who did not answer our letter. Twice by Italians who volunteered immediate compensation and paid in full. The problem is that chasing compensation in foreign countries, in foreign languages and via post is a most unrewarding and frustrating pastime. Better to do a modest deal on the spot while the other fellow's conscience is still troubling him, than to hold out for full and complete indemnity. Most yachtsmen are decent types, thank God, and long may it last.

Major damage is a different matter. Here insurance is a very definite help, for even if the perpetrators cannot be traced or brought to book, underwriters can be expected to settle in the terms of the policy, or even a little more in some cases. If you commit the damage yourself, to another vessel or a person, then you will probably appreciate being insured. This is a mischance all the more likely as yachting centres get more crowded and increasing numbers of novices take to the sea with certificates obtained at evening classes, fondly believing they are competent. To sail without good third party cover is foolhardy and anti-social, especially as more and more people new to the sport bring a motor-car mentality to sea with them. One must also remember the fortune that many modern yachts represent in money terms, and the high cost of even cosmetic repairs.

Personal accidents

Minor damage to the person is discussed in Chapter Fifteen, which is mainly about prevention within on-board resources, rather than even minor first aid. But one can have major accidents or mishaps that require surgery or hospital treatment, and though this cannot be considered a minor matter it will have to go in that chapter too, together with some comments on health insurance. Not all accidents to the person happen on board, or even to your own crew. Everyman's mishap diminisheth me, to bastardize a good quotation. We once had a difficult time helping fellow British yotties coping with the problems involved when a singlehanded yachtsman was killed in a motor accident in Italy. The British Consul at Florence was not merely unhelpful, he was positively discourteous.

Laurel and I frequently travel about together in little excursions from our ship, and it is always a possibility that an accident to one would involve the other too. Such accidents do not have to be fatal to be bothersome to strangers. And the problems ensuing, if temporary neighbours whom you have only met the day before, or local officials, have to trace your relatives or whatever, are so very great that some small precaution should be taken.

Each short-handed cruising yacht should have displayed close to the main hatch a small, semi-permanent notice saying, 'In case of urgency or difficulty, contact...'. One should also leave a will in a place of safety, and in the case of couples (because the likelihood of both dying at the same time is greater than for shore-dwellers) consult a lawyer about whether special clauses should cover this aspect. If so, draw up compatible wills.

On a less gloomy note, it is a good idea to have a square foot or so of surface, close to the main hatch, painted in blackboard paint. We leave messages on it in chalk, or at appropriate moments write up announcements of pure joy.

Accidents at Sea: the Legal Position

I have mentioned already the obligation to go to the assistance of a vessel in distress. This is detailed in Section 6 of the [British] Maritime Conventions Act of 1911, the terms of which will have been enacted by all nations signatory to the Convention. We are obliged, so far as we can without danger to our own vessel, to render assistance to every person (even if such a person be a subject of a foreign State at war with Her Majesty) who is found at sea in danger of being lost. Failure to do so is a misdemeanour. This is further amplified by the Merchant Shipping (Safety Convention) Act 1949, which should be read. (It is too long and detailed to include here: copies can be had from Her Majesty's Stationery Office.)

The procedure for dealing with casualties on board is in Section 73 of the Merchant Shipping Act 1970. Casualties (and note that the ship herself can be a casualty) must be reported to the Department of Transport as soon as possible, and in any case not later than 24 hours after arrival at the next port. The report should contain a description of the incident, give details of injuries to personnel and damage to the ship, the name and official number of the ship, her position, next port of call and ETA, and should go to any DoT Marine Office, or to the Marine Directorate at Sunley House, 90 High Holborn, London WC1V 6LP.

Births, deaths and marriages

Also coming under 'accidents' we have births, deaths and marriages at sea. The law covering deaths is given in the Merchant Shipping (Returns of Births and Deaths) Regulations 1979. A master is required to make a return of births in a ship, or of deaths in or from a ship. It should be made as soon as practicable (but within six months) to either a Marine Superintendent in the UK, a British Consular Office in foreign countries, or the equivalent of a Marine Superintendent in a Commonwealth country. There will also be local procedures if a body is landed at a port (the Regulations warn), but the UK regulations apply whether or not the body is landed, buried at sea, or not recovered.

The official record of a birth or death is in the register entry made by the Registrar following the receipt of such a return from a Master. Marriages on board have a legal basis only when conducted by an authorized person, and when the ship is in the territory covered by that person's authority, and the official record would be held under the law of that territory. A British shipmaster is not, and never has been, an authorized person, and there is no UK machinery for recording marriages at sea. An entry in a log book is not, of itself, legal evidence of a marriage.

There is no legal obligation to recover a body sighted at sea, because of the dangers of capsizing, disease etc, but sightings should be reported to the nearest authorities. Do so by radio, if possible. If reporting by person, the report in a foreign country should be made to the British Consul in the hope of avoiding local problems. That is the official position; there must always be a strong incentive not to sight bodies at sea.

If wrecked, the yachtsman is normally not entitled to be treated as a ship-wrecked mariner for the purpose of repatriation, and any in this unfortunate difficulty would be treated by a Consul as a normal distressed British subject. And God help them if my experience of British Consuls is anything to go by. It is worth noting that while on the high seas a British registered ship is considered an extension of British Law, but once she enters the territorial waters of another state the situation is not so clear, particularly if citizens of that state or their property are affected.

Loss of Skipper

A particular disaster that worries a lot of wives, mates and less experienced members of a crew of two, is the loss of the skipper, whether permanently overboard or temporarily through injury or sickness while at sea. It is such a real worry to some that it justifies a word or two.

The crew must be able to handle the craft, even if only under power or with reduced sail. Even for a novice this is not so impossible as it might seem, especially when needs must. Some people are afraid to discuss this, particularly wives with their husbands, but it is worth making the effort because the conclusions will never be forgotten.

In any event there are a few simple precautions to be taken. In big ships it is normal for the radio room to be given the ship's position every watch so that in emergency they have an approximate position always at hand. In a yacht I always plot the position at least once every four hours in the oceans, and at least every two in soundings, whether by fix or DR. I always have in the ready drawer charts for diversionary ports to which I might have to go for some emergency, and my plan for the voyage lists some of them. Because Laurel is the Met Officer she is always aware of wind patterns and the weather; because she often works out a sun-sight alongside me, she knows how to do it; because I insist she uses the VHF from time to time she is not nervous on the radio (and a lot of people are). She is not so hot on engineering but she can start, stop and use the engine.

Loss of anyone aboard is a terrible disaster. Its effect and the awful fear of it can be mitigated by a discussion and decisions of what to do if the disaster happens. That is probably enough to make sure it never does.

Internal Damage to the Yacht

The water's coming in Even with good care and maintenance, things do go wrong in ways that are dangerous. I once had a shaft coupling disintegrate off Ushant. It had been badly machined by someone I was entitled to expect to do it well, and the chatter of the bad fit destroyed the metal. The shaft dropped back leaving a 5 cm diameter hole through which the water came in gallons per second. One of my crew on that occasion was a professional cabinet maker: I have never seen a wooden plug made so fast, but it took a lot of getting in against the water pressure. It could not be put in the outer end. The lesson I drew from this was to have ready-made plugs for all the openings in the hull.

Fire down below Perhaps the most frightening possibility is fire, particularly at sea. We had one in *Fare Well*'s engine room and I was fortunate in having been trained in ship fire-fighting. The experience is instructive. I had fitted a ventilating fan above the batteries, and the exhaust side had Tannoy brand ducting secured by clips supplied by the manufacturers. The ducting consisted of a wire spiral thinly covered by plastic. In the compartment there was a deckhead-mounted Noxfire automatic extinguisher.

At about 0330 when somewhere northwest of Corsica (we always have a bad time round there), sailing in a very rough sea at the tail end of a gale, Laurel, who was on watch, called me to say there was a smell of burning. I opened the hatch to the engine room and found the whole space full of flame and smoke. I shut the hatch; the fire was clearly beyond the capacity of extinguishers and I naturally thought that the automatic one had gone off but had failed to cope. In fact, it never did go off.

After some time I managed to get the fire under control using a very fine spray of sea water. As the smoke cleared I saw the cause. The ducting had fallen out of the clips, which were clearly not adequate for the extra strains of violent motion in bad weather (a feature that is distressingly common in items designed by whizz-kids who have never had a wet shirt). The ducting had dropped on to the battery terminals, rolled about and soon worn away its thin plastic coating; the wire had shorted across the terminals, igniting everything nearby, helped by the contents of a plastic can of paraffin that I had been idiot enough to stow there.

Lessons Learnt

(Some of them I knew already, but needed a reminder.)

- Cheap and flimsy fastenings just will not cope with the violent movement of a small boat in bad seas.
- Contrary to popular advice, it is a good precaution to cover batteries, but the covers must permit the passage of gases. A strong plastic mesh would be effective.
- Paraffin and any cans of any fuel, particularly in plastic containers, should be on deck.
- Automatic extinguishers, even when in date, cannot be relied on and are therefore not worth the money.
- Butyl insulated wiring, specified by Lloyds as being fire resistant, burns as merrily as other, less expensive, plastics but is more difficult to extinguish.
- Our thick-walled plastic diesel fuel lines did not ignite or melt, even though damaged. This may be because the engine was running and the tubing was cooled by the flow of oil in it.
- The sort of fire extinguishers that can be carried in a small craft, while adequate for a minor outbreak in the early stages, cannot cope with a serious blaze.
- Crew intending to cruise a lot need to have actual experience of putting out electrical (the most frequent cause) and fuel fires using only a water spray. Not a jet, but a spray of as fine droplets as one can get. It is cheap and effective, but it is a definite skill which the long-cruising yachtsman should acquire.
- Boiled batteries do not work.
- The mess from a fire is horrible, and very hard to clean up.
- We were in more physical danger from the fumes of burning plastic battery cases, wiring insulation etc) than we were from heat and flames.

Some Brief Comments on Fighting Fires in Small Craft

'Captain, we are fowle on each other and the shippe is on fire.'

The nature of fire

To start, a fire needs three essential elements: fuel, oxygen and a source of heat. I think that for our purpose we can ignore some of the more esoteric chemical fires which the full-time fireman may have to deal with, and consider the more simple ones. In a yacht there are fuels galore for a fire: diesel oil, plastic linings, foam upholstery, the resin in fibreglass, paints, wood, cooking fat and gas to name the more obvious ones.

Heat is necessary in two ways: the fuel has to be raised to its ignition temperature, below which it will not burn. This varies with the material, and for some is remarkably low. In addition a source of heat has to be applied (even if momentarily) at a temperature known as the flash point and this triggers the flame. This also varies with the material and again can be quite a low temperature.

To extinguish a fire, break the triangle of fuel, oxygen and heat. One can remove the fuel, cut off the supply of oxygen or lower the temperature of whatever is burning, or preferably do a combination of these. Even if the flames are put out, if the temperature of the fuel is not lowered below its ignition temperature the fire can re-start. We remove the fuel by, for example, throwing it overboard. Very effective, but sometimes not practicable. We can remove the oxygen by smothering the fire, with a fire blanket or foam, for instance. We can cool the fuel with water or certain chemicals.

Fire extinguishers

These are essentially for first aid. They are useful and necessary to provide a very quick means of dealing with minor outbreaks which have been detected in the early stages. Of course they are also helpful even with major fires, for in these circumstances every little helps.

Given that their chief effectiveness is against small fires, one should choose extinguishers that do not themselves cause a great deal of damage, inconvenience or mess. In every case that I have seen a dry powder extinguisher used on a small fire, it has caused more mess and damage than the fire. This experience cannot be extrapolated indefinitely because the fire, if unchecked, would obviously have gone on to cause a great deal of damage, but it does contain a lesson. One should also get an extinguisher that is easy to use. Instructions to beat the top on the floor, shake for a minute, then point away from the fire for five seconds are too complex to remember, and far too difficult to absorb if on the edge of panic.

Extinguishers with certain chemicals are dangerous to the user. Carbon tetrachloride (Pyrene) is a close and poisonous relative of chloroform, and must not be inhaled for any length of time, especially if there is any alcohol in the body. There are extinguishers loaded with halene or Halon, an inert gas similar to the freon used in refrigerators. We used it when careless welding in the engine room of *Hosanna* set alight some rags soaked in spilled diesel oil. It was extremely effective; only one squirt was required. It is, however, supposed to affect the ozone layer several miles up, and is to be banned before long. It has already been so in some countries. The gas is much heavier than air; no one has yet explained how it gets up to the ozone layer since it does not rise! Yes, I know all about the Brownian diffusion of gases, but that does not necessarily apply in an infinite atmosphere. Carbon dioxide and Halon are similar in effect and very good material in a boat. Both are very heavy gases and do no damage. Because of weight they do not leak away from the boat, as they would do in a caravan, for example. Both are very effective against fat fires in the galley. It is possible to use some of the contents on a small fire and still have the remainder usable if you are unlucky enough to have another; a very important point at sea where replacements are unobtainable. They both work on all oil fires, but do not cool the fuel, so after putting out the flames that has to be done. The failure to cool means that they are not so good for dealing with fires in carbonaceous or solid materials, unless some other method of cooling is subsequently used. Both replace oxygen so you need to watch out you can go on breathing.

Foam extinguishers are really only for oil and petrol fires. They make a horrible mess and do not cool effectively. They need a certain skill to be fully effective and are probably not really suitable for small yachts.

Automatic extinguishers usually work by having a fusible plug which melts in heat, or by having an electronic actuator which senses smoke. I have known the former go off by accident, and also to fail to go off, but I have never heard of a case on a boat where they went off as promised. In my view they are a snare and a delusion and are best avoided. I have no field experience of the other type in action, but I mistrust electronics in small craft. I have rather more faith in my wife's nose.

So, what sort do I have? I have five Halon. They are easy to see if up to pressure and ready to work. One must be sure to renew extinguishers according to the makers' recommendations. In my professional career I fought two very serious fires at sea, and have spent much of my life since thinking about the problems. I disapprove strongly of the banning of Halon as a result of 'Green' pressure. It should be permitted for use at sea. There are alternative fire-fighting techniques for use on shore which are not available to the ship-firefighter. When off-shore, and with no outside help available, the seaman is *entitled* to use the very best material available. This is undoubtedly Halon. To forbid its use at sea is tantamount to sentencing seamen to death. Let's be green, yes, but with some common sense.

Any other firefighting materials? Yes, a fire blanket is worth keeping, both to smother a small fire or to use as a means of removing burning material. It's cheap and has nothing to go wrong. But remember a blanket does not cool the fuel: this must still be done, and very quickly. Sprinkler systems, which ought really to be called spray systems, are worth installing in large yachts, especially in machinery spaces when it may not always be possible to get in to fight a fire. They give off a spray of very fine droplets of water, usually sea water. As their effect is not carefully aimed they do a fair amount of devastation, particularly to furnishings, so in my view are not recommended for automatic use, when they could be expected eventually to go off unasked.

For an automatic system in the engine room I would prefer Halon or carbon dioxide, but remember that engines cannot run on it. If the access is down a hatch, do not go leaping gaily down when the fire is out. There will be no oxygen for you to breathe, and maybe toxic smoke as well. Again the burning material will not be cooled, and could therefore reignite if the gas is dispersed.

Big fires

In the context we define this as a fire beyond the capacity of your hand-held extinguishers. It may not be very large, but perhaps it is very intense and very soon could be large. In a yacht there is only one firefighting material available in sufficient quantities: water. You are surrounded by it, but to succeed you must use it skilfully. Water can be used against almost any type of fire if used well.

Fire Brigades are occasionally called to deal with ship fires in port. Very soon there are dozens of 3 inch hoses snaking aboard, and before long the weight of water in the vessel either sinks her or destroys her hydrostatic stability by creating free surface which capsizes her in her berth. The Bootle Fire Brigade hit the jackpot in 1953 with the *Empress of Canada*. It certainly puts the fire out, which enables the firemen to call it a success. It usually writes off the ship, puts a busy berth out of action, and may cause more financial damage than letting the fire burn itself out.

At sea one is rather obsessed with preserving the ship, so make sure every bit of water let into her will be used to the maximum advantage. The jet of water used so often and so dramatically on fires in buildings has a point in enabling firemen to get water to the seat of a blaze they could not otherwise reach. It also blasts apart solid material and cools it. In its place, it is the right way of doing things. In a ship, and especially in a small ship, it is very seldom the right way. Notice I do not say 'never' or 'always': there is no such conception in fire-fighting. Water serves the important purpose of cooling. Its most effective way of doing this is not by conducting heat away but by evaporating, which uses up a very large amount of heat energy. In most circumstances, therefore, it pays to deliver the water in an ideal form for instant evaporation: this is as a very fine spray. A fine spray also acts as a sort of curtain. As the fire uses oxygen, it draws in more air and feeds itself. The spray curtain, though not a complete screen, reduces the flow of air to the fire. As the water droplets evaporate efficiently they turn almost instantly to steam which, because it has many times the volume of the water it came from, helps to create a quite effective barrier to air.

Jets of sea water conduct electricity well. A perfect spray of fine droplets, because the droplets are separate from each other, will not conduct. In practice, of course, a spray is never perfect, but I have taken part in experiments showing that a fine spray of sea water can approach to 75 cm away from a high-voltage source without the nozzle giving more than a mild tingle to a person holding it with bare, wet hands. It is not for repetition with backyard lash-ups: it is potentially a very dangerous thing to do and the experiments were very carefully controlled, but it demonstrates that in the presence of low-powered electrics it is acceptable as a fire-fighting method.

The conclusion I draw from these last three paragraphs is that a fine spray can be used effectively against any likely fire aboard a yacht. Ideally the spray should be under some pressure: it can be pumped by hand using a galley pump. If enough pressure is obtainable the JetSpray hose 'gun' used aboard many boats for washing down decks and paintwork is good. If pressure is low, then a shower fitting is better than nothing. A rose from a watering can is good, but something of a rarity aboard a yacht. Rather than chuck buckets of water over a small fire (which can actually help it spread) I have found that dribbling water from a sponge can be more effective.

How do you use a spray? The spray's weakest effect is against solid materials. In this case use it to drench the burning items and to keep wet the adjacent area. Even when the flames are out, continue cooling until the surfaces stay wet. If in doubt remove charred matter with a knife or coarse rasp and cool again because it might still be very hot inside.

Galley fires

Of course halon, CO_2 or the fire blanket are best used first. One must also cut off the supply of fuel to the stove. A lot depends on the state of a fat fire. If it is entirely inside a saucepan (and one should endeavour always to use deep cooking utensils in a boat) put a lid on it and cool the pot down. Don't let any water get in the fat or it will spatter explosively. If the fat has spilled and spread, then we have an oil fire.

Electrical fires

There is not really any such thing: electricity provides the initiating heat and flash point and it is other matter that burns. The problem is usually that the electricity goes on supplying a source of great heat, which hinders attempts to extinguish the fire and also constitutes a hazard. Usually the trigger of the fire is a shortcircuit, which may or may not be arcing and therefore may not be easy to see. Try to identify the problem point and cut off the power to it. Smoke can prevent one from being able to see, so this is not always by any means easy. It is possible to use a spray curtain to contain the smoke to some extent, enabling one to see the seat of the fire. Apart from the regenerative potential of a continuing short-circuit, this type of fire usually turns into one of the others. A particular problem is that when plastic electrical insulation burns it gives off poisonous fumes.

Oil fires

If the area of oil that is burning is large, use the fine spray curtain as if one was holding an umbrella against a very strong wind, and slowly sweep the surface of the oil to try to reduce the burning area and to 'gather' the burning part into an ever-decreasing area. Do not leave any burning patches behind; go back and sweep again, slowly. You are both cooling it and reducing the oxygen supply. You will not succeed quickly. Try not to use more water than the fire is evaporating. If the oil is sloshing about in a moving boat this can be helpful because it is assisting cooling somewhat, but it does make containment with the spray more difficult. If there is a lot of oil (and water) in the bilge try to pump it out; ecology comes a poor second just now. The oil, even if hot, is unlikely to cause problems in the pump. It is important to cut off as soon as possible any supply of fresh oil to the fire, so it may be necessary to concentrate on cooling the site where the isolating cocks are before tackling the main blaze, if more oil is actually leaking into it.

Smoke

It is a sad thing that many of the comforts of modern life produce toxic smoke when they burn, for example fabrics, upholstery and mattresses, plastic linings. Others produce carboniferous smoke which is not necessarily poisonous but which stops us breathing. Incomplete combustion can produce carbon monoxide which is poisonous. Sea water mixed with battery acid gives off chlorine, which is deadly as well as choking.

Some of these toxic gases are lighter than air, and in fire conditions, when they are hot, can be expected to rise. Under most conditions it pays to approach fires giving off a lot of smoke by keeping as near the deck as possible. Wet cloth over mouth and nostrils will filter particles, but will not stop most toxic gases. It hardly seems worth lumbering up a boat with breathing apparatus, but if necessary, it may be possible to improvise with a diving face mask and some tubing.

Of course all these are easy at a fire-fighting school. The important thing about actual fire-fighting, when every fire is different, is to be aware of the principles, to know the methods (and if possible to have exercised their use) and then to use your intelligence. The tradition of rushing to a fire is a very good one, but on arrival do not go mad and waste your resources. A few seconds to determine the nature of the fire and to plan the battle will be amply repaid.

The point at which you call for outside help depends on what help is available, what means you have to call it, and the relationship of the fire to your resources. If in doubt about your ability to cope and help is available, take a moment to call it. Most port authorities insist on a Fire Brigade being called, because they have an obligation to protect other vessels. They usually have power to tow away a burning ship to a safe berth and similar draconian rights. In these circumstances, ie in port, you must summon help, but unless the fire is beyond your control remember you are still in command of the ship.

In Case of Fire

- Call the whole crew.
- Get to the fire quickly, but calmly.
- Determine the generative centre of the fire.
- Assess the dangers of toxic gases and take precautions.
- Cut off any outside supply of fuel, or potential fuel.
- Select your fire-fighting apparatus.
- Attack the generative centre if it can be reached. If not, determine your route to it. *It is important to attack the centre.*
- Keep on until flames are out.
- Thoroughly cool the previously burning material.

Check at frequent intervals afterwards that you have not overlooked any hot spots that are smouldering.

'The fire is out, God be thanked.'

Dismasting

Other mishaps to the yacht involve the loss of mast, and canvas. We carry enough spare or alternate sails to get by, perhaps less efficiently but nevertheless practically, if some are blown out. Loss of a mast is more serious, and is best dealt with by getting them strong enough at the start. The extra cost will probably be less than the excess on one's insurance policy. Cruising boats should not go around with the bendy fishing rods sported by the racing folk. It helps to have a two-masted rig too, but only if there is no triatic stay. (I am not sure triatic stays contribute very much anyway.)

What to do if you lose a mast is very well covered in salty books on seamanship. Racing yachtsmen write about it frequently in magazines, but mostly they have large crews of gorillas to heft spars about. All the more reason for the cruising man to consider his double-strength masts and rigging, and then double again to be on the safe side.

Yes, I have been dismasted. Twice. Once while racing, and once recently in *Hosanna*, and both in almost exactly the same place off the Kentish Knock Light Vessel. Racing, we were grossly overcanvassed and deserved it. Recently *Hosanna*'s solid wood foremast had rotted round a knot under the paint, and the vibrations of motoring (yes!) into a short, steep sea brought it all down. At 0400 of course. The two of us managed to get all 400 kg of it back inboard, and we continued south to Ramsgate. We have a steel mast now. No mucking about.

Lightning

During the various talks we have given we have been surprised at the interest shown in lightning at sea. *Fare Well* was struck once, and Bill was struck once before in a small warship; it is one of those very rare sea-going experiences which seems to fascinate everyone.

Quite a long while ago *Yachting Monthly* had a correspondence on what policy to adopt when entering a violent thunderstorm, and one writer advocated donning rubber gloves and boots. Bill, being rather a rude sort of sailor, wrote in, suggesting that someone had forgotten to include a condom. The then Editor, Des Sleightholme, doyen of yachting wits, wrote back that he felt the comment a little ripe for his readers, and finished with the following:

> *The lightning flashed, the thunder crashed,*
> *The mate of the watch turned pale,*
> *For St Elmo's fire struck his rubber attire*
> *The moment he touched the rail.*

What happens in a lightning strike? It is St Elmo's fire (a brilliant display from the masthead looking like a 'sparkler' type of firework), that one is more likely to encounter, especially in a steel boat. I was on deck both times when struck, and it was difficult to assess exactly what was happening. Both times there was an enormous display, several metres across, of St Elmo's fire at the masthead, and it went on some time. In *Fare Well* (then in the Gulf Stream) the sparking increased rapidly in intensity as I watched. I felt the sensation usually described as one's 'hair standing on end', even though I was wearing a cap. It was an extraordinarily strong sensation. It developed into a feeling of being lifted off the ground a few inches, of stopping breathing, of being held by the back of the neck like a rabbit, of being absolutely unable to move at all. Those below felt nothing.

During this time I was aware that the sparking at the masthead had turned into a brilliant ball of light about seven metres in diameter, and that the rigging was glowing white. Suddenly, as if by throwing a switch, it all turned off. I fell to the deck in a state of shock, and all the fire and sparks at the masthead disappeared. Notice that I have given no time-scale for these events. I was not aware of any sensation of time passing. It is possible the whole sequence took place in a second, it might have taken ten or twenty; I have no idea.

What was the damage to a steel boat?

To me personally, nothing that a good breakfast could not put right. We all had headaches, but there are few things that do not yield to a good breakfast. The problem was: no breakfast yet. The only interior part of the boat affected was the wiring, which suggests to me that the current flowed in the skin of the boat and set up a strong magnetic field that induced current into some, but not all, of the wiring. It must have done so at great speed, for in some cases the wire had melted before the fuse had blown. Generally wires melted or insulation blew open at sharp corners, and the damage took the form of a directional blast along the wire. It was as if the current had a linear momentum and could not negotiate the tight bend, mounted the banking and left the track like a racing car. Some physicists I have discussed this with deny that such an effect is possible, but I have seen it, and I have found one scientist who says there is some evidence that very violent flashes of current have what he called a 'plasma effect'. Well now.

Question: Was that a strike or a very bad attack of St Elmo? Answer: Who knows? Next question: What can one do about it?

If it was just very bad St Elmo, then in the thunderstorm going on at that time, it suggests to me that a good electrical path up to the top of the mast, together with a good area of conductor in the water (we had recently had a spectacular grounding in coral which had taken a lot of paint off our keel), inhibits a strike by organising a very effective discharge. If it was a proper strike, then compared with the devastated condition of both wooden and GRP boats that have been struck (all I have seen have taken fire), I cannot help feeling that a boat built of a good conducting material has advantages for the tropics.

What else was damaged? All the electronic fittings on the mainmast were blown apart, but to my amazement I found that some of the instruments them-selves (those which had been switched off) survived the blow. All the electronics on the mizzen mast, including the Decca radar, survived. Our radio sets all survived (they were switched off, and their aerial plugs removed: my practice in storms). Several electric motors did not. The stator coils in the generator had to be re-energised. As for the standing rigging, it appeared to be undamaged, possibly because the current was flowing over the surface rather than inside the wire, and of course the wire was soaking wet in the heavy rain, which may have cooled it. Anyway it survived several more years of use and abuse.

There was one other important effect which does not go under the heading of damage. The whole ship became highly magnetised and the compass was wildly in error. Fortunately we had logged the direction of the swell a couple of hours before the storm, so we had an angular reference. Without that, in completely overcast conditions that lasted for days, and 400 miles from land, we would have had absolutely no idea of which way to go. It turned out the compass deviation was about 90° to start with, but within an hour this had fallen to 35°. A week later it was about 15°, but it took three months to fall below 5°. It never did return to its former state; after about six months we adjusted the magnets to remove the last couple of degrees.

It wasn't much fun clearing up the mess, but it was a fascinating intellectual exercise trying to sort it all out. All in all I feel there is not enough objective evidence in existence to justify any heavy expenditure on this problem. One can, however, take the simple precautions which follow. At least they won't do any harm. And doesn't it pay to keep the log up to date?

In a GRP boat or a wooden one, there is a lot to be said for having a bond between the sea water and the top of the mast. Of course the standing rigging does this if the mast is not metal, the only link required being between the chain plates and the water. The reason for such a bond is to keep the electric current flow on the outside of the boat.

Thunderstorms in the tropics, and also in the Med, can be very much more violent than we in temperate zones are used to. One hazard is sheeting rain of such intensity that visiblity is nil, and even the radar cannot cope. Another is the huge potential difference between the atmosphere and the sea, we once counted 42 lightning flashes within one random minute. It is only when this potential difference is unable to disperse peacefully that it runs riot and produces strikes. During a night thunderstorm one will often see St Elmo's fire. This dispersed discharge is helping to prevent a more violently damaging strike.

Emergencies Outside the Boat

These are emergencies which can lead to the abandonment of the enterprise, its interruption or a temporary trip home for one of the crew. Illness of a close relative, for example. It really is impossible to give advice to cover so many different problems in so many possible places, and at widely varying times. We have only had to make two out of routine or emergency trips home in 22 years, one from a Greek island, and one, half-expected, from southern France. I would counsel maintaining a contingency fund of cash on board to cover both fares and additional costs that will be entailed in such an event, if there is any chance of it occurring. It is possible that a real family emergency while cruising the South Pacific could be ruinous. (See Finance chapter.)

The Panic Bag

Having advised that a good rigid dinghy is in many respects better than an inflatable liferaft, I have to remind you that the latter does have a survival pack of sorts on board. Therefore if you use a rigid dinghy as a lifeboat, you should have a pack to help you survive. We call ours the panic bag. Some people object to the use of the word panic in this context, saying that it is the last thing one should be aware of in this circumstance, but I disagree. Actually using the word reminds one of the danger of panic, and inhibits its formation.

Ours actually consists of two bags: the First Panic Bag, which is kept in the dinghy on passage, and the Second which is kept reasonably handy for grabbing if there is time. For those with an inflatable liferaft, it might be worth comparing my lists with the contents of the provided survival pack, and making up a bag to contain the difference. (You cannot check the raft's pre-packed supplies: they aren't always as promised.)

Our lists are based on consultation with a survivor friend, and also my own 600 ocean miles in an open boat.

The First Panic Bag

4 x 8 pint water in opaque plastic bottles
2 strong drinking cups (Melaware)
4 red flares, 4 orange smoke day markers
Torch, spare bulb, spare batteries
200 multivitamin pills in plastic jar
100 Horlicks tablets
1 lb boiled sweets
Swiss Army knife, dinner knife, spoon
Tweezers
Small compass, mirror
Needles and thread
Cotton wool
Small bottle TCP antiseptic
Tube of Aureomycin antibiotic cream
100 tablets Tetracyclin
Tube of sun screen ointment
Seasick pills
Sponge (bailer is already in dinghy)
2 small hand towels
2 'space blankets'
300 ft codline
Fishing line, spoons, hooks
Greek style foul-hooks for fishing
Greek 7-pronged harpoon head (a barbed miniature Poseidon's fork)
Gaff for fishing
Set of small chartlets in a plastic bag
Survival type solar still (RAF surplus type)

The Secondary Panic Bag

2 inflatable cushions
2 single blankets
2 wool sweaters
3 sq yds 4 oz canvas
Some fresh lemons in foil
2 parachute flares
Small funnel

Candles, matches in screw-top jar
Araldite (epoxy glue)
More boiled sweets
4 more pints water
More sunscreen ointment
8 assorted tins of food
Can-opener
2 pairs sunglasses
Bucket

Items which deteriorate must be replaced when time-expired. And let's hope that, like us, you get twenty odd years of cruising and never have to use your bag.

Chapter Twelve

Navigation

'If you don't know where you are going you will probably end up somewhere else.' — Peter and Hull, The Peter Principle

Being a professional Navigator, I cannot help putting in my two pennyworth on the subject, especially as all those who can row a boat seem nowadays to set themselves up as experts. Many people I have talked to who are contemplating the cruising life but have so far cruised only local waters, have expressed nervousness about their navigation. They need have no fear if they are prudent.

This is not a navigation primer, but I can add something to what can be found in any good book on navigation; involving points that have particular relevance to long-cruising.

Navigation has in common with medicine that the experienced practitioners have set up an elaborate mystique to defend their monopoly, and frighten off would-be amateur interlopers. In medicine the process seems to be strengthening itself, but I am glad to say that among navigators there is now a much healthier attitude. You do not need to be BCh., FRCS, to put a couple of stitches in a cut, and you certainly do not need a Maths degree to get an astronomical position line.

I pay homage to a lady, the Blessed Mary Blewitt, whom I consider the first person to write for the layman about navigation succinctly, sensibly and well. And for choosing to include in her book *Navigation for Yachtsmen* an Appendix on compass adjusting, by another expert, that is a lesson in clarity.

Types of navigator

To return to the problems of the far-ranging navigator. First decide what type of navigator you are: there are two broad types, those who shit when they can see land, and those who shit when they can't. It is rare to find anyone fitting neither category, and usually such a person is too unintelligent to recognize danger. There are a few who fit both categories and stay at home.

The first type tends to favour navigational aids that reassure them of perils comparatively close to; ie radar and echo-sounder, while not bothering much about accuracy when they are over 100 miles from the nearest danger. The second type, however, are nervous without frequent fixes, and end up with so many electronic aids that their masts look like Christmas trees.

Electronics

What is an old fashioned navigator? Answer: someone (not you, of course) who uses methods that were out of date before you started. I had always proudly considered myself an old-fashioned navigator (though I preferred the word 'traditional'), and then two things happened.

First I came to notice that there was a blank spot the size of a penny in the centre of any page I was reading. This is due to 'navigator's eyeball'. It is the result of having 4300 sunsights in my work-book, and though I have always taken reasonable care, the sun would sometimes flash out from behind a cloud and bounce off one's retina via the ten-times telescope in the sextant. Apparently, doing this a few times is enough to burn out the centre of the retina completely. To go on doing it is to risk cancer of the retina. This was all a well-known syndrome in the old sextant days, but ophthalmologists have forgotten about it now.

Secondly I made a passage in bad conditions, using GPS. During the night we were dismasted, and with only Laurel, who though very able as regards steering and cooking is of limited use when it comes to rough seas up on deck. I was soon exhausted. It was a tremendous relief being able to set waypoints and watch them from the seat in the wheelhouse as we made painfully slow way across the tide towards Ramsgate.... So, here am I, a renegade from the Old Salts Union, siding with those people who talk about cross-track-error and think in milli-amps. However did I manage before?

So now we have GPS, radar (it's a very old one), Echo-sounder, Navtex, Wind instruments, and autopilot. Not over the top, but I've bitten the electronic bullet. The fact is that nowadays electronic gadgetry costs less than the traditional ones. GPS can be bought for much less than the cost of a good sextant, and with the latter you have to have books of tables, almanacs, and a chronometer, all weighing quite a bit. But don't we still need a back-up for the GPS?

During the Gulf War we were making a passage across the Ionian Sea one February day, and I was plotting GPS fixes every two hours as I always do, when I noticed that we hadn't apparently moved since the last fix. A glance over the side showed water sluicing past quite reassuringly. The instrument reported itself working well, 4 satellites. When we berthed in Levkas we were told by the AWAC crews that Uncle Sam had pulled the plug for a few hours. The transmissions were still being made, but civilian receivers would not have been able to decode them. Oh fine! Couldn't Stormin' Norman have put out a 'Normal service will be resumed as soon as possible' sign?

So a second GPS receiver, even if operated on dry battery, wouldn't solve the problem. Perhaps a set operating the Russian system (GLONASS) might. Or, one day, the European system. But that's a long way off. In the meantime it seems a sextant could still come in handy.

If starting from scratch I would buy one of the quality plastic ones, Ebbco, for example. Not the very cheapest, but one of the better ones. It is lightweight, quite cheap, and tolerably accurate. The requirement is not for an instrument that can fix you within 100 yards, such accuracy may be possible on shore or a big ship, but it is unachievable in a yacht in a seaway. Use a programmed calculator, or very simple tables, such as those in the French *Livre de Bord*, and forget stars. If buying second-hand tables, or calculators, beware the millenium: many of these will run out of data in 1999.

The trouble is that one has to be in practice to take a usable sunsight. And one must remember the arithmetic. For this reason we still include the sight reduction form at the back of this book. They may be a disappearing feature, and one might come in handy to remind you what to do.

I would say that the clutch of electronics we have is now the working outfit for a well-fitted yacht. Notice we have no log instrument. GPS, backed up by DR does all that. Distance through the water is less important than distance over the ground. Smaller boats, especially if staying in the tropics, might dispense with the radar, but fog is quite frequent in the Med. And there is another point: much of the world is charted from ancient surveys that do not conform to modern geographic datums, and anyway yachts tend to wander around using out of date charts bought second- or even fourth-hand from a previous passer-by. We have observed that GPS positions are often miles out from the charted lat and long grid. In the Ukraine we found that *Hosanna* was apparently in the local railway station, instead of the river Danube. It can be very confusing and dangerous if you are not aware of the problem. In these circumstances, a radar set, which gives position relative to the land, independently of the lat and long, can be very reassuring.

I wish the Hydrographer would suspend metrication, which dilutes his resources, and concentrate on producing charts with up-to-date geographical datums. Then we could soon forget that problem.

The Broader Aspects

A problem for the long-cruise navigator is that many of the techniques he will (or ought to) use, are not those within most courses in Britain or the USA. In Britain the chief aim of most courses is to fit the student for the Yachtmaster's Certificate in one or other of its forms. These naturally have a home waters emphasis, and this applies to some extent to the Ocean syllabus too.

While the navigational content of the RYA yachtmaster qualification should not be at the leading edge of technology, it is at present too far behind, about as relevant to today's navigation as that of Vasco da Gama. The rate of change in the science and craft of navigation is frightening, even to professionals. With serious consideration being given to unmanned computer-driven 100,000 tonne bulk carriers (not in my life-time I hope), and proposals to change the collision regulations to suit computer navigated ships (ditto), yachtsmen will have to do something to keep abreast of developments. Even if they do not use them, the other guy may be doing so. More on latest developments later.

Further inadequacies of the RYA syllabi concern the problems associated with waters that are inadequately surveyed, ill-provided with marks and lights, with meagre tidal data, and where the expected, conventional and prudent arrangements for keeping up to date are not available. Few people have any experience of these problems nowadays.

Although the Hydrographer of the Navy is beginning to consider the requirements of his yachting customers (who in some parts of the globe constitute the majority of users), this consideration applies so far only to home waters; he is still publishing new charts of overseas areas that are, from a small craft point of view, very much worse than the old ones. For example BA1703 (Majorca and Minorca) is a poor job compared with 1317 which it replaced, and not only because the scale was reduced from 193,000 to 300,000. The whole field of books of navigational data is an ergonomic nightmare: it was never planned, it

A log working on the Pitot principle, which one can make. A ¼" ID metal tube extends 2" below the hull, and has an expansion chamber and pressure gauge above the waterline. The detail sketch shows the twin weed deflectors in relation to the tube opening.

just grew piecemeal, and is badly in need of a complete review. The trouble is that the professionals are so familiar with the present chaos that they will resist change.

Navigational Publications

It is necessary to do a bit of planning before leaving home waters because charts and other works are not readily available or are very much higher priced overseas. I do not infer that you have to stick to an itinerary; it is possible to cover a lot of variations in one's planning, and this is desirable because one does not get to know a lot of the good things about an area until you get there.

It might be thought that the hydrographic services of Great Britain and the USA, the only countries maintaining effective world coverage of navigational data and both with advanced business outlooks, would have devised an effective marketing and/or distribution system for their wares. Brilliant surveyors these gentlemen are, businessmen they evidently are not. It is virtually impossible to buy US Defence Mapping Agency or National Oceanographic and Atmospheric Administration charts or publications outside the USA, and even there the ordering system (computerised, of course) is so ludicrous that it should be turned into a party game.

The typical DMA chart gives the appearance of having been drawn by a long-sighted computer that has forgotten its reading glasses. It uses bottom contours extensively and, for example on the Bahamas Banks, shows large blank areas between shallow contours when the variations in the bottom between these limits are many, various, and of the highest value to small craft. That this type of inshore data is not without military value was demonstrated in the Falkland Islands.

British charts and publications have a slightly better availability, but suffer from a random system of numbering that leads to mistakes when ordering large numbers of charts. Even at major stock-holding agents it is possible to find charts out of stock far too frequently, and some neighbouring agents have a friendly and sensible reciprocal arrangement to help out customers when the Hydrographic Department have let them down. The charts themselves vary from work-of-art standard to virtually useless outline diagrams, but though the basic surveys are sometimes very old, I find that British charts, on the day of purchase, are more up-to-date than American ones.

Admiralty charts are published in a hodge-podge of metric and natural units. (Each individual chart is consistent within itself.) To be totally metric, or totally natural would be quite indifferent to me, but the present confusion between charts is irritating and dangerous. The interim changeover period has gone on far too long. The whole unnecessary exercise must have been a major cause of the quite indecent rise in the price of British charts, which are now among the most expensive. On the other hand though there are individual bad ones in the Admiralty catalogue, as a general collection of small-craft charts they are a lot better than any others. They have the advantage of being printed on strong paper, but why are they not printed on both sides to save both cost and storage space? Quite a good feature of British charts is that they are almost entirely of a standard and very convenient size.

In certain areas it pays to buy locally produced large-scale charts of the coastal waters, and this is a policy approved by the Hydrographer. Some countries have very good hydrographic services. I have found Turkish and French charts clear, reliable and easy to use. Italian charts are more confused and their boundaries are not well planned. Greek charts, though otherwise quite good, suffer from an inability to convey information to foreigners due to their alphabet and the oddities of the language. Unfortunately British charts transliterate Greek grammatical constructions (particularly the genitive case in its three genders) and thus proliferate the confusion of Greek place names.

The law, and other considerations

Notice to Mariners no 18 of each year lists those publications that all British registered ships over 12 metres in length are obliged to carry. These requirements would astonish many yachtsmen, as well as leading to the serious overloading of a typical yacht of 12 metres overall. Common sense has to prevail in selection. I have used the International Code of Signals (one of the obligatory volumes, and a large one too) on only one occasion in the last ten years, and that was to find a flag hoist for Christmas Day in Bequia. (We hoisted MOX meaning 'a child has been born' and about 150 other craft had to ask us what it meant). Merchant shipping notices are not really appropriate to a cruising yacht, and the Mariner's Handbook is something to read before going, unless you plan to navigate in ice. It is a fairly slim volume at least.

The Nautical Almanac and Navigation Tables are essential, even if you prefer milliamps and computers for everyday use. The Lists of Radio Signals are very bulky and mostly irrelevant to a yacht, particularly those with no radio transmitter. Too often the details of radio beacons are out of date on publication even if Her Majesty's Sationery Office is not on strike, and the whole publication lags behind commercial almanacs. Lists of Lights, tide tables and atlases are necessary, but again the commercial publications are better where the coverage is available.

Charts carried must be of appropriate scale to identify hazards and marks and they must be up to date, which leads to the next requirement. Notices to Mariners *must* be carried. This is an example of a regulation drafted by well-meaning blue-suited gentlemen in comfortable offices in London. Just try getting Notices to Mariners in the Bongo Bongo Archipelago. Better still, just try getting them anywhere: Consulates? You're joking; in Budapest they'd never heard of them. I called in at Potters in London and found only a meagre selection. Notice to Mariners no 14 in each year (if you can get it: I succeed one year in three) has a list of places where Notices may be consulted, and this list is pure romantic fiction. I have made a particular point over the years of visiting these places when in the vicinity, and in the vast majority no Notices were available. Even when they were one was not permitted to take away a copy, and you cannot correct charts on your knees while seated in a windy Consulate hallway. The fact is that Consuls do not give a damn.

The volumes are so heavy that having them sent airmail is out of the question, and seamail never catches up with a cruising yacht. The whole system of chart correction, based on the facilities of a world-wide empire and on a plenitude of labour which no longer exist, is badly in need of redesign.

Correcting charts

Correcting an outfit of charts is a big job. Warships carry a specially trained rating to do this, which with 500 charts is a full-time occupation. Something has to give in a yacht with a crew of two, and having fallen behind when I had only some 200 charts I never managed to catch up, so I gave up. Here is how I try to keep as up to date as I can, in the special circumstances of our cruising life. It is not ideal, it is merely a practical partial solution to an otherwise insoluble problem.

First, I make the reasonable assumption that only a small proportion of Notices affect a yacht. Whenever I return to England or Gibraltar I get every Notice I can, and throw away those sections that do not deal with areas in which I navigate. I then cut out those Notices that might affect a yacht, ignoring for example the instruction to insert a sounding of 250 metres somewhere, and divide these into batches according to which Admiralty Pilot is involved. When on board I pencil in the Pilot, on the appropriate page, either a precis of the chart correction or a reference. I can then throw away a lot more paper. I never use a chart for pilotage (ie for coastal navigation) without also using the Pilot book *with its latest Supplement*. Taking care, and keeping fully aware of the limitations of the system, I think it is the best way of coping with a large folio of charts in a small yacht.

The Admiralty Pilots (Sailing Directions, to give them their proper title) are very good, much improved on the last editions. However, their price has risen out of all proportion to their usefulness in small craft. They are much better written than heretofore, but the layout is confusing, while the policy on place-naming is positively idiotic. Considerable improvement is necessary. They are sometimes the only aid available, and they should be carried, with their latest supplements, if you do not keep your charts up to date. Sometimes the very old Admiralty Pilot Books are very informative, especially where they were written in the days of sailing ships. Often they contain very good advice on how to beat round a headland, for example. If you come across them in a second-hand book shop, get them.

A significant entry for the electronically minded is that all operating and maintenance manuals for any Navaid carried *must* be on board. Try getting a proper maintenance manual from some of the cowboy manufacturers about in the industry.

Chart agents

Buying charts abroad, as already mentioned, is fraught with difficulties. Notice no 2 in each year, as well as the catalogue, gives a full list of agents and is again a bit of a humourless frolic. Most of these agents have only a very few local charts in stock, mostly aged and dog-eared, uncorrected, and at outrageous prices. It is little wonder so many yachts are navigating on photocopies of other people's charts. This is unavoidable, being preferable to going chartless; I have done it and hated it.

The Admiralty Chart Depot at Gibraltar has now closed, but a good selection of charts is available there from commercial sources. The commercial department of the Admiralty needs to get itself into the twentieth century, before the twenty-first overtakes it.

The best source of British charts in the Med is from Cdr Mike Healy, 10 Rue Jean Bracco, 06310 Beaulieu-sur-Mer. Tel 04 93 01 30 00, Fax 04 93 01 30 01. He also stocks a large range of English Language nautical books including this one (I hope), though beware, books in France cost more than in England, partly due to VAT.

Pilotage

Now a little on coastal navigation, particularly in poorly charted waters. It was big-ship practice to try to fix the ship visually at least every twenty minutes when inshore, and more often than that if going fast. In a yacht one does not change position enough to make such a frequency appropriate except in conditions of very strong tides or when very close to the shore, where even so a different method of navigating is desirable. Even with GPS, I would try to chart position every now and then, the exact time intervals depending on speed, visibility, tides, other traffic etc.

It is unfortunate that many ill-charted or ill-marked coasts have offshore dangers that are also unmarked by buoy or beacon, so that although fixing may not be practical, one cannot relax attention. In any case there may not be sufficient identifiable marks on which to fix. Even if you have Loran C or GPS, the system error, coupled with possible geographic errors in an old survey, would make reliance on electronics foolhardy.

Clearing bearings

The best way of sailing such waters is to keep a network of clearing bearings (I write them on a notepad by the compass). Using clearing bearings, one may not always know where one is but one does know very well where one is not.

A clearing bearing is a compass bearing of a fixed object such that, provided you stay to the appropriate side of that bearing, you cannot strike a danger situated closer to you than the fixed object (see diagram). Some of my charts are inked in with clearing bearings ready for use. They are also marked with transits (objects in line with each other, called 'ranges' by our American cousins) which are very useful for giving a position line proof against any compass error, and also for checking the compass (which should be done frequently, if possible once a day at least). It is far too easy in the relaxed atmosphere of a cruising yacht's cockpit for someone to leave something magnetic close to the compass.

Navigating by clearing bearings is an ideal complementary system alongside GPS, and is particularly appropriate to short-handed sailing, when it is difficult to leave the cockpit to do detailed chartwork.

True bearings

Note that most charts and pilot books give bearings in their true form, and these must be converted to magnetic and compass form by corrections of variation and deviation. This system has grown because variation due to the earth's magnetism varies from year to year, and because each vessel has to correct for its own deviation anyway; most navigators like to do both corrections together as a

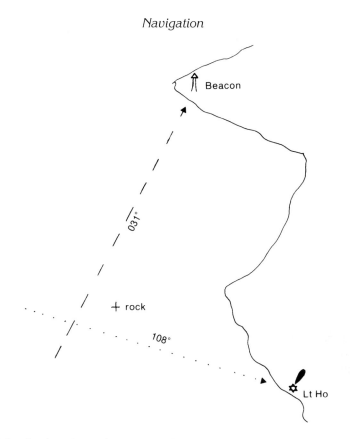

Example of clearing bearings taken on two shore points, to avoid a dangerous rock

sort of ritual. Did you know that the earth is overdue for a complete reversal of polarity: the North magnetic pole will move to the southern hemisphere, and vice versa, and that the move will be comparatively sudden? A mere hundred years or so? It does not look as if it has started yet, so this little snippet is for amusement only.

A few more words on the reliability of charts, which should never be assumed to have oracular authority and which are not claimed by their most devoted surveyors to be more than aids to navigation. Look at the date of survey in the legend (title), or on newer charts the data source diagram. This will give some idea of the methods of survey used, and in the older charts the number of soundings printed will give some idea of the comprehensiveness of the survey. As the British Hydrographer is also moving towards (less useful) bottom contours, this indicator is no longer valid for new editions. In old surveys, which were often made under very hard conditions, straits and channels were usually surveyed one side at a time, and the correspondence between the two sides may not always be exact: it is better to fix using marks from one side or the other, but not both, if it can be avoided. Much of this advice about getting the best from older charts will not concern those who navigate home waters, but it is rarely taught these days, and it could come in handy far from home where the grotty yotties sail.

Outward Bound

Now let us go deep-sea, that is out of the danger of hitting land. There is an old saying, 'Outward bound, don't run aground'. This means that if you are going to be at sea on a 20 day passage it is not worth cutting across a dangerous sandbank when leaving harbour, just to save ten minutes. But people do it! A yacht moored inside us at Ramsgate got us up at 0400 in order to sail for the Caribbean. When we followed him four hours later we found him stuck on a sandbank just off the pierhead, and though tempted we did not have the heart to leave him there. We delayed our departure and pulled him off.

Astro

Forget about starsights. The only starsights I have taken since retiring have been for amusement or practice, or in order to fix the geographical position of somewhere when I suspect the chart to be in error. (It very seldom is.) To cross the ocean in a sailing craft at an average speed of 5 knots, the sun will suffice. The moon can be useful but is by no means essential.

Do not worry about the theory of astronomy unless you wish to get pleasure from knowing more than the minimum required. Sunsights can be taken entirely by rule of thumb and my form (see Appendix). It is desirable to take a morning sight, a noon meridian passage and an afternoon sight in each day. The times will vary according to how high the sun is when it crosses the meridian (your north-south line), but in general one does not want to take the sun when it is too low down, say under 30° from the horizon, because of refraction errors in the atmosphere which cannot be predicted with complete reliability; nor when its altitude is very high, for then it becomes difficult to bring the sun down to the horizon, and to get it to sit comfortably right beneath itself, especially if the ship is rolling. This problem has to be faced at the meridian passage, when the sun is at its height, but there's no need to look for trouble.

The compass bearings (azimuths) of the sun at the morning and afternoon sights should ideally be 60° or more from the meridian, but do not worry if cloud or breakfast hold you up. Perfectly good results are obtainable with angles down to about 30°. Likewise, do not fret if you take too long over your afternoon inspection of the inner surface of your eyelids. Even if the sun does get a bit low, it is still observable; though the position line should be treated with a little caution, it is still worth having.

Strictly speaking it is not necessary to take sights as often as this in good weather at the start of a voyage, but it does become important towards the end when making a landfall, when conscientious daily sight-taking will have you so expert and confident that you stand a good chance of making the right harbour without getting emotional and having to swear at your partner.

Spurious accuracy

There is such a thing as excessive, unnecessary or spurious accuracy in any form of navigating. A sextant reading to a tenth of a minute of arc is overkill when used with the Air Navigation Tables (AP 3270), even supposing one has the manual skill to get that accuracy from a sight of a body at high altitudes from a small boat in a seaway.

Nevertheless, do not get too careless. Even most pros take three or more shots for each sight and check that the differences of both altitude and time are consistent. A convenient way of doing this is to set the sextant for fixed intervals of either 3 minutes of arc or 4, and then to record the times as the sun kisses the horizon. With equal intervals of altitude, it is easy to check that the intervals of time are about right. You would be very skilled indeed if the intervals, or differences, were all exactly right; such fine accuracy is virtually unobtainable.

However, accuracy over time is important. Near the Equator 4 seconds of time can mean about 1 nautical mile when translated into a position line. But a chronometer is hardly required any more. Even quite cheap quartz watches will maintain sufficient accuracy for a 30 day passage, and with a shortwave radio receiver one can get frequent time checks. (I would not be without means of getting the BBC World Service news from time to time: just think of arriving at some small island in the middle of an invasion by gung-ho Marines.)

When plotting a sunsight it is not normally satisfactory to use an ocean chart for the scale is too small; it is likely the whole day's run will fit into an inch or so. Navigation textbooks say that one should use a plotting sheet, which has a compass rose in the centre and a latitude scale without any numbers on it. After inserting degrees of latitude to choice, one is then faced with constructing a longitude scale because this will vary with latitude.

Well, all this is good to keep idle navigators busy. I find it simpler to use a large-scale chart of the same latitude as I am in, but for a different part of the world. I then have only to change the numbers on the longitude scale to suit my position and I can do my plotting on that, later transferring the position to the ocean chart. It is hard to make an error as one is keeping a daily check on progress, and on transferring the position any mistake would be immediately apparent. One has to get used to the idea of plotting a position line in the middle of a desert, but the idea rather amuses me. Navigation schools and shore-bound experts may scream with dismay, but I have used this method for thousands of sights for over almost 50 years without mishap.

There are errors in electronic navigation, too. GPS is not really accurate to 20 yards as I have seen advertised. I have never found it any use for warning me of dragging anchors, not before our five senses give the alarm. Differential GPS would be but that is a more expensive story, and would be rather overkill for a yacht. When using radar one should be aware that range is much more accurate than bearing, the latter depending on beam-width.

Even in sight of land the sextant can be a great deal of use if you are familiar and easy with it. I used mine for vertical danger angles or for obtaining the ranges (distance off), of mountains using Lecky's Tables. It is a very fast method and much less trouble than switching on radar, but the tables are virtually unique and out of print.

In bad weather, when maybe you or the crew are feeling unwell, take especial care. One French destroyer I served in had notices plastered round the ship saying '*Valeur et Discipline*'. Whether such notices achieve anything depends, I suppose, on those to whom they are addressed, but if you are the sort that responds to exhortation then stick them up.

If you are tired and unsure of your position, then, however miserable you may feel, *do not put the ship on a course that could be dangerous*, as you would be that much less able to cope with an emergency should one arise. Even if it means standing off in discomfort, that is better than the Shipwrecked Mariners' Hostel, supposing one exists. Do not cry for help because you are miserable: go out to sea where you will be safe as long as the ship remains seaworthy.

If you are Lost

This is particularly relevant to making a landfall, and is a branch of navigation that is insufficiently treated in textbooks, perhaps because professionals either do not get lost so do not know how to cope, or more likely, do not wish their fellows to know that they have been lost. There have been several occasions when I have not known where I was, so here goes.

First, remember that if any navigator happens to be exactly where he thinks he is, it is purely accidental. This is true. Navigation is not an exact science, it is a craft in which judgement plays a very important part. All systems and aids contain the possibility of errors and all human beings make them. What makes one a professional is being aware of the possible or likely errors in the method one uses and subconsciously being completely aware of the degree of reliability of one's position. In theory, this is complex mathematics, but there are plenty of practical wrinkles. It is impossible to give complete, generalized counsel as to what to do in any or all cases of being lost: there are too many variables. One thing to do before getting into this state is to keep charts and pilot books up to date; that can make it a lot easier to get out of it.

If you are clearly well offshore you have a problem, it is true, but it is not urgent and too early to start worrying. Provided weather conditions are reasonable and the shore is not a lee to a very strong wind, approach it with care. The problem may even solve itself. We will not discuss night-time. My advice with a doubtful position close to unlit land by night or in bad visibility is to b***** off out to sea and wait till conditions improve.

If, having raised the shore, you cannot identify any feature or find your chosen haven, then you certainly have a problem. If it is a question of visibility, wait and stand off. But if the weather is fair, and if the coast is not a dead lee with known or suspected offlying unmarked dangers, then approach it cautiously at an angle. I, personally, would go downwind in such a situation, but know of competent friends who would do the opposite. It may be something to do with whether you describe a bottle as half full or half empty: I always believe things will improve. One good reason I have for approaching downwind is that if one does come across a danger one has more scope for hauling clear very quickly. To do so going upwind puts limits on one's manoeuvrability without tacking, which is not always the work of a minute when short-handed. Another reason is that one changes one's position faster. If landmarks are not distinguishable in one place, then get somewhere else as soon as reasonably possible. Still another reason is that the motion will be less, making observation and chartwork easier.

Where are you not?

In this process there is the advisability of changing one's outlook. You do not know where you are, but there are plenty of places where you know you are not. Start eliminating: huge areas go at once. The length of time since your last known position should give you a radius of possibility, and even if you had lost your compass, for example, I am sure you would have been able to have found an approximate direction. It is probable that the unknown area that you occupy is less than 100 miles along the coast; it is almost certainly less than 200.

Inspect all the relevant large-scale charts and the pilot books for any features in this sort of distance. There may be reference to a chimney or radio mast. Unless you are very unlucky and they have just been demolished, you can cross off those bits of coast within their visibility distance. And so on. Things will narrow down. Is part of the coast hilly, or swampy with offlying banks? Are there soundings? Are there ships in sight? Are they on courses that might converge at a point? If so, they are almost certainly going to or from a port; that is a position line of sorts, and I once found Colombo that way under an overcast sky, though this is the first time I have ever confessed it.

Don't forget the simple things. Is there a river estuary? This often brings discoloured water as well as a lot of floating rubbish. If approaching Italy you will see many floating plastic bags, and you can recover a few to see the address of the shops printed on them; known in the trade as 'bag of buns navigation'.

This general problem does not always follow ocean crossings. We once headed for Majorca after being hove-to for a time. Approaching at right angles to a coast with many similar features is almost as bad as approaching a coast without any at all. This was a virtual cliff of highrise buildings. After studying the chart, 'I think we're either off Cape X or Cape Y', I called up to Laurel, who was on watch. 'It's Cape X,' she said, looking through binoculars. 'How do you know...?' 'Well, that hotel with the red balconies is the Cape X Hotel. There's a sign that says so.'

We once drifted in the little yacht *Phoenix* which had no engine, for two full days in the Malta Channel, completely blanketed by thick fog. At the end of this we had only a vague idea where we were, but as the fog began to clear one evening we saw over the horizon the signs of fireworks. Someone had given us a Roman Catholic calendar which had the Saints' Days on it. It took only a moment to identify which parish church was busy beating the hell out of the Devil, and then we had quite a reasonable position line.

Once at night well off a coast I saw what appeared to be the loom of a lighthouse where none should be. (The loom of a light is the beam in the sky when the light itself is out of sight below the horizon.) It was oddly irregular. In fact it was a busy main road with a sharp rising bend and the beams were the headlights of cars going round it. Jokes about navigating by road maps are out of place: not all valuable information is published by the Hydrographer. For another example: nautical charts do not show the flight paths of aircraft. With a low fog it is very useful to be able to pinpoint where aircraft turn for a final approach; this is helpful off the mouths of the Tiber, near Fiumicino Airport, off the French Riviera, and Athens, among many other places.

Ferry timetables can be of value. Apart from being a rare potential fixing aid, the ABC shipping guide helps one to avoid these tracks, for ferries are notorious for being selfishly and inconsiderately driven.

Latest Developments

GPS is becoming cheaper and better, with smaller receivers, even handheld ones. It is likely that Differential GPS will be within the financial reach of the average yottie before long. In the meantime, if you wish for better accuracy, the Russian GLONASS system is not downgraded for civilian use, and one can get receivers capable of receiving both systems. With one of these you have effectively got a built-in back-up. For detailed info on GPS or GLONASS there are internet websites:

US coastguard Nav Info Service: http://www.mavcen.uscg.mil/
Russia: http:/www.rssi.ru/sfcsic main.html

Electronic charting

It is already with us, and working. The British Admiralty ARCS system is probably the best. Having bought the hardware and a programme from a commercial service provider, one gets the charts one requires on a card or disc. Unfortunately, being a government department, the Hydrographer does not know much about marketing. This system will become very effective as more people use it, but the present pricing structure is prohibitive. The Hydrographer needs to seed the market a bit to get the system into general use, then hardware and service prices will fall, and a commercially appropriate level will be established. At the moment commercial shipping is obliged to have paper chart backups in case the electronics fail. When this rule changes, as it will, yachtsmen will be virtually the only users of paper charts, and their prices will rise even more.

Navigating for the millenium

We do have a serious warning for anyone buying any equipment with a computer programme inside it, especially if buying second-hand. Watch out for the year 2000! And talking of the year 2000, which isn't so very far away, note that it will be a year of unusually strong solar activity with severe electro-magnetic storms. These might possibly interfere with navigation systems, and will certainly interfere with radio communications.

Which brings us to GMDSS (Global Maritime Distress and Safety System), navigation has become a world of acronyms: professional navigators no longer speak English to each other, they talk only in strings of letters. Aviators are even worse!). This system will affect yachtsmen by providing a search and rescue organisation which will be more effective and less expensive than heretofore. Even if, like us, you like to extricate yourself and do not want the search and rescue people to bloodhound after you, you could get searched for whether you like it or not. It will also affect all VHF coastwise radio traffic, which we do use, and so it is necessary to read all about it.

We do not carry an HF transmitter, preferring to look after ourselves on the Arthur Ransome principle: If not duffers, won't drown; if duffers, better drowned. Others may not feel so purist.

For books about GMDSS see the Appendix.

Those readers not contemplating oceans, but who are more interested in the world's inland waters, should be on their guard, for the whole system of licensing both ships and captains is in process of change. Why should they be exempt, everything else is changing?

We have a situation where the Collision Regulations (Colregs), which have been agreed by treaty, and which are legally binding on all states, and which apply as a basis in all waters navigable by seagoing vessels (see Reg 1(b)), have been disturbed by a United Nations Congress which proposed alterations to be applicable to Europe only. These regulations (SIGNI) have no international standing, not being subject to treaty status, but have nevertheless been implemented by certain countries, notably France. To confuse matters further, the French call these rules CEVNI, as they don't like anything written in any language but their own. Speaking recently (May 97) to the acknowledged world expert on this subject at the International Maritime University at Malmo in Sweden, I was told that the matter would have to be regularised, but that the European Commissioner for Transport was not exactly being very industrious about it.

In the circumstances, get whatever certificates you can. Make a collection of them, overload your boat with the nasty little pieces of paper. When you are asked to produce your qualification by a gendarme who does not know one end of a boat from the other, shower him with bureaucratic confetti, preferably with lots of stamps on it. It will still be wrong, but at least you will have tried. We feel that not only the RYA and the Marine Safety Agency should issue certificates, but also each yacht club, the Barge Cruising Association (whose certificates for English members should, with any luck, sow complete confusion throughout Europe), and perhaps the RSPCA, who should certify British pets as competent ships' cats. I am getting carried away again.

Good sailing!

Hydrographers Again

Another word or two about the Hydrographer in charge of BA charts. I am critical of the organization, and occasionally of the design or printing of charts, but the standard of surveying is generally excellent and has been so, given the instruments available, for a very long time. There are few serious errors on charts, and I am sceptical when I hear someone say (and it happens quite frequently) that they ran aground because the chart was wrong. Mostly they were not where they thought they were. But things do change, and at an alarmingly increasing rate, while the Hydrographer cannot keep survey ships up every little by-water. If you do come across a change, or an error which you are *sure* is a chart error, then drop a line to the Hydrographer. It is called an H note, and a blank form is found at the back of all Supplements to Admiralty Pilot Books. This form should be used if you can, for it is a reminder of the background details that H would like to know. You may be a novice, but if you are off the beaten track you may be the first to report something that may save a ship; you are keeping up the standard of charting and helping to keep down costs.

Remember that navigating is not a mystery any more. There are many techniques that will come with experience, but the cautious novice, exercising common sense and using intelligently the little knowledge he already has, will get by and gently learn more. It is an old axiom that there are old navigators and bold navigators, but no old and bold navigators. *Prudence* is the word.

Chapter Thirteen

Social Life and Entertainment

'... then all the rest may do what they will til midnight.'

Entertainment might seem an odd subject for those to whom sailing itself is an entertainment, but when the navigation of a vessel from one place to another is the prime motive, some forms of diversion are needed.

Reading is the most obvious. People used to books cannot easily manage without. There are no libraries available to the wanderer, so one has to have reference volumes to taste. Most yachts carry a paperback library comprising those loved books which one keeps to read over and over again, and a box of less loved books that are enjoyable once and are then swopped with other yachts for similar works. Many yachting centres have second-hand bookshops, where your nearly new paperbacks may be swapped for a fee. Swopping paperbacks is a continuing process. It is sad that British and American paperback publishers now use a form of unsewn binding that falls apart. To bind reference books in this way is little short of fraud, and they are completely unfit for the purpose for which they are sold. Continental paperbacks are better bound.

If you are going where books in English are unobtainable or very expensive, it may be worth sending for the Good Book Guide (address in Appendix). This well produced independent magazine comes out seven times a year, and not only gives excellent reviews of new books but will send you any book on their current list for the UK published price plus the postage, by airmail if you wish. There is no obligation to buy any book at all. If it is not on their list, they will get any book in print for a 50p surcharge: this can solve problems both with education and birthday presents, also gifts back home. You would need a good postal 'drop' however; Poste Restante would not be reliable enough.

More and more reference books are becoming available on CD for use in computers. This is a very good way of carrying a library in a boat, for once you have the computer, an idea that no longer makes hardened sailors hoot with ribald disbelief, it saves enormously on space and weight. It costs a lot, though.

Apart from reading, games are played rather more by the typical yottie than by his land-dwelling friends. A lot of chess is played. Some, including myself, indulge themselves with a chess computer, but it is not the same thing as playing with real live people. Draughts (or checkers) and backgammon (or tavla) are played a lot. We are occasionally asked to play bridge, but as we do not play we are unaware of the extent to which it is enjoyed.

A very popular game is Scrabble. There are certain difficulties playing it with Americans owing to their inability to spell. We solved the problem by using the *Shorter Oxford Dictionary* when aboard *Fare Well*, and *Webster's* when in an

American boat, but they had the worst of it because *Webster's* is kind enough to have both American and English spellings. Bridge and Scrabble can be got for playing against a computer. Personally I find computer Scrabble unsatisfactory owing to there being no choice of dictionary. It uses *Chambers*, which has some extraordinary words in it and omits ordinary ones.

The Royal Cruising Club has a song book, and at a suitable time aboard their boats the skipper may hand them round like hymn books so that the anchorage resounds with song. The accompanying instrument for sailors' songs has traditionally been portable and easily stowed; a pipe, concertina or harmonica. Later a fiddle came in. Then, of all things, the yacht piano, which solved the ballast problem I suppose. Now we have electronic keyboards (where will it end?) and guitars. The traditional Spanish guitar, of thin wood put together with non-waterproof glue, is surprisingly popular considering it has minimal aptitude for life in a yacht. Ours was stowed in the shower in a moment of crisis, and of course someone had left the pump switched on, so the next use of the generator sprayed the guitar. Innumerable boats have one, occupying valuable space. Someone should invent one, the inside of which can be used as a locker. Not content with the guitar, Laurel bought a dulcimer kit in the USA and amused herself building it while coming back over the Atlantic. I hold my breath every time we see a double bass.

Hobbies

Sailors of old did not have a lot of spare time, or daylight to play in, but they had various diversions including decorative knotting (macramé), knitting, scrimshaw and wood, bone and ivory carving. These are all enjoyable pastimes today, though real whales' teeth are getting as scarce as hens'. They all have the virtue of taking up little space, and when well done the products can be sold.

The first problem is that more and more of the old seafaring hobbies are condemned as environmentally unfriendly (scrimshaw is an example, as is carving in bone and ivory) and are therefore banned by landlubber legislators. (Don't they realise that whale skeletons can be found?) The next problem is that many well practised shoreside hobbies do not translate to the seagoing life. Collecting is difficult because of space and the importance of protecting vulnerable and valuable items from sea damage. Postage stamps and books, for example. I have not heard of anyone actually having a model railway in a yacht, but I expect one exists somewhere. I sometimes wish I had an old-fashioned Meccano set.

Almost any art or craft except possibly stained glass, fresco painting, mosaic and monumental masonry can be practised (we met a German sculptor who carved stone in his old Baltic Trader, and have heard of a potter with full-blown kiln). Painting depends a bit on the medium: oils are very vulnerable to getting sat on while wet, water colours are easily ruined by damp, and need storing in strong plastic folders. If you want to be a serious painter, you will not regret investing in really good quality handmade paper. Laurel uses acrylic paints. They have the advantage that they dry quickly and stand up to a certain amount of wet, but some people don't like the texture. Craft and technical pens, with the size of nib marked in millimetres (03, 05, 07 etc), are often fast to light and water, which is a good idea.

If you have a skill, even a small area can make a workshop.

Fabric crafts are particularly appropriate to a boat. Laurel once did a lot of patchwork; she says it is an occupation which can be done in any corner at any time and is easy to put down or take up. Let your imagination run along those lines and do as you will. Take any special tools with you, and spares too for they are sometimes unavailable or hard to trace.

One of the chief entertainments while cruising is the social life, meeting and getting to know other yotties or passers-by. Whatever their background, the chat with the people in the next boat is of the sea and common experiences, richly educational.

When on board on our own the radio is valuable. It is wise to keep some track of world events; you do not want to arrive somewhere in the middle of a coup d'état. The BBC World Service has many news broadcasts, mainly and maddeningly political and apt to stress the Third World at the expense of the other two. Reception of music can be bad enough to switch off. The broadcast frequencies for any area vary during the day, and also from month to month as they have trouble from sunspots or human interference. A magazine, which used to be called *London Calling* is published by the BBC, which gives a lot of programme information, and there is a monthly sheet listing frequencies in use. Both these can be got from the BBC World Service, Bush House, Strand, London WC1. Other shortwave radio reception varies with locality and time.

Local national and provincial radio is heavily dependent on taste. In the West Indies one gets reggae morning, noon and night. In Europe all countries have an approximate equivalent to the BBC Home Services, and most countries have a programme with cultural leanings. France Musique is excellent, and has the great asset that its announcers have almost perfect diction which is a great help in learning the language. How foreigners get on trying to learn English from the BBC, who seem to favour regional accents, we cannot imagine. The area of the announcer's accent should be attached to his name, as newspapers always add

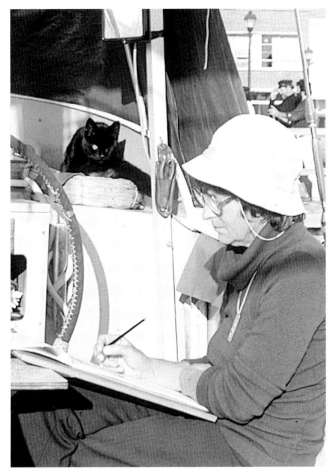

Laurel sketching.

one's age, just as impertinently, ie: Tess d'Urbeville (Wessex), Bill Sykes (East London), Peter de'Ath Bredon (Eton and Balliol), Emily Brontë (Yorkshire).

Turkey and Greece both have cultural Third Programmes. The Greek one *was* excellent, but its former director is apparently out of favour politically. Now the service is only obtainable near Athens and is musically much less interesting, seeming to consist of interminable readings of avant-garde poetry. The Turkish programme put out a lot of trad jazz when I last heard it.

Radio in Italy is chaos. Everyone seems to start their own station, mostly to broadcast rock music and advertisements, and they are so unregulated that frequencies overlap. Some transmitters are so poorly modulated that the marine distress frequencies are affected, but no-one bothers. Near Rome there is Canale 5 which has non-stop classical music all day, and is very good when not subject to interference. Also near Rome, if you have TV, is all night porn, for what it's worth.

In the USA the radio situation is a pale copy of the Italian; much the same in principle, but with some order superimposed, though not much is apparent to the outsider. For those with mental pretensions above the moronic there is

Public Radio, which we thought good in quality and not only because they sometimes use BBC material.

The best domestic radios are those with digital tuning and 'save' buttons. There are several on the market. We carry a JVC multi-system miniature television set, which works everywhere except France. I like to pretend it is for watching weather forecasts, which are often more easily absorbed if one can see a synoptic chart.

But television is also an effective language teacher. By watching children's programmes one gets talk in a simple vocabulary with simple grammar, usually spoken slowly and clearly. Advertisements can be in simple language, and repeat phrases over and over again, with pictures. This can be a great help.

There is not much entertainment from television abroad. One finds an occasional piece of excellence that is relevant to us, the foreigners, but not often. If you have video to go with your TV there are now many video libraries in places where yotties winter, and a thriving swop-and-borrow system, so they are evidently popular.

Yacht Clubs

Talk of social life leads us to consider clubs and associations of interest to the long-cruising yachtsman. There is a tendency not to belong to clubs. We are thus exceptions, though we question just what benefit we get from some. Loyalty dies hard.

We have to consider this mainly from a British point of view, as we know less about other countries' clubs than citizens of those countries. It is likely that the generalities we make about British clubs will apply to all. Clubs (other than local ones) which set out to, or actually do, help the cruising yottie are:

- *The Royal Cruising Club*, the most senior of them all. Limited membership, mutually supportive, but not at all snobbish. Its members really do get about the world, and tend to be well-informed.
- *The Cruising Association*. After being nearly asleep for some time, it is now much more active. It has an excellent clubhouse in London with a great many charts and much information for consultation by those planning a voyage. We meet quite a lot of members, who display creditable levels of skill.
- *The Little Ship Club* has also been kissed by Prince Charming and is now wide awake, and extending its influence. For the long-cruiser it possesses the asset of having premises with comparatively cheap bunks right in the centre of London. When one has sold up and sailed, a base in town can come in handy. It also has excellent courses for those wishing to improve their skills. The dues are a little expensive if you live near London.
- *The Royal Naval Sailing Association* is a very active club (it originated and organised the Whitbread Race for example), and has a fantastic spread of Hon Local Officers world-wide, almost all of whom are superior in every respect to those attached to imitating clubs. Though supposedly for serving or retired Navy, Reserves, and those associated with the Navy, these qualifications are so loose that virtually anyone can join. They even let wives in!

- *The Ocean Cruising Club* is a classless, and somewhat international club for those cruising the oceans. Qualification is a port-to-port voyage exceeding 1000 miles in a small yacht. It is run by people more interested in sailing than administration, which is fine till the admin goes wrong. It disseminates a lot of valuable information through its magazine *Flying Fish*, and constitutes the second largest batch of members that we meet in harbour and on the high seas. It ought to offer Apprentice membership.
- *The Seven Seas Cruising Association* is run from the USA and is specifically for live-aboards. All members are Commodores, and we find the sensation that all are Chiefs without there being any Indians rather eccentric. One ceases to be eligible if one moves ashore, even for short periods, and that is a good idea. The membership qualification is loose, so that one finds a high proportion of live-aboards are house-boat dwellers on the US east coast waterways. A very friendly lot.

We were once in favour of a club for European live-aboards, but were nervous of initiating anything that would either fail because all the membership were so busy sailing that there was no administration, or alternatively it would, like so many clubs, end up by administering itself into the position of taking in its own washing, thus achieving nothing at great expense.

For many years I was a personal member of the Royal Yachting Association (I joined when it was still called the Yacht Racing Association in 1948, and sometimes feel it ought not to have changed its name), but have become disenchanted, especially when I discovered that many of their policies are actually detrimental to the interests of the long-term cruiser. The Secretary General in 1984 told me that long-distance cruisers were a minority and they couldn't be bothered with them. But so are ocean racers, olympic helmsmen, windsurfers, the disabled sailors, and indeed most types of sailors when you classify them. The yachting fraternity is a collection of minorities. I found that most long-term cruisers did not feel quite so strongly as I did about the RYA, possibly because they have not involved themselves. But general opinion is that the RYA has little relevance if you are out of British waters.

One must give the RYA its due and say that they have been very helpful to yachtsmen in the major changes of VAT legislation in the EU, and they are the only body capable of seeing through the nightmare of European compulsory qualifications. I have therefore rejoined, believing in President Johnson's saying about a protesting aide: 'Better to be inside the tent pissing out, than outside pissing in.'

Magazines

It is surely right that authors should review yachting magazines, since they in turn review our books. But doing so imposes the duty of being fair.

No yachting publication specializes in matters of interest to long-cruising folk, though various journals have periods of temporary enthusiasm, which have gotten longer as they realise we are a bigger group than they at first thought. The American *Cruising World* is probably the most consistent, but suffers a little from feminism. It is well produced, and is probably the nearest to a truly international

It isn't all balmy breezes in the Med. Here in Ibiza a bad squall has an American and a South African yacht in trouble. Everyone turns out to help.

yachting magazine. British magazines are generally more inward looking, perhaps a little parochial, but there are often some brilliant contributions. Other countries have some good magazines too; the French and Scandinavian ones are very good, but parochial in their turn: as we said, there isn't a truly international magazine, and this is perhaps a lack.

The main problem with magazines is getting them. With their weight of advertising they cost the earth to post, and are hardly to be found in bookstalls overseas, even in established yachting centres. One does not wish to discard the advertisements which are often rather valuable and informative, except for double page spreads about motor-cars, cigarettes or whisky. Somehow, we wish the advertisement print could be smaller, and the layout tighter: maybe an airmail edition on tissue paper! We might then buy more of them!

Amateur Radio

Many live-aboards are radio amateurs or 'Hams'. There are regular 'nets' or times during which enthusiasts get in touch with one another. Apart from the nets, it is possible in some countries to 'patch in' to the telephone network (officially) and call the folks back home (but not in Britain). A problem lies in the nature and origins of amateur, non-VHF radio. Nowadays some countries actually like their people to use radio and get an interest in modern subjects like electronics. Grandma Britain, however, believes it will rot our teeth or send us blind, and it is made as difficult and expensive as possible to get examined for a licence and stay legal, especially if one is travelling or out of the country for some time each year.

This is a pity, for it is an ideal pastime for the cruising yottie. I asked the RYA to suggest to the licensing authority that there should be a special simplified, limited qualification for cruising yachtsmen to allow them to use only the established 'maritime mobile nets' and only when outside territorial waters. They were not interested, even though it would clearly be a major and inexpensive contribution to ocean sailing safety.

The inevitable outcome is that some yotties broadcast while unlicensed. They are deemed radio pirates and are liable to prosecution if caught, but with a modicum of prudence and cunning there is little likelihood of that. Licensed amateurs are prohibited from communicating with the 'pirates', but in practice have a hard job checking all of them because many pirates 'borrow' real call signs from someone of the same name.

If you are interested in this activity, and it can be fascinating, then it is much better to be licensed, but do try to get your licence while still living ashore. Most places in Britain have amateur radio clubs whose members are usually delighted to help, and there are sometimes courses at evening classes. More information on Amateur radio can be obtained from the Radio Society of Great Britain, Lambda House, Cranbourne Road, Potters Bar, Herts, EN6 3JN or less formally from David Jolly, Little Russel, Lytchett Minster, Poole, Dorset, BH16 6JD (Fax 01202 622142), who will also advise on, and supply most forms of radio communication equipment. The Secretary of State for Trade and Industry also produces an excellent booklet on the subject, but I would try the other sources first.

Electronic Communications and the Internet

The GSM digital phone system has transformed *Hosanna*'s communications. We have used it throughout much of Europe and in Greece and Turkey, but it does not yet work in some of the ex-Soviet bloc countries. (Although some, such as Poland and Hungary, have adopted it as a cheaper way of expanding an antique national telephone system.)

One can use it up to 20 or 30 miles offshore, sometimes a bit more. When we were dismasted off the Kentish Knock, way out in the North Sea, we were able to inform our contacts ashore that we would have to change our expected arrival port, and all our plans. Had we wanted to make a distress call (we did not), it would have been easier to have dialled 999, asked for the coastguard, and had a two-way conversation with him, rather than the one-way-at-a-time stilted and slow VHF marine radio.

To get a GSM phone, one must have a contract with a service provider, such as Vodafone (there are others), but to do this you would need a credit rating and an address in Britain, or whatever country you are based in. This is not as easy as it sounds for live-aboards with no fixed abode. We are considered untrustworthy because we do not fit any category the service providers have put on their form. So get your phone organised before you sell your house.

It is now possible to send and receive fax, and E-mail in a boat at sea. It is also possible to send 'documents' down line from one computer to another without anything anywhere being written down. Because we wanted to communicate with our publishers otherwise than by poste restante, we went into this quite deeply. It took some doing for no service provider, or anyone in any sort of technically authoritative position, was the least bit interested in providing facilities for mobile users on yachts. Or even thinking about it. (They have a funny concept of the uses to which a mobile phone might be put.) We became quite a nuisance, asking questions to which no one seemed to know the answer.

In theory one should be able to connect to fax or the internet using a mobile phone of the GSM (digital) type. It would need to be a special sort of phone, and be compatible with the fittings on your computer. Not impossible, but in practice, not very convenient because the mobile phones do not have a very high baud rate: the speed at which they can transmit data. This would mean that over international phone lines the transmission would take a long time and prove very expensive. And while taking a long time there is always the chance of part of it being garbled, for mobile phones do not have a constant clarity; in certain areas reception is bad.

We know of one journalist who takes his lap-top computer to a public phone booth, and arranges the contact via the phone system, before introducing a fitting on his computer which feeds a noise into the telephone handset which transmits the fax or the E-mail. Apart from the problems of finding a phone booth that works, he has to balance some heavy bits and pieces, probably without the aid of a shelf. Still, it worked after a fashion.

A fellow member of one of our clubs has just transmitted a fax to the Club Secretary from his yacht about 50 miles off the coast of Hawaii. He did this by satellite telephone. This service is getting cheaper and more convenient all the time. The dishes are getting smaller. It is still too expensive for us, but we expect this to improve soon. The progress in communication, whether by word or by data transmission, is faster than one's ability to write about it, and very exciting. By the time you read this, the foregoing paragraphs will probably be history.

Flags and things

If there is one thing that the old guard keep banging on about, it is so-called flag etiquette. People who write for the RYA or pontificate in club journals on this subject seem never to have left Cowes, or else believe that no one else in the world goes sailing other than 'English gentlemen'. In the real live world, Britain now comes some way down the list of countries where yachting is popular: the amount of boats actually under way in some parts of the world greatly exceeds our own backyard fleets. We are no longer entitled to be the arbiters of taste in such a matter, because etiquette is, by definition, the generally accepted code of behaviour and these days the traditional British code is no longer the generally accepted one. Now I am very fond of flags, but I have come to accept that the old traditional etiquette has had its day. Here is the situation as I see it:

Legally, a British ship has only to show an ensign on entering or leaving a foreign port (Merchant Shipping Act 1894). The ensign she may use is also laid down, and the Royal Navy is supposed to, but no longer does, police this. In addition, a lot of countries expect to have their ensign displayed by visiting vessels, and in some cases (Turkey is one), the courtesy ensign is a legal requirement.

I have said that etiquette is the 'generally accepted code of behaviour', so that if one belongs to a club or association which expects its members to conform, that is a reason for conforming. It is, in any event, economical to lower the ensign at night when nobody can see it, because they cost quite a lot, and soon wear out if left flying all the time. An exception could be appropriate in Mediterranean ports when one is lying stern to the main town quay which is well lit, and on which the local population is taking their evening stroll. I like to have the ensign on a good

LEFT
A common Continental method of flying an ensign in a ketch. It is both practical and sensible. Sometimes the downhaul of the halyard is inside the tubular fitting.

RIGHT
Not often seen: the pilot jack in the bows, which is the approved jack for civilian vessels.

sized staff, so that I can dip it to warships (usually with no response; it seems to be a courtesy that has died nowadays), and also to half-mast it on occasions such as the funeral of the mother of the taverna keeper on the other side of the quay. If one half-masts an ensign, one also must half-mast the courtesy ensign, do not forget.

Courtesy ensigns by tradition were flown at the fore masthead. In yachts this was traditionally kept for the club burgee, but nowadays few cruising yachts belong to clubs, and if they do they usually fly the burgee at the port crosstrees. The starboard crosstrees are then for the courtesy ensign. This is because mastheads are now often cluttered with electronic decorations.

Many smaller yachts have their ensign tied to the standing backstay, where it stays until it rots. This is almost the current etiquette, so if you do the same no one is likely to notice. But it does add to the cost of living, and it seems to me desirable to have some sort of halyard so that when one remembers one can haul the flag down to prolong its active life.

International Code Flags are a waste of money, unless you wish to dress ship for a celebration. You will need flag Q on arrival in some countries, though no longer within the European Union, unless coming from outside the Union. Apart from that most flags carried will be courtesy ensigns, which have become a bit of a nuisance since so many former colonies have become jealous little republics.

The best way of dealing with the problem of multiple courtesy ensigns, since they are so expensive, is to follow our previously given advice and carry a sewing machine and a couple of yards of material of each of the primary colours, plus some different coloured fabric marking crayons (Vogart is a trade name of a suitable brand) to do the intricate bits without which no modern flag seems to be complete. If possible arrive in a country with its courtesy ensign hoisted. Try not to be mean with size; flags are generally hoisted high and can look very tiny, which hardly seems a courtesy. In some places yachtsmen have been fined for having a ragged courtesy ensign; this raises several thoughts about what is a courtesy, and to whom.

Recently the whole question of flag etiquette has come under debate in the journal of the RNSA. The fact that old-and-bold naval officers are at last questioning an outmoded practice should augur well for a change in the position.

Dressing ship

It is a present day nautical convention to hoist strings of decorative flags between mastheads and down to stem and stern in order to celebrate various occasions. Not many observe it, except a few British and Dutch with the odd American or German. We do it because I am a flag nut and think it looks good, but we do not always do it for those formal occasions laid down by the Admiralty. We did it at Meganisi in Greece where we were staying at the time of the Feast of Saint Bissarion, the local patron, just as we halfmasted the ensign for Good Friday, as the local boats do. It is an island of merchant navy men, and on both occasions several called by to thank us for the courtesy. It all helps to make the yottie more welcome.

We once did it on Trafalgar Day while in France, and a French Naval Captain observed 'This is a good day for the France.' '*Comment?*' we replied, a little surprised. 'Well, we shot Nelson that day, and if we had not, we might well now be a British colony.' Everyone enjoys a sense of humour; we made another friend.

The usual form for dressing lines is to alternate the flags of the code with the pennants and substitutes. The order does not really matter — just make a colourful show.

Our dressing occasions are: the birthdays of crew, Trafalgar Day, St George's Day, Christmas Day, New Year's Day (when we also hoist a full string of courtesy ensigns for places visited during the past year), plus any special dates for the country or port we are visiting.

How to be a Popular Yottie

The considerations that apply to flag etiquette apply also to yacht etiquette — the arbiters are no longer those elderly blimps from Cowes or the New York Yacht Club who have for so long arrogantly imposed their values on Anglo-American yachting. The arbiters now are the people who actually sail, and they comprise many nationalities. The form nowadays can be summed up:

- Cause the minimum inconvenience to other yachts' crews.
- Help another yacht berthing close by you.
- Give assistance willingly, and without legal haggling, to anyone in difficulties.

These three tenets are obvious to most people who want to sail. In more detail certain usages have grown up around them, and I will give those I have noticed. If I have missed any, then I apologise to whomever I have offended.

Generators Their use is growing as they become smaller and quieter, and it has to be faced that many yachts have them and need them. In general most confine generating to the forenoon. There is a growing tendency for a second run in the dog watches, between about 1600 and 1800, which is not so nice, but tolerable. In port you should not run generators before 0830, between 1230 and 1600, or after 1800 unless you want to incur the justifiable wrath of your neighbours.

In 1997 the use of generators at *all* hours has become more common. Charter yachts are likely to run their air-conditioning 24 hours a day, and even among the smaller yachts the practice is on the increase. There is a law in Greece forbidding the running of noisy machinery anywhere between 1400 and 1700, the better to further the Ipnos, or afternoon sleep. We suggest this should be observed in boats, extended to include the late evening and night-time. At anchor, when yachts are some distance apart, the convention can be relaxed, particularly if it is windy, but in close anchorages such as Bequia or Union Island it ought to be observed.

Dinghies In Europe, dinghies left ashore are inviolable, at least from other yotties. You should make yours fast on a long painter so that it can be shoved to one side to allow room for others to get alongside to land. In areas where Americans abound, and particularly where their racing circuses congregate, the unsolicited borrowing of dinghies is not uncommon, like bicycles at Oxford. Americans seem to tolerate this noxious practice, which is generally anathema to our older civilization. Either take precautions or be surprised.

Anchors Be particularly careful when berthing bows or stern to a quay not to lay your anchor cable(s) across others. In many places it cannot be avoided, however. The first to arrive at Navpaktos, in the Gulf of Corinth, is obliged to be the last to leave; the centre of this tiny harbour resembles a diagram for a multi-part Matthew Walker knot, tied in cable. A great deal of tolerance is needed.

Untangling foul anchors is an example of the willingness of yotties to help each other. Usually anyone with a dinghy down will paddle out to do his stuff. Greek yachtsmen are particularly good about this.

If you are moored stern or bows to with the usual taut cable, and someone fouls it when weighing, you have an obligation to respond to reasonable requests from the fouler, who is probably in the best position to know how he is foul. He will probably ask you to give him some slack, for a yacht without a power windlass is unlikely to be able to haul a tight chain to the surface so that he can unhook his anchor. Even if he has power, if he hauls up a tight cable he is likely to haul up your anchor with it, so some slack is usually desirable. If wind conditions are troublesome run your engine at modest revs to hold your stem off the quay. If you are the fouler, and haul out the anchor of a berthed boat, try to re-lay it as close to its original position as possible.

One does *not* buoy anchors in a busy port; the chaos if all did so can be imagined. If you are worried about foul anchors use a trip line taken back to your bow. In an open anchorage an anchor buoy can be of help to another yacht in avoiding anchoring too close because sometimes one's cable lies in a curve on the bottom. In a crowded anchorage it is a help to a newcomer shaping up near you to tell him how much cable you are lying to. It is the responsibility of the latecomer to keep clear of those already anchored, and this continues unless the first-comer changes the state by veering or shortening cable, or by letting go another anchor.

The last to haul or the last to veer,
He's the one who must keep clear.

Berthing It is usual to help with the ropes of a yacht berthing next to you. In the Med, where harbours are often crowded, it is anti-social to berth alongside the quay instead of stern-to. There are exceptions, such as Poros in the Aegean, or Khalkis, but for special reasons. Anyone berthing in this way has to be prepared for others to berth alongside them without any ceremony. In the Azores, Bermuda, Baltic and some Canaries harbours, yachts sometimes lie alongside six or more abreast. Outside yachts (other than tiddlers) must have breastropes to the quay, and springs to their neighbours. Utmost co-operation is needed, and is usually forthcoming to a measure that breeds friendships.

The old convention of always crossing over the foredeck of a neighbour is gone: many voyagers now have a proper sleeping cabin in the fore part of the yacht, and in warm climates often a wide-open hatch. It is proper to enquire (by day) how you should cross, and the responder should also pass on the information he has already got from yachts inside him.

Polite Footwear The real seaman wears deck shoes because he knows that stubbed toes can be disabling, and also that quaysides are often fouled by disease-ridden dogs. Dilettante yachtsmen who spend more time polishing their yachts than sailing them have an elaborate ritual of donning or doffing shoes like a crowd of Japanese on their doorsteps. But you cannot expect an outside crew to take off their boots just because you bagged the inside berth. Face the fact that if the deck of your yacht will not stand up to deck shoes it is not fit for its purpose. (A little small grit is very good for teak; it roughens it, improves its nonslip qualities.) On the other hand the shoe wearer has an obligation to see that his shoes are clean.

Smoking Do as you like in your own boat, but in harbour do not throw cigarette ends overboard. Many yachts put their dinghies down in harbour, and it's too easy to make a bad shot and start a fire in one. While not inflammable, peach stones and olive pips are irritating, too.

Greek ladies washing using tubs and washboards. It's back to basics without a washing machine.

Garbage The French and Italians tend to leave plastic bags of garbage loose on the quay, thereby encouraging rats, stray dogs and cats, and the wrath and disrespect of others who mostly look for the garbage skip. This is often full, when there is nothing to be done except to leave the garbage alongside it. In the Caribbean and elsewhere, pay no heed to little boys who paddle out to your anchorage and offer to dispose of your garbage for a fee. They will rummage through it for anything of interest, and then leave the rest on that pretty little beach where you wanted to swim.

Quiet Quiet times vary from place to place. Some are still beating at 0300. A few miles away, at another port, the inhabitants will all be asleep by 2130. Local people may well welcome the income from tourism, but do not want to pay too high a price for it. Ascertain and respect the local convention. And join the anti wet-bike campaign.

Helping There is a tradition of helping others with navigation information. Where they are otherwise unobtainable, charts etc are loaned for photocopying. Linguists pass on the weather reports, and any yacht who has been in the port more than a few days passes on the whereabouts of sources of essentials (water, or gas bottles) or even non-essentials that are particularly interesting.

Cruising in Company

It had (truly) never occurred to me that anyone would be seriously nervous about an Atlantic crossing in the tradewind belt until we invited a relative to cross with us in *Fare Well* in 1982. He brought his wife, an experienced dinghy sailor, and a valuable member of the crew during very rough weather between Gibraltar and the Canaries, which didn't frighten her at all.

Three days out from Tenerife, she appeared on deck with a face of thunder; she had just learnt that our destination was Barbados, twenty days away. Her shame-faced husband confessed that the only way he had been able to get round her fear of crossing the Atlantic was to tell her that we were making a short trip round the Canaries. She had been shanghaied! It was a calm crossing, as they mostly are; and we are glad to say she enjoyed it; we had already endured the only rough bit between Gibraltar and Tenerife, running before a wild Levanter (east wind).

Given that sort of feeling, we should have expected that someone would propose a trans-Atlantic voyage in company. Jimmy Cornell, an experienced ocean sailor, started the Atlantic Rallies for Cruisers (the ARC) which, backed by *Yachting World*, have been a great success, and have pleased many people. We do not propose to carp at this aspect of the ARC. How could we? It would not be our way of cruising, because we like to be on our own at sea. We like to pick our ports of departure and arrival. The ARC organisers changed the latter from Barbados, which was the logical destination, to a very commercial marina in St Lucia, which we think is not, and for reasons we find unconvincing. Also there is a substantial fee (when last we heard — 1995 — it was up to £400 per boat plus about £30 per person in the crew). We would not feel personally happy with the competitive atmosphere (prizes for the first boat and so on) that is developing.

The ARC cannot provide any real services while on passage that are not already there. If one is in danger or distress, then all vessels are bound by law to come to your assistance, including, on both sides of this 'equation', those in the ARC. Essentially one is paying for a grand party at either end; if that suits you, go to it. In addition, we understand from those who have joined in, that one's boat is inspected before the start. To us that would be an impertinence. At present the sole arbiter of whether or not a vessel is suitable for her voyage is the Captain. No other has any competence, except that in certain special cases, a Coastguard Officer (or equivalent in some countries) can prevent an obviously unseaworthy craft from leaving port; a draconian power that is very seldom used.

The fitting out of craft is a very personal thing, and I can think of nobody I would deem capable of making judgements in all possible cases. It would be arrogant to claim such plenipotentiary power. This is the aspect of the ARC which, to us, is a little threatening because, before long, some government department is going to use the fact that those running the ARC find it necessary to inspect craft before departure to justify a universal system of small craft inspections, such as already exists in certain countries. I have recently been much involved with the way continental authorities' minds are moving towards limiting the pleasure boat communities' freedoms, and they move just as I have suggested above. Woe betide, then, the owner of an unusual craft; anything out of the ordinary would be suspect. This aspect of the ARC should be re-considered. It would be far better to emphasise individual responsibility, beside which little else matters.

Nevertheless, the fact that so many have taken part indicates that there are many yachtsmen who welcome Jimmy's initiative. If you feel you would like that way of cruising watch *Yachting World* for details. If the ARC is treated as a sort of apprenticeship or initiation, then it can hardly do any harm to the community of yotties.

There are other cruising 'rallies'. One runs from Hampton, Virginia to Bermuda and Tortola, but we have no details. There have been others on a 'round the world' basis, making several stops en route. These latter attract more criticism than the ARC. They remind us of the flotillas, which have changed for the worse the cruising atmosphere in the Ionian Islands. They bring to yachting the concept and atmosphere of the package holiday, and gradually 'benidorm' the places they touch. These events are very expensive, and the participants are in holiday mode. They call in at well-known ocean-yottie stops, and quite frankly spoil things for the independent yottie following them.

Yachts had traditionally paid peanuts for their Suez Canal passages until after one such group had negotiated a 'special deal' for a transit en masse ('Special for you, Effendi!'). They ended up paying three times the normal rate, and the old price has gone for ever. We have met Australian and New Zealand boats which have arrived in the Med angry about the don't-care atmosphere these yachting circuses leave behind them.

We have to face it that yachting in all its forms has expanded greatly over the past 50 years. Many coastal yacht clubs and marinas are full; almost the only yachting activity still with growth potential is the long-haul cruising world. It is all going to get more and more crowded as more and more countries take up yachting. But, though some control is going to come in respect of personal qualifications, let us try to keep this a pastime for individualistically minded folk. Wait until it really catches on in Japan, Korea and China: it's starting already.

Chapter Fourteen

Routeing

*'It is to be supposed by this time the ship is victualled and manned,
the voiage determined... and all things else ready to set sail.'*

This chapter is concerned with ways of getting between the various cruising grounds we have discussed in Chapter Ten, and is meant to provide outline guidance only. There are now a number of ocean routeing guides that provide comprehensive information, and one should not overlook the British Admiralty, or US Navy routeing charts which have a statistical coverage of weather and currents for all the world's oceans.

Some people will perhaps wish to remain in one area, but most who are seriously infected with the wanderbug will one day want to try somewhere else — it's what the business is all about. Sometimes one can make a sheltered passage from one area to another, but there are a few occasions where an ocean passage is an option. For a Briton or European, the first problem to be faced is getting away. If I say that a voyage direct to North America is contrary to the spirit of the casual wanderer, I think most readers will by now know what I mean. So we rule out 30 days of beating into the winds of a series of depressions. This means that, even if bound across the Atlantic, the first stage is a voyage south, not necessarily as far as Gibraltar but in that direction.

This is also the open-sea route to the Mediterranean. There are other ways of getting there, and they will be mentioned under inland water routes. For the moment, then, let us look at a passage to Gibraltar, or its vicinity.

The Bay of Biscay, Your First Challenge

It is a sad fact of geography that the first ocean crossing which northern Europeans make on setting out is the Bay of Biscay, a difficult stretch of water for sailing vessels.

A sad fact also that if you, a cruiser climbing a learning curve, are plucked out of trouble by helicopter, your fifteen minutes of fame will be attended by castigation, condemnation, little respect, and a week later oblivion; whereas a racing yachtsman (an expert who should know better), whose Southern Ocean rescue involves expenditure in megamillions, is treated as a hero and there will be a book and a film. It seems hard.

The reputation of the Bay of Biscay stems from the depressions that are characteristic of its weather patterns, causing strong westerly winds which blow craft into the bay. With a long gale, or a series of short ones in quick succession, the average yacht has difficulty not only in getting out of the Bay, but also in surviving the gale itself, for room to manoeuvre gets steadily less and less the more one is embayed. Further into the bay it shallows, making the seas steeper and more dangerous, and the last part of a typical gale has the wind from the north-west, the worst possible sector.

Old sailing captains leaving the English Channel in weather other than a set-fair anti-cyclone would steer west until longitude 8° west, when they would turn south. It took longer, but that way they stood a fair chance of not becoming a statistic. It seems to us that cruising yachts manned by *small inexperienced crews* should think of doing just that. Top quality yachts with huge crews of experienced gorillas do as they please, but families, especially with children, should play safe at the beginning of their world cruise.

An alternative is to coast to Cork in Ireland, getting gradually accustomed to the life and having shelter to run to, and then start from there. They're lovely people in Cork, and it's well worth a visit.

In any event, keep well outside the Ushant traffic separation scheme and special tanker channel; it is better to double Ushant out of range of Ushant light. You should do so even if the separation scheme were not in operation, because if bad weather comes the wind is more likely to be west than any other, and it will almost certainly be accompanied by a current pushing a vessel into the Bay.

Above all, be prudent.

I would pass down the Portuguese coast well out to sea, out of sight of land, and only close the coast near Cape St Vincent. This headland has a traffic separation scheme round it, which is of doubtful necessity and a hazard of itself. Sailing vessels should round this cape very close to with an easterly wind, in which case they are obliged to foul the badly planned north-bound lane, though there is seldom very much traffic. With a northwesterly wind, which is the most likely, it is well to stay offshore out of the way of the north-bound traffic; keep a good offing if bound for Gibraltar in order to avoid the Banks, for though there is depth for a yacht the seas can be very unpleasant there.

The distance from Falmouth to Gibraltar is 1080 miles, and from Cork it is 1098 miles. Most cruising boats average between 100 and 130 miles per day. I had my best day's run ever in *Fare Well* south-bound some 30 miles off the Portuguese coast, logging 190 miles with only 37 square metres of canvas set. But we still took 12 days for the passage because we were hove to for 48 hours in the Bay.

The Mediterranean

Within the Med, routeing is comparatively simple. There are a few caution-worthy spots. When crossing the Gulf of Lions check not only the weather forecast but also that you know the bad weather signs (see Admiralty Pilot, Mediterranean Vol. II). Watch the Bonifacio Strait in rough weather for it seems to act like a funnel: the weather is always bad, and I always suffer damage to either myself or the yacht off Cape Corse. This last is, I think, a purely personal affair, but you never know.

There is often fog in the Sicilian Channel and in the Malta Channel, even in summer, and the east-going current can be strong in both. They are both encumbered with shipping and fishing boats, and good watch-keeping is required. One occasionally gets very strong westerly winds in spring or autumn, with seas that can damage even big ships.

The Straits of Messina is one of the few in the Mediterranean with a very strong tidal stream. I have personally measured 6 knots at springs. Consult the Admiralty Pilot (the tidal information is based on Gibraltar), and try to go through with a fair tide. Scylla and Charybdis, the whirlpools, may be seen, but since the earthquake in 1783 are no longer as menacing as heretofore, and one can sail right through the vortices, even at springs, with no ill effects other than being rotated a bit. In strong wind-against-tide conditions, however, a small yacht could find itself in trouble. There is a strict traffic control scheme in operation: one must have a motor ready for use, and keep watch on VHF. The ferries are frequent, arrogant, and difficult to cope with as they leave the port of Villa san Giovanni at full speed.

Navigation of the Dardanelles is only difficult because of the volume of traffic, particularly large Russian ships. There is often a strong south-going current. One's passage is controlled with all the strictness expected of Air Traffic Control. One must report on VHF to each station as one approaches, and be passed on from one controller to the next. Language English; very efficient.

West-bound across the Atlantic

Go south until the butter melts, then turn right: there is not much more to it. If leaving Gibraltar, it is better to wait for a Levanter (east wind), but that often brings poor weather generally. If coming from the north, it pays usually to keep well out and one can sometimes carry the Portuguese Trades almost down to the Canary Islands.

Most yachts call at the Canaries, if only to stock up, and it can be quite a social scene there in November. The tradewind belt moves north in winter, and it is better to wait for it to establish itself up to 15°N or so, which usually happens during November. The wind increases, and by January, is much stronger. If going to the Caribbean for a long stay it might be worth spending a couple of months or more in the Canaries, or making a diversion via the Cape Verde Islands.

Only really freak weather should disturb the easy tedium of the passage. The occasional squall enables everyone to strip off and have a free shower, but make sure there is enough rain to wash the soap off before putting it on.

For the nervous or extremely social, there is the ARC (Atlantic Rally for Cruisers) which we have commented on earlier.

North-bound from the Caribbean

If bound for Florida it is better to go south of the Bahamas Islands. There are some doubts about the surveys east of the Bahamas; ever since a flag officer of the Royal Cruising Club was wrecked there the charts have been assumed to be wrong.

Seriously, though, there have been quite a few yachts lost in those parts; one should think carefully before closing the low-lying banks. Whether the charts are wrong, or there are unrecorded strong currents, I do not know; nor, I suspect, does anyone else yet. It is not one of the most important bits of ocean.

If bound for the Bermudas, it is as well to start from east of Puerto Rico to be reasonably expectant of a reach. There are no problems. The Bermudas are well lit and clear of off-lying dangers to the south.

Heading to the USA from the Bermudas ought not to be difficult, though we once took 12 days for the 630 miles. I know from bitter experience that this is a passage where one should take a lot of care about the weather. Excellent forecasts are broadcast from Portsmouth, Virginia by voice on SSB, and some of them are in English. The others are in what my American friend called 'Dixie'. One of the important features of these forecasts is the relaying of the positions of the edges of the Gulf Stream. This ocean-going river flows at up to 3 knots in this part of the world and makes a lot of difference to a yacht's course made good. The edges are well defined: the northern edge particularly can be recognized with some exactitude by observing the sea-water temperature, which will fall several degrees in a few hours when bound northwards out of the stream. Because of the current flow, very nasty seas can build up when the wind is opposite this current. Gales from the northeast quadrant can be particularly dangerous.

Watch out for fog in the colder waters approaching the New England coast. As soon as possible get the local weather forecasts from the special coastal VHF stations. Also beware of shipping bound to or from New York. There are off-lying dangers near the New England coast so do your homework first and carefully. Take note that by some administrative lunacy, the offshore buoys off Nantucket that would be so useful for a position check in bad weather all have the same light characteristic: flashing white, every four seconds.

If having left Bermuda you are tempted to return for any reason, then consider very carefully before doing so. The offlying reefs to the northwest of the islands are dangerous; and very dangerous in bad weather, being poorly lit and comparatively steep-to.

East-bound over the Atlantic

The most common route is via the Bermudas and the Azores. The passage to Bermuda poses few difficulties that we have not already discussed in the reverse direction. From Bermuda head northeast until the latitude of 40°N is reached, then steer along the parallel until a couple of days or so west of the Azores. The popular time for this voyage is May/June and then the weather will not be hot: often it is jersey weather all the way, and the winds can be variable and sometimes irritatingly light. There is always a chance of some strong winds, but most of the severe depressions should pass well to the north. (I do not guarantee that.)

Shipping is mostly light especially compared with the yacht traffic in May or June when something like 150 yachts arrive in the Azores each month from the west. The Azores are an easy landfall, and Mount Pico is a very impressive one after some 18 days at sea. Nevertheless they have been missed completely; I do not know how, but they have. The welcome is good and the living is cheap. From the Azores to Gibraltar, Portugal or the English Channel presents no special problems in the summer months.

Inland Passages

For passages through the French canals and rivers to the Mediterranean there are so many books giving detailed advice, written by people with great knowledge of these waterways, that much comment here is not appropriate.

It is not a quick passage: there are very many locks, and navigation at night is not permitted. In my view it should be a lingering cruise, not to be taken at the rush. The French canals are an experience in themselves. The quickest passage from North Sea to the Mediterranean I know of is via the Marne, mast down to mast up 19 days, but how they must have sweated, and what delights they must have missed. The maximum length should not worry the type of cruising yacht that falls in our categories, but beam is limited to 5 metres, and draught officially to 1.8 metres, though over 1.6 may involve some ploughing. The lowest bridge obstruction is 3.4 metres, and there are facilities for striking masts at both ends of the system.

Some yachts have sailed into the Bay of Biscay and passed to the Mediterranean via Bordeaux and the Canal du Midi, emerging at Sete. Not all yachts who do this originally intended to, it being sometimes difficult to get out of the Bay any other way. The Gironde estuary with its many banks can be dangerous for small craft in strong westerly winds. One catamaran with the spoonerish name of *Cupid Stunts*, bound for Gibraltar in autumn, was carried to leeward by several days of bad weather and actually blown into the Gironde River willy-nilly. Her crew, who were mostly inexperienced, learned a lot, and enjoyed their passage through this marvellous canal. Bear in mind that the Canal du Midi might be closed in times of drought, as in 1989.

The Rhine-Main-Danube Canal has opened, and vessels should be able to navigate across Germany, Austria, Yugoslavia etc and down to the Black Sea. We have done it (see our book *Back Door to Byzantium*, published by Adlard Coles Nautical), and it is by no means the relaxing journey that one would have via the

French canals. From sea to sea it is 4000 kilometres (2162 nautical miles), and both the navigation and the old Iron Curtain countries present difficulties. It took us five months.

Elsewhere

The Panama Canal is a substantial undertaking for a yacht, and I have done it only in big ships. Some people have had uneventful passages; others have had events and damage. The Panama is not an expensive canal to pass through because the charge is tonnage based, but yachts without engines capable of 5 knots or more have to be towed, which is another matter.

The long passage across the Pacific does not appeal to me much, although it does not seem to cause many problems to the large numbers who have sailed it. I have spent a lot of time in the Indian Ocean and thoroughly enjoyed it. Political uncertainties in the area would detract from the pleasure today.

There is nowadays quite a bit of yacht traffic from Australia via Galle in Ceylon and on into the Red Sea. A good alternative is the route via Christmas Island, the Cocos Keelings, Mauritius and Cape Town. A practical problem is the Agulhas Current off the southeast coast of South Africa; here the seas in bad weather can cause difficulties even for big ships.

The main problem about the Suez Canal route to Europe (provided one is not daft enough to try to cross the ocean against the Monsoon) is getting up the Red Sea. In spite of the political complexion of the government yachtsmen are usually well received at Aden, but a similar welcome cannot be relied on at any Red Sea ports. This is a pity, for with the virtual certainty of head winds most will want to make a stop or two. Even Port Sudan, which was once quite popular, has to be approached with caution nowadays, and Saudi Arabia, for all its wealth and its religious teaching, and in spite of the millions of pounds worth of yachts owned by their citizens, has not learned yet how to give a civilized welcome to travellers.

The Suez Canal necessitates having an agent, unless one has unusual persistence, patience and a very cool head. The big trouble is that Egypt is openly and unashamedly corrupt. The actual cost of the transit is modest, but the agency fee will probably exceed the canal dues. A pilot is compulsory (I was one once, for a short time), who will have little to do except watch the signal stations. You may be lucky and get a pleasant fellow for half the journey; you would be very lucky indeed if both pilots were congenial. The chances are that local pilots will demand and expect 'gifts'.

The reverse voyage, down the Red Sea, presents few problems and is best done non-stop in the present world disorder.

I offer no advice on rounding Cape Horn. In my view it is a rotten part of the globe, and the only reason I can think of for going there is to prove something that one ought not to have to prove.

	Aden	Barbados	Bermuda	Brindisi	Chesapeake	Cork	Cristobal	Dover	Fayal	Genoa	Gibraltar	Istanbul	Madeira	Malta	Marseilles	New York	Las Palmas	Plymouth	Port Said
Aden																			
Barbados	6550																		
Bermuda	6230	1220																	
Brindisi	2320	4530	1220																
Chesapeake	6630	1680	640	4210															
Cork	4400	3400	2730	2380	4600														
Cristobal (Panama)	7630	1220	1640	5620	1750	4310													
Dover	4600	3710	3080	2580	3390	450	4660												
Fayal (Azores)	4430	2250	1800	2400	2220	1180	3260	1480											
Genoa	2810	4100	3770	750	4170	1950	5180	2140	1980										
Gibraltar	3300	3250	2930	1280	3330	1100	4340	1230	1130	850									
Istanbul	2190	5050	4730	790	5140	2900	6150	3030	3000	1310	1810								
Madeira	3900	2630	2520	1900	2880	1250	3740	1400	670	1450	600	2420							
Malta	2330	4230	3910	360	4320	2080	5330	2220	2110	670	990	850	1590						
Marseilles	2900	3940	3620	840	4020	1790	5030	1920	1820	200	700	1390	1290	650					
New York	6500	1830	700	4480	260	2820	1970	3250	2100	4050	3200	5010	2770	4190	3900				
Las Palmas (Canaries)	4000	2640	2560	1980	3060	1480	3800	1610	900	1550	710	2500	290	1680	1390	2930			
Plymouth	4400	3501	2870	2380	3430	233	4450	225	1275	1950	1038	2840	1205	2020	1730	3051	1421		
Port Said	1400	5150	4830	930	5240	3000	6240	3140	3040	1430	1900	790	2500	940	1500	5100	2610	2945	
Ushant	4230	3420	2810	2200	3120	230	4380	310	1170	1770	920	2720	790	1910	1610	2990	1310	110	2830

Chapter Fifteen

Health and Welfare at Sea

*'The Chirurgeon is to be exempted from all duty but to attend the sicke
and cure the wounded; and good care would be had he have a certificate
from the Barber-Chirurgeon's Halls of his sufficiency... for which neglect
hath beene the loss of many a man's life.'*

Nowhere is it more obvious than on a long-distance cruise that sickness is
more a state of mind than of body. Most cruising people find that as the pace
of life slows to 5 knots on average and the world shrinks to the size of their boat,
many bodily ills dwindle and disappear. On the other hand, you have a better
chance of doing yourself an injury on a boat of cruising size than might be the
case if you had stuck to golf and lawnmowers.

Consequently, while you need no longer exempt your Chirurgeon from all other
duty, it would be well, as Capt John Smith points out, that he have a certificate;
nowadays from the Red Cross or St John's Ambulance Brigade, at least. It has to
be said that the Red Cross and St John's courses are not enough for the long-
distance cruiser. Even if we have access to advice by radio, we are likely to need
practical skills such as giving injections, administering a drip, stitching wounds,
and the control of pain and infection. Many doctors in the British Isles have a
deep-seated mistrust of allowing any Tom, Dick or Harriet to acquire such paramedical skills or even read about them. In the USA there is a crash course
designed by a Doctor/sailor: the *Intensive Survey of Medical Emergency Care*.

In the first edition we wrote that there were no medical courses in UK for
long-distance yachtsmen. The scene is changing, though we think there is still a
need for more and better. The RYA is still barely interested in long-distance
cruising, but now runs a course called Small Craft First Aid. The Department of
Trade approve a course called First Aid at Sea. In the days before these Laurel
attended the Lowestoft Nautical College to take the Ship Captain's Medical Course,
which is not specifically intended for yachtsmen, but is wonderfully reassuring.

She reported: The course is based on the *Ship Captain's Medical Guide*
(known as The Book) which all British Merchant Ships are required to carry. We
always had a copy on board for long cruises in *Fare Well* and latterly in
Hosanna, and found it very useful in emergencies. Embarking on our travels
again, I felt I wanted some practical knowledge to add to the drugs and equipment which we had carried on *Fare Well*. It was all very well having the stuff on
board, but did I know how to use it all? No, I did not. Many people ask how we
cope with sickness or accidents. The only response that we can make is: 'As best
we can, it doesn't happen often.' One knows that help is not within reach, and
that the High Street surgery is 4,000 miles away. When the crunch comes you

are your own barefoot doctor — you, with the worried look and the shaking hands. I ought, I felt, to be able to give an injection, and take a stitch-in-time with a suturing needle.

So I enrolled on the course, and began badly. I was ten minutes late, and I'd missed the whole of 'Preparing a Cabin for a Patient' and half of 'Vital Signs'. Yes, the course was dense and intense. There were six of us on the three-day course, four Merchant Navy Officers, and two yacht ladies: Caroline of *Heartsease* and me. We went at the pace of a motorcycle scramble. The breathless speed made us reel.

We learned how to take blood pressure, record temperature, pulse and breathing, how to test urine and why. (Nurses in the old days used to taste it to find what was in it, said Rosie SRN, our Mentor, thank God we now use Labstix.)

We did Observation of Specimens, and Care of Bed Patients; we learned to face the enema, and to give rectal infusions (to fight the Demon Dehydration, the killer in many and varied diseases and conditions). We learned how to cope with Malaria, we saw a slide cassette on Heat Exhaustion and Heat Stroke.

Fortified by lunch, I then discovered more than I care to know about Sexually Transmitted Diseases. This lecture was beautifully sung by a Welsh doctor, who accompanied it with extraordinary slides. He began *pianissimo* with the diseases we'd all heard of, went into a fugue of oddities that were new to some of us, and ended up with a threnody on AIDS.

We then pelted through Poisons, including many gases that were relevant to the cargoes of Shipmasters, but not very likely on a yacht. We roared past Resuscitation, hurtled through Haemorrhage, and halted for a while for Hypothermia (something that anyone who goes boating on the lake ought to know about, let alone long-distance cruisers).

We galloped past Gallstones, shot through Surgical Emergencies, were mesmerised by Mental Illness and Myocardial Infarction (which up to then we had called heart attack). We were petrified by Palpation of the Abdomen, bemused by Bodies (disposal of) and bothered by Burial at Sea. And all the time Caroline and I would ask: 'But suppose you haven't got room on your boat for all that apparatus/equipment/vast array of drugs?'

Improvisation can save your bacon, as I well know, and Rosie often assured us with examples. I remembered once leaving Port Mahon (on a Friday of course) when Bill was freeing the anchor from a heavy rope encrusted with barnacles, when a huge fish-hook caught deep in the pad of his middle finger. My first action had to be taking the strain off the rope, and therefore the finger. The second was to check that the boat was still safely anchored. The third was to sit down and think a bit.

'Push the hook through the skin (if no vital organ is endangered), nip off the barb, and withdraw', said the First Aid book. But they hadn't seen stainless steel Spanish fish hooks; they're more like something you find at the butcher's, with a whole ox hanging from it. Which was not far from the truth, as I pointed out to the Skipper at the time: he was not amused. A brief effort to obey the First Aid book with the aid of bolt cutters threatened to amputate the finger and was quickly abandoned for a Stanley knife, 'sterilised' with brandy.

Both patient and 'doctor' then drank some of the brandy (not recommended in The Book) and, shaking like leaves, cut out the hook, which was baited with something slithery that looked very evil. I wish I knew what, as the wound healed clean and with great rapidity, and we might have made a fortune selling it to a drug company. Observe that it never occurred to us to row ashore and find a doctor. One loses the habit.

I also recalled putting the Skipper's neck in traction with a handy billy and a seven kilo gas bottle over a pulley, and under 'Burns' you will find an ingenious use for the rain gauge.

Back to the course. In two and a half crammed days we learned to stitch gaping wounds in surprisingly resistant foam rubber (very like the real thing, said Rosie) and *not* to put our finger on the knot. Knowledge of stitching I could have used on a couple of occasions for small wounds.

We learned to inject oranges. We learned to approach the plastic model of Resusci-Annie with confidence, despite her lying on the floor with her lungs exposed and a feral grin on her face. Her bared rubber teeth looked as if they could bite you if she didn't care for your technique, or your aftershave. I added the Brooke Airway to our first aid list. When it came to exam. time, we all regurgitated sufficient material (some of it only half-digested) to pass; Caroline and I were the first women to do so at Lowestoft who were not Shipmasters.

What does all that make me? Certainly not the Doc. But next time something happens, I shall have a modicum of confidence to add to common sense. I will hope to reassure my victim that my panicky search through 'The Book' will bring help and relief. Raising morale is my strong point. Even without the brandy. And I am more determined than ever to harp (to the point of boring my readers) on *prevention* of accidents and illness at sea. Stop it happening, and you don't have to treat it.

If you are within reach of land, English speaking doctors who have been properly trained may be found world-wide by joining (for the cost of a donation) IAMAT, the International Association for Medical Assistance to Travellers whose address will be found in the Appendix. Otherwise advice *may* be available by radio: a call of 'Pan Pan Medico' should produce results if any doctor is monitoring, or any merchant ship or shore station picks up your call.

It is to be hoped that you will have gone to sea in a state of good health, as far as can be ascertained by check-ups and dental work before you go. Cherish this happy state of affairs by thinking 'prevention' rather than 'cure'. Catch it before it happens. Eliminate the chances of sickness and bodily damage to your utmost. Since this attitude goes hand in hand with the watchfulness that every good seaman cultivates, the quicker it becomes second nature to you the sooner, paradoxically, you can relax and enjoy your cruise. By 'looking for trouble' you are avoiding it!

MASTA (Medical Advisory Services for Travellers Abroad) is a world-wide advisory health service for travellers. Approved by (and next door to) the London School of Hygiene and Tropical Medicine, they will tailor a Health Brief to your individual requirements, with details of all inoculations you will need, information and a list of medical items to take with you, and up-to-date 'health newsflashes' from all over the world, via their computer bank. They can also organise your membership of the Blood Care Foundation, and supply antimalarial and other equipment. Address in the Appendix.

Take with you 'The Book', and/or *The First Aid Manual* published by the Red Cross and St John's.

A–Z of Preventive Measures

There follows, in alphabetical order, not the First Aid advice you will get from the above books, and others specially written for yachtsmen, but a useful list of preventive measures, which is less often come across.

AIDS and STD's

It used to be sailors who spread Sexually Transmitted Diseases (STD's). Now that everyone travels, it is the tourists and the businessmen who spread the plague. Take the obvious precautions, remember that condoms have a limited shelf-life, and are hard to find in remote places. If you intend going to certain parts of the world where AIDS is especially rife, take with you your own syringes, needles, blood giving set, sterile swabs and plasma. You might consider joining the Blood Care Foundation, a charity to provide screened and tested blood in countries where it is not usually available: £99 covers two adults and two children for a year, see address of MASTA in appendix.

Appendicitis

This is the great bugaboo that frightens everyone. Many transatlantic yachtsmen have an 'elective appendectomy' in order to avoid any possibility of trouble. This would need to be discussed with your doctor. We feel that nowadays hospitals take away the disease you came in with and give you several new ones in exchange: this is even acknowledged by the medical profession in a fearsome Greek-derived term: Nokosogenic (meaning arising in the hospital) disease. Stay out of hospital and stay healthy, we say. However, it is a worry. We know of no-one who has died of peritonitis at sea since the sixties: it seems that modern antibiotics may be able to hold the situation until help is at hand.

Births

It is very difficult to get contraceptives in large areas of the world. To be safe, take a good supply with you, and have several different kinds in case you run out.

Lady, if you are seasick to the point of vomiting, or have even a short attack of diarrhoea, or vomiting, or both, the effectiveness of your Pill could be endangered. Talk to your doctor before you go about the possible effect on your sort of Pill: it might be necessary to use a supplementary method for the rest of the cycle.

Bodily damage

A yacht is made of hard and unyielding substances, which in bad weather get up and hit you, causing bruises, cuts, concussion, cracked ribs or broken bones. The old Salts used to say: One hand for yourself, and one for the King. Learn the motion of your boat, when she may jerk or spin, as in a gybe all-standing or the wash of a big ship, or a sudden squall. Make sure that handholds are numerous, in the right place, and that these and anything that can be used as such are strong

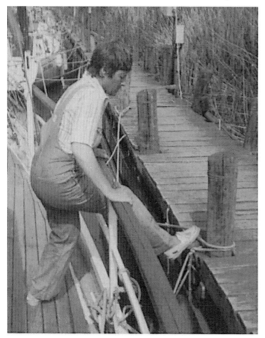

This was posed to illustrate a very dangerous, but common practice. Never, never get feet or hands between the boat and the quay. Note the strong midship springing cleat — a rarity in production craft

enough. We have seen (for instance) tables on production boats that collapsed into matchwood when crashed into by a seven stone weakling.

Expect the Captain to warn you if at all possible, that a big wave or jerk may be coming. Climbing the mast at sea should be attempted only in dire necessity.

The deck of a yacht is never smooth. It is dotted with cleats, rings, bitts, upstands, screwplates and deadeyes, all waiting to bite your feet. Wear good deck shoes to protect them from damage, as well as for traction. Bare feet are fine in harbour or at anchor, but get your shoes on for manoeuvres. Shipboard work often cannot wait while you hop around holding your toe and yelling.

A yacht big enough to go cruising in is under the sway of enormous forces. If something breaks or casts loose it can cause serious damage to people or boat. Part of seamanship, therefore, is learning how to approach and tame your tiger whether it be a flogging sail or twin boom; with the minimum of danger. Use preventers and guys to limit the swing of spars, and prevent gybing. Again prevention is better than cure, so check halyards for weaknesses, ropes for chafe, wire for kinks and broken strands (the latter are a constant source of lacerated fingers), replace bent shackle pins, and tape up protruding split-pins or enclose them neatly in plastic tube. If the weather threatens, shorten sail early to lessen the forces you have to control. Even a handkerchief of canvas in a force 8 can bat around like a tin roof in a hurricane, and a rope can assume the murderous quality of an iron bar wielded by a maniac.

Listen to the Flotilla. They believe that nothing can hurt them: after all, what could possibly happen on two weeks' holiday? 'I'm coming in a bit fast: stick your foot out and hold her off, will you, Harry?' The luckless Harry tries to stop 5 tons of fast-moving boat in zero seconds: oh dear, he's hurt his foot. Dad is too busy at the other end to help him: 'Maud, can you let a bit more anchor line out? What? No more? Well tie another rope to it then — be quick, I can't quite reach the quay. *Hold on!* What did you let go for? Stop crying, it's only a rope burn. Fred, take a line ashore will you. No I can't seem to get any nearer, we've run out of anchor line: can't you jump it?' Fred, challenged, jumps at the precise moment when the cleated anchor line brings the boat up short. He is lucky if he is precipitated into the water rather than onto the rough concrete quay, which will result in numerous cuts and abrasions if not worse. The same abrupt halt has probably thrown Mum against the cockpit coaming, a frequent cause of cracked ribs. All it needs now is for Sandra to stub her bare toe against a cleat, and on leaving, for Susan to jam her fingers in the anchor cable roller and Dad to get a hernia heaving up the anchor, unaware in all the excitement that the ferry has come in and laid several hundredweight of chain across it. We have watched all these things happen, and a lot more, but not all to one boat, at one time, mercifully.

Even a simple thing like filling a bucket of water from the sea, if you are sailing at 5 knots, can almost dislocate your shoulder; so can an unexpected gybe if you are holding the mainsheet in your hand. 'Never cleat the mainsheet' goes back to our dinghy days: it is not valid for bigger boats.

Anchor chain can crush fingers or hands: I have a healthy respect for ours, which is very heavy. I keep my hands well away from it by looping a short length of codline through the links when I need to move it: this can be let go instantly if the cable began to run out unexpectedly, or even cleated up to stop it if you are quick. You know those dinky little elastic sail gaskets with a plastic knob at each end? Release them with care, or they will snap back and knock your teeth out and probably break your glasses as well.

Finally, wearing a lifejacket can save you a few bruises, as will a padded jacket with integral buoyancy.

Body odour

This delicate matter must be mentioned, since the chronic water shortage on board often prevents normal bathing and showering.

First, be aware that your clothing affects your smell. Man-made fibres all engender smells in the smalls after a couple of hours. Cotton, wool and linen may be worn for much longer before they need washing. You may decide that the easy-care qualities of polyester/cotton mixtures are worthwhile, but you will have to wash them oftener, thus using more water.

Canvas shoes need washing whenever you have access to a shoreside hose, otherwise the smell can become intense enough to glow in the dark; leather deck shoes are more expensive, but kinder to plates and mates.

Personal hygiene can be assisted by moistened wipes. Do not, in the interests of economy, use those saved from restaurants on anything except your hands: I shudder to think of the effect of the lemon flavoured variety on certain tender portions of the anatomy. There are specially made ones for this purpose such as Bidette and Femfresh. For ladies, throwaway Brief Savers are a godsend, one wishes there was a male equivalent, a sort of paper jockstrap. My greatest contribution to cruising is probably the discovery that the Debutante brand plastic bowl (withstands boiling water and is graduated in pints and litres) fits exactly into the Lavac bowl to form a bidet. I was so excited by this discovery that I bought a second plastic bowl, but the first one has lasted ten years without breaking.

Bill is under the delusion that underarm deodorants are effective. Overuse can cause dermatitis.

Breaking nails

You need strong nails at sea. There are preparations to paint on and strengthen them, but you can also 'eat' them strong by including plenty of gelatine in the diet: eat straight jelly (Jello) cubes if you like, or dishes in aspic such as *oeufs en gêlée*, brawn or pig's trotters. Wearing gloves can spare you damage: not the delicate little pair from the Yotte Shoppe, but a strong leather or plastic palmed pair, such as the yellow ones sold for bargees in European waterways to prevent injury either when dealing with wire rope, or that popular French mooring system called the *Pendille*, where you pick up a fixed rope between the quay and a mooring buoy, and slide it through your hands to bring it to the forward anchor winch to make fast. As the rope spends a lot of time in the water, it is covered with coral and small, sharp crustacea. Those on shore can be heard tittering as you lacerate your hands and bleed into the scuppers.

Burns and scalds

Every cook must evolve her own way of coping with hot pans in a choppy sea. Some advocate seats and straps in the galley, but I prefer to be free to leap aside. With good fiddles it is not the pans that move, it is their contents, so have deep, tall pans, with well-fitting lids, and don't fill them too full.

Pressure cookers are excellent because the lid stays on. A wide-based kettle with a whistle closing the spout keeps boiling water in the right place. You need a safe place to put a hot pan down where it will not slide, and insulated pan and pot handles. A large cover-all apron of tough plastic will protect you from splashes.

Should you be unlucky enough to sustain a burn or scald, get it into cold water immediately and you may prevent blistering. It is also important to prevent dehydration. When Bill accidentally barbecued me four hours away from civilization, we were acutely conscious of this. Following instructions in 'The Book', he fed me lemon squash with a little salt in it, half a pint every half hour, and measured my output in the rain gauge, driving the boat at maximum speed all the time, I should point out. He also radioed ahead for assistance. On arrival (at an Eastern Mediterranean port with a hospital) we had waiting for us a French doctor, an English doctor, an English nursing sister, and an American nurse (all live-aboards or on holiday in yachts). All of them advised us not to go near the hospital, and were delighted with Bill's lemonade, now satisfactorily coming through me every five minutes, and tickled by the rain gauge idea. With such good care, the burns on thighs, arms and hands healed in no time. I convalesced in the cockpit on a clean sheet.

Burns can occur if you have an on-board barbecue (usually the kind that gimbals on a stern rail). We know of two cases of burns caused by thoughtless use of methylated spirit: firelighters are much safer. We keep a blanket extinguisher near the cooking stove in case of galley fires. (For firefighting see Chapter 11.)

Ciguatera poisoning

This is caused by eating fish from coral reefs near the Equator. It manifests not only with the usual food poisoning symptoms: nausea, vomiting and diarrhoea; but can also produce tingling and numbness in the fingers, toes, lips and tongue; joint and muscle pains, weakness and cramps; fatigue, fainting and headaches; and itching made worse by alcohol. To confuse the issue even more, any or all of these symptoms may be present, and they may be so slight as to be barely noticed, or severe enough to include breathing difficulties. Some sources say the death rate (mostly from breathing difficulties) is 2–3%, others 1%; others say that it could be less as the milder cases are not reported. In by far the majority of cases, unpleasant as these symptoms are they will go away in time, though muscular weakness may persist for quite a while.

Ciguatoxin is found in a small organism that attaches to the algae on certain coral reefs, where it is eaten by small fish. These are then eaten by larger fish, and as the food chain gets longer the toxin is concentrated until in the larger predatory fish it becomes a danger to those who eat it.

Distribution This is the hard part, as the distribution of the affected reefs is sporadic and capricious: it is not yet understood what factors make some reefs harbour the organism, and others (though quite close by) not. So while one can say with truth that ciguatera is present in reefs in the Pacific, Japan, Queensland, the Great Barrier Reef and the Caribbean, that is not the whole story. North of Antigua in the Caribbean, ciguatera is present in some reefs. To the south, the Windward Islands and the Grenadines are free of it. French Polynesia is widely affected, Raratonga is not.

What is certain, in all the myth and rumour which abounds on this subject, is that the local fishermen, be they Polynesian, Caribbean or Floridans, know with fair exactitude which reef and which fish species to avoid. They will also volunteer much folklore on testing fish for poison, ranging from cooking it with a silver coin (which turns black if the fish is toxic) to trying it out on the Mother-in-law. No reliance can be placed on these methods, as only very sophisticated laboratory tests can detect whether the fish is affected. Neither heating nor canning destoys the effects of the toxin. So what to do?

Local knowledge from a reliable source is vital. If in any doubt, do not eat the larger predatory fish: Grouper, Barracuda, Emperor, Sailfish etc. (One source describes over 10 kilos as large.) Do not eat Moray eel. Do not eat the roe, liver or other offal especially from large fish. Research is going on in Queensland, Tahiti, Japan and Hawaii, among other places, to establish accurate tests for ciguatera.

Colds

Just go to sea. The virus disappears after a week to ten days.

Cystitis (a urinary tract infection)

If you are subject to this, make sure you drink a lot of water.

Dental problems

Some old Salt Horses, chiefly from the New World, used to suggest having all your teeth out before a long cruise. This seems to us a draconian solution, especially as teeth seem to last much better nowadays. It should suffice to ensure that you are 'dentally fit' before you leave. Tell your dentist your plans, and he will be careful to miss nothing.

Thereafter, look after your teeth. I will not insult your intelligence by telling you how, since we are all over-exposed to dental hygiene. Here are some thoughts that might not occur to you, however. If you wear dentures, take them out if you feel seasick, they are too easily chundered overboard. Of course you will take a spare set in case of accidents.

A dental first aid kit should contain cement to repair bridgework, or even broken teeth. Lost fillings may be temporarily replaced by equal parts of oil of cloves and powdered zinc oxide. Mix this well, and work it into the well dried cavity. It will set in about a quarter of an hour, and last until you can get it seen to. Oil of cloves on cottonwool is a harmless local painkiller.

Departure stress

Leaving home and friends can be grievous. Husbands and lovers could help a lot by trying to understand how serious a bereavement this is; the male has no roots, it seems, certainly not the ones who go to sea, and feels less pain on upheaval. The tumbleweed male should allow plenty of time for his partner to adjust to transplantation (in the gardening sense). Unlike plants, this will be worst before the actual uprooting; on sailing day the relief will be balm to everyone's pain but the weeks or even months *before* you go will be hard. Bereavement is a sense of loss, of people and things that are loved and respected. It is not necessary for the people to actually die, or the things to be destroyed for you to feel bereft; bereavement is also caused by leaving treasures behind, whether human, animal, abstractions or objects. Bereavement is something to be reckoned with. It is a very germane consideration. Men come up against it with a jolt when they unexpectedly lose their jobs. Some people suffer severely from bereavement when they retire, and grieve for their lost jobs and status. If they have no absorbing hobby they can die of despair. In the same way women will grieve for family, friends and the house they leave behind.

Happy are they who are encouraged and comforted while they work their way through this painful stage. Grief is extremely hard work, and very time-consuming for the person undergoing it; and the support group will need great patience. He will need to check the urge to say: 'Aren't you making rather a meal of this?' or 'Dear oh dear, you are going on a bit.' Of course she is. That is how she will work through it.

Diseases, avoidable

'They fall sicke of one disease or another...'

Unless there are positive medical objections, it makes sense to acquire vaccination, immunisation, and inoculation against smallpox, tetanus and typhoid (TAB).

Some parts of the world will not allow entry without an International Certificate of Vaccination, against smallpox and/or yellow fever. It may also be advisable, according to where you intend to travel, to have shots against cholera and polio, and gamma globulin shots against hepatitis and some other viral infections. Babies should have the triple vaccine (diphtheria, whooping cough and tetanus) unless your doctor advises otherwise. It is not considered advisable for babies under nine months to have yellow fever shots, but you may insist, in writing. Children should have the triple vaccine, plus immunisation against polio.

Discuss with your doctor the advisability or otherwise of all these precautions, and whether to include shots against tuberculosis and German measles for your children (tuberculosis is making a disturbing comeback) and whether you should do something about malaria.

Detailed lists are available in a leaflet from your local Department of Health and Social Security. Try also the Hospital for Tropical Diseases and MASTA (Medical Advisory Services for Travellers) whose addresses will be found in the Appendix. See also Rubbish and Hygeine in the Chapter on victualling.

Ear itch

Many people get this infuriating complaint when swimming. Otosporin (on prescription) seems to work.

Eye damage

Whether you wear glasses or not, have your eyes tested before departure. You will need good sight by night as well as day, and if glasses help, wear them. Tell the optician your plans and discuss with him whether the lightness and toughness of plastic lenses outweighs their tendency to scratches. Take spare pairs (and your prescription) with you. Keep them on with chain, elastic or string: whatever suits you. Do not keep them in a breast pocket: I have seen many a pair of specs go to the bottom as their owner bent over a rail. Fix a steel tag to them and you might get them back with a Sea Searcher magnet (on the other hand you might give the compass a nervous breakdown each time you look at it). We have rescued not only spectacles but keys, fountain pens, bolts and wing nuts, fish traps and bicycles.

When using the sextant for sunsights be extra careful not to glimpse the sun directly through the telescope. This is easy to do on days when the sun is fitful and can burn the retina, causing irreversible damage which may not be noticed at the time. Professional seamen seldom wear sunglasses, preferring to train their eyebrows to jut like yardbrooms and to observe the world through slitted eyes. I, Laurel, feel that Polaroids can be helpful if you are looking up-sun. If bright reflections give you headaches, add a broadbrimmed hat or an eye shade.

There's nothing that drives you out of your senses
Like constantly losing your contact lenses.

Talk to your optician about the advisability or otherwise of using these at sea, and ask him to check for colour blindness, which would preclude unsupervised night watchkeeping. Eyes are priceless: guard them well.

Falls

Much of what was said under Bodily Damage is equally valid for falls. Apart from damage to fingers from tools, we observe falling to be the major cause of damage to yachtsmen, resulting in a wide variety of lesions, from bruises and scrapes to the very common cracked ribs, through broken bones of all kinds up to skull and vertebral fractures. Good handholds and the right shoes go a long way to avoid these injuries. In weather when the ship's motion is very jerky, clip on and hold on, and only move when necessary.

Bill and I hold opposite views about cockpit cushions: I like plenty of them to cushion me when I get thrown off balance; Bill thinks there are too many, as he falls over them if they get dislodged. A padded coat or lifejacket can save bruises to the upper part of the body. I sometimes inflate my pilot jacket a little to enable me to bounce off hard edges.

Your steering or helmsman's seat should be difficult to fall out of, as well as comfortable to sit in.

> *Mop, ah, mop those spills away,*
> *Before you crack your vertebrae.*

Flip-flops are for wearing ashore only. They are highly dangerous. We knew a paraplegic who acquired his injury by catching the rung of a ladder between his toes and the sole of his flip-flops. He fell 30 feet.

Peeing over the side in a rough sea is an excellent way to fall overboard, however alluring it might be not to have to go below. There is evidence to show that attacks of faintness can occur during this process, which make it even more dangerous. How about constructing a 'pig's ear' as the Navy calls it? Make a funnel from the top of a plastic bottle: an opaque one for aesthetic preference; attach it firmly to a length of hose which will reach over the side, then hang the business end within reach of the cockpit. A little ingenuity with the design of the funnel even allows us disadvantaged females to use it, instead of getting our bottoms splashed by the rollicking seas in the toilet bowl.

Heat exhaustion

This is nothing to do with sunstroke, it is caused by working in hot humid conditions. The danger arises with temperatures of over 27°C (80°F) combined with high relative humidity. Increasing bad temper and bolshiness on the part of a normally cooperative crew is an indicator. A sufferer will be cool, sweaty, and pale. Prevention is a question of allowing the cook a heavier hand with the salt, and plying the crew with anchovies and highly seasoned salami. Keep cool and stay in the shade if possible. Stokers in the Navy used to be given pints of salty lemonade to prevent heat exhaustion.

Heatstroke, sunstroke

More catastrophic, but less common than heat exhaustion. The sufferer will not be sweating, and become very hot. Acclimatise yourself gently to hot weather and strong sun. Wear light clothing and a hat. Stay in the shade and keep decks and crew cool with buckets of sea water. Drink plenty of fresh water and don't be mean with the salt.

Herpes (cold sores)

Avoid sun on the lips, as it excites the herpes virus into action. So does wind, dryness, and a raised body temperature. Wear a shady hat, and use a sunscreen or lipsalve. Zovirax is now available off prescription.

Hypothermia

'Not so much as a cloth to shift him, shaking with cold.'

In our young days, something vaguely termed 'suffering from exposure' attacked mountaineers, fell walkers, and shipwreck survivors. Old people and babies died, too, in their homes. After years of study and research, it is now called hypothermia and is recognized as a killer. Not only in cold climates, take note. It is now suggested that yachtsmen at risk, whether in the water or in a liferaft, actually succumb to hypothermia oftener than drowning. If they are in the water, it is hypothermia which probably causes them to drown. Since the former is at present the most likely cause of death at sea, know the enemy. Hypothermia is a serious loss of heat from the deep areas of the body. If the inner body temperature falls below 32°C (87°F) the prospects are not good. Your clinical thermometer is no use for these deep body temperatures, which are caused by heat being leached away from the body without being replaced. This can happen when immersed in cold or even cool water, when exposed to wind without proper clothing, or, as in the case of the very old and the very young, through malfunctioning of the body's heat regulators.

The time it takes to get into this condition is idiosyncratic; if you are strong and physically fit, even dare one say, fat, you will last longer than someone of smaller build who is equally fit. Well-covered people have an initial advantage as they store more heat, but lose their edge when they tire more rapidly and become exhausted. Children cool faster than adults. Cold water leaches the heat away faster than cold dry air, and wind chills you very fast.

Prevention: Your sailing clothes are important. They should protect you from wet and wind, and have some insulating (air-retentive) properties. The former is provided by waterproof foul weather gear, and the latter by wearing under it anything that will trap air, such as a knitted garment, or a foam lining. Those furry garments sometimes called Polar suits trap the air in the pile, and are comfortable. However as they are of man-made fibres, a woollen jersey over them is a good idea, as wet wool is a better insulator than wet nylon and actually generates a little heat.

Even on a warm night, a sudden strong wind can chill you rapidly. It is as well to have a windproof jacket and a woolly hat handy. Preventing loss of heat from head (20% heat loss is through the scalp), hands and toes becomes important in colder climates, and there is no substitute for wool. Wet nylon socks will not keep you warm, but having said that, once you get to survival level anything is better than nothing.

Signs to watch for:

- The person may not realize that he is dangerously cold.
- He may be shivering. (This is beneficial, as it generates heat.)
- He may be awkward and clumsy, and his movements and speech be very slow.
- His mind may feel like porridge, and a state of lethargy can set in, preventing self-help.

If you suspect hypothermia, *prevent further heat loss*. Remove the person from the water or wind. Get him below. If possible replace wet clothes with dry ones, otherwise wrap him in a foil Space Blanket. Cover the head with a woolly hat, and mouth and nose with a closely wound scarf, to prevent heat loss from the lungs. Do not leave him alone, as he is capable of irrational behaviour, including removing all his clothes. Encourage a little activity if he is not exhausted. If he is conscious, give hot, sweet, drinks but *no alcohol*, which causes central heat loss and a dangerous fall in the blood sugar.

It is much more important to prevent further heat loss than to try artificial warming by means of hot water bottles or baths, as this can bring the heat to the body surface at the expense of the deep organs. If the sufferer can get into a warm bath without help, it is safe for him to have one.

Survival in the water Float, don't swim. Swimming dissipates heat. If you are not alone cluster with the others, and try to roll into a ball, to reduce the heat loss from your body.

Infantile diarrhoea

This is probably the most dangerous thing that could happen to your baby or toddler, apart from severe sunburn. The baby becomes progressively dehydrated until he is seriously ill. To combat dehydration in children (and adults as well if need be) you can obtain a double-ended plastic spoon which has been developed for Third World mothers. Salt goes in one end, and sugar in the other, and both are stirred into a glass of water until dissolved. One glass for a child, and two for adults is taken after every attack of diarrheoa. This cheap and simple device has saved more lives than kidney machines. The address to send for the spoon is in the Appendix, but if you encounter any difficulties here are the quantities: ⅓ coffee spoon salt, 1 level teaspoon sugar, *dissolved in a glass of water*. (Dissolving is important because your body cannot use the salt otherwise.) Alternatively ask your Chemist for Dioralyte sachets, a ready-made mixture of sodium chloride (salt), potassium chloride, soda bicarbonate and glucose, for mixing with 200 cc (7 oz) water. They will be more expensive than the salt and sugar mixture, but can be used even for tiny babies.

Legionnaire's Disease

This risk is present if the boat is left for a few months, when plastic water tanks and pipes encourage the growth of the *Legionella* bacteria. They are then spread in the spray from the shower. Empty tanks, disinfect by chlorination, and flush well.

Low morale

'For when a man is ill or at the point of death, I would know whether a dish of buttered rice with a little Cynamon, ginger and sugar... bee not better... than salt fishe...'

Sooner or later the time comes when nothing goes well, and every one feels low and grouchy. I have said earlier that food and drink are important: now is the time to break out something special for the next meal. In the meantime, splice the mainbrace or have a coffee with some rum in it, or eat a whole candy bar.

The aftermath of bad experiences takes its toll of all the crew, not always in the same way. Some talk a lot, some do not talk at all. Some sleep at once, some cannot sleep. Some are elated because it is over, others worry in case it happens again. All need comfort and reassurance. What we sailors have known about for years has now a fancy name: post-traumatic stress, and become the province ashore of professional consultants, but tact, understanding, mutual support, and a recognition that it takes different people different ways, is at the heart of everyone's recovery.

If we found it hard to sleep after an exhausting (even frightening) experience, a tablet of Serene or Kwells was an effective calmer. If something stronger was needed 5 mg of Diazepam usually did the trick, without fogging our heads in the morning as stronger tranquillisers are apt to do. Usually, however, our practice after such events was to talk the shock away for an hour or two over a stiff brandy or gin, to cut the adrenalin. When we felt sufficiently unwound, we went to bed and usually slept like logs.

Morale on board is a delicate flower. It has to be nurtured and tended with care. We have met yachts where it seems to have broken down completely: everyone moving well away from each other in a heavy silence, speaking to us and other strangers without looking at us, in tones that are too loud. Someone is often crying down below; and you can bet she will be the first to recover.

I have said something already about mutual support between skipper and crew. This must extend, gentlemen, to allowing your ladies a good cry, after an exhausting or terrifying experience. Most women are immensely strong mentally and can also call on more physical strength than might be thought, if need be. They will do whatever is necessary, beyond what you could have hoped for. They will fight fires, pump valiantly, bail like demons, staunch the blood, and hang on to the uttermost. They will cope, beyond the point of pain and exhaustion, like the human beings they are. When there is no more to be done, they are likely to burst into tears. Men react indignantly to this. They feel it as a reflection on their actions; but crying is no more a criticism of him than his heartfelt swearing at a sulky generator is a reflection on her. What is more, tears are as beneficial as a cold beer on a sweltering day. Better, since there is some evidence to show that a natural anaesthetic is released into the brain when someone cries. No wonder it is such a relief. Try crying a bit more, chaps: it's good for you.

After the storm is over
 Indulge in a real good cry,
Swallow a whisky and water
 And dinner with lots of pie.
Comforting words should be spoken
 Helping you sleep till morn,
Harmony need not be broken
 After the storm.

Malaria

There are pills to prevent malaria. You must start them in advance, and continue after you leave the area known to be infested. IAMAT, previously mentioned, and MASTA, have very good information. Unfortunately malaria is becoming resistant to the present range of remedies and must be taken seriously.

Malnutrition and deficiency diseases

Most ocean passages last less than a month, so it is very unlikely that you are going to stagger ashore with Beri-beri or Pellagra at the end of your voyage, especially if you paid attention to the chapter on victualling. However, multivitamin pills take up no space at all and might be useful. One of the really long passages is that made by cruisers from Australia and New Zealand, who come across the Indian Ocean and up the Red Sea to the Mediterranean. The time for this is the dry Northeast Monsoon, which means that water is critically short and hard to replace. These folk sometimes arrive in the Mediterranean in poor shape, skinny (easily remedied) but with salt water boils and ulcers that are hard to heal. The protein-rich cereal mixtures in Chapter Nine could help to prevent these. For the boils see Skin Problems, below.

Noxious diseases of all kinds

Your life will be changing completely. Would it be so hard to use this opportunity to stop smoking? Apart from the good effect it will have on your health and finances (and you will not find low-tar and filter tips in the remoter areas) smoking in the confined space below decks of a small yacht is literally nauseating. Think about it.

Rabies

Get your ship's cat or dog vaccinated (see Chapter Seven), and in areas where rabies is endemic warn the children not to pet animals they may find ashore. At the same time, they must understand the necessity to report bites, especially from 'oddly' behaving animals.

Seasickness

This above all can spoil your enjoyment of (anyway) the first two days of your voyage. There is much that can be done to minimise its likelihood and shorten its duration. You could be one of those who are never ill at all, or one of the unfortunates who are very sick indeed for a long time.

It is a comfort to know that on a long voyage the large majority of people are over the worst on the second day. Thereafter a sensible regime will prevent its recurrence, even in rough seas, unless prolonged galley or engine room work are attempted.

To cut seasickness down to a minimum:

- Don't go to sea with a hangover.
- Go into a rough sea with the stomach warm and comfortably full of something fairly stodgy: stew with lots of potatoes, or pilaf, or pasta or porridge.
- Have an extra jersey handy; it is important not to get chilled and you might not want to go below for it. Best start off too warm: you can always discard.
- Try not to get too tired. Do whatever is necessary, and rest between tasks, up on deck if you can.
- Spell the helmsman, drive a bit. Drivers are seldom sick.

Remedies The most effective drug, statistically, is Hyoscine Hydrobromide. The stronger pills need a prescription, milder ones are available over the counter as Kwells (tablets) or Scopoderm TTS (skin patches) which are better if you are likely to vomit. Avomine (Promethazine Theoclate) and Dramamine (Dimenhydrinate) are almost as good; it is a question of finding out what suits you and taking it at least half an hour before it is likely to be needed. Sea Legs (Meclozine) may be taken the night before sailing. Stugeron, Marzine (both Cinnarizine) and Valoid (Cyclizine) are less likely to make you drowsy, and are therefore less useful as mild sedatives. None of these drugs should be accompanied by alcohol, which is anyway not a good idea in bad weather. Some people find pressure wrist bands to be very effective.

> *When storms begin*
> *Lay off the gin.*

If you can, keep eating. If you cannot face real food, nibble dry crackers or crispbread, and have an occasional sweet fizzy drink: a swallow or two of beer (the Eurofizz kind) is surprisingly good, ginger ale not far behind; it's the fizz that counts.

As a last resort, lie down, for'd if running before the wind or aft if going to windward. (This takes one set of the semi-circular canals in your ear out of action, and so you feel less giddy.)

> *Take in time your seasick pill*
> *Otherwise you will be ill.*
> *Tummy warm and full of food*
> *Helps to keep you feeling good.*
> *Too much booze the night before*
> *Makes you toss your cookies more.*
> *Cold your body, head and toes,*

> *Overboard your breakfast goes.*
> *Nibble, nibble all the day*
> *To hold your queasy tum at bay;*
> *A gill of beer or ginger ale*
> *Will stay your stomach through the gale.*
> *Should you feel that death is near,*
> *Lying down you'll feel less queer.*

Skin trouble

Ulcers and boils (gunnel bum, in the racing world) are caused by constant contact with salt water, such as occurs on the long run from Australia up to the Red Sea. With water so desperately short, none can be spared for washing to remove the salt from the skin. It would be well worth taking a large quantity of travel tissues: the moistened kind; even one a day would get some of the salt off. Paper underpants make a lot of sense, too. Cocoa butter is soothing, and speeds healing.

Stomach upsets

'... and then if their Victuals be putrified it indangers all'

Assuming that you have had your TAB shots, get further immunity by eating and drinking locally. Take the normal precautions of washing or peeling fruit and vegetables just before you eat them. Boiling the water we have not found necessary anywhere, but with a small baby you may feel it essential, or if you yourself are susceptible and worried about the water source. Purifying tablets are available, both for large and small quantities of water. Most are based on chlorine. Since a chronic water shortage leads to skimping the washing up, it is sensible to have two separate chopping boards. (The new Microban impregnated bug-killing ones will be a boon to yachts.) Keep one strictly for raw meat, fish or chicken and stow its appropriate knife with it. The other is for cooked meat, bread and cleaned raw vegetables for salads. It too has its own knife.

Stomach disorders are usually caused by one of the F's: food, flies or faeces, so keep the first clean and cool, murder the second mercilessly (see 'Pests') and don't skimp the personal hygiene and hand washing. Put some medicated wipes in the heads as well as a towel, and a bin for used ones.

We ran into trouble with stomach disorders on our return from America, when we visited Tangier. We had obviously lost our resistance in the two years we had spent in the ultra-sanitised States, and Tangier is not a good place to be sensitive in. We suffered somewhat, but our Mediterranean immunity soon re-established itself.

Remember that alcohol is a great bug killer. 'Take a little wine, for thy stomach's sake, and thine often infirmities,' as St Paul advised St Timothy. Our eminent authority states that 'a little wine' can be reckoned as up to half a litre a day!

Stress

You have gone to a great deal of trouble to leave stress behind. Make sure that you also leave behind such lingering habits of the old life as hurrying to get somewhere, working from morning till night, or putting the engine on merely because it is faster. There will be quite enough to challenge you in the months ahead without looking for extra work.

Use the lazy windless days to store well-being and energy, as well as learning how to cope when the weather turns foul, things go wrong and everyone is needed to the utmost. This is certain to happen, even if you neither girdle the earth nor round Cape Horn. If you do decide that you want to do these heroic things, beware that a sense of compulsion does not creep in, and with it a loss of that carefree feeling that you are doing what you want and not what you must. That is not the way of laid-back cruising. Nor is the driving urge to 'get your ticket punched', as we have heard circumnavigation described: trying to do this in a limited time probably causes as much pointless hassle as staying in the cut-throat world of business or fighting for your job ashore.

The way to circumnavigate or cruise without stress is to have no time limit and do it almost by accident, strolling from island to island and continent to continent.

> *Blue sky and green water pour into your mind;*
> *The balm of the world, landsman's daughter,*
> *You sought so long to find.*

Sunburn

Millions of words of warning are printed every year, yet one sees the boiled-lobster effect wherever there is a bit of sun and wind. Patience and a good sunscreen lotion (and the latter is not essential) are all that is required; you cannot get a deep water suntan in three days, you will merely have your skin crispy-broiled. Take a total screen cream: apart from prevention it can alleviate even a nasty sunburn. Protect noses, lips, bald pates and the tops of your feet. If you stayed in the shade for a fortnight in hot sunny weather, you would still achieve a pleasant tan and no burns.

Sun is not always beneficial. Even with a good protective tan you can get skin cancer, which is on the increase. This is less likely if you are black, lucky thing.

Thrush (Vaginal Candidiasis)

This distressing complaint can be discouraged by wearing loose-fitting cotton (never man-made fibres) next the skin. The Pill can predispose you to Thrush. Take with you something to cope with it, like Canesten.

Water contamination

Do not let the water hose fall in the dock. Keep the hose clean. It will last much longer if you don't leave it in strong sunlight. Before you top up, direct a jet at the tap or standpipe to clean it: shore people can be very careless where they walk their dogs. Thirty grains of stabilized chloride of lime to 100 gallons of water will destroy all organisms in it, but so will a little alcohol in your drinking glass and it tastes better.

Worms

See page 139.

The Medicine Chest

'... also that his chest be well furnished bothe for Physicke and Chirurgery and so near as may be proper for the clime you go for.'

Here follows a list of what we took (after much discussion with our doctor and other authorities); what we used it for; and whether we used it at all. In the twenty years since our first departure many improvements and discoveries have been made, so I also give an update, and a list of additions that we found necessary. + means a prescription was necessary, 0 means that we never used it. Ampoules are for injections.

+ 0 Adrenaline ampoules: 1:10,000: Shock or severe drug reaction.
+ Ampicillin: Broad-spectrum antibiotic. Update: + Amoxil.
Aspirin tablets, soluble: Headache and colds, minor aches.
+ 0 Atropine: Narcotic, relaxes gastro-intestinal tract. Update: + ProBanthine.
+ 0 Benzedrine, 4 tablets: For emergencies requiring short-term prolongation of alertness.
+ 0 Benadryl Antihistamine: For allergic reactions. Update: Triludan.
Codeine: Now withdrawn from sale. See Paracetamol.
Cream of magnesia: Indigestion. Update: Aludrox.
Burrow's Solution: Still available as Aluminium Acetate lotion, for fungus infections. Update: Canesten cream.
Chloramine tablets: For water purifying. Update: Sterotabs, Katadyn Micropur.
+ 0 Decadron: Severe allergies, shock and venom. Update: Piriton.
+ Diazepam 5mg capsules: Tranquilliser (for sleeping in severe storms).
+ 0 Diazepam ampoules: Potent tranquilliser.
0 Dioralyte powder: Against dehydration.
+ Distalgesic tablets: For moderate to severe pain. Update: +
Dihydrocodeine. + 0 Gelusil tablets: Antacid. Update: Aludrox tablets.
+ Hyoscine Hydrobromide (Scopolamine): For seasickness.
+ Kaolin and Morphine mixture: BNF: 'Concrete mixture', for diarrhoea.
Kwells tablets: For seasickness, also useful as a mild sedative.
+ 0 Lasix: Diuretic, for use after near-drowning in salt water.
+ 0 Lomotil: For severe diarrhoea.
Multivitamin tablets: To prevent deficiency diseases.
+ 0 Naprosyn tablets: Muscular and skeletal pain (eg discs).
+ 0 Nitrazepam, 5 mg capsules: Sleeping tablets.
Paracetamol capsules: For headache, toothache, colds, etc.
+ 0 Penicillin V.K. tablets: Antibiotic. Update: + Magnapen.
+ 0 Pethidine ampoules: Narcotic for pain relief.
Scopoderm TTS: Hyoscine Hydrobromide skin patches.
0 Senokot tablets: Constipation. A rare condition, we found.
+ 0 Septrin tablets: For those allergic to Penicillin. Update: Methoprim.
Stugeron (Cinnarizine): For seasickness.
+ Tetanus vaccine.
+ Tetracycline tablets: Broad spectrum antibiotic.
+ 0 Xylocaine ampoules: Local anaesthetic. Later we also added:
+ Xylocaine cream: Local anaesthetic.

SYMI

About one-third of this list was never used in twenty years of travel from America to Turkey. The more heroic measures were there if they were needed, kept in a locked drawer (and we were told later that we would have been justified in using one of the narcotic pain-killing ampoules on one occasion) but it was run-of-the-mill remedies we mostly needed: antibiotics, paracetamol, kaolin mixture and so forth. As it should be.

Thorough discussion with a qualified person will be necessary, not only because you will need prescriptions (and not necessarily on the National Health Scheme either) but also an explanation of how and when to use these things.

The First Aid Kit

Whatever container you keep this in, it ought to be fairly near the cockpit (which tends to become the casualty centre) and easily accessible. A list of the where-abouts of more bulky items (large dressings, bandages, and the applicators for the larger sizes of tubegauze, for example) should be stuck into the lid or otherwise firmly attached. List One is what we took when we started, Lists Two and Three were later additions due either to increasing age or experience. + means we needed a prescription, 0 means it was never used.

List One

Acriflavin ointment: For burns.
+ Aureomycin ointment: Antibacterial, for cuts and abrasions.
Calamine cream: Minor skin itch, and sunburn.
Fisherman's Friend: Rubbing ointment (no, not the pastilles!) for sprains, wrenches and muscle pain.
+ Furacin ointment: Antibacterial, for burns or wounds.
Golden Eye ointment: withdrawn. Update: + 0 Chloromycetin ointment.
Ice Pak: (added later) A once-only shake and apply ice pack for bad bruises. No need to store in the fridge. We got ours in the States, but now obtainable in the UK (see Appendix).
Mercurochrome stick: Used like Iodine, stays on better in sea water.
TCP antiseptic liquid: For disinfecting minor cuts.
+ Neobacrin Eye ointment: see Golden Eye ointment.
+ Nystan ointment: Thrush and athlete's foot. Update: Canesten cream.
Adhesive dressing strip and Elastoplast (finger plasters): We used hundreds of these.
Tubegauze bandages and applicators, in four sizes from toes to torsos. We used only the two smaller sizes. A particularly neat form of bandage.
Crepe bandages: Can be washed and reused.
Butterfly sutures: Never successful, as the victim was always sweating and no matter how much we swabbed they would not stick.
Cotton Wool.
Sterile packs of wound dressings in several sizes. (Used 1 small one.)
Roll of adhesive plaster (tape): The Bandaid type from America came unstuck within ten minutes: we were glad to get back to Elastoplast.
Eye bath: For washing out foreign bodies with saline solution.
0 Disposable hypodermic syringes, with needles.

Safety pins.
Scissors and tweezers: never to be taken away and used elsewhere!
Clinical thermometer.
Anti-sting cream: Mosquito bites, wasp stings, jellyfish.

List Two

0 Prepacked sutures, already attached to needle. For closing wounds.
0 Sterile burn dressings: Sofra tulle, Opsite etc.
0 Aerosol burn spray: Now kept near the stove.
Nobecutane spray: Forms a sterile plastic coating over wounds or burns.
0 Disposable scalpels: After the fishhook episode.
Fever Tester: A temperature-sensitive plastic film; takes up no room, is
unbreakable, but cannot be used rectally. There are several kinds of plastic
thermometers nowadays.
Cicatrin: Antibiotic powder for wounds.
Oil of cloves and zinc oxide powder: for temporary tooth filling.

List Three

0 Disposable mini enemas (Microlax).
0 A rectal thermometer (Blue bulb): for measuring Hypothermia.
0 Fluorescein stain: for finding damage to cornea.
0 Labstix: for testing urine.
0 A Brooke Airway, for resuscitation.
A low voltage electric blanket.

As you can see, we really needed nearly everything in the first list at least once.
Murphy's Law being what it is, since we got the scalpels and sutures we have not
required them again.

May you also never need what you have prudently taken with you.

Epilogue

A night in harbour is a precious thing,
  No waves to rock the boat, a full night's sleep:
But we are wishful to be journeying,
  With islands yet unknown a tryst to keep.

They call and beckon, coax and draw us forth,
  A pull as strong as the relentless tide.
They draw us like a magnet, South and North,
  Their soft insistence cannot be defied.

We'll sail the ancient ways, the quiet ways
  By dolphin path, salty, and silver blue;
The saffron sun shall circumscribe our days
  Of hopeful travelling to Xanadu.

A night in harbour is a precious thing,
  But when we go to sea again we sing!

⸃⸂ Appendix ⸃⸂

Book List

In the first and second editions we gave a comprehensive book list. So many yachting books are being published these days that it would be a wonder if you could not find 20 books on How to Sail, and at least five on painting wooden boats, for example. This time we are limiting the list to 'must have's' and those books that you will not find in a Nautical Publisher's list, but which may prove helpful, rather than attempt a 'best in each category'.

If you wish to read widely on cruising before committing yourself to a lot of expenditure, the four serious publishers of yachting books in Britain: Adlard Coles Nautical; Imray, Laurie, Norie and Wilson; Waterline Books; and Fernhurst, will send you a catalogue of their books in print. Libraries can be helpful in getting them for you to borrow. In the USA there are two main nautical publishers: Sheridan House Inc, and International Marine, part of Tab Books.

However, seeing the book before you buy presents difficulties. Few book-sellers keep much of a stock of sailing books. We recommend finding a specialist nautical bookseller. In the United States, Armchair Sailor in Newport, Rhode Island and Seattle, Washington, and Bluewater Books and Charts in Fort Lauderdale, Florida have large selections.

Some possible reading:

The boat herself

Metal Corrosion in Boats by Nigel Warren (Adlard Coles Nautical/Sheridan House)

The Rigging Handbook by Brion Toss (Adlard Coles Nautical/International Marine)

The Marine Electrical and Electronics Bible by John C Payne (Adlard Coles Nautical/Sheridan House)

Seagoing

Heavy Weather Sailing by K Adlard Coles and P Bruce (Adlard Coles Nautical/International Marine)

The Handbook of Offshore Cruising by Jim Howard (Adlard Coles Nautical/Sheridan House)

Yachtsman's Ten Language Dictionary by B Webb (Adlard Coles Nautical/Sheridan House)

Celestial Navigation for Yachtsmen by Mary Blewitt (Adlard Coles Nautical/ Sheridan House)
Where There is No Doctor (published by Teaching Aids at Low Cost, PO Box 49, St Albans, Herts AL1 4AX Tel 01727 853869
Where There is No Dentist (published by Teaching Aids at Low Cost, address above)
The Ship Captain's Medical Guide (HMSO)
First Aid Manual, Joint Voluntary Aid Societies. (Dorling Kindersley)
Your Offshore Doctor by Dr Michael H Beilan (Adlard Coles Nautical/Sheridan House)
Advice to the Sealorn by Herb Payson (Adlard Coles Nautical/Sheridan House)
Understanding GMDSS by Tetley and Calcutt (Arnold/Hodder Headline)
The GMDSS Handbook by Denise Brehaut (Adlard Coles Nautical)

Catering

Charcuterie and French Pork Cookery by Jane Grigson (Penguin)
Mediterranean Seafood by Alan Davidson (Penguin)
North Atlantic Seafood by Alan Davidson (Penguin)
Diet for a Small Planet by Francis Moore Lappe (Ballantine Books, Random House Inc)
Recipes for a Small Planet by Ellen Buchman Ewald (Ballantine Books, Random House Inc)
The Great Cruising Cookbook by John C Payne (Adlard Coles Nautical/Sheridan House)

Some Useful Addresses

Clubs and associations

Seven Seas Cruising Association 521 South Andrews Avenue, Suite 8, Ft Lauderdale, FL 33301 Tel 305 463 2431
E-mail: sscaassn@aol.com
Http: //www.mgend.com/SCA/home.html
US Sailing PO Box 209, Newport, RI 02840 Tel 401 849 5200
E-mail: ussailing@compuserve.com
Http: //ussailing.org
Cruising Association CA House, Northey Street, London E14 8BT, England Tel 0171 537 2828 Fax 0171 537 2266
E-mail: office@cruising.org.uk
Website: www.crusing.org.uk
Little Ship Club Bell Wharf Lane, Upper Thames Street, London EC4R 3TB, England Tel 0171 236 7729 Fax 0171 236 9100
Website http: //www.oceanware.co.uk/lsc/
Ocean Cruising Club PO Box 996, Tiptree, Essex CO5 9XZ, England
Tel/fax 01206 331108

Health care

Hospital for Tropical Diseases 4 St Pancras' Way, London NW1 OPE
Tel 0171 387 4411

Institute of Child Health 30 Guilford St, London WC1N 1EH Tel 0171 242 9789

IAMAT (International Association of Medical Assistance to Travellers)
188 Nicklin Rd, Guelph, Ontario NIH 745, Canada

IAMAT (International Association of Medical Assistance to Travellers)
417 Center Street, Lewiston, NY 14092 Tel 716 754 4883

Life-Fax 200 Market Place, Suite 140, Roswell, GA 30075 Tel 800 487 0329

International SOS Assistance PO Box 11568, Philadelphia, PA 19116
Tel 215 244 1500

Ministry of Agriculture (Animal Health Division) Government Buildings,
Hook Rise South, Tolworth KT6 7NF Tel 0181 330 4411

MASTA (Medical Advisory Services for Travellers Abroad) Bureau of Hygiene
and Tropical Diseases, Keppel St, London WC1E 7HT Tel 0171 636 8636.
MASTA Traveller's Health line: 01891 224100

Education

Worldwide Education Service 35 Belgrave Square, London SW1X 8QB
Tel 0171 235 2880

National Extension College 18 Brooklands Ave, Cambridge CB2 2HN
Tel 01223 316 644 Calvert School 105 Tuscany Rd, Baltimore, MD 21210, USA

Sun Sight Reduction Form

A   Latitude nearest whole degree ....▶ | ° N OR S

Local Date ....▶

B   Watch time in GMT ....▶ | h m s

Date if changed for GMT
(Greenwich Date) ....▶

C   Watch error ± ....▶

D   Calculate B ± C..............................▶

E   Declination ....▶ | ° 'N OR 'S

......Look up Declination for exact time D: in this case, interpolate.

F   Hour Angle ....▶ | ° '

......From Almanac, on Greenwich Date look up Hour Angle at time D hours; do not interpolate.

G   Hour Angle interpolation ....▶

......Obtain from back of Almanac for the minutes and seconds.

H   Calculate F + G ....▶

I   Assumed Longitude ....▶

......The idea is to get a whole number of degrees by subtracting I from H if Longitude is West or by adding I to H if Longitude is East.

J   Calculate H – I or H + I
as appropriate.................................▶

......For numbers over 180° subtract from 360°.

Now consult Nav Tables and open for your Latitude (A). Choose side for Latitude either same name (N or S) as Declination, or contrary name.

Enter Table in column for Declination less than your figure (E). Opposite entry for Hour Angle (J) look up K, L, and M.

K   Altitude ....▶ | ° '

Q   Sextant reading...............................▶ | ° '

L   Interpolation factor Δ.....................▶

R   Index error of sextant ....▶

M   Azimuth ....▶ | °

S   Calculate Q ± R ....▶

N   From Interpolation tables in back of book use excess declination over that used to get KLM, relate it to factor L to get corr N ....▶

T   1st Sun correction ....▶

U   Add S + T ....▶

V   2nd Sun corr & monthly corr.........▶

P   Calculate K ± N** get CORRECTED ALTITUDE ....▶

W   U – V, THE OBSERVED ALTITUDE ....▶

X   Calculate the difference betwee P and W, the INTERCEPT........................▶ | ' | (OR MILES) | TO° FROM°

Y   If sight is before noon re-enter M. If sight is after noon, subtract M from 360°, giving SUN'S TRUE BEARING ....▶ | °

*If W is larger than P, delete FROM, if smaller, delete TO (above right, the INTERCEPT)

**K + N if Declination same name as Latitude, K – N if opposite name.

Now, on chart draw in prencil position of Latitude (A) and Longitude (I), and mark with the symbol ☐

Draw in the bearing (Y), towards the bearing if TO, otherwise draw the reciprocal. Measure from the symbol ☐ the Intercept (X), marking it Δ

Through Δ draw a line at right angles to the bearing (Y). Put an arrow head on each end of it. This is your position line at the time of the sight. Write that time along the line.

Position lines can be transferred by moving them in the direction of the Course Made Good, a distance of the Distance Made Good, and drawing the transferred line parallel to the original.

NB This form is suitable for use with British Admiralty and US Nautical Almanacs, and commercial Almanacs such as Reeds, MacMillans, and Browns. And for the Air Navigation Tables, HO 249, HO 214, HD 486, Spanish Publication Especial Num 4 and NP 401.

Index